OCCUPATIONAL FORENSIC

ENCYCLOPAEDIA OF FORENSIC SCIENCE -

OCCUPATIONAL FORENSIC

By

Ashok Kumar

Dept. of Zoology
Bundelkhand University
Campus Department
Jhansi (India)

DISCOVERY PUBLISHING HOUSE PVT. LTD.
NEW DELHI-110 002

Published by:

DISCOVERY PUBLISHING HOUSE PVT. LTD.
4383/4B, Ansari Road, Darya Ganj
New Delhi-110 002 (India)
Phone : +91-11-23279245; 23253475; 43596065
E-mail : discoverybooksindia@gmail.com
discoverypublishinghouse@gmail.com
namitwasan9@gmail.com
web : www.discoverypublishinggroup.com

First Published: **2010**
Reprinted: **2022**

ISBN: 978-81-8356-422-9 (Set)

ISBN: 978-81-8356-568-4

Occupational Forensic

Printed at:
Infinity Imaging Systems
Delhi

Preface

The present title *"Encyclopaedia of Forensic Science"* has been written for undergraduate, post-graduate students and those engaged in pharmaceutical, pathological, and clinical research. Actually the explosion of new technologies with their vast potential has brought with it the need for forensic scientists to equip themselves and their laboratories with a whole array of new expertise. With the high discriminating power of the DNA systems has come high potential in evidentiary terms, high profile status for many investigations, and not least, a high degree of professional scruting of evidence produced by such technology. The present book provides protocols for the major methods of DNA analysis that have been introduced for identity testing in forensic laboratories. It also deals with the developments intersecting with the neighbouring fields of law inforcement and the justice system. This book will prove a useful guide for public awareness, health authorities, professional and industrial organizations. The aim of writing this book has .been to show how it is possible to enjoy the benefits of technology in detecting the criminals. The language used in it is simple and lucid, and illustrations are clear and labelled.

To make the work more comprehensive and informative, the author has consulted many authoritative books, research journals, abstracts, monographs etc., so there can be no claim to originality except in the .manner of treatment.

The author expresses his thanks to his friends and colleagues whose continue inspirations have initiated him to bring out this book.

The author expresses his gratitude to Mr. Wasan and staff of M/s Discovery Publishing House Pvt. Ltd. for their whole hearted co-operation in the publication of this book.

In the mean time, the author will remain sincerely responsible for any shortcomings of the book and be grateful to the readers for their suggestions and constructive criticism for the continuous betterment of the book. He takes this opportunity to appeal to the readers to send their suggestions straightaway to his Publisher.

Author

CONTENTS

1

INTRODUCTION

The main objective of industrial toxicology is the prevention of health impairments in workers handling or exposed to industrial chemicals. This objective can only be reached if conditions of exposure or work practices are defined that do not entail an unacceptable health risk. With the possible exception of carcinogenic substances, for which it is still debatable whether "safe" conditions of exposure can presently be defined, this implies in practice the definition of permissible levels of exposure to industrial chemicals. These levels can be expressed either in terms of allowable atmospheric concentrations (maximum allowable concentrations—MAC; threshold limit values—TLV; time-weighted averages—TWA; short-term exposure limits—STEL; emergency exposure limits—EEL) or in terms of permissible biologic levels for the chemicals or their metabolites (biologic TLV). To evaluate with some degree of confidence the level of exposure at which the risk of health impairment is negligible, a body of toxicologic information is required that derives from two main sources, experimental investigations on animals and clinical surveillance of exposed workers (including retrospective studies on previously exposed workers). In some circumstances, limited investigations on volunteers can also be considered.

The large-scale use of any chemical in industry should be preceded by certain types of toxicologic investigations on animals in order to establish a tentative "no-adverse-effect" level. Other important information that may also be derived from these investigations concerns methods of biologic monitoring and preexisting pathologic states that may increase the susceptibility to the chemical animal testing can provide only an estimate of the toxicity of a chemical for man. For example, there is a great risk of missing allergic reactions in testing new materials in animals. Thus when the compound is actually handled in industry, monitoring of the work places and careful surveillance of the workers are essential.

The main objectives of the clinical work are (1) to test the validity of the provisional permissible level of exposure based on animal experiments; (2) to detect as early as possible hypersensitive reactions unpredictable from animal investigations; and (3) to confirm the usefulness of biologic methods of monitoring workers. One must, however, recognize that for many chemicals toxicologic investigations on animals have not been performed before the chemical's use in industry. In that case clinical work (retrospective epidemiologic studies; historic prospective studies) is aimed at defining the no-adverse-effect level directly in man.

In some circumstances exposure of volunteers can be considered when the information, e.g., threshold for upper respiratory tract irritation, is not easily obtainable by other means and when the experiments entail no risk for the volunteers (which means that extensive biologic information should already be available before any experiments on volunteers are undertaken). Experimental investigations on animals and clinical studies on workers or volunteers are closely related, and I will illustrate below how collaboration between disciplines or approaches helps accomplish more rapid progress in the field of industrial toxicology.

Preliminary Testing on Animals

It is evident that certainly as to be the complete safety of a chemical can never be obtained, whatever the extent of toxicologic investigations performed on animals. Nevertheless, some basic requirements can be suggested to estimate with some degree of confidence the level of exposure at which the risk of health impairment is negligible and thus acceptable. We are excluding from the following considerations chemicals that have only very limited use, as in a research laboratory, and can be handled by a limited number of skilled persons in a way that prevents any exposure.

General guidelines for assessing experimentally the toxicologic hazards of industrial chemicals have been recommended. Their principles do not differ much from the investigations presently required for evaluating the toxicity of substances to which the general public can be exposed (drugs, food additive, pesticides residues, etc.)

The need for performing some (or all) of those investigations should be carefully evaluated for any industrial chemical to which workers will be exposed. The toxicologist is guided in selecting the studies most relevant for safety evaluation by an understanding of he physicochemical properties of the chemical; the conditions of use and degree of exposure including the possibility of generating toxic derivatives when the chemical is submitted to various chemical and physical factors (heat, pH change, etc.); the type of exposure, which may be continuous or accidental and possibly toxicologic information already available on other chemicals with similar chemical structure and reactive chemical groups. It should be stressed that conclusions drawn from any toxicologic investigation are valid only if the exact composition (e.g., nature and concentration of impurities or degradation products) of the tested preparation is known precisely. The assessment of the toxicity of 2,4,5,-T illustrates this point. Its teratogenic hazard is estimated differently depending on the content of the highly toxic impurity 2, 3, 7, 8-tetrachlorodibenzodioxin in the preparation tested. Accurate methods of analysis of the chemical in air and in biologic material should also be available.

Flexibility of approach is essential in deciding the duration of tests necessary to establish a reasonable no-effect level for occupational exposure. This depends mainly on the type of toxic action that is suspected, but it is generally recognized that subacute and short-term toxicity studies are usually unsatisfactory for proposing permissible exposure levels. Subacute and short-term toxicity tests are usually performed to find out whether the compound exhibits some cumulative toxic properties and to select the doses for long-term exposure and the kind of tests that may be most informative when applied during long-term exposures. Several studies have recently drawn attention to the fact that the reproductive system may also be the target organ of industrial chemicals (e.g., anesthetic gases, monochlorodibromopropane, vinyl chloride). Studies designed to evaluate reproductive performance and teratogenic action should therefore also be considered during routine toxicologic testing of industrial chemicals.

Information derived from similar exposure routes (skin, lung) to those sustained by workers is clearly most relevant. For airborne pollutants, inhalation exposure studies provide the basic data on which provisional permissible levels are based. Experimental methodology is certainly much more complicated for inhalation studies than for oral administration experiments. For example, in the case of exposure to aerosol, particle size distribution should be estimated and the approximate degree of retention in the respiratory tract of the animal species selected should be known. Ideally, particle size should be selected according to the deposition pattern of solid or liquid aerosols in the particular animal species used. It should also be kept in mind that the concentration of the material in the air and the duration of exposure do not give a direct estimate of the dose, which is also dependent on the minute volume and percent retention. The appropriateness of other routes of administration (usually oral) in combination with limited data from tests by inhalation or skin application must be scientifically evaluated for each chemical (depending on its main site of action, metabolism, etc.). The morphologic, physiologic, and biologic parameters that are usually evaluated, either at regular intervals in the course of the exposure period or at its termination, have been reviewed. It is evident that investigations that can make use of specific physiologic or biochemical tests based on the knowledge of the "critical" organ or function produce highly valuable information and hence increase confidence in the TLV derived from them. In the field of industrial toxicology, knowledge of the metabolic handling (absorption, distribution, biotransformation, excretion) of the chemical and/or its mechanism of action is of major interest. Indeed, as indicated in the introduction, the main objective of occupational toxicology is to prevent the development of occupational diseases. In this respect the biologic monitoring of workers exposed to various industrial chemicals may play an important role, by detecting excessive exposures as early as possible, before the occurrence of significant biologic disturbances, or at least when they are still reversible or have not yet caused any health impairment. A rational biologic monitoring is possible only when sufficient toxicologic information has been gathered on the mechanism of action and/or the metabolism of xenobiotics to which workers may be exposed. These studies must be performed first on animals.

Observation on Workers

When a new chemical is being used on a large scale, careful clinical of the workers and monitoring of the work places should be planned. In addition to the specific actions immediately taken if any adverse effect on the health of the workers is discovered, a clinical survey may have two main general objectives; to evaluate the validity of the "no-adverse-effect" level derived from animal experiments, and to test the validity of a biologic method of monitoring.

Evaluation of the Validity of Animal Experiments

Evaluation of the validity of the "no-adverse-effect" level derived from animal experiments is certainly the prime objective since, as stated by Barnes (1963), "studies and observations on man will always be the final basis for deciding whether or not a MAC set originally on the basis of tests on animals is, in fact, truly acceptable as one that will not produce any signs of intoxication." This means that behavioural, clinical, biochemical, physiologic, or morphologic tests that are considered to be the most sensitive for detecting an adverse effect of the chemical should be regulatory applied to the workers at the same time their overall exposure is evaluated to provide personal monitoring of airborne contaminants.

Since the adverse effects under scrutiny for the early detection of health impairment are subtle, and since individual variations exit in the response to a chemical insult, results can only be evaluated on a statistical basis. This means that the dose-response curves found among exposed workers should always be compared to similar responses in a group of unexposed workers matched for other variables such as age, sex, socioeconomic status, and smoking habits. The importance of selecting a control group that is well matched with the exposed group and that undergoes exactly the same standardized clinical, biologic, or physiologic evaluation at the same time as the exposed group must be emphasized. Since an employed population is a group selected to a certain degree for health, comparison with the general population is not valid. Since such a survey lasts for several years (prospective survey or observational cohort study), the importance of good standardization of all methods of investigation, such as questionnaries related to subjective complaints, instrumentation, and analytic techniques, must be stressed before the start of the survey.

If labour turnover is too high to allow a typical cohort study (i.e., regular examination of the same exposed and control workers), repeated cross-sectional studies of exposed and matched controls should be undertaken. If exposure is above the threshold level of response, these studies may permit (1) establishment of the relationship between integrated exposure (intensity × time) and frequently of abnormal responses, and consequently (2) a redefinition of the "no-adverse-effect" level.

When this surveillance program has been planned before he introduction of a new chemical, it is more difficult to obtain the desired information through investigations designed after the fact.

Indeed, in this case, evaluation depends on retrospective cohort studies or, more usually, simple cross-sectional studies. Since the information regarding the past exposure of the workers is often incomplete, a correct evaluation of the no-effect level is much more difficult. Whether or not clinical investigations are planned from the introduction of a new chemical or process, it is essential to keep standardized records of workers occupational histories and exposures. The need may arise for mortality or case history studies in order to answer an urgent question on a suspected risk. The evaluation of the "no-effect" level of vinyl chloride in man illustrates this point.

In addition to these clinical surveys, it is useful to report in case studies any particular observations resulting from exposure to the chemicals (e.g., accidental acute intoxication). Although such isolation observations are not helpful for determining the "no-effect" level in man, they are of interest, mainly for new chemicals. They may indicate whether human symptomatology is similar to that found in animals, and hence may suggest the functional or biologic tests that might prove useful for the routine control of exposed workers.

Testing the Validity of a Biologic Method of Monitoring

Experimental work may have suggested a biologic method for monitoring of workers (e.g., evaluation of current exposure, internal load, or early biologic response by measuring a metabolite or the compound itself in urine or blood, or by determining blood enzyme activity). Clinical investigations must then be made to test the applicability of such methods in industrial situations. A brief review of the main biologic monitoring methods presently available for evaluating exposure to some industrial toxicologic hazards is presented at the end of this chapter.

Experimental Studies on Volunteers

Experimental studies on volunteers are usually designed to answer very specific questions, e.g., time course of metabolite excretion during and after exposure; threshold doses for blood cholinesterase inhibition; evaluation of the threshold concentration for sensory responses (odor, irritation of the nasal mucosa, etc.); effect of solvent exposure on perception, vigilance, and the like. For evident ethical reasons, such studies can only be undertaken when the same results cannot be obtained through other means and under circumstances where the risk for the volunteers can reasonably be estimated as nonexistent. The experimentation should comply with the Declaration of Helsinki (1964), i.e., it should be carried out under proper medical supervision on duly-information volunteers.

Interest of Close Collaboration between Experimental Investigations on Animals and Clinical Studies on Workers (or Volunteers)

Perhaps in the field of industrial toxicology more than in other areas of toxicology, close collaboration between experimental investigation on animals and clinical studies on workers plays an important role in explaining the potential risk linked with overexposure to chemicals, and hence in suggesting preventive measures to protect the health of the workers. A few examples will illustrate the complementarity of both disciplines in occupational toxicology.

The firm identification of an occupational carcinogen requires both epidemiologic and experimental evidence; an excess of cancer is found in a group exposed to a known chemical and tumors can be produced in experimental animals by the same chemical. The carcinogenicity of vinyl chloride was first demonstrated in rats and a few years later epidemiologic studies confirmed the same carcinogenic risk for man. This observation stimulated several investigations on its metabolism in animals and on its mutagenic activity in various *in vitro* systems. Identification of vinyl chloride metabolites led to the conclusion that an epoxy derivatives is first formed that is suspected to be the proximate carcinogen. This report triggered a number of investigations on the biotransformation of structurally related chemicals extensively used in industry, such as trichloroethylene, vinylidene chloride, vinyl benzene, and chlorobutadiene. It is likely that all give rise to reactive epoxy intermediates.

Retrospective epidemiologic studies on persons who are or have been occupationally exposed to these chemicals are therefore indicated. Furthermore, several of these chemicals or their metabolites exhibit mutagenic activity *in vitro*. This observation stimulated the search for chromosomal aberrations in workers. Such anomalies were indeed found in workers exposed to vinyl chloride, and an epidemiologic study suggests that vinyl chloride can induce genetic damage in man. Again, in view of the results of the experimental studies cited above, extension of these clinical studies to chemically related compounds is highly desirable.

Dioxane is an industrial solvent with a variety of industrial applications. When it is administered at high doses, the principal toxic effects in rats are centrilobular hepatocellular and renal tubular epithelial degeneration and necrosis and induction of hepatic and nasal carcinoma. The major metabolite in rats was identified as either β-hydroxyethoxyacetic acid (HEAA) or p-dioxane-2-one, depending on the acidity and the alkalinity of the solution. It was found, however, that the biotransformation of dioxane to HEAA may be saturated at high doses of dioxane. This observation led Young to suggest that the toxicity of dioxane occurs when doses are given sufficient to saturate the metabolic pathway for its detoxification. On the premise that similarity of the metabolic pathway of dioxane in rats and humans would greatly facilitate the extrapolation of toxicologic data from rats to man, the same authors examined the urine of plant personnel exposed to dioxane vapor.

In urine of workers exposed to a time-weighted average concentration of 1.6 ppm dioxane for 7.5 hours, they found the same product (HEAA) as found previously in the rat. Furthermore, the high ratio of HEAA to dioxane, 118 to 1, suggests that at a low-exposure concentration dioxane is rapidly metabolized to HEAA. The authors concluded that since saturation of the metabolism of dioxane in rats was correlated with toxicity, their results on man support the hypothesis that low levels of dioxane vapor in workplace pose a negligible hazard. This conclusion is debatable, however, since dioxane is a carcinogen and the existence of a threshold level for such chemicals is still controversial.

Furthermore, Woo et al. (1977) have reported that p-dioxane-2-one is more toxic than dioxane and its production *in vitro* may be related to dioxane toxicity and/or carcinogenicity, in view of the fact that a number of lactones with similar structure are known to be carcinogenic. If it can be shown that p-dioxane-2-one is really a proximate carcinogen workers found to excrete the metabolite will have to be considered risk.

Dimethylformamide (DMF) is an hepatotoxic solvent extensively used in laboratories and in the production of acrylic resins. Exposure of workers occurs mainly by inhalation of vapor and through skin contact. Its metabolism was first investigated in rats and in dogs *in vitro* and *in vivo*. These investigations demonstrated that DMF is rapidly metabolized *in vivo*. The biotransformation consists of a progressive demethylation, possibly followed by the hydrolysis of the amide bond. The main urinary metabolite is the monomethyl derivative, N-methylformamide (NMF). The animal studies stimulated human studies to evaluate whether *in vivo* biotransformation could lead to workers investigated the metabolism of DMF on volunteers. They both found that the majority of the absorbed substance is eliminated within 24 hours and that the main urinary metabolite is NMF. Its concentration was related to the intensity of exposure. The next logical test was to evaluate the practicability of this biologic monitoring method on workers. A preliminary investigation in an acrylic fiber factory confirmed that NMF in urine is a sensitive biologic indicator of exposure since its presence could be easily detected, even when the average airborne DMF concentration was below the current ACGIHTLV (30 mg/m^2). Furthermore, in a group of workers, the amount of DMF excreted at the end of the shift seems to reflect the intensity of exposure of the same day.

These examples (vinyl chloride, dioxane, dimethylformamide) demonstrate that the study of the metabolic handling of an industrial chemical in animals is very important because it may lead to the characterization of reactive intermediates, suggesting yet—unsuspected risks, or it may indicate new methods of biologic monitoring, which must first be validated by a field study.

Conversely, clinical observations on workers may stimulate the study of the metabolism or the mechanism of toxicity of an industrial chemical in animals. This may help in predicting the human response to structurally related compounds or in evaluating the health significance of a biologic disturbance. In 1973 an outbreak of peripheral neuropathy occurred in workers exposed to the solvent methyl butyl ketone (MBK). Metabolic studies were then undertaken in rats and guinea pigs and some MBK metabolites (2,5-hexanedione, 5-hydroxy-2-hexanone) were also found to possess neurotoxic activity.

Similar oxidation products are formed from n-hexane, the neurotoxicity of which is probably due to the same active metabolite as that produced from MBK. According to DiVincenzo et al. (1977), the most probable active intermediate is 2,5-hexanedione. Since methyl isobutyl ketone and methyl ethyl ketone cannot give rise to 2,5-hexanedione, they should preferably replace MBK as solvent, n-Hexane derivatives that are oxidized to 2,5-hexanedione are probably also neurotoxic for man.

Investigations on volunteers and on workers have shown that for same level of exposure to lead the accumulation of free erythrocyte porphyrin (FEP) is more important in women than in men. Whether this finding justifies the proposal of different permissible levels of exposure to lead for women and for men is debatable, since its health significance is still unknown. A study on the mechanism of the sex difference could clarify its health significance. A joint experimental and clinical approach seems very promising in being able to yield an understanding of the mechanism of this sex-lead interaction. A difference in the level of the iron pool between men and women was first proposed as the main mechanism of the different susceptibility to lead. A relative iron deficiency in women could synergize the action of lead on the enzyme chelatase in the bone marrow. Two arguments, one clinical and one experimental, suggest that the lead-sex interaction may also involve other biologic factors. In women moderately exposed to lead who did not suffer from iron-deficiency anemia, no correlation was found between FEP and plasma iron, nor between concentration of lead in blood and plasma iron.

Furthermore, it was possible to reproduce the sex difference in FEP response to lead in rats. In this species under normal feeding conditions the action of lead on FEP accumulation is apparently independent of the iron pool but is influenced by sex hormones, in particular progesterone. Such hormonal influence is in agreement with the finding that in women a slightly increased excretion of δ-aminolevulinic acid (a heme precursor) is also found during pregnancy and this is associated with a slight increase in plumburia (unpublished results). The mechanism by which sex hormones interfere with the action of absorbed lead in the heme biosynthetic pathway deserves further investigation. It is possible that sex hormones influence the distribution of lead in blood and increase the proportion of ultrafiltrable lead in plasma. A preliminary clinical observation compatible with this hypothesis is the finding of a greater urinary excretion of lead in women than in men for the same level of lead in blood. Further *in vitro* investigations on lead distribution in plasma and *in vitro* studies on animals under different stages of hormonal impregnation are required to validate this hypothesis.

Other examples of fruitful collaboration between experimental and clinical studies in the area of industrial toxicology can be found in a recent review article. I am convinced that more rapid achievement of the control of occupational hazards can be accomplished if close collaboration between both disciplines is further stimulated.

Practical Applications

We have already stressed two important types of applications of toxicologic investigations, i.e., the proposal of permissible levels of exposure and the development of methods for the biologic evaluation of the intensity of exposure to chemicals.

Permissible Levels of Exposure to Airborne Industrial Chemicals

It is a cliche to say that the best practice in occupational hygiene is to maintain concentrations of all atmospheric contaminants as low as is practical, but even this does not always preclude overexposure to toxic levels of chemicals. The industrial physician must have guidelines to judge the potential health hazards industrial chemicals and to evaluate whether the general preventive methods in use in the factory are adequate or must be improved or must be complemented by the use of personal protective devices. An important objective of experimental and clinical investigations in industrial toxicology is the proposal of "safe" levels of exposure.

Various private and official institutions review regularly the toxicologic information on chemicals in order to propose permissible levels of exposure. Critical evaluation of these data can be found in the following publications: various NIOSH criteria documents on specific chemicals, documentation on TLV's prepared by the American Conference of Governmental, Industrial Hygienists, and reports prepared by the Deutsche Forchungsgemeinschaft. It is evident that with the accumulation of new information on the toxicity of industrial chemicals, the proposed permissible levels must be reevaluated at regular intervals. It should also be made clear that these levels are only guides and should not take the place of close medical surveillance of the workers.

Biologic Monitoring of Workers

Measurements of industrial chemicals or their metabolites in biologic material (expired air, blood, urine) allow estimation of the intensity of exposure to these chemicals. Biologic monitoring may also be used to detect early biochemical changes (e.g., acetylcholinesterase inhibition) before the occurrence of adverse health effects. As indicated above, the applicability of such monitoring methods requires detailed clinical investigation. For example:

(a) If a biologic parameter is proposed for evaluation of the total uptake (lung, skin, etc.) of a foreign chemical or its degree of retention in the organism (body burden), the relationship between these parameters (uptake, body burden) and the rate of variation of the biologic parameters in man must be evaluated. In some circumstances this evaluation may be performed in the field under routine working conditions.

(b) When a biologic measurement is principally intended for evaluating uptake, the relationship referred to under (a) must hold for exposure below the maximum tolerable exposure; hence a biologic threshold limit value can be proposed. Other problems must also be considered when proposing new methods for the biologic monitoring of workers. It a biologic parameter is intended to evaluate the intensity of a biologic disturbance, some consideration should also be given to the health significance of the biologic change in order to propose a meaningful threshold value for the selected parameter. For evident practical reasons a selected parameter should be sufficiently stable to allow storage of the biologic samples for a certain period of time and it should be amenable to a non-time consuming analysis by a not-too-sophisticated technique. The precision and the accuracy of the analysis should be satisfactory. Several intercomparison programs for the analysis of industrial chemicals in biologic material have indeed stressed the analytic difficulties associated with these measurements. Unfortunately, relevant toxicologic information on metabolism and mechanism of action for many industrial chemicals is lacking and thus no biologic method can yet be proposed. Furthermore, even if preliminary investigations suggest the usefulness of a biologic monitoring method, quite often no meaningful biologic limit value can yet be proposed because clinical studies are insufficient to elaborate the close-response curves.

When such specific biologic measurements are feasible, the approach offers important advantages over monitoring the air of the workplace. The two main advantages are (1) that it takes into consideration absorption by all the routes, not only through the lungs; and (2) that it may consider individual differences in the sensitivity to the chemical or differences in its rate of absorption, distribution, biotransformation, and excretion. Each worker is thus his own integrator of the total exposure. Biochemical or physiologic tests specifically designed to detect a toxic response (e.g., lung function tests in case of exposure to lung irritants; proteins in urine of cadmium-exposed workers) have not been dealt with. The values indicated in the third column should be considered only as tentative values based on our current scientific knowledge as it has been summarized in recent publication. Like the airborne TLV's, these values should be subject to regular revision in the light of new scientific data.

The working environment will always present the risk of worker's overexposure to various chemicals. It is self-evident that the control of these risks cannot wait until epidemiologic studies have defined the no-adverse-effect level directly in man. However, extrapolation from animal data has its limitations. A combined experimental and clinical approach is certainly the most effective for evaluating the potential risks of industrial chemicals, hence for recommending adequate preventive measures and for applying the most valid screening procedures on workers.

Thus the field of industrial toxicology provides many opportunities for scientists with different backgrounds (physicians, chemists, biologists, hygienists) who are convinced of the usefulness of working in close collaboration to understand and prevent the adverse effects of industrial chemicals on workers' health.

2

Detection of Biomaterial

The sensitivity and evidential power of DNA profiling have impacted on the way in which crime scenes are investigated. Because only a few cells are required for DNA profiling, crime scene examiners now have a much wider range of biological evidence to collect and also have a much greater chance of contaminating the scene with their own DNA.

Sources of Biological Evidence

The human body is composed of trillions of cells and most of these contain a nucleus, red blood cells being a notable exception. A wide variety of cellular material can be recovered from crime scenes.

Each nucleated cell contains two copies of an individual's genome and can be used, in theory, to generate a DNA profile under optimal conditions. In practice, 15 or more cells are required to generate consistently good quality DNA profile from fresh material. Forensic samples usually show some level of degradation and with higher levels of degradation, more cellular material is required to produce a DNA profile. If the material is very highly degraded then, even with the high sensitivity of DNA profiling, it may not be possible to generate a DNA profile.

The biological material encountered most often at scenes of crime is blood. This is mainly because of the violent nature of many crimes and also because it is easier to visualize than other biological fluids such as saliva.

Other frequently encountered samples include seminal fluid, which is of prime importance in sexual assault cases; saliva that may be found on items held in the mouth, such as cigarette butts and drinking vessels, or on bite marks; and epithelial cells, deposited, for example, as dandruff and in faeces. With the increase in the sensitivity of DNA profiling the recovery of DNA from epithelial cells shed on touching has also become possible. Hairs are naturally shed, and can also be pulled out through physical contact and can be recovered from crime scenes. Naturally shed hairs tend to have very little follicle attached and are not a good source of DNA, whereas plucked hairs or hairs removed due to a physical action often have the root attached, which is a rich source of cellular material.

The four most common nucleated cell types that are recovered from scenes of crime are white blood cells, spermatozoa, epithelial cells and hair follicles.

Collection and Handling of Material at the Crime Scene

The high level of sensitivity that makes DNA profiling an invaluable forensic tool can also be a potential disadvantage. Contamination of evidential material with biological material from another source, such as an attending police officer or scene of crime officer, is a very real possibility. It is vital that the appropriate care is taken, such as maintaining the integrity of the scene and wearing full protective suits and face masks during the investigation of the scene. Improper handling of the evidence can have serious consequences. In the worst cases, it can cause cross contamination, lead to sample degradation, and prevent or confuse the interpretation of evidence.

Identification and Characterization of Biological Evidence

Searching for biological material, both at the crime scene and in the forensic laboratory is performed primarily by eye. In the laboratory, low power search microscopes may help to localize stains and contact marks. Alternative light sources have been found to assist with finding biological material both in the field and in the laboratory. Epithelial cells, saliva and semen stains may fluoresce at different wavelengths of light compared with the background substrate and therefore may become visible. A range of light sources is available and these can either operate at fixed wavelengths or a variable number of wavelengths that are suitable for detecting different types of stain.

Searching a crime scene or items recovered from a crime scene for blood can be aided by the use of luminol (3-aminophthalhydrazide). This chemical can be sprayed onto a wide area and will become oxidized and luminescent in the presence of haemoglobin, which is found in red blood cells. It is necessary to be able to darken the area that is being searched in order that the luminescence can be detected. Luminol can also be used in the more controlled environment of the forensic laboratory and can be particularly useful when searching clothing for trace amounts of blood.

The success in finding biological material depends upon the search method employed and also on the integrity and state of the scene. In the UK, biological material is found at approximately 12% of investigated crime scenes, this figure can go up significantly if the crime scene is exhaustively searched.

Evidence Collection

The methods used for collection will vary depending on the type of sample. Dry stains and contact marks on large immovable items are normally collected using a sterile swab that has been moistened with distilled water; in other cases, scraping or cutting of material may be more appropriate. Lifting from the surface using high quality adhesive tape is an alternative method for collecting epithelial cells. Liquid blood can be collected using a syringe or pipette and transferred to a clean sterile storage tube that contains anticoagulant (EDTA), or by using a swab or piece of fabric to soak up the stain, which should be air dried to prevent the build up of microbial activity. Liquid blood can also be applied to FTA paper that is impregnated with chemicals to prevent the action of microbial agents and stabilize the DNA.

Smaller moveable objects, such as weapons, which might contain biological material are packaged at the scene of crime and examined in the controlled environment of the forensic laboratory. The same range of swabbing, scraping and lifting techniques as used in the field can be employed to collect the biological material. Clothing taken from suspects and victims presents an important source of biological evidence. This is also analysed in the forensic biology laboratory where stains and contact areas can be recorded and then cut out or swabbed.

Sexual and Physical Assault

Following sexual assaults the victim should be examined as soon after the event as possible. Semen is recovered by a trained medical examiner using standard swabs; fingernail scrapings can be collected using a variety of swabs; combings of pubic and head hair are normally stored in paper envelopes. Contact marks, for example bruising caused by gripping or bite marks, can be swabbed for DNA. The same types of evidence (except semen) can be taken after cases of physical assault.

Presumptive Testing

Identifying a red spot on a wall or a white stain on a bed sheet might indicate the presence of blood or semen. A range of presumptive tests are available that aid the identification of the three main body fluids encountered; blood, semen and saliva. Ideally presumptive tests should be safe, inexpensive, easy to carry out, use a very small amount of the sample, and provide a simple indication of the presence or absence of a body fluid. The presumptive test should have no negative effect on DNA profiling. In addition to helping to locate material for DNA analysis, stain characterization can also provide important probative and circumstantial evidence.

Blood

The presumptive tests used to detect the presence of blood take advantage of the peroxidase activity of the haem group which is abundant as part of the haemoglobin molecule within red blood cells – there can be as many as 5 million red blood cells in 1 millilitre of blood. In addition to luminol, two main presumptive tests are available for blood and they work in a similar manner. The haem group can be detected using the colourless reduced dyes Kastle–Meyer (KM) and *leuco-malachite green* (LMG). If haem is present the colourless substrates are oxidized in the presence of hydrogen peroxide and become coloured. In the case of KM a purple colour develops, and when LMG is used a green colour develops. Any of the tests for blood should be considered as a presumptive test and does not confirm the presence of blood because other naturally occurring compounds, such as plant extracts, coffee and some cleaning fluids, can produce the same colour change or light reaction, thus reducing the specificity of the reaction.

Semen

The positive identification of semen can be extremely important evidence to support an allegation of sexual assault and both presumptive and definitive tests are used. A simple test involves assaying for the presence of the enzyme seminal acid phosphatase that is present in high concentrations in seminal fluid. Other body fluids, such as saliva and vaginal secretions, contain the enzyme albeit in significantly lower concentrations and so can give a positive result. Another marker for the identification of semen is the protein P30 that is a *prostate specific antigen* (PSA). The advantage of using PSA compared to the reaction involving acid phosphatase is that PSA is produced independently from the generation of sperm and therefore it can be used for both spermic and azoospermic samples. A definitive test for semen involves treatment with dyes that stain the spermatozoa and allows them to be visualized using a high power microscope; commonly used dyes include haematoxylin-eosin and Christmas tree stain.

Saliva

Saliva is a fluid produced in the mouth to aid in swallowing and the initial stage of digestion. A healthy person produces between 1 and 1.5 litres of saliva every day and can transfer saliva, along with epithelial cells sloughed off from the buccal cavity, in a number of ways. Transfer may be by contact; such as on food products when eating, drinking vessels, cigarette butts, envelopes or in oral sexual assaults. Transfer may also be by aerial deposition of saliva such as on to the front of a mask when worn over the head or onto a telephone when talking into the mouth piece.

Presumptive tests for saliva make use of the enzyme á-amylase which is present at high concentrations and digests starch and complex sugars. The digestion of starch can be measured by the release of dyes that have been covalently linked to insoluble starch molecules. The release of the dye causes a colour change that can easily be detected. Amylases are present in other body fluids such as sweat, vaginal fluid, breast milk and pancreatic secretions; however amylase is present in saliva at concentrations greater than 50 times that in other body fluids.

Epithelial Cells

When an object is touched, epithelial cells can be deposited. The amount of cellular material transferred depends upon the amount of time the skin is in contact with the object; the amount of pressure applied; and the presence of fluid such as sweat to mediate the transfer. Some people transfer their skin cells more readily than others; these people are classified as good shedders. This material can be collected from evidential material by swabbing or by tape lifting. Surfaces that the perpetrator(s) of a crime are likely to have had contact with include door handles, the ends of ligatures, the handles of weapons and contact marks on victims. These are all potential sources of epithelial cells. In most cases the number of cells is very low and the success rate of DNA profiling is limited. Screening methods, for example using the reagent ninhydrin, which detects the presence of amino acids (and is routinely used to develop latent fingerprints), can be helpful in identifying samples that are likely to contain epithelial cells.

Reference Samples

In order to identify samples recovered from the scene of crime, reference samples are needed for comparison. Reference samples are provided by a suspect and, in some cases, a victim. Traditionally, blood samples have been taken and these provide an abundant supply of DNA; however, they are invasive and blood samples are a potential health hazard. Buccal swabs that are rubbed on the inner surface of the cheek to collect cellular material have replaced blood samples in many scenarios. In some circumstances plucked hairs may be used but this source of material is not commonly used.

FTA cards can be used to store both buccal and blood samples. The FTA card is a cellulose based paper which is impregnated with chemicals that cause cellular material to break open - the DNA is released and binds to the card. The chemicals on the card also inhibit any bacterial or fungal growth and DNA can be stably stored on FTA card for years at room temperature as long as the card remains dry.

Storage of Biological Material

Biological material collected for DNA analysis should be stored in conditions that will slow the rate of DNA degradation, in particular low temperatures and low humidity. A cool and dry environment limits the action of bacteria and fungi that find biological material a rich source of food and can rapidly degrade biological material.

The exact conditions depend on the nature of the samples and the environment in which the samples are to be stored. Buccal swabs and swabs used to collect material at a crime scene can be stored under refrigeration for short periods and are either frozen directly or dried and then stored at –20°C for longer term storage. Blood samples will normally be stored at between –20 and –70°C. Buccal and blood samples collected using FTA cards can be stored for years at room temperature. Some items of evidence, like clothing, can be stored in a cool dry room; in temperate regions of the world DNA has been recovered from material stored at room temperature for several years. When samples are not frozen, for example clothing, they are stored in acid-free paper rather than plastic bags, to minimize the build up of any moisture. Once the DNA has been extracted from a sample, the DNA can be stored short term at 4°C but should be stored at –20 to –70°C for long term storage.

3

INHERITANCE IN FORENSIC SCIENCE

The directions for reproduction and metabolic processes in organisms are contained in *nucleic acids*, which are huge biopolymeric molecules consisting of *nucleotide* units each composed of a sugar, a nitrogenous base, and a phosphate group. There are two kinds of nucleic acids. The first of these is deoxyribonucleic acid (DNA), in which the sugar is 2-deoxyribose and the bases may be thymine, adenine, guanine, and cytosine. The second kind of nucleic acid is ribonucleic acid (RNA), in which the sugar is ribose and the bases may be adenine, guanine, cytosine, and uracil. A nucleic acid molecule, which typically has a molecular mass of billions, consists of many nucleotides joined together. Alternate sugar and phosphate groups compose the chain skeleton, and the nitrogenous base in each nucleotide gives it its unique identity. Since there are four possible bases for each kind of nucleic acid, the nucleic acid chain functions like a four-letter alphabet that carries a message for cell metabolism and reproduction.

The structure of DNA is that of a double helix, in which there are two complementary strands of DNA counterwound around each other. In this structure, guanine (G) is opposite cytosine (C), and adenine (A) is opposite thymine (T) in the opposing strand. The structures of these nitrogenous bases are such that hydrogen bonds form between them on the two strands, bonding the strands together. During cell division, the strands of DNA unwind and each generates a complementary copy of itself, so that each new cell has an exact duplicate of the DNA in the parent cell.

2-Deoxyribose (sugar in DNA) **Ribose (sugar in RNA)**

T C U

Thymine (DNA only) **Cytosine** **Uracil (RNA only)**

Single-ring bases called pyrimidines

A G

Adenine **Guanine**

Fused-ring bases called purines

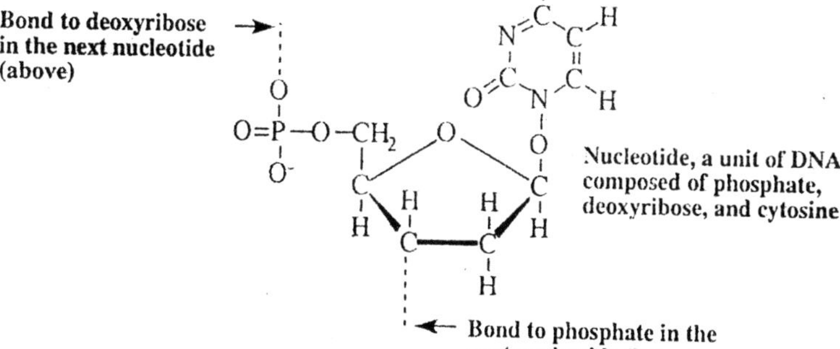

Fig. 3.1. The two sugars, five nitrogenous bases, and phosphate that occur in nuceic acids. Each fundamental unit of nucleic acid is a nucleotide, an example of which is shown.

Chromosomes

The nuclei of eukaryotic cells contain multiply coiled DNA bound with proteins in bodies called *chromosomes*. The number of chromosomes varies with the organism. Humans have 46 chromosomes in their body cells (*somatic cells*) and 23 chromosomes in each *germ cell*, the eggs and sperm that fuse to initiate sexual reproduction. During cell division, each chromosome is duplicated and the DNA in it is said to be *replicated*. The production of duplicates of a molecule as complicated as DNA has the potential to go wrong and is a common mode of action of toxic substances. Uncontrolled cell duplication is another problem that can be caused by toxic substances and can result in the growth of cancerous tissue. This condition can be caused by exposure to some kinds of toxicants.

Genes and Protein Synthesis

The basic units of heredity consist of segments of the DNA molecule composed of varying numbers of nucleotides called *genes*. Each gene gives directions for the synthesis of a particular protein, such as an essential enzyme. Cellular DNA remains in the cell nucleus, from which it sends out directions to synthesize various proteins. The first step in this process is *transcription*, in which a segment of the DNA molecule generates an RNA molecule called *messenger RNA* (mRNA). The nucleotides in a gene are arranged in active groups called *exons*, separated by inactive groups called *introns*, of which only the exons are translated during protein synthesis. In producing mRNA, adenine, thymine, cytosine, and guanine in DNA cause formation of uracil, adenine, guanine, and cytosine, respectively, in the mRNA chain.

The mRNA generated by transcription travels from the nucleus to cell *ribosomes*. The mRNA attached to a ribosome operates with *transfer RNA* (tRNA) to cause the synthesis of a specific protein in a process called *translation*. Sequences of three bases on a chain of mRNA, a base triplet called a *codon*, specify a particular amino acid to be assembled on a protein. Each codon matches with a complementary sequence of amino acids, called an *anticodon*, on a tRNA molecule, each of which carries a specific amino acid to be assembled in the protein being synthesized. For example, a codon of GUA on mRNA pairs with tRNA having the anticodon CAU. The tRNA with this anticodon always carries the amino acid valine, which becomes bound in the protein chain through peptide linkages. So by matching successive codons on mRNA with the complementary anticodons on tRNA carrying specific amino acids, a protein chain with the appropriate order of amino acids is assembled.

There are 20 naturally occurring amino acids that are assembled into proteins. If codons consisted of only two base pairs, each of which could be one of four nitrogenous bases, directions could be given for only $4 \times 4 = 16$ amino acids. Using three bases per codon gives a total of $4 \times 4 \times 4 = 64$ possibilities, which is more than sufficient. This provides for some redundancies; for example, six different codons specify arginine. Codons also signal initiation and termination of a protein chain.

Toxicological Importance of Nucleic Acids

In discussing the toxicological importance of nucleic acids, it is useful to define two terms relating to the genetic makeup of organisms and their manifestations in organisms. The *genotype* of an individual describes the genetic constitution of that individual. It may refer to a single trait or to a set of interrelated traits. The *phenotype* of an individual consists of all of the individual's observable properties, as determined by both genetic makeup and environmental factors to which the individual has been exposed. Until relatively recently, genetic effects were largely inferred from observations of genotype, such as by observations of strange mutant offspring of fruit flies irradiated with x-rays. With the ability to perform DNA sequencing, it has become possible to determine genotypes exactly through the science of *genomics*, which gives an accurate description of the complete set of genes, called the *genome*. This capability makes possible accurate observations of the effects of toxicants on genotype.

Nucleic acids are very important in toxicology for two reasons. The first of these is that heredity as directed by DNA determines susceptibility to the effects of certain kinds of toxicants. This phenomenon makes different species respond differently to the same toxicant; for example, the LD_{50} for dioxin in hamsters is 10,000 times that in guinea pigs. In addition, differences in genotype cause substantial differences in the susceptibilities of individuals within a species to effects of toxicants. The second reason that nucleic acids are so important in toxicology is that the intricate processes of reproduction and protein synthesis in organisms as carried out by nucleic acids can be altered in destructive ways by the effects of toxic substances. This can result in effects such as harmful mutations, uncontrolled replication of somatic cells (cancer), and the synthesis of altered proteins that do not perform a needed function in an organism.

Destructive Genetic Alterations

Toxic substances and radiation can damage genetic material in three major ways: gene mutations, chromosome aberrations, and changes in the number of chromosomes. Each of these has the potential to be quite damaging. They are discussed separately here.

It should be kept in mind that cellular DNA is susceptible to damage from spontaneous processes that are not caused by xenobiotic toxicants. These include hydrolysis reactions, oxidation, nonenzymatic methylation, and effects from background ionizing radiation. To cope with these insults, organisms have developed a variety of mechanisms to repair DNA. These fall into two broad categories, the first of which is *reversal*, consisting of direct repair of a damaged site (such as removal of a methyl group from a methylated DNA base). The second category of coping with damage to DNA is *excision*, in which a faulty sequence of DNA bases is removed and replaced with a new segment, a process called *nucleotide excision*, or *base excision*, in which the damaged base molecule is removed and replaced with the correct one. In both cases, the remaining strand of DNA is used as a template to replace the correct complementary bases on the damaged strand.

Gene Mutations

When the sequence of bases in DNA is altered, a *gene mutation* (also called *point mutation*) may result. One way in which this may occur is through a *base-pair substitution*, where a base pair refers to two nitrogenous bases, one a purine and the other a pyrimidine, bonded together between two strands of DNA. If the purine–pyrimidine orientation remains the same, the alteration is called a *transition*. For example, guanine (G) always pairs with cytosine (C), whereas adenine (A) always pairs with thymine (T), switching an A:T pair on DNA with a G:C pair results in a transition. A *transversion* occurs when a purine on one strand is replaced by a pyrimidine, and on the corresponding location of the opposite strand, a pyrimidine is replaced by a purine. For example, the switch of A:T → C:G means that the purine adenine on one strand is switched with the pyrimidine cytosine on the second strand, whereas the pyrimidine thymine on the first chain is switched with the purine guanine on the second chain.

The two possible consequences of base-pair substitution are that the gene encodes for either no amino acid or the wrong amino acid. Effects can range from minor results to termination of protein synthesis.

The loss or gain of one or two base pairs in a gene causes an incorrect reading of the DNA and is known as a *frameshift mutation*.

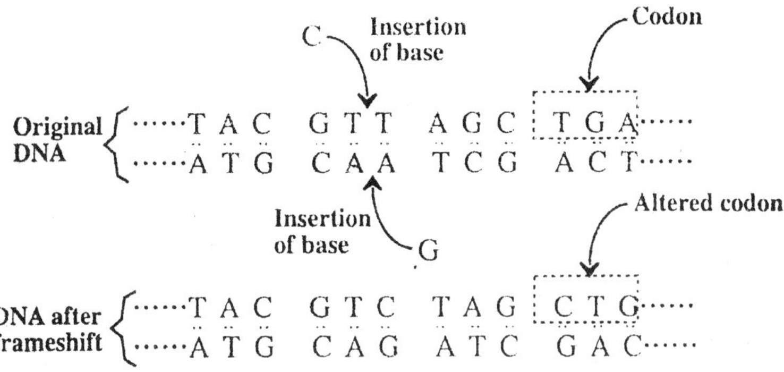

Fig. 3.2. Illustration of a framework mutation in which a base pair is inserted into a DNA sequence, altering the codons that code for kinds of amino acids in a protein.

It is seen that subsequent codons are changed, which almost always means that there are "*nonsense*" codons that specify no amino acid. So either no protein or a useless protein is likely to result.

Chromosome Structural Alterations, Aneuploidy, and Polyploidy

Chromosome structural alterations occur when genetic material is changed to such an extent that visible alterations in chromosomes are apparent under examination by light microscopy. These changes may include both breakage of chromosomes and rearrangements. In some cases, chromosome alterations can be passed on to progeny cells. Chromosomes may break during replication and then rejoin incorrectly.

Not only can there be changes in structures of chromosomes, but it is also possible to have altered numbers of them. *Aneuploidy* refers to a circumstance in which a cell has a number of chromosomes differing by one to several from the normal number of chromosomes; for example, a human cell with 44 chromosomes rather than the normal 46. *Polyploidy* occurs when there is a large excess of numbers of chromosomes (such as half again as many as normal).

Genetic Alteration of Germ Cells and Somatic Cells

Genetic alterations or abnormalities of germ cells, some of which can be caused by toxicant exposure, can be manifested by adverse effects on progeny. The important health effects of these kinds of alterations may be appreciated by considering the kinds of human maladies that are caused by inherited recessive mutations. One such disease is cystic fibrosis, in which the clinical phenotype has thick, dry mucus in the tubes of the respiratory system such that inhaled bacterial and fungal spores cannot be cleared from the system. This results in frequent, severe infections. It is the consequence of a faulty chloride transporter membrane protein that does not properly transport Cl^- ion from inside cells to the outside, where they normally retain water characteristic of healthy mucus. The faulty transporter protein is the result of a change of a *single amino acid* in the protein.

Genetic alteration of somatic cells, which may also occur by the action of toxicants, is most commonly associated with cancer, the uncontrolled replication of somatic cells. Replication and growth of cells is a normal and essential biological process. However, there is a fine balance between a required rate of cell proliferation and the uncontrolled replication characteristic of cancer, that is, between the promotion and restriction of cell growth. The transformation of normal cells to cancer cells results from the excessive growth-stimulating activity of *oncogenes*, which are produced from genes called *proto-oncogenes* that promote normal cell growth.

The body has defensive mechanisms against the development of cancer in the form of *tumor suppressor genes*. Whereas the activation of oncogenes can cause cancer to develop, the inactivation of tumor suppressor genes disables the normal mechanisms that prevent cancerous cells from developing. Both the activation of oncogenes and the inactivation of tumor suppressor genes contribute to the development of many kinds of cancer.

Gene mutations, chromosome structural alterations, and aneuploidy may all be involved in the development of cancer. These effects are involved in the initiation of cancer. However, they may also be involved in the progression of cancer through genetic effects such as damage to tumor suppressor genes.

Toxicant Damage to DNA

Toxicants can cause destructive alteration of DNA, specifically the nitrogenous bases on the DNA nucleotides. There are three ways in which this may occur. One of these is *oxidative alteration*, in which a functional group on a base is oxidized. The other two modes of damage are by binding of electrophilic molecules or molecular fragments to the electron-rich N and O atoms on the bases to form *DNA adducts*. There are two major kinds of such adducts. One kind is produced by *alkylating agents* that add methyl ($-CH_3$) groups or other alkyl groups to bases. The other kind of adduct is that in which a *large bulky group* is attached.

Methyl group to guanine in DNA is an alkylation reaction in which the small methyl group is attached. The attachment of a large

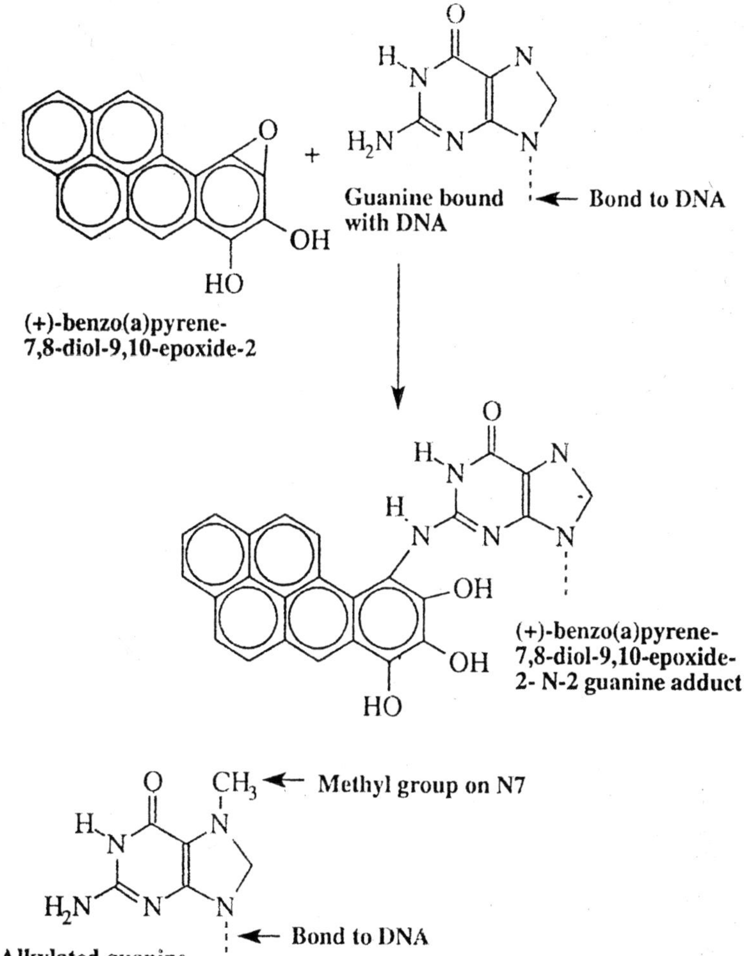

(+)-benzo(a)pyrene-7,8-diol-9,10-epoxide-2

Guanine bound with DNA

Bond to DNA

(+)-benzo(a)pyrene-7,8-diol-9,10-epoxide-2- N-2 guanine adduct

Methyl group on N7

Bond to DNA

Alkylated guanine

Fig. 3.3. Formation of the bulky guanine adduct of (+)-benzo(a)pyrene-7,8-diol-9,10-epoxide-2.

bulky group is illustrated by the binding to guanine of benzo(a)pyrene-7,8-diol-9,10-epoxide, a substance formed by the epoxidation of the polycylic aromatic hydrocarbon benzo(a)pyrene, followed by hydroxylation and a second epoxidation. There are actually four stereoisomers of this compound, depending on the orientations of the epoxide group and the two hydroxide groups above or below the plane of the molecule. Only one of these stereoisomers, designated (+)- benzo(a)pyrene-7,8-diol-9,10-epoxide-2, is active in binding to guanine to initiate cancer.

A major effect of binding of a base on DNA can be altered pairing as the DNA replicates. For example, the normal pairing of guanine is with cytosine, a G:C pair. Guanine to which an alkyl group has been attached to oxygen may pair with thymine, which subsequently pairs with adenine during cell replication. This leads to a G:C → A:T transition, hence to altered DNA, which may initiate cancer.

Another effect on DNA can result when alkylated bases are lost from the DNA polymer. For example, guanine alkylated in the N^7 position has a much weakened bond to DNA and may split off from the DNA molecule:

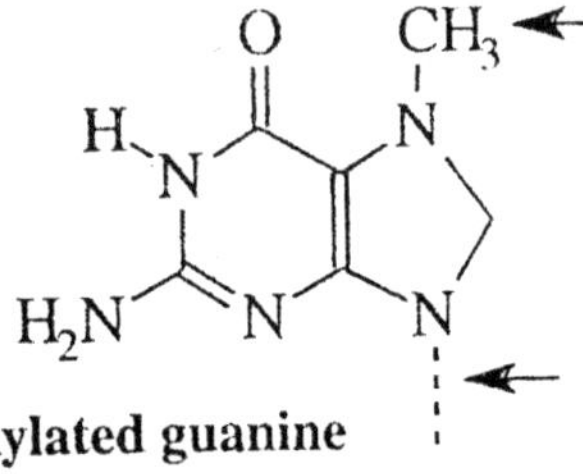

O CH$_3$ ← **Methyl group on N7**

H N N

H_2N N N

← **Bond to DNA**

Alkylated guanine

This leaves an AP site (where AP stands for apurinic or apyrimidinic). This site may become occupied by a different base, leading again to alteration of DNA.

The DNA alterations described above have involved covalent bonding of groups to nitrogenous bases. Another type of interaction is possible with highly planar (flat) molecules that are able to fit between base pairs, a phenomenon called *intercalation*. This can cause deletion or addition of base pairs, leading to mutation and cancer. A compound known to cause this phenomenon is 9-aminoacridine:

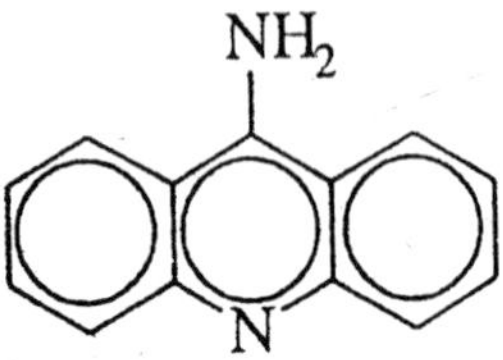

NH_2

N

9-Aminoacridine

Predicting and Testing for Genotoxic Substances

The ability to predict and test for genotoxic substances is important in preventing exposure to these substances. One way in which this is done is by the use of *structure-activity relationships*. Several classes of chemicals are now recognized as being potentially genotoxic (mutagenic) based on their structural features. The single most important indicator of potential mutagenicity of a compound is electrophilic

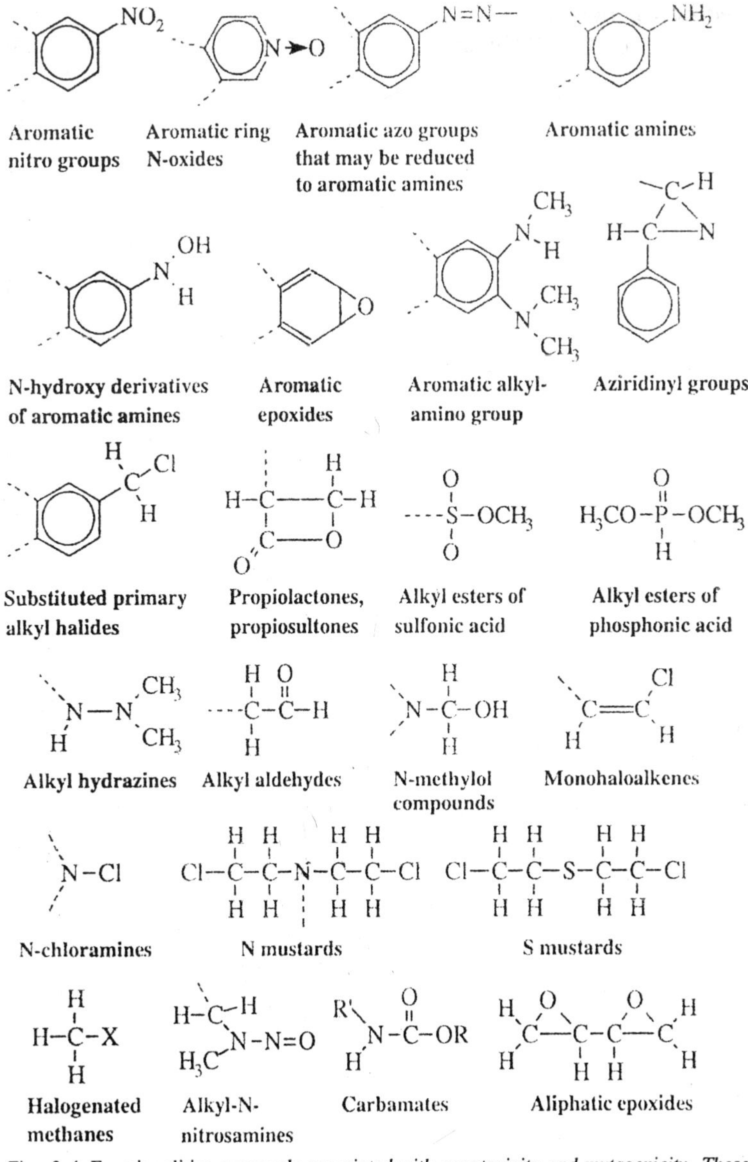

Fig. 3.4. Functionalities commonly associated with genotoxicity and mutagenicity. These groups are used in structure-activity relationships to alter for possible carcinogenic substances.

functionality showing a tendency to react with nucleophilic sites on DNA bases. Steric hindrance of the electrophilic functionalities may reduce the likelihood of reacting with DNA bases. Some substances do not react with DNA directly, but generate species that may do so. Compounds that generate reactive free radicals fall into this category.

Tests for Mutagenic Effects

In addition to structure-activity relationships, dozens of useful tests have been developed for mutagenicity to germ cells and somatic cells and inferred carcinogenicity. The most straightforward means of testing for effects on DNA is an examination of DNA itself. This is normally difficult to do, so indirect tests are used. One useful test measures the activity of DNA repair mechanisms (unscheduled DNA synthesis); a higher activity is indicative of prior damage to DNA.

Commonly used tests for mutagenic effects are most effective in revealing gene mutations and chromosome aberrations. Mammals, especially laboratory mice and rats, have long been used for these tests. As sophistication in cell culture has developed, mammalian cells have come into widespread use for genotoxicity testing. Insects and plants have been used, as well as bacteria, fungi, and viruses. Tests on insects favor *Drosophila* (fruit flies), on which much of the pioneering studies of basic genetics were performed. For reasons of speed, simplicity, and low cost, tests on microorganisms and cell cultures are favored.

Microorganisms used in genetic testing may consist of wild-type microorganisms that have not been preselected for a particular mutation and mutant microorganisms that have a readily identifiabie characteristic, such as an inability to make a particular amino acid. These classes of microorganisms give rise to two general categories of mutagenicity tests based on observation of phenotypes (offspring after exposure to the potential mutagen). The first of these involves *forward mutations*, in which the organism loses a gene function that can be observed in the phenotype. The second type of test entails *back mutation* (*reversion*), in which the function of a gene is restored to a mutant. Testing of cultured mammalian cells usually involves forward mutations that confer resistance of the cells to a toxicant, that is, some of the cells exposed to the test compound reproduce in the presence of another substance that is normally toxic to the cells. Testing with microorganisms favors reversion with restoration of a gene function that has been lost in a previous mutation through which the test microorganisms were developed. Microbial tests are particularly useful for changes that occur at low frequencies because of the large number of test organisms that can be exposed to a potential mutagen.

Bruce Ames Test and Related Tests

The most widely used test for mutagenicity is the Bruce Ames test, named after the biochemist who developed it. A number of variations and improvements of this test have evolved since it was first published. The Bruce Ames test and related ones make use of *auxotrophs*, mutant microorganisms that require a particular kind of nutrient and will not grow on a medium missing the nutrient, unless they have mutated back to the wild type. The Bruce Ames test uses bacterial *Salmonella typhimurium* that cannot synthesize the essential amino acid histidine and do not normally grow on histidine-free media. The bacteria are inoculated onto a medium that does not contain histidine, and those that mutate back to a form that can synthesize histidine establish colonies, which are assayed on the growth medium, thereby providing both a qualitative and quantitative indication of mutagenicity. The test chemicals are mixed with homogenized liver tissue to simulate the body's alteration of chemicals (conversion of procarcinogens to ultimate carcinogens). Up to 90% correlation has been found between mutagenesis on this test and known *carcinogenicity* of test chemicals.

Cytogenetic Assays

Cytogenetic assays use microscopic examination of cells for the observation of damage to chromosomes by genotoxic substances. These tests are based on the cellular *karyotype*, that is, the number of chromosomes, their sizes, and their types. The standard test cell for cytogenetic testing is the Chinese hamster ovary cell. In addition to a well-defined karyotype, these cells have the desired characteristics of a low number of large chromosomes and a short generation time. In order to test a substance, the cells have to be exposed to it at a suitable part of the cell cycle and examined after the first mitotic division. (Mitosis refers to the process by which the nucleus of a eukaryotic cell divides to form two daughter nuclei.) This means that the examination is performed on cells in the metaphase of nuclear division, in which the chromosomes are conducive to microscopic examination and abnormalities are most apparent. Abnormalities in the chromosomes are then scored systematically as a measure of the effects of the test subsance. A complication in these assays can be the requirement to use such high doses of a test substance that it is toxic to the cell in general, resulting in chromosomal aberrations that may not be due to specific genotoxicity. In addition to performing cytogenetic assays on cell cultures, it is often desirable to perform *in vivo cytogenetic assays* consisting of microscopic examination of cells of whole animals — most commonly mice, rats, and Chinese hamsters — that have been exposed to toxicants. Bone marrow cells are commonly used because they are abundant and replicate rapidly. A disadvantage to in vivo cytogenetic assays is that the system is much less controlled than in assays on cell cultures. The major advantage is that the test substance has had the opportunity to be metabolized (which can produce a more genotoxic metabolite), and normal processes such as DNA repair can occur.

Transgenic Test Organisms

As discussed above, in vivo assays reproduce the metabolic and other processes that a xenobiotic substance undergoes in an organism. However, microbial systems are much simpler and more straightforward to detect mutations. A clever approach to combining these two techniques makes use of transgenic recombinant DNA techniques to introduce bacterial genes into test animals for chemical testing, and then transfers the genes back to bacteria for assay of mutagenic effects. Genes most commonly used for this purpose are the *lac* genes from *Escherichia coli* bacteria. These genes are involved with the expression of the *β-galactosidase* lactose-metabolizing enzymes, which consist of three proteins. Either the *lacI* genes, which suppress formation of the enzymes, or the *lac*Z genes, which allow formation of the enzymes, may be used. When *lacI* genes are used that are inserted transgenically into the test mouse (known by the rather picturesque brand name of Big Blue Mouse), the mouse is treated with potential mutagen for a sufficient time to allow for mutant expression. Samples are then collected from various tissues of the mouse. The segment of DNA involved with the *lacI* genes is then extracted from these samples and put back into *Escherichia coli* bacteria, which are grown in an appropriate medium containing lactose. The bacteria with unaltered *lacI* genes (*lacI*$^+$) do not produce *β-galactosidase*, whereas the mutants (*lacI*$^-$) do produce *β-galactosidase*. Another kind of mouse (brand name MutaMouse) has been used that contains *lac*Z genes that encode for expression of *β-galactosidase*. In this case, the procedure is exactly the same, except that the nonmutants (*lac*Z$^+$) produce *β-galactosidase* and the mutants (*lac*Z$^-$) do not produce it.

One reason for the popularity of this test is the facile detection of *β-galactosidase* activity. This is accomplished with the chromogenic substrate 5-bromo-4-chloro-3-indoyl-*β*-D-galactopyranoside, which is metabolized by *β-galactosidase* to form a blue product. Therefore, when colonies of the *Escherichia coli* bacteria are grown in an assay, the *lac*$^+$ colonies are blue and the *lac*$^-$ colonies are white.

Despite the rather involved nature of the *lac* test described above, it has several very important advantages. The simplicity of assaying microorganisms is one advantage. The fact that the potential mutagens act within a complex organism (the mouse) where they are subject to a full array of absorption, distribution, metabolism, and excretion processes is another advantage. Finally, the procedure allows sampling from specific tissues, such as liver or kidney tissue.

Genetic Susceptibilities and Resistance to Toxicants

The discussion in this chapter so far has focused on the toxicological implications of damage to DNA by toxic agents. However, the genetic implications of toxicology are much broader than damage to DNA because of the strong influence of genetic makeup on susceptibility and resistance to toxicants. It is known that susceptibility to certain kinds of cancers is influenced by genetic makeup. Mention was made of *oncogenes*, associated with the development of cancer, and *tumor suppressor genes*, which confer resistance to cancer. Susceptibility to certain kinds of cancers, some of which are potentially initiated by toxicants, clearly have a genetic component. Breast cancer is a prime example in that women whose close relatives (mother, sisters) have developed breast cancer have a much higher susceptibility to this disease, to the extent that some women have had prophylactic removal of breast tissue based on the occurrence of this disease in close relatives. It is now possible to run genetic tests for two common gene mutations, BRCA1 and BRCA2, that indicate a much increased susceptibility to breast cancer.

Another obvious genetic aspect of toxicology has to do with the level in skin of *melanin*, a pigment that makes skin dark. Melanin levels vary widely with genotype. Melanin confers resistance to the effects of solar ultraviolet radiation, which is absorbed by DNA in skin cells, causing damage that in the worst-case results in deadly melanoma skin cancer. Skin melanin is a chromophore (a substance that selectively absorbs light and ultraviolet radiation) that absorbs visible light and, more importantly, ultraviolet radiation in the UVB wavelength region of 290 to 320 nm. Melanin's presence confers resistance to sunburn and other toxic effects of ultraviolet radiation.

Genetic susceptibilities exist to the chemically induced adverse effects of ultraviolet radiation and visible light, a condition known as *photosensitivity*. *Porphyria*, an abnormal extreme sensitivity to sunlight, can result from chemical exposure in genetically susceptible individuals. Lupus erythematosus, a heritable disease manifested by red, scaly skin patches, is characterized by abnormal sensitivity to ultraviolet radiation. Porphyrias in genetically susceptible individuals, which can be induced by chemicals such as hexachlorobenzene and dioxin, occur through the malfunction of enzymes involved in producing the porphyrin heme used in hemoglobin. This results in the accumulation of porphyrin precursors in the skin. Exposed to ultraviolet light at 400 to 410 nm, these precursors reach excited states, which may generate damaging free radicals through interaction with cellular macromolecules and O_2. Phototoxicity can also be caused by xenobiotic substances either applied to skin or distributed systemically. Photoallergy is a condition in which exposure to a xenobiotic substance, either through application to skin or systemically, results in sensitization to ultraviolet radiation.

Although many smokers develop lung emphysema with age, some do so extremely early, suggesting a genetic susceptibility to this malady. It is now believed that early onset of emphysema occurs with a rare mutation that prevents production of the protein $alpha_1$-antiprotease in the lungs. In normal individuals this substance retards the protein-digesting activity of elastase enzyme. The elastin protein that constitutes elastic tissue in the lung is readily destroyed by the action of elastin enzyme in the lung in individuals with the mutation that does not allow for generation of $alpha_1$-antiprotease. This allows for the loss of lung elasticity characteristic of emphysema at a very early stage of smoking.

Since the early 1940s, it has been known that there is a genetic predisposition to allergic contact dermatitis, a skin condition that is one of the most common maladies caused by workplace exposure to xenobiotics and to cosmetics. A study published in 1993 revealed that some individuals have a genetic predisposition to produce human leukocyte (white blood cell) antigen, resulting in allergy to nickel, chromium, and cobalt.

TOXICOGENOMICS

Genomics was mentioned as the science dealing with a description of all the genes in an organism, its genome. Because of the known relationship of gene characteristics to disease, the decision was made in the mid-1980s to map all the genes in the human body. This collective body of genes is called the human genome, and the project to map it is called the Human Genome Project. The original impetus for this project in the U.S. arose because of interest in the damage to human DNA by radiation, such as that from nuclear weapons. But from the beginning it was recognized that the project had enormous commercial potential, especially in the pharmaceutical industry, and could be very valuable in human health.

The sequencing of the human genome has been done on individual chromosomes. Each chromosome consists of about 50 million base pairs. However, it is possible to sequence only about 500 to 800 base pairs at one time, so the DNA has to be broken into segments for sequencing. There are two approaches to doing this. The publicly funded consortium working on the Human Genome Project identified short marker sequences on the DNA that could be recognized in reassembling the information from the sequencing. The private concern involved in the effort used a process in which the DNA was broken randomly into fragments, each of which was sequenced. The data from the sequencing were then analyzed using powerful computer programs to show overlap, and the complete gene sequence was then assembled.

In 2001, a joint announcement from the parties involved in the Human Genome Project revealed that the genome had been sequenced. Details remain to be worked out, but the feasibility of the project has been demonstrated. This accomplishment is leading to a vast effort to understand genetically based diseases in humans, to develop pharmaceutical agents based on genetic information, and to develop other areas that can use information about the genome. The benefits and consequences of mapping the human genome will be felt for many decades to come.

The mapping of the human genone, as well as those of other organisms, has enormous potential consequences for toxicology. This has given rise to the science of toxicogenomics, which relates toxicity and the toxicological chemistry of toxicants to genomes at the molecular level. More broadly, toxicogenetics relates genetic variations of subjects in their response to toxicants. Toxicogenomics has the potential to revolutionize understanding of toxic substances, how they act, and how to develop effective antidotes to them. Techniques are being developed to examine at the molecular level the interaction of specific toxicants and their metabolites with genes, even including genetic material such as DNA arrays printed on plates.

It may be anticipated that much of what will eventually be learned about toxicogenomics will be based on knowledge acquired through the science of pharmacogenomics, in which genetic variabilities to pharmaceuticals are determined in an effort to develop much more effective, sharply focused drugs. Such variations arise from differences in targets or receptors and differences in drug-metabolizing enzymes. Pharmacogenomics applies to both pharmacokinetics, which is how an organism processes a pharmaceutical agent, and pharmacodynamics, which is how the agent affects a target in an organism or a disease against which the agent acts. By analogy, toxicogenomics can be applied to toxicokinetics, the metabolism of a toxic agent, and toxicodynamics, its effect on a target.

Genetic Susceptibility to Toxic Effects of Pharmaceuticals

Pharmaceuticals have provided numerous examples of genetic susceptibilities to toxicants. This is because major pharmaceutical drugs are given to hundreds of thousands, or even millions, of people so that genetic defects that result in toxic effects will show up even if only very small fractions of the population (estimated to be 1 in 10,000 or less for cases of toxic effects to the liver) are genetically predisposed to adverse effects. Unfortunately, at such low levels of occurrence, there is as of yet no good way to predict such rare adverse effects in advance.

An example of genetic susceptibility to toxic effects of a drug is provided by mercaptopurine drugs, such as 6-mercaptopurine, used as antitumor agents. The active forms of these drugs are the methylated metabolites, as shown for the methylation of 6-mercaptopurine:

SH → SCH_3

Thiopurine S-methyltransferase
SAM cofactor

6-mercaptopurine **6-methylmercaptopurine**

The methylation reaction occurs by the action of thiopurine S-methyltransferase enzyme with the S-adenosylmethionine (SAM) cofactor, discussed as a methylating agent. In some children, the gene responsible for making the enzyme is mutated, the enzyme is not synthesized, and toxic effects occur due to the accumulation of 6-mercaptopurine. A knowledge of this genetic condition prior to treatment could prevent this toxic effect. In general, genetic screening for adverse drug reactions could be very helpful in increasing the safety of medical treatment. The most common adverse effect of drugs in genetically susceptible individuals is hepatotoxicity (toxic effects to the liver).

The reason that the liver is damaged in these cases is that it is the first major organ to process substances taken orally and has an abundance of a wide variety of active enzymes that metabolize drugs (or fail to do so, as is the case with 6-mercaptopurine). Although total liver failure from toxic side effects of pharmaceuticals is rare, somewhat more than half the cases seen at liver transplant centers are caused by drugs. However, far more people are afflicted with liver disease as the result of taking prescribed drugs. Many drugs have been

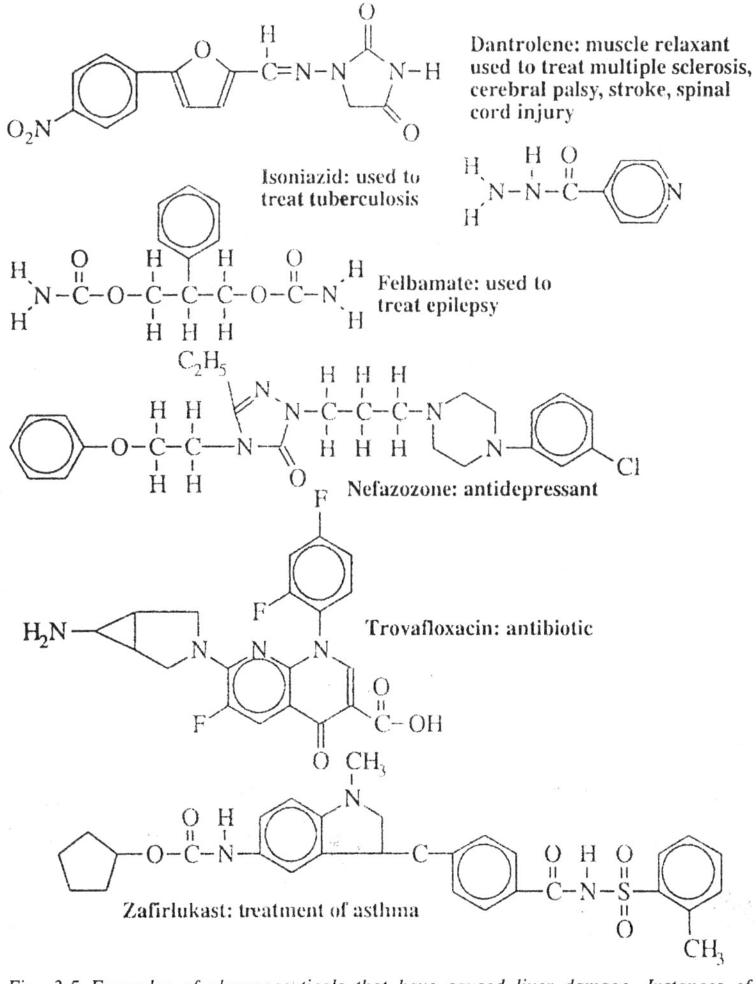

Dantrolene: muscle relaxant used to treat multiple sclerosis, cerebral palsy, stroke, spinal cord injury

Isoniazid: used to treat tuberculosis

Felbamate: used to treat epilepsy

Nefazozone: antidepressant

Trovafloxacin: antibiotic

Zafirlukast: treatment of asthma

Fig. 3.5. Examples of pharmaceuticals that have caused liver damage. Instances of hepatotoxicity have been rare, suggesting a genetic susceptibility in some cases.

implicated in liver damage to relatively few individuals, many of whom probably have a genetic susceptibility to adverse effects from the drugs.

One of the most prominent examples of a drug that caused liver failure in a small percentage of genetically susceptible people is Rezulin. This oral diabetes drug was approved for use in 1997 and rapidly became very popular. However, within three years it had been implicated in 90 cases of liver failure, of which 63 were fatal. This led to the withdrawal of Rezulin from the market in March 2000. Not long before the problems with Rezulin surfaced, Duract, a pain killer, and Trovan, an antibiotic, were withdrawn from the market. Four deaths from liver failure were attributed to Duract, and eight other patients required liver transplants. Trovan was implicated in 14 cases of acute liver failure.

Arguably, the most cases of liver toxicity from drugs occur from ingestion of acetaminophen, a widely used pain killer and fever reducer. About 800 cases of acute liver failure each year are attributed to this drug, and fatalities have been around 80 to 90 annually. Most of these cases are probably not attributable to genetic susceptibilities because most of them have been due to accidental or intentional (suicidal) overdoses. An interesting aspect of acetaminophen toxicity is that chronic heavy drinkers can tolerate only about half the dose of acetaminophen that causes liver failure in nondrinkers. The reason for this is that chronic ingestion of alcohol increases the activity of cytochrome P-450 enzyme, which breaks acetaminophen down into products that can be toxic to the liver, leading to significantly higher levels of these toxic breakdown products.

4

Forensic Pathology

Knowledge of the *postmortem interval* (PMI) is absolutely essential in criminal investigations for further measures of tracing, collection of evidence and inclusion or exclusion of suspects. However, the current methods for estimating PMIs - particularly longer ones - are far from accurate and straightforward. Therefore, the boards of prosecution deem a new method that may solve these problems extremely important. Additionally, the procedures and results of forensic examinations have a strong impact on relatives and friends of a victim, influencing the process of mourning and the management of sentiments of real and imagined guiltiness. Questions such as 'would an earlier visit have saved my beloved person?' are often as fundamental as the cause of death itself. The value of a reliable evaluation of the PMI for relatives has been shown in a study where 43% of the interviewed persons wanted to know the circumstances of the unexpected death, including the exact time. It is obvious that a determination of PMI using non-invasive techniques would further reduce the trauma for relatives and friends, resulting in an increased willingness to agree with the forensic investigation. We will report here the estimation of PMIs using *magnetic resonance spectroscopy* (MRS), a non-invasive method that acquires metabolic data from tissue *in situ*. Since magnetic resonance imaging (MRI) is increasingly used to examine bodies in forensic investigations, MRS can be combined with these imaging methods during the same examination.

Classical Methods for the Determination of PMI

Traditionally, time of death was defined by an irreversible termination of circulation caused by a cessation of cardiac function.

This definition had to be modified in intensive care medicine where circulation and respiration were maintained artificially. The resulting working definition uses brain death as the moment that characterizes individual death. Nevertheless, cessation of cardiac function still represents the time of death in the vast majority of forensic cases and thus the transition of the body into the so-called supravital state. Supravital reactions are, by definition, phenomena that can be observed in the time between irreversible loss of function of the organ systems and the actual death of the cells in a particular organ. Since the resistance of various tissues to oxygen deficiency differs greatly, these phenomena in different tissues can cover a time span from a few minutes to some hours following the irreversible loss of brain function.

In the early PMI, i.e. during the first 3 days postmortem, estimation of the PMI in forensic medicine is mostly based on the evaluation of supravital signs (e.g. livor mortis, rigor mortis) and the decrease of body temperature after death. The medico-legal significance of livor and rigor mortis is limited by non-standardized and subjective examination techniques and various ante- and postmortem factors. The decrease of body temperature after death – alone or in combination with non-temperature-based indicators – is a reliable and thoroughly investigated phenomenon. Considering the weight of the body and environmental factors, the body core temperature permits a retro-

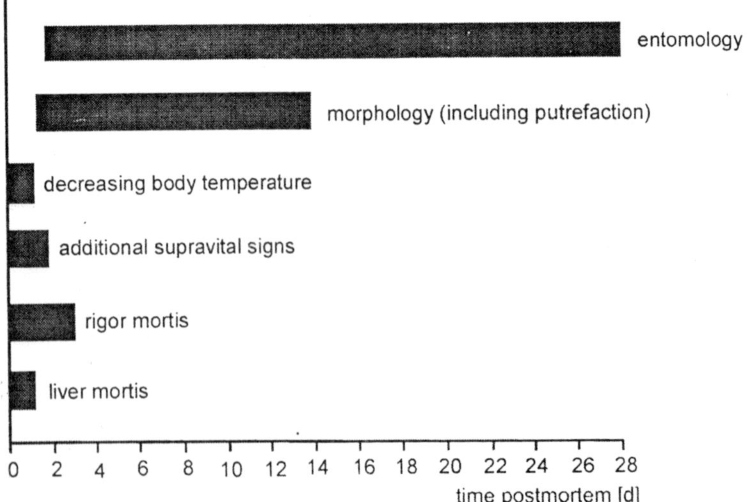

Fig. 4.1. Overview of the periods in which the classical forensic methods can be used for estimation of the postmortem interval (PMI).

calculation of a time span within which death occurred. However, body temperature approaches ambient temperature approximately 30 hours after death and thereafter is no longer of value for assessing time of death. A survey at the Institute of Forensic Medicine at the University of Bern revealed that 16% of 559 bodies were not found before two or more days after death. This corresponds to a significant number of cases where an objective method for determination of the PMI is missing. In that later postmortem phase, an estimation of the PMI has to rely on the evaluation of putrefaction signs of the body, fragmentary criminological information from witnesses or, in certain cases, entomological studies of insects colonizing the body.

Putrefaction signs can be observed starting at 2–3 days postmortem, however, while the general sequence of their appearance has been described frequently, a review of the forensic literature showed that no systematic description of morphological changes during decomposition of the body giving precise time frames for each sign had been established. This finding was additionally documented by an internal survey including nine experienced forensic pathologists. It was found that even common changes being observed in the majority of cases led to an uncertainty of up to 5 days for PMIs of the same time range. Thus, it is generally accepted that morphological signs cannot be used as reliable and objective indicators of the PMI, particularly since they are strongly dependent on external (e.g., temperature, humidity) and internal factors (e.g., antemortem treatment and diseases). Forensic entomology uses the fact that insects colonize bodies during the process of decomposition in various waves, depending on the stage of decomposition of the corpse. While this method allows for an estimation of the PMI in certain cases, it is extremely time-consuming and demanding. In addition, insect populations vary with geographical region, season and environment, making standardization almost impossible.

The disintegration of the chemical, physical and morphological organization starting immediately after death is known as '*autolysis*' and results from the action of endogenous enzymes and the cessation of oxygen-dependent biochemical processes. The failure of the body to maintain homeostasis leads to a breakdown of the internal equilibrium as well as to the degradation of proteins, carbohydrates and fats. This results in an increase of breakdown products. Chemical analyses for the purpose of a PMI estimation based on concentration changes have been performed on body fluids such as blood and blood serum, vitreous humor of the eyes and skeletal muscle. Some projects concentrated on specific groups of metabolites, e.g. the decomposition of fats or proteins. Collection of body fluids can be very difficult depending on the PMI and the state in which the individual body is found. While this could be less problematic in brain tissue due to the protection by the skull, only a few studies were published that analysed brain tissue chemically for an estimation of the PMI. On the other hand, examinations of the brain would be particularly interesting because inter-individual differences in tissue composition are very small compared to other tissues of the body (e.g. skeletal muscle or liver).

To date, none of the chemical methods have become generally accepted, nor are they routinely applied for PMI estimation. One reason for this disappointing outcome may be the fact that most of these methods attempted to characterize PMI by a few or even just one specific parameter. It seems that chemical methods based on multiple metabolite concentrations lead to more successful PMI estimations while methods based on a single metabolite failed to be used regularly in the past.

Magnetic Resonance Spectroscopy

Magnetic resonance became an established tool in diagnostic radiology and clinical research. Since it is so popular in medicine, it is often ignored that clinical magnetic resonance is just one of many applications of the '*nuclear magnetic resonance*' (NMR) effect. In chemistry and biophysics, so-called '*high-resolution*' NMR spectroscopy is one of the most important methods to study the structure of organic and inorganic substances. Today, the development and analysis of chemical compounds is unthinkable without NMR technology; even complicated three-dimensional structures of large biological molecules can be understood with the help of this potent method. In medicine, *magnetic resonance imaging* (MRI) is nowadays a particularly valuable and versatile instrument in diagnostic radiology, due to its detailed and accurate representation of *in vivo* anatomy and function. *Magnetic resonance spectroscopy* (MRS) combines the volume-selective data acquisition of MRI with the chemical information provided by NMR. Without reaching the sensitivity and resolution of high-resolution NMR, *in situ* MRS allows for a non-invasive examination of the chemical composition from selected volumes in humans.

In principle, the above-mentioned applications of the NMR effect are all based on the fact that stable atomic nuclei have a magnetic moment and an angular momentum, called '*spin*'. When a material is placed in an external magnetic field, these '*spins*' begin to tumble in a precession. This motion enables the nuclei to absorb and emit electromagnetic waves with a frequency in the MHz range, depending on the strength of the magnetic field and the type of isotope. While MR images are generated in the majority of cases from the signals of hydrogen nuclei (^{1}H) in water, MR signals can also be obtained from various other stable isotopes, including phosphorus (^{31}P), carbon (^{13}C), fluorine (^{19}F), sodium (^{23}Na) and others. Magnetic resonance spectroscopy makes particular use of ^{1}H, ^{13}P and ^{31}C. Depending on the local chemical environment, different atoms in a molecule resonate at slightly different frequencies, resulting in the so-called '*chemical shift*'. This chemical shift is resolved in spectroscopic applications (NMR and MRS), however it is neglected in standard imaging. It is measured in relative units (parts per million, ppm), and represents the x-axis of a spectrum. The spectrum of butyrate, a molecule that has three types of hydrogen atoms: an H–C–H group close to the carboxyl group C=O, a second H–C–H group in the middle and a CH_3 group at the end of the molecule. The hydrogen atoms in each of these groups are identical and resonate at a specific position on the chemical shift axis. Since the area of the resonance peak under specific experimental conditions is proportional to the concentration of the chemical species, butyrate should show three single resonance lines with a 2:2:3 ratio of the areas. The reason why the lines are further split into so-called '*multiplets*' is a mutual influence of the nearest hydrogen atoms. This effect complicates the spectrum; however, it also helps to identify chemical species.

In other words, spectroscopy (either NMR or MRS) uses frequency information of absorbed and emitted radio waves to identify different chemical compounds – the position of the signal in the spectrum defines the chemical nature while the signal area reveals the amount of molecule. The width of a resonance line is another important experimental factor since it defines the resolution of the spectrum, i.e. how many chemical species can be observed separately. In addition to the type of chemical compound, the homogeneity of the magnetic field influences the width of the lines, i.e. the resolution of a spectrum. The homogeneity of the magnetic field can be improved by technical means, called '*shimming*', in turn biological tissue can introduce additional inhomogeneity of the field, particularly at air–tissue borders. As we will see below, gas bubbles that are produced during the process of body decomposition can severely decrease the homogeneity of the magnetic field such that spectral resolution becomes a problem.

While high-resolution NMR uses small sample tubes in vertical magnets up to a magnetic field strength of 22 Tesla, *in situ* and *in vivo* MR spectra are acquired in horizontal bore magnets with typical field strengths of 1.5 or 3 Tesla. Selection of the signal-generating tissue ('*voxel*', 'region of interest ROI') is achieved by techniques that are common with MRI. The voxel can be placed at the desired anatomical location based on a series of localizer MR images and contains typically a few millilitres in ^{1}H-MRS. An MR spectrum can be acquired by technicians in much less than an hour without the need for sample preparation and a ^{1}H-MR-spectrum contains information on about 20 metabolites simultaneously. Depending on the automation of the spectral analysis, final data can be obtained in less than an hour.

In order to estimate the PMI, ^{1}H-MRS of the brain is particularly advantageous:

1. ^{1}H-MRS provides high relative sensitivity, allowing the selection of small voxels.
2. Established MRS sequences for ^{1}H allow for a robust and easy selection of spectroscopic volumes with subsequent absolute quantitation of the metabolites.
3. A majority of clinical MRS investigations are performed on the brain, resulting in widespread experimental experience and a large collection of reference data in healthy and pathological brain tissue.
4. About 20 different characterized substances can be observed and quantified.
5. Inter-individual differences in brain tissue composition are rather small and can partly be attributed to the aging process, which can be corrected for.
6. The brain is protected by the skull after death, i.e. destruction by environmental factors (scavengers, external microorganisms) is minimized, and when the brain tissue becomes decomposed and liquefied the skull guarantees a certain fixation.

A determination of late PMIs by means of ^{1}H-MRS of the brain is based on the fact that MRS reveals concentrations of multiple metabolites in a single spectrum. If there are calibration curves of metabolite changes following death, it should be possible to compare the measured concentrations in a brain with an unknown time of death with the calibration curves. The following paragraphs will illustrate how calibration curves are established in an animal model, how first cases of human bodies are studied and which statistical procedures are used to compare actual metabolite concentrations and calibration curves.

Sheep Model

Ethical reasons prevent the storage of human bodies longer than necessary for a regular forensic examination, making it almost impossible to establish calibration curves of metabolite changes over a longer time based on human bodies. An animal model allows decomposition processes of the brain to be followed repeatedly and under standardized conditions at different, optimally spaced points in time.

While in the following study a sheep model is used, there have also been reports on studies in pigs. For practical reasons, the animal has to be a mammal and should be available in a slaughterhouse. The size of the animal brain should be as large as possible to optimize voxel selection; however, the complete head should still be within the size of an MR head-coil. As described in detail by Ith *et al.* (2002), the heads used in the following study were harvested from healthy sheep, which died in the course of the normal slaughtering process. The heads were separated from the bodies and stored at constant temperature (21 ± 3°C). *In situ* brain spectra from the frontal lobe and the parieto-occipital region were acquired regularly up to 18 days postmortem. A striking increase of the signal amplitude shows how decomposition of brain tissue makes many more metabolites MR-visible.

In order to obtain quantitative data, absolute concentrations of the metabolites had to be determined. This is achieved by a comparison of the signals with the signal from water (fully relaxed) from the same volume and with an estimation of the resonance area by a mathematical modelling of the experimental curve, i.e. by a fitting procedure. A well-known fitting algorithm is 'LC Model' that uses linear combinations of model-spectra, a so-called '*basis set*' of spectra from measurable substances. The basis set, which in clinical practice is used to fit brain spectra, consists of about 25 metabolites: acetate, alanine, aspartate, cholines, creatines, phospho-ethanolamine, ethanol, gamma-aminobutyric acid, glucose, glutamine, glutamate, glutathione, glycine, lactate, myo-inositol, scyllo-inositol, *N*-acetyl-asparates, taurine, and valine. However, during the particularly interesting late postmortem phase, several substances appeared that had not been observed in brain spectra before then, and had to be identified by means of high-resolution NMR as trimethylamine, propionate, butyrate and isobutyrate. Since the additional metabolites are detected only after the third day postmortem and do not contribute significantly to spectra before then, they are most likely of bacterial origin. A chemical identification of substances is not only necessary for a deeper understanding of the underlying processes, but also to analyse the spectra mathematically. An incomplete set of theoretical spectra results in a poorer fit, and spectral features could be wrongly attributed to substances that are included in the basis set. This would lead to an under-estimation of the unknown substance and, subsequently, to an erroneous over-estimation of an included substance with similar spectral features. Therefore, a complete set of spectra improves the accuracy for all substances in a spectrum. Inclusion of the newly identified metabolites and succinate (corrected for pH and temperature effects) resulted in a significantly improved fit quality and reliable quantitation of up to 30 metabolites.

The time course of the observed metabolites has then been followed up to 18 days postmortem. While some of the time courses are ambiguous or too scattered, others show a clear and unequivocal time dependence, such as NAA/NAAG or butyrate. Obviously, the decomposition process follows certain rules that can be used for an estimation of the PMI. In the early postmortem phase metabolic changes probably due to autolytic processes are observed, i.e., a decay of the '*neuronal marker*' *N*-acetyl-aspartate into acetate and aspartate and the build-up of lactate during glycolysis. Later, starting at about 3 days postmortem, bacterial decomposition processes, i.e. heterolysis, come up in addition to autolysis, leading to an observation of substances that are associated with the action of bacteria, e.g. butyrate, trimethylamine or propionate.

How to Predict the PMI Based on MRS Measurements

Following the acquisition of MR data, the time course of the metabolite concentrations has to be described by mathematical functions. Since the exact biochemical mechanisms are not yet known, it is reasonable to chose functions with the smallest number of parameters that still lead to an appropriate description of the time course. The concentration of NAA+NAAG is described by a decreasing exponential function - it may serve as an indicator for the period below 70 h. Butyrate starts to increase at about 50 h postmortem and reveals an unequivocal function up to 400 h that is parameterized by a quadratic function.

As soon as such a calibration curve is established, a measured metabolite concentration corresponds to a specific point in time when the metabolite is expected to have this concentration. These error ranges can now be used to estimate the error of the resulting PMI. It is obvious that equivocal, scattered or flat parts of the time course

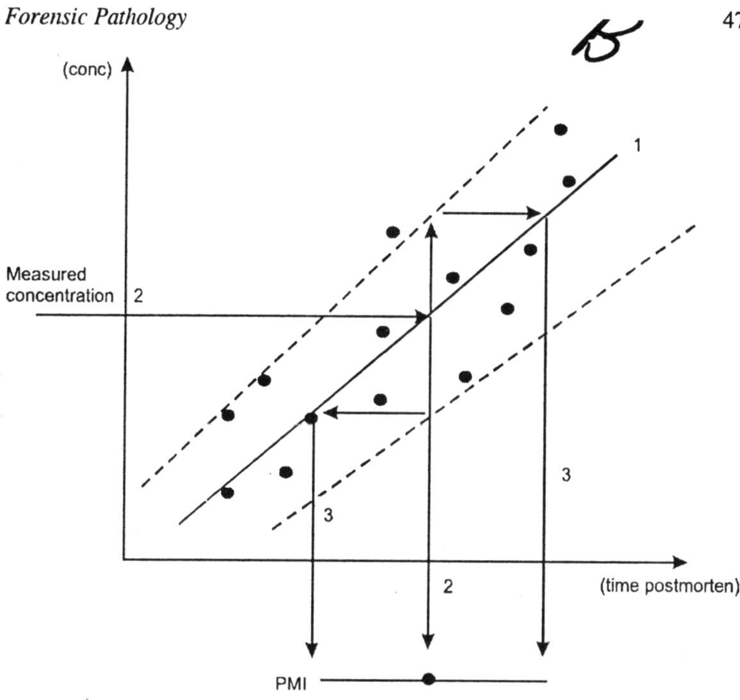

Fig. 4.1. Schematic representation of the mathematical calculation of the predicted PMI.

cannot be used as a calibration curve. Therefore, from the 30 visible metabolites, just about 10 are fitted by mathematical functions and 5 of them are used for further analysis.

Since experimental data from different metabolites will not predict exactly the same PMI, it is necessary to combine the predictions obtained from different metabolite curves by a robust procedure. In addition, and in order to restrict the fit to meaningful (i.e. unequivocal) parts of the measured time course, limits for concentrations and times are applied – full details about this procedure can be found in Scheurer *et al.* (2005) but to summarize: final estimations for the PMI are calculated on the basis of PMIs from the different metabolites, weighted by their accuracy.

The correlation coefficients of the predicted time versus true PMI are $r = 0.93$ for the whole time period (0–300 h) and $r = 0.97$ for the time period below 250 h. Predicted times combined from these five metabolites correlate very well with true times postmortem up to 250 h. In contrast, PMIs of >250 h are systematically underestimated in this model system. It is surprising that this result is almost independent for various combinations of metabolites ($r = 0.87$–0.97, mean 0.92), showing that the influence of the choice of metabolites is almost negligible. Obviously, a larger number of metabolites leads to smaller variances, however the robustness of the method is convincing. Eventually, a combination of acetate, alanine, butyrate, trimethylamine and propionate is used for evaluation of the experimental data.

Human Bodies

In order to test the applicability of the sheep model to human bodies, four selected human cases from the Institute of Forensic Medicine were examined. The human cases were selected in order to match the ambient conditions of the animal model, i.e. were found in closed areas and the skull and brain were not injured. The forensic PMI was estimated by traditional forensic methods, i.e. by evaluating livor and rigor mortis, putrefaction signs and criminological information. After arriving at the Institute of Forensic Medicine the bodies were stored at 4°C for 20–70 h before being examined by MRS. To make human data comparable to the sheep model, storage times in the cold have been subtracted from the total forensic PMI based on the experience that bacterial decomposition is massively reduced at low temperatures. The MR data acquisition was done the same way as for the sheep heads.

The same metabolites occur at comparable points in time, in particular metabolites that are not found *in vivo* can be found postmortem in sheep as well as in human spectra. This is not self-evident since the bacterial colonization in an animal body could be different from humans. This qualitative agreement leads to the conclusion that the sheep model can be used to construct calibration curves, which then could be used for estimating PMIs in humans.

The four substances trimethylamine, propionate, butyrate and isobutyrate are generally not observed in healthy human brain tissue, however they are known as products of microbial activity. In addition, trimethylamine is almost exclusively found in bacterial metabolism. Succinate, another substance specifically seen in brain abscesses, could also be measured in sheep and human brain postmortem.

When calibration curves from sheep data are used to estimate PMIs in the four human cases, the estimated PMI can be compared with 'true' PMIs that have been mainly determined from criminal evidence. The comparison shows an acceptable agreement, however the large error bars of forensic PMIs demonstrate that the determination of PMIs in forensic medicine is often very imprecise, covering time spans of several days or even weeks. This is an inherent problem and illustrates that a real '*gold standard*' for validation of the MRS data is largely missing. It takes a prohibitively long time to wait for a large number of the rare cases where a human body is found after a long time, while it is still possible to restrict the time of death to a reasonable period. It will be necessary to collect these rare cases in order to validate the time curves established in the sheep model, however it is completely unrealistic to define the calibration curves directly in humans.

Outlook

The influence of environmental (i.e. external) factors such as ambient temperature, humidity, air motion, clothes, blankets etc. upon the processes of decreasing body temperature and decomposition is undisputed. However, in order to take these factors into account, it is necessary to consider additional information, e.g. from weather reports, etc. In forensic practice, the influence of temperature has been studied in detail, particularly the effect of temperature on specific processes, e.g. the degradation of muscle tissue, the increase of potassium in the vitreous humor, etc. Many authors also studied the effect of ventilation, humidity and clothing and tried to classify the extent of the influence of these factors on the decomposition rate. Experience shows that the overall decomposition rate in tissues of human bodies stored at 4°C is significantly slower than at 20°C. However, since the changes observed by ^{1}H-MRS include two different mechanisms, i.e., autolysis and heterolysis, it is not at all obvious that the time courses of the metabolites from the two processes are affected in the same way by variations of the temperature. This is at the same time a complication as well as a chance. If the two processes proceed independently, the interpretation of the calibration curves would get much more complicated and, in turn, independent calibration curves for autolysis and heterolysis would contain additional information that could, in principle, be used to estimate the influence of the ambient temperature. In an ongoing study the influence of temperature on brain decomposition tissue is investigated with sheep heads in order to extend the sheep model.

Although it is generally accepted that internal factors may change the progress of decomposition, the influence of most of them is not well documented. Among them are antemortem diseases, which in some cases may even provoke death, such as diabetes or alcoholism. In contrast, the influences of drugs such as antibiotics have been proven to be insignificant for the later postmortem period since they are degraded within a short time. The influence of other drugs is still unclear. The cause of death can promote decomposition by facilitating bacterial colonization, i.e. in the form of injuries of the skin or enhanced blood fluidity in asphyxia. Systematic studies of the influence of the different factors are difficult, because they interfere and can hardly be standardized.

While it is obvious that calibration curves cannot be obtained with human cases, it is nevertheless necessary to validate the curves obtained from the sheep model with human cases at specific points of time. As described in the previous section, it is unlikely that the time of death can be determined exactly in a body that is only found several days or weeks after death. A delay in locating a human body is often due to limited or non-existent social contacts, which makes an exact determination of the PMI very difficult. Since restriction of the PMI is often based on criminal evidence that is not immediately available when the body is found, bodies have to be included in a study with the hope that a further restriction of the time span is possible. To date, 40 human bodies from the Institute of Forensic Medicine have been investigated by means of *in situ* ^{1}H-MRS of the brain - in many of these cases it is not possible to restrict the possible PMI to a short period in time, therefore it is necessary to acquire a larger number of bodies in future.

Despite the fact that many factors such as ambient temperature influence the results and that a gold standard is almost missing in human cases, the simple concept of a non-invasive and simultaneous observation of multiple metabolites during decomposition of the brain is promising. Since MRI is increasingly used to examine bodies in forensic investigations, the additional effort and expense to obtain a ^{1}H-MR spectrum of the brain are acceptable and can provide crucial information on the time of death, particularly during the later postmortem phase.

5

Clinical Forensic Studies

Clinical and forensic toxicology is concerned with the detection, identification, and measurement of toxic compounds and their metabolites in human body fluids and tissues. Most often the toxic compounds are drugs taken either accidentally or intentionally in quantities sufficient to cause an adverse reaction or death. Analysis and identification of a possible drug or drug combinations, toxicological drug screening and confirmation should encompass as many different classes of drugs as possible. The most important classes being salicylate, paracetamol, antiepileptics, antidepressants, neuroleptics, hypnotics (benzodiazepines, barbiturates, diphenhydramine), digoxin, and theophylline, as well as many illicit drugs, such as opiates, methadone, D-lysergic acid diethylamide (LSD), cocaine, and/or its major metabolite benzoylecgonine, cannabinoids and amphetamines. Currently, urinary drug monitoring has established itself as the basis of clinical and forensic toxicology.

It is also the method of choice for drug testing of employees at the workplace, athletes at sports events (such as the Olympics), and patients in drug-substitution programs. Since positive urine tests for an illegal drug can result in severe penalties and drastically change the life of the presumed abuser, urine drug testing must be as free from error as possible. Positive results from an initial screening process should always be confirmed by another method that is more selective and possibly also more sensitive than that used for rapid screening. Furthermore, monitoring of drugs and metabolites in urine is a useful approach for the assessment of drug metabolism and to investigate the patient's compliance.

Comprehensive approaches, such as immuno- and chromatographic assays, for the analysis of illicit and licit drugs in urine, have been developed and are routinely used in clinical and forensic laboratories all over the world. Typically, immunological techniques, including those based on *fluorescence-polarization immunoassay* (FPIA), *enzyme-multiplied immunoassay technique* (EMIT), *cloned enzyme donor immunoassay* (CEDIA), and *kinetic interaction of microparticles in solution* (KIMS), are employed because of their ease of use and speed of analysis. Immunoassays, however, often lack specificity and sometimes sensitivity. Thus, they are inappropriate for confirmation of the presence of a specific drug or metabolite. Moreover, most commercial immunoassays are by nature unsuitable for the simultaneous monitoring of multiple drugs and metabolites. Chromatographic approaches, such as *thin-layer chromatography* (TLC), *high-performance liquid chromatography* (HPLC), and *gas chromatography* (GC), can provide results for multiple components. These methods typically require extensive sample pretreatment, are characterized by a modest sample throughput, and are difficult to automate. Despite the widespread use of TLC as a screening method in forensic science, due to difficulties inherent with the technique, it is not routinely used in clinical laboratories. HPLC, on the other hand, is widely applied for drug screening. Automated HPLC with multiwavelength detection is commercially available and has been successfully employed as a drug profiling system for emergency toxicology. Although these methods are useful for screening, gas chromatography with mass spectrometry (GC-MS), and to a minor extent, liquid chromatography with mass spectrometry (LC-MS), are employed for confirmatory testing in clinical and forensic laboratories.

Capillary electrophoresis (CE) has been used to separate and identify many drugs, including drugs of abuse, in a variety of body fluids, including urine. Thus many CE-based assays for drugs of toxicological interest have emerged. A comprehensive concept for toxicological drug screening and confirmation has also been developed and applied to the monitoring of drugs of abuse in patient urine. In this chapter, CE-based assays for analysis of illicit and abused drugs and their major metabolites in urine are described. Usually two CE methods are employed: *capillary zone electrophoresis* (CZE) and *micellar electrokinetic capillary chromatography* (MECC). Examples discussed in this chapter come from data gathered in our laboratory and were selected to provide insight into the strategies employed for sample preparation and drug detection.

ANALYSIS OF URINARY DRUGS AND METABOLYTES BY CAPILLARY ELECTROPHORESIS WITH OPTICAL DETECTION

Assays with No or Minimal Sample Detection

When using CE, urine specimens can often be injected directly into the separation column or may require only minimal pretreatment, such as dilution, centrifugation, or filtration. The data represents MECC data of a urine from a patient with suspected salicylate intoxication. This sample tested markedly positive (> 1 mM) for salicylate employing the modified spectrophotometric method of Trinder. Using a *fluorescence polarization immunoassay* (FPIA), the serum of the same patient was found to contain 3.0 mM salicylate, a value that is above the recommended therapeutic range of 1.1–2.2 mM. After direct urine injection, MECC revealed an overloaded, completely unresolved electropherogram in which the presence of salicylate was difficult to identify. However, after 10-fold dilution, clear separation of salicylate and two of its metabolites, gentisic acid and salicyluric acid, were obtained. In addition, an endogenous marker substance, uric acid, could also be identified. For all four compounds, there was excellent agreement of the normalized absorbance spectra with those of pure compounds allowing identification as well as purity assessment of these zones. Comparison of panels A and B also reveals the impact of the sample matrix, showing that detection time by itself is not adequate for analyte identification. However, in conjunction with multiwavelength detection it is possible to identify analytes unambiguously. Analysis of the same sample by CZE at pH 8. 3 also gave comparable data.

Currently, the most popular optical detection method is on-column UV absorbance. However, due to the short optical pathlength within the detection cell, the lowest detectable concentration (without preconcentration or stacking of solutes) is in the 1–10 μM (low μg/mL) range. This sensitivity is 1–2 orders of magnitude less than found using HPLC. Other optical detection techniques include fluorescence (F) and *laser-induced fluorescence* (LIF). When compared to UV absorption detection, sensitivity enhancement using F and LIF can be between 10- and 1000-fold, respectively. These two detection modes can also provide increased selectivity that is useful for identification of selective analytes. Both UV absorption data (wavelength of 220 nm) and the fluorescence data (emission wavelength of 450 nm) reveal the presence of salicylate. By using fluorescence detection molecules of similar structure, including the metabolites salicyluric acid and gentisic acid, can be recognized. Thus the simultaneous monitoring of UV

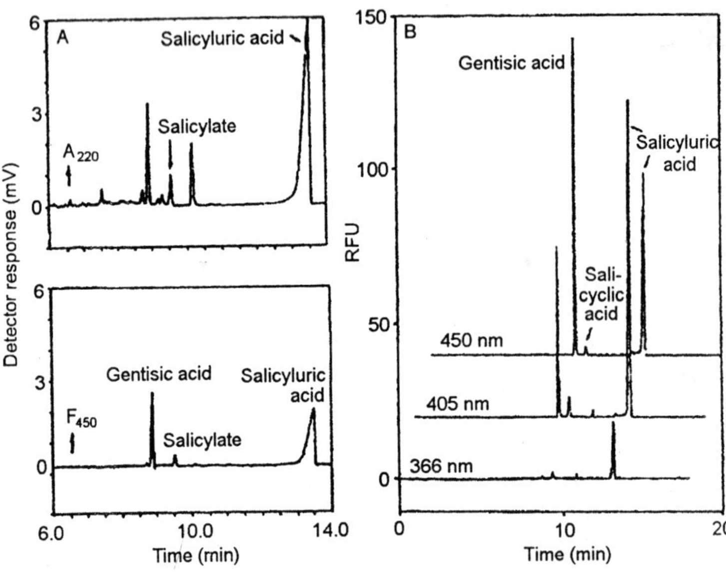

Fig. 5.1. Monitoring of urinary salicylate and metabolites by CE with fluorescence detection.

absorption and fluorescence provides valuable information for drug monitoring as well as for the determination of metabolites. Comparison shows that LIF detection provides a significantly higher sensitivity compared to that obtained by UV and F detection. The same urine used was analyzed after 30-fold dilution with water and detected with a HeCd laser (excitation 325 nm line). Using various narrow bandfilters (emission), it can be shown that salicylic acid, salicyluric acid, and gentisic acid have differences in their emission spectrum. Recording multiple electropherograms with different filters can provide multi-wavelength fluorescence data, permitting analyte identification. Thus, instrumentation with wavelength-resolved fluorescence detection would provide straightforward data that could be employed for spectral identification in a way comparable to UV absorption.

Although LIF provides the highest sensitivity, it is of limited use as there are only a few laser lines available for analyte excitation and there are only a limited number of the compounds of interest that fluoresce without derivatization. Using laser-induced resonance energy transfer as described by Petersen et al., the LIF application range can be expanded to nonfluorescing solutes. In this approach, the energy absorbed by a donor molecule is transferred to an acceptor compound (e.g., terbium or europium) which subsequently fluoresces. The feasibility of this method was demonstrated in a CZE setup by detecting salicylic acid, gentisic acid, salicyluric acid and 4-aminosalicylic acid after direct injection of fortified urine. A HeCd laser (325 nm) was used and the terbium ion luminescence at 547 nm was monitored. In the absence of terbium, no fluorescence at 547 nm was detected. The analysis of drugs of abuse in real world samples, however, has not yet been studied. The same is true for CE configurations with indirect fluorescence or absorbance detection, which have been employed extensively in other applications.

Assays Based on Extraction, Hydrolysis, and Stacking

Analytes that cannot be monitored by direct sample injection or after minimal sample pretreatment have to be extracted and often concentrated. Depending on application, analytes may also have to be hydrolyzed. Conventional liquid-liquid or solid-phase extraction procedures are typically employed when extraction is found to be necessary. Another method that is being investigated and thus not yet used routinely for analyte concentration is on-line extraction and preconcentration of analytes. On-column preconcentration can also be attained by various electrokinetic injection and stacking procedures.

The urine was from a patient who received 1.5 mg racemic MDMA/kg body weight and was collected 12 h after drug administration. After direct injection of untreated urine, MDMA (22.5 μg/mL) could be determined easily. By using solid-phase extraction (2 mL urine with reconstitution in 200 μL of 10-fold diluted running buffer) MDMA and its metabolite 3,4- methylenedioxyamphetamine (MDA) could be detected. However, the major metabolite, 4-hydroxy-3-methoxymethamphetamine (HMMA, a compound that is mainly excreted as conjugates), could only be monitored after enzymatic hydrolysis prior to solid-phase extraction. These data illustrate the impact of the various extraction procedures. With extraction, interfering endogenous substances are removed and analytes of interest concentrated by reconstitution of the dried extract in a volume that is smaller than the initial urine volume. After hydrolysis, metabolites can be analyzed that—because of lack of a specific extraction process or lack of appropriate reference substances—could otherwise not be monitored.

Many assays have been developed that are based on pretreatments. Of particular interest is an assay for multiple classes of drugs that include opiates, methadone, cocaine, and benzoylecgonine, amphetamine and analogs, methaqualone, 11-nor-Δ^9 -tetrahydrocannabinol-9-carboxylic acid (THC), benzodiazepines, barbiturates, diphenhydramine, and so

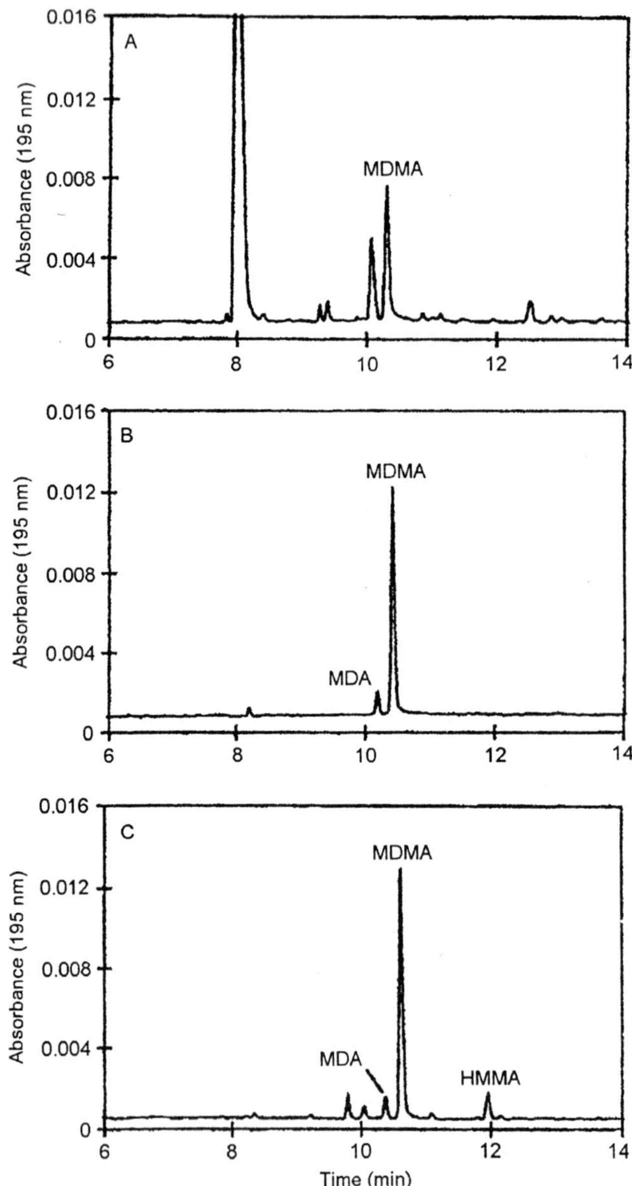

Fig. 5.2. CZE assay for Ecstasy (MDMA) and its major metabolites in human urine. Data shown were obtained after direct urine injection (A) solid-phase extraction (B), and enzymatic hydrolysis and solid-phase extraction (C) of a urine that was collected 12 h after ingestion of 1.5 mg recemic MDMA per kg body weight.

on. This assay was developed in our laboratory and has been used to analyze urine samples received for drug screening from the local University Hospital. It is based on a two-step, solid-phase extraction with a copolymeric sorbent followed by analysis of the two concentrated extracts by MECC or CZE with on-column fast scanning polychrome detection. The spectral information obtained in this approach is used to help identify the substances. From the same aliquot of urine, the two-step extraction procedure allows analysis of barbiturates, some benzodiazepines, THC and methaqualone (in the first eluate), as well as opiates, cocaine and benzoylecgonine, selected benzodiazepines or their metabolites, methadone and its primary metabolite 2-ethylidene-1,5-dimethyl-3,3-diphenylpyrrolidine (EDDP), diphenhydramine and amphetamines (in the second eluate). MECC data of a urine specimen from a hospitalized patient that was found to be (i) markedly positive for cocaine, opiates, methaqualone, and methadone using EMIT; (ii) EMIT negative for amphetamines, barbiturates, and benzodiazepines; and (iii) positive for cannabinoids employing an FPIA immunoassay. Using 5 mL urine and the two-step extraction procedure with methylene chloride as first elutant and methylene chloride/isopropyl alcohol (80:20) containing 10% NH_3 as second elutant, the presence of methaqualone, benzoylecgonine, and opiates was confirmed. Peak assignment was achieved through comparison of retention times and absorption spectra of eluting peaks with those of computer-stored control runs. The presence of 6-acetyl morphine indicates the possible consumption of heroin. The peak denoted with M was found to have the same normalized spectrum as methaqualone. Furthermore, peaks M_1 and M_2 were determined to have spectra that are very similar to that of methaqualone. Thus, the assay is assumed to confirm not only the presence of methaqualone, but also some of its many metabolites. For detection of THC, the urine would have to be hydrolyzed prior to extraction. Methadone and EDDP (which were found in the second fraction) elute in the micelle peak and, therefore, would have to be analyzed by CZE.

Compared to GC-MS, CE instrumentation is less expensive and somewhat simpler to operate. However, in addition to the structural information provided by MS, the GC-MS detection sensitivity is higher than that of MECC and CZE with on-column UV absorption detection. Nevertheless, for most compounds, the sensitivity of our MECC and CZE assays (about 50 ng/mL with application of 5 mL urine) is equal to or better than those of commercial immunoassays, which are typically employed for rapid urine screening. LSD is an exception as the required cutoff value for that compound is 0. 5 ng/mL. In the two-step extraction procedure, LSD appears in the second fraction with a comparable detection limit as that for other illicit substances. Thus, this generalized procedure is not adequate for analysis of LSD in the required concentration range. However, electroinjection in conjunction with LIF has recently been shown to permit the determination of urinary LSD in the low ppb concentration level. Also the two-step extraction procedure in combination with CE was found to be capable of recognizing false-negative results from immunological screening processes.

Electrophoretic mass transport is highly regulated, allowing charged solutes to be concentrated (stacked) across an electrolyte discontinuity. This also includes the boundary initially produced between sample and running buffer. In CE, this inherent feature of electrophoresis may take place when the sample compounds encounter isotachophoretic conditions (isotachophoretic sample stacking is based on differences in electrophoretic mobilities) or when the conductivity of the sample is less than that of the buffer (field-amplified sample stacking). After hydrodynamic sample introduction, stacking techniques are not only dependent on sample composition, but also on the sample volume injected and are thus limited by the capillary volume. Experimentally determined enhancement factors associated with these on-column stacking techniques typically do not exceed 100. Head-column, field-amplified sample stacking (also referred to as field-amplified sample injection) associated with electrokinetic sample introduction takes place at the tip of the column removing the limitation of injection volume. It is typically performed with a sample of low conductivity and a short plug of water at the capillary inlet. During electroinjection, analytes are stacked at the interface between the low-conductivity zone and the running buffer. With this type of injection, very little sample solvent is co-injected because the net electroosmotic velocity is typically much smaller than the local electrophoretic transport. Using this approach, a 1000-fold sensitivity enhancement can easily be obtained and ng/mL drug levels can be determined using UV absorption detection. Based on this principle, a microassay for urinary dihydrocodeine and nordihydrocodeine employing microliter urine volumes has recently been developed. In addition, Taylor et al. and Wey and Thormann demonstrated that a lower detection limit is obtained when extracted opiates are injected electrokinetically instead of hydrodynamically. The same was found to be true for analysis of urinary amphetamines. It is important to realize that detection limits in CE are not only dependent on the type of optical detector used, but also on the matrix of the sample and the injection procedure employed.

CE-Based Immunoassays for Urinary Drugs of Abuse

The combination of immunochemistry and CE has lead to the emergence of a number of competitive binding drug assays using labeled drugs as fluorescent tracers. These procedures incubate small amounts of urine (20–50 μL), antibody solution, and tracer prior to application of an aliquot of the mixture onto the capillary. After separation of the unbound fluorescent tracer and antibody-tracer-complex by CZE or MECC, detection is by LIF detection. Chen and co-workers reported the feasibilities for immunological determination of urinary morphine and PCP, in addition to morphine, PCP, THC, and benzoylecgonine by CZE using drug-cyanine conjugates as tracers and LIF detection with a He-Ne laser (excitation: 543 or 633 nm; emission: 590 or 690 nm). Other approaches employed fluorescein-labeled tracers and LIF detection with an Ar ion laser (excitation: 488 nm; emission: 520 nm). Using this approach, monitoring of urinary benzoylecgonine by CZE, urinary methadone, and amphetamines by MECC- and CZE-based immunoassays, and a CZE four-analyte immunoassay for urine screening using reagents from Abbott's TDxFLx FPIA kits, is possible. Furthermore, Choi et al. described the use of various antibodies for CZE-based immunological analysis of methamphetamine in urine.

Typically the automated solution-based immunoassays for drugs of abuse that are in widespread use are based on FPIA, EMIT, CEDIA, and KIMS. All of these methods represent one analyte immunoassays (e.g., for methadone or benzoylecgonine) or assays for one group of analytes, such as opiates and amphetamines. Other approaches, such as those with discrete placement of antibodies in spatially separated zones on a solid support onto which binding of different antigens can take place (e.g., the Triage 7 and 8 systems comprising immunoassays for seven and eight analytes or group of analytes, respectively) permit simultaneous screening for multiple components or multiple groups of analytes. Alternately, the Testcup-5 system of Roche Diagnostic Systems combines a cup for urine collection and a panel with five assays. These noninstrumental multianalyte immunoassays were developed for on-site testing of drugs of abuse. CE has also been found suitable for the performance of simultaneous immunoassays of more than one analyte (or more than one group of analytes) in a single sample. Our four-analyte CE-based immunoassay uses four different sets of reagents, namely those for methadone (M), opiates (O), the cocaine metabolite benzoylecgonine (C) and amphetamine/methamphetamine (A) and was thus referred to as the MOCA assay. It was applied to the screening of drugs of abuse in fortified blank urines, commercial-quality control urines and patient samples and was validated. Data obtained with the MOCA assay were found to be quantitative and to be in agreement with data resulting from routine urinary screening using EMIT and FPIA. The electropherograms were obtained with a blank urine, with a low-level control urine containing 300 ng/mL methadone, 250 ng/mL morphine, 500 ng/mL D-amphetamine, and 500 ng/mL benzoylecgonine (center graph) and with the external quality control urine No. 106. For all four analytes, small peaks for the free tracers were noted

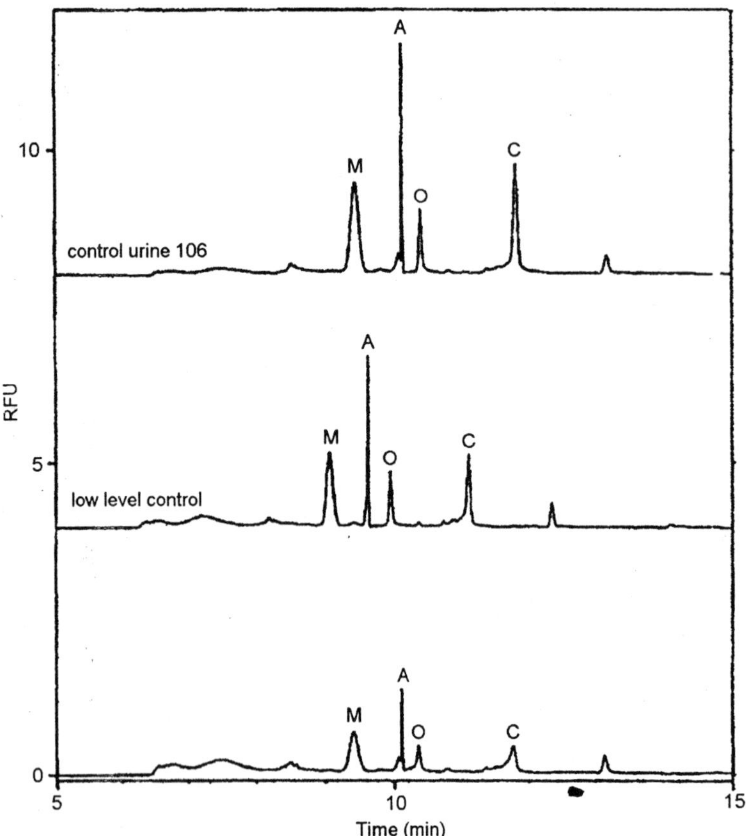

Fig. 5.3. CZE four-analyte immunoassay.

when the urine blank was analyzed. Significantly increased responses for the free tracers were obtained with both the low-level control urine and the external-quality control urine that is known to contain all four classes of drugs (chromatographic data for methadone, free morphine, benzoylecgonine and amphetamine being 2.29, 5.64, 2.46, and 2.38 μg/mL, respectively). Thus, the multianalyte CE immunoassay provides meaningful data and can be used to screen patient urines for the various classes of drugs of abuse. In this case, threshold values of the peak heights relative to the peak height of an internal standard should be defined and applied for urine classification.

CE-based multianalyte immunoassays are limited by the ability of CE to separate labeled antigens from each other and from the antibody-antigen complexes. CE-based immunoassays are simple, rapid, sensitive, and reliable approaches for multianalyte screening of drugs in body fluids. The principle employed lends itself to configure custom-made screening reagents that include the specific antibodies and the labeled tracers. To increase versatility, but at the expense of instrumental complexity, strategies with different tagging of tracers together with LIF detection with multiple laser lines and/or wave-length resolved fluorescence detection could represent interesting approaches for simultaneous selective detection of many different types of solutes.

Chiral CE of Urinary Drugs and Metabolites

CE has proven to provide a simple, inexpensive, and effective approach for the separation of enantiomers after the addition of a chiral selector to the buffer. The separation by CE of the enantiomers of several drugs of interest in toxicology and doping control has been investigated. By using various cyclodextrins it was possible to effect the chiral differentiation of the optical isomers of racemethorphan and racemorphan, amphetamines, cathine, cathinone, cocaine, and others, as well as of urinary mephenytoin and phenytoin, urinary methadone, urinary MDMA, and various amphetamines in urine.

Chiral discrimination has a number of possible applications in clinical and forensic toxicology. For example the antitussive dextromethorphan (an allowed drug) and the narcotic analgesic levomethorphan (a banned drug), are the d-(+) and l-(-) isomers of 3-methoxy-N-methylmorphinan, respectively. Aumatell and Wells demonstrated that these enantiomers could easily be distinguished using a chiral CZE assay that was developed for urinary analysis of the optical isomers of racemethorphan and racemorphan. Distinction of these compounds is not only of interest in forensic science (such as the elucidation of the cause of death after intake of levomethorphan), but also for the treatment of intoxicated patients. In addition, dextrorphan (allowed drug) and levorphanol (banned drug) can easily be separated by MECC using β-cyclodextrin as chiral selector. Other compounds, such as (+)-propoxyphene (a narco-analgetic and a controlled substance) and (-)- propoxyphene (an antitussive and an allowed compound), have been separated by chiral CE. Finally, the ability to separate the enantiomers of amphetamine and methamphetamine has forensic applications as well. The S-(+) enantiomers (d-enantiomers) of amphetamine and methamphetamine have about five times more psychostimulant activity than the R-(–) enantiomers (l-enantiomers) and are thus banned or controlled substances, whereas R-(–)-methamphetamine is found in the Vicks Inhaler sold in the United States. Furthermore, selegiline is known to metabolize to the R-(–) enantiomers of methamphetamine and amphetamine.

Recently we developed an assay comprising a pH 2.5 buffer containing 8.3 mM (2-hydroxypropyl)-β-cyclodextrin (OHP-β-CD) as chiral selector. This assay was able to separate enantiomers from urinary extracts containing methamphetamine, amphetamine, methadone together with its major metabolite EDDP, in addition to 3,4-methylene-dioxymethamphetamine and other designer drugs. Enantiomer identification was based on comparison of UV absorption data along with comparison of the electropherograms with those obtained by re-running spiked extracts. The suitability of the chiral electrokinetic capillary method for drug screening and confirmation is demonstrated with the data. Analysis of the unhydrolyzed quality control urine 106 in the achiral buffer revealed the presence of amphetamine, methadone, and EDDP. By using the chiral assay it was possible to show that both enantiomers were present for all three compounds. These data indicate that a much-increased resolution is obtained with the chiral buffer. Furthermore, morphine and other substances found in alkaline urinary extracts can only be monitored in the chiral buffer. Using the chiral assay to analyze a urine from a patient on selegiline pharmaco-therapy, the presence of the R-(–)-enantiomers of methamphetamine and amphetamine could be unambiguously identified. Thus, ingestion of an R-enantiomer or other drugs that metabolize to the R-enantiomers can be distinguished from the ingestion of S-(+)-enantiomers (due to drug abuse) or prescribed drugs that metabolize to the S-enantiomers of methamphetamine and amphetamine. The approach is simple, reproducible, inexpensive, and reliable (being free of interferences of other major basic drugs that are frequently found in toxicological urines) and can be used to screen for and confirm urinary enantiomers in a routine laboratory.

Analysis and Confirmation of Urinary Drugs and Metabolites by CE-MS

Interfacing a CE with a mass spectrometer (MS) has been shown to be an attractive approach, analogous to the use of LC-MS, to gather structural information of compounds, and to use the MS as a CE detector. The best examples are CE-MS determination of urinary N-1-hydroxyethylflurazepam (the major metabolite of flurazepam), haloperidol, anti-inflammatory drugs (ibuprofen, flurbiprofen) and their metabolites, paracetamol and metabolites, nonopioid analgesics, methadone, and methylphenidate. In addition, the feasibility of using MS as the detector for the enantiomers of terbutaline spiked into a urine blank has been demonstrated. In this instance the use of the chiral selector (heptakis (2,6-di-O-methyl)-β-cyclodextrin) in addition to the use of MS gave the selectively needed to verify the chiral composition in complex matrices.

CE-MS instrumentation employed thus far for urinary confirmation testing of drugs of abuse and/or their metabolites uses CE interfaced to a MS with atmospheric pressure electrospray ionization. This is followed by identification of protonated molecular ions and/or their fragments using a triple quadrupole or an ion trap MS. In the first approach, fragmentation of methadone and EDDP was determined by MS-MS. Confirmation was achieved with in-source fragmentation. The first quadrupole was operated in the selected ion monitoring mode by switching between the respective parent/daughter ion masses for methadone (m/z = 310, 265) and EDDP (m/ z = 278, 249, 234). The CE-MS-MS approach has been successfully applied to the confirmation of methadone and EDDP in urines that were positive for methadone using CE-based immunoassays, FPIA, EMIT, and CE with UV absorption detection. Using an ion trap MS, the presence of amphetamine, MDMA, MDA, methadone, EDDP and morphine in urine could easily be confirmed by the full ion scan mode followed by MS-MS of the protonated molecular ions. An example is the alkaline extract of the quality control urine 106, where the presence of amphetamine, methadone, EDDP and morphine could unambiguously be confirmed by CE- MS. In addition, CE-MS was shown to be capable of detecting amphetamine and nicotine, compounds that co-migrated under the conditions employed. This was not the case using CZE with UV detection. After sample extraction, urinary drug concentrations of 50–100 ng/mL can be detected by CE-MS, comparable to that observed by CE with UV detection. This sensitivity is sufficient for confirmatory testing of most urinary drugs of abuse. The use of a volatile buffer was not found to be a limitation in the separation. CE-MS instrumentation with a single quadrupole MS does not permit unambiguous confirmation since no structural proof via fragmentation is possible. A single quadrupole MS can, however, be used as detector.

As is shown by the examples, CE provides high-quality data that would be of interest to clinical and forensic drug toxicologists. The obvious tests to be replaced by CE involve methodologies that are too expensive, inaccurate, and/or prone to interferences. Prime examples include applications that require enantiomeric resolution, methods that consume high amounts of organic solvents, and assays that lack specificity. Before widespread adoption of CE assays in clinical and forensic drug toxicology can occur, however, validation and the quality assurance aspects of CE based assays have to be addressed. This is especially important for assays that are used for screening and/or confirmation of the presence or absence of illicit, abused, and banned drugs in urine. In this work, data produced by electrokinetic capillary assays were found to be in agreement with the results of other techniques. Despite these encouraging results, additional efforts in exploring the use of CE in the clinical and forensic areas needs to be continued. Of critical importance is that analysis of a large number of external quality control urines, e.g., those offered by Cardiff Bioanalytical Services or College of American Pathologists (CAP), should be undertaken.

Currently the use of optical detection is the most popular detection mode employed. UV absorbance in the single and multi-wavelength formats as well as fluorescence and laser-induced fluorescence has been successfully used in a number of publications. Also, based upon the commercial availability of benchtop instrumentation, the use of MS is currently increasing and soon will establish itself as the detection method of choice for confirmation testing. Thus far, electrochemical detection, which is highly sensitive and selective, has received only cursory evaluation for detection of drugs in urine. This is mostly due to the lack of commercial detectors. The use of amperometric detection, however, has recently been demonstrated for the analysis of urinary promethazine and thioridazine.

Analysis of illicit and abused urinary drugs and their metabolites by CE offers many attractive features. CE offers separation methods that are amenable to the analysis of ionic (CZE, MECC) and neutral (MECC) solutes, including compounds that are difficult to analyze by GC. Furthermore, CE provides extremely high efficiency, resolving power, and separation speed when compared to HPLC. CE is also complementary to existing analytical methods, such as HPLC, GC, and high-throughput, automated immuno- and photometric assays. CE methods performed in capillaries of 25–75 μm ID are considered nanoscale separation techniques, the capillary and sample plug volumes being 0.1–5 μL and 1–10 nL, respectively. Versatility, high efficiency, and the possibility of direct urine injection or minimal sample preparation are appealing features for clinical and forensic analysis. Although CE is appealing for routine clinical and forensic use, the limit of detection is somewhat not as good as that of other separation techniques. This often calls for either on-line or off-line preconcentration of analytes prior to analysis. Fortunately, electrophoretic techniques feature a unique concentration effect (inherent to electrophoretic mass transport and very rarely seen in other separation techniques), which can provide compensation for the lack of sensitivity. Having instrumentation with a single fused silica capillary, sample throughput is limited since analyses can only be performed in a sequential mode. Having multiple capillaries in parallel would allow increased sample throughput and/or to permit the simultaneous analysis of a urinary extract in different buffers. Alternatively, the use of microchips in the single or multilane formats would provide even faster analyses and thus the highest throughput.

Serum Drug Monitoring

Since it was found few decades ago that optimization of serum antiepileptic drug levels reduced the number of seizures and drug side effects, the field of *therapeutic drug monitoring* (TDM) has flourished. Historically TDM started with the spectrophotometric analysis of phenobarbital and phenytoin. However, due to the inability to use spectral data to differentiate closely related drugs, chromatographic techniques such as *gas chromatography* (GC) and *high-performance liquid chromatography* (HPLC) were introduced. These methods required skill, sample preparation, and a long *turn-around time* (TAT) from receipt of sample to reporting of results. Thus despite their high cost, immunoassays, which provided quicker TAT, have slowly replaced chromatographic methods. Although easier to perform and suited for automation, immunoassays are usually not available when a new drug is first released to use in the treatment of patients.

Capillary electrophoresis (CE) is a very versatile technique and can potentially be used to analyze not only the drug but also its metabolites. In fact, drug analysis represents one of the best potential applications of CE. However, as with any analytical method, CE has not only advantages but also drawbacks. The advantages and disadvantages of CE and the types of drugs suited for analysis by this technique are discussed here. In general, CE offers speed, ease of analysis, low cost of operation, and very high resolution. CE can also offer basic information on the physicochemical properties of the drug such as protein binding and ionization. However, it suffers from matrix effects (especially when using serum), poor detection limits, and less than desirable precision. To use CE successfully for the analysis of drugs, four areas require careful attention: (i) choice of the separation type (CZE, MEKC, Chiral); (ii) sample preparation (especially critical for serum samples); (iii) instrument setup (optimum voltage, maximum injection volume); and (iv) precision (choice of capillary wash and internal standards).

Comparison of CE and HPLC

In the past, small molecules, such as drugs, have not been analyzed by electrophoretic techniques due to the lack of sensitivity. Generally, drugs were analyzed by chromatographic techniques, such as HPLC, that are based on the interaction of the compound with the column packing (e.g., hydrophobicity). CE, on the other hand, utilizes charge (directly or indirectly) to separate and identify the drug of interest.

Several studies have shown that for TDM, CE is better than HPLC, being faster and easier to use. CE also has better resolution, especially for polar compounds, and costs less to operate. Wynia et al. determined the precision, linearity, ruggedness, and detection limits for CE and HPLC using the antidepressant drug mirtazapine. They found that the *relative standard deviation* (RSD) for CE was higher than that for HPLC, 0.6 vs 0.2, respectively. The linearity for CE (10–1400 μg/mL) was also different than HPLC (4–800 μg/mL). Altria and Bestford reviewed the analysis of a variety of pharmaceuticals and found that CE has many advantages over HPLC. Many researchers have also found that CE has advantages in terms of reduced sample pretreatment, consumable costs, and analysis time. Additionally, CE has the ability to separate a wide range of compounds using a single set of operating conditions. Most workers however, agree that in general

HPLC tends to give better precision and better sensitivity. Because CE and HPLC can analyze the same molecules, in many instances they can seem complementary to each other. CE is better suited for the analysis of polar or charged compounds with high molar absorbitivity or those that are present in a relatively high concentration. Nonpolar compounds or those with low molar absorbitivity may be better analyzed by HPLC. However, by using a combination of stacking methods and special flow cells with extended light path, CE can achieve sensitivity close to that found for HPLC.

CE Problems for TDM

The poor sensitivity and matrix effects are two major problems that may seem insurmountable to newcomers to the field of CE. This is especially true for TDM. In addition, CE also has less than desirable reproducibility. These problems and how to overcome them are discussed later.

Sensitivity

Owing to the narrow path length of the detection window in the capillary, the absorbance signal in CE is not very strong. Sometimes in order to improve the separation efficiency (theoretical plate number) or to speed up the analysis, the capillary diameter is decreased. This in turn causes a further decrease in the signal. To overcome this problem, capillaries with an extended light path, e.g., Z-cell, bubble cell, or the high sensitivity cell, have been developed for some CE instruments. Even with these new detection windows, many of the drugs routinely analyzed for TDM are present in serum at concentration of 0.01–1 mg/L, well below the detection limits. Thus, the majority of the drugs have to be concentrated before analysis by CE, either on or outside the capillary. Fortunately electrophoretic techniques offer a very simple means called stacking to concentrate the analyte directly on the capillary.

Initial studies with two commonly used drugs, theophylline and phenobarbital, have demonstrated that detection of therapeutic levels are attainable with simple stacking methods and little sample preparation. Some drugs, however, still require complex extraction and concentration steps.

Matrix effects

In CE, unlike most other techniques, many basic parameters such as resolution, plate number, migration time, and precision are greatly affected by the sample matrix, especially when inorganic ions or proteins are present. As the sample size increases, matrix effects become more significant. Generally CE easily analyzes pure standards. However, analysis of serum samples, the usual sample matrix for TDM is more difficult. The salts present in serum ($\sim$150 mmol/L) affect the field strength and consequently the velocity of the analyte causing band broadening. Proteins in the serum ($\sim$60 g/L), on the other hand, bind to the capillary walls, producing secondary interactions, and affecting the reproducibility of the method.

Forms of CE Used to Separate Drugs

In the analysis of drugs and other small molecules, three basic forms of CE, capillary zone electrophoresis (CZE), micellar electrokinetic capillary chromatography (MEKC), and chiral separation are often used.

Capillary zone electrophoresis (CZE)

In CZE, separation is based on charge of the analyte in a buffered solution. The method is used for analysis of drugs that either have a positive or negative charge.

Micellar electrokinetic capillary chromatography (MEKC)

MEKC is where separation is based on the differential distribution of the drug of interest between the aqueous phase and micelles formed using a surfactant such as sodium dodecyl sulfate (SDS). Separation in this system is based on hydrophobicity. This method can be used for analysis of neutral as well as charged molecules. Serum can be injected directly, provided the migration of the serum proteins does not overlap with the drugs being analyzed. The correct amount of SDS, ionic strength of the buffer, and modifiers are manipulated to achieve this effect.

Chiral separation

Chiral separation is a form of CE where special additives, e.g., cyclodextrins (CD) or proteins, are incorporated into the separation buffer affecting the migration of one isomer more than the other isomer. Chiral separation by CE is much easier to perform than by HPLC. To date, it is most often used in the pharmaceutical industry and has yet to be used in TDM.

Serum Sample Preparation

One of the advantages of CE is the simplicity of the sample preparation. For example, sometimes the sample can be introduced directly without preparation. However, due to matrix effects, analysis of drugs in serum often requires special preparation such as dilution, protein precipitation, or extraction. Drugs such as the antifungal fluconazole have been analyzed after a variety of sample preparation methods to illustrate the differences in speed, linearity, detection limits, and precision. For example, direct injection of plasma or supernatant after protein precipitation by acetonitrile has detected fluconazole levels of >5 μg/mL. Using liquid–liquid extraction (dichloromethane), the detection limit is about 1 μg/mL. However by using disposable solid-phase C18 cartridges and 1 mL of plasma to extract the drug, levels as low as 0.1 μg/mL can be detected.

For MEKC, if the drug concentration is high enough the serum can be simply diluted in buffer before injection onto the capillary (direct serum analysis), minimizing the matrix effects. This is because the small amounts of serum are solubilized by the micelles of the surfactant. Thormann and colleagues have successfully applied this technique to the analysis of several drugs such as theophylline, caffeine, and barbiturates by directly injecting serum. Similarly, we applied this technique in the analysis of the new antiepileptic drug felbamate. The simplicity, high resolving power, and the small sample size used for the assay render this method suitable for monitoring the levels of these drugs in pediatric patients.

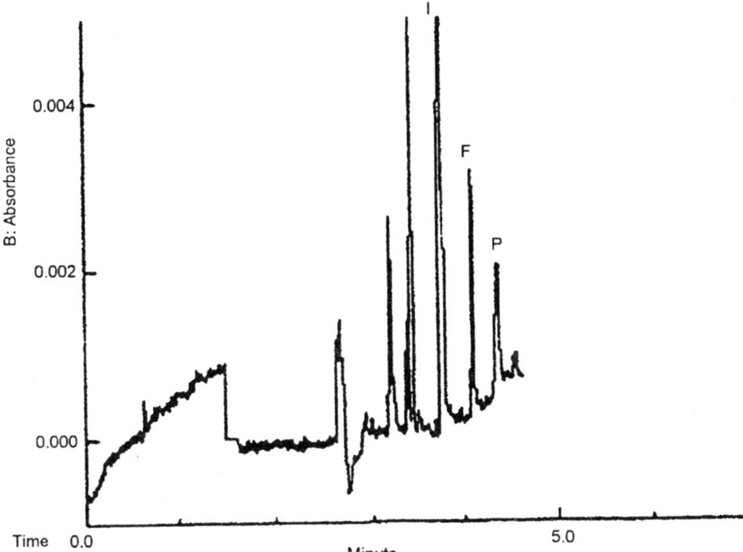

Fig. 5.4. Felbamate analysis by CE with direct serum injection after the addition of an internal standard. Patient receiving felbamate (53 mg/L, F) and phenobarbital (18 mg/L, P), (I, internal standard).

In CZE, small amounts of proteins (<3 g/L) can be tolerated provided the ionic strength of the buffer is high enough and the capillary is washed thoroughly with sodium hydroxide after each injection. Ions in the sample also decrease the field strength and can cause band broadening. To minimize these effects, the sample is diluted in a low ionic strength buffer while the ionic strength of the electrophoresis buffer is increased (typically >100 mM). If the protein concentration is too high, they can bind to the capillaries, modifying the surface charge and affect the separation of subsequent samples. Proteins can be removed before injecting the sample by precipitation with acids, heavy metal ions, or alcohols. However, acids and heavy metals ions add salt to the sample that can degrade the separation.

To overcome the problem of sample matrix, several strategies have been developed by using membranes, protein precipitation, and extraction methods.

Use of membranes

Membranes with a low molecular weight cut-off can be used to remove proteins and other large molecules. However, salts that can interfere in the separation remain in the filtrate. Membrane filters are also relatively expensive, and can require a long time to filter the serum. As an example, the membrane filters have been used in the analysis of serum nitrate by CE. Membrane filtration to remove protein bound drugs can also be used to separate free drugs for further analysis by CE.

Protein precipitation

Precipitation of proteins by acetonitrile is an effective and simple method to pre-treat serum samples for analysis by CZE. In addition to removing proteins, acetonitrile, also permits injection of a large volume of sample (5–20% of the capillary volume) leading to 5–20-fold concentration by the capillary because of "stacking," as discussed later. The use of this simple method of concentration allows many drugs to be determined at concentrations of approaching 0.5 mg/L. Deproteinization also decreases the need for washing of the capillary between samples, thus speeding the analysis. This method, however, is limited to analysis of small molecules by the CZE and is not suitable for MEKC.

Extraction

Use of an organic solvent or by a solid phase to extract drugs from serum also removes the proteins and salts present. In addition to sample clean-up, extraction methods can also be used to concentrate the drug. In routine analysis, solvent and solid-phase extractions followed by solvent evaporation are usually avoided as much as possible because of the time, labor, and skill required. However, drugs present in serum below 1 mg/L usually require extraction and concentration. Different strategies of sample pretreatment and methods for direct injection of bio-fluids for drug analysis by CE have been recently reviewed by Lloyd.

Concentration by Capillary Stacking

As mentioned earlier, electrophoretic techniques offer a relatively simple means to concentrate the sample directly on the capillary by injecting a large volume of sample. Under nonstacking conditions, the sample volume is kept below 1% of the capillary volume. However this volume can be increased to 10–30% of the capillary volume using stacking conditions. The drug "stacks" at the interface of the injection buffer and the run buffer. This helps to alleviate the poor detection limits of CE. Stacking, however, requires careful planning and an understanding of the method. For example, the field strength should be very high in the injected sample relative to the electrophoresis buffer so the drugs migrate rapidly to the solvent interface before the separation step takes place. Buffers, that do not generate much Joule heating, such as, e.g., borate, become important for this step. Methods have been described for stacking by: low ionic strength buffer in the sample, stacking by inclusion of acetonitrile in the sample, and isotachophoresis. Stacking in MEKC is more difficult but a few methods have been described recently.

Low ionic strength buffers

Dissolving the sample in the separation buffer, but at a 10 times lower ionic strength, or conversely, by injecting a small plug of water before the sample, increases the peak height 3–10 times by stacking. A similar stacking can be obtained in the electrokinetic injection, provided the sample matrix is free from salts. For example, Zhang et al. used this technique to increase the sensitivity for amiodarone analysis by several orders of magnitude. This type of on-column stacking is best suited for analysis of compounds present in a clean matrix, e.g., extracted samples.

Acetonitrile-salt

Addition of acetonitrile to the sample (not in the electrolyte) leads to stacking, especially when inorganic salts are present at concentration of ~1%. Thus, acetonitrile stacking is useful for samples with physiological amounts of salts and proteins such as serum. The acetonitrile and salts (~50 mmol/L of NaCl in the final mixture) allow for increasing the sample size (using hydrodynamic injection) up to 50% of the capillary volume, yielding a 5–20-fold concentration.

Acetonitrile stacking depends on several factors, such as the pH and ions in the sample, in addition to the ionic strength of the separation buffer. Weakly anionic compounds are easier to stack using acetonitrile in borate buffer compared to cationic compounds. The latter group stacks better in buffers containing amines and zwitterions. Stacking by acetonitrile, allows many drugs to be analyzed in serum at the low level of ~0.5 mg/L.

Field-amplified injection in presence of salts

Recently, we found that electrokinetic injection in presence of physiological amounts of salts (~1%) can give sharp peaks provided the sample contains 66% acetonitrile. The advantage of this type of injection over the previous hydrodynamic injection is a better theoretical plate number.

Transient isotachophoresis

Isotachophoresis is a powerful method for concentrating drugs on the capillary. It is well-suited for samples with a high salt content. However, coupling it to CE is difficult. A transient isotachophoretic step or self-stacking occurring in the early stages of the electrophoresis is more practical. Under these conditions a suitable, complementary ion is added to the sample to act as a leading/terminating ion and a large volume is injected. The conditions for ITP can be fulfilled before the separation is changed to CZE. Knowledge of migration rate of the different ions and a clever choice of the buffers are important for the success of this technique.

Stacking in MEKC

Stacking in MEKC is more difficult than in CZE. However, several methods have been described recently by Terabe and others. They are based on solubilizing neutral molecules in micelles with accelerated micelle migration using a lower conductivity matrix. For example, Quirino and Terabe described the use of low conductivity in the sample (dissolved in water) in the normal injection mode. Liu et al. dissolved the sample in a solution containing SDS with a concentration lower than the separation buffer and injected at a negative polarity. After a brief period needed for analyte stacking and removal of the sample matrix, the polarity is switched to positive for separation and detection. Quirino and Terabe have also described a similar stacking method, including the use of high molecular weight surfactants. They also described a simpler approach by using reversed-migration micelles for stacking. In this technique, the pH of the separation buffer is acidic so the micelles have a higher electrophoretic velocity than the *electroosmotic flow* (EOF). A large sample, prepared in water or dilute buffer, is injected under reversed polarity allowing a concentration factor of ~100-fold.

Precision

The precision of both peak area (used for quantification) and migration time (used for identification) in CE is not as good as that in HPLC. However, studies aimed at understanding this problem will improve precision, as has been the case with other emerging techniques.

In many instances, imprecision in migration time is related to the interaction of the compound with the capillary wall and to changes in the EOF. Fortunately, in CE the migration time is more predictable than the peak height (area). By employing one or more references points or internal standards, precision can be improved. Dose and Guichon reported that a RSD of 1% for migration time and peak area is possible by using two internal standards. Siren et al. also showed that using multiple standards whose migration time closely brackets the compound being analyzed improves the reproducibility to <1%. Migration time can also be more reproducible when a constant current is used than a constant voltage. In addition, calculations based on the effective mobility are more reproducible than migration time giving a RSD of mobility of 0.01–0.03%.

Imprecision in peak height or area on the other hand is related to two factors: injection volume or time and capillary wall effects. It has been found that the RSD of peak height (area) is inversely related to the sample concentration. Thus, as the sample concentration increases precision improves. This is especially true when peak area instead of peak height is used. Stacking methods that concentrate the sample on the capillary improve the precision for peak area. In general, peak area shows less variation than the peak height with a wider range of linearity. In the absence of the sample extraction, internal standards will improve slightly the precision of peak height or area.

Several other factors can affect precision in CE. Controlling the temperature of the buffer inside the capillary has been found to be a critical factor in reproducibility. Kunkel et al. compared the RSD of several CE instruments. They pointed out that the technology for the detector has been improved and the main source of error for most of the instruments is sample injection, which can be decreased by using internal standards.

Changes in the capillary surface can also affect precision. A thorough wash with NaOH (0.1–1 M), phosphoric acid (100 mM), acetonitrile, or SDS decreases the wall effects and improves greatly the reproducibility of the migration time and peak height (area). Kelly et al. presented data on electrolysis of the buffer and its effect on the precision. They found that high ionic strength buffers at low current or zwitterionic buffers (which generate low current) improve precision. They also presented several suggestions to decrease the effect of electrolysis. Water injection (2–3 s) after the sample also improves precision.

Drugs Analyzed by CE

A single drug can be analyzed for different purposes, e.g., TDM, metabolic, forensic, pharmaceutical, or pharmacological. In the pharmaceutical industry CE is used to determine drug purity or to study its metabolism. The same conditions used for these studies, buffer, pH, voltage, internal standards, and so on, can be extended or modified for use in separation of therapeutic drugs. However, unlike the pharmaceutical industry, the emphasis in TDM is on speed, precision, automation, and sample clean up. However, it turns out many of the methods developed for the different drugs are very similar to each other. For this reason, Altria et al. described a general CE method employing a high pH borate buffer, which was validated to allow analysis of a wide range of acidic pharmaceutical compounds using a variety of internal standards. They also validated a similar procedure for the analysis of basic compounds. Based on our experience for TDM, anionic drugs are separated best in borate buffer, 200 mmol/L, after sample deproteinization with 2 vol of acetonitrile. Sample loading can be from 1–10% of the capillary volume. Cationic compounds, on the other hand, are better analyzed using triethanolamine buffers. Neutral compounds can be analyzed in either borate or phosphate buffers containing SDS (MEKC). Standards are added to the serum directly to reduce problems with matrix effects. Obviously it is easier to analyze a single compound than several at the same time. In most of these methods ultraviolet (UV) detection has been utilized, although in a few procedures, fluorescence or *laser-induced fluorescence* (LIF) detection has been used. The majority these methods have been validated for their linearity, detection limits, accuracy, and precision. A few of these methods used sample extraction although most injected serum with or without acetonitrile treatment. Use of on-line sample clean up and concentration for drugs is a very attractive procedure due to its simplicity and speed. It has been described by Strausbauch et al. and Morita (48) and reviewed by Guzman et al.

Growing interest in the analysis of drugs by CE is indicated by the publication of several review articles in addition to a whole journal issue dedicated to CE and drug analysis. The practical aspects of TDM analysis by CE has been described. Studies, that have dealt primarily with TDM are discussed more in detail later.

Anti-epileptic

The two antiepileptic drugs, phenobarbital and phenytoin, were among the first drugs to be analyzed by CE for TDM. They have been analyzed using both CZE and MEKC. Several of the antiepileptic drugs (ethosuximide, phenytoin, primidone, valproic acid, phenobarbital, and carbamazepine) were analyzed by MEKC after extraction with ethyl acetate in phosphate buffer, 25 mM, pH 8.0, containing SDS. The separation was completed in 14 min. Barbiturates, i.e., phenobarbital, pentobarbital, amobarbital, and butalbital, in serum and urine were measured by Thormann et al. by MEKC using borate, phosphate, and SDS at pH 7.8. Serum could be injected directly on the capillary, whereas urine required extraction. Evanson and Wikotorwicz also separated several anti-epileptic drugs by MEKC using a borate buffer, pH 9.3, containing SDS and 30% acetonitrile. Serum samples were injected after solid-phase extraction with separation completed in about 15 min. Pentobarbital was analyzed by CZE in about 5 min after acetonitrile deproteinization using an electrophoresis buffer of 300 mM borate at pH 8.5. The epoxy and the diol metabolites of carbamazepine, difficult to detect by HPLC or immunoassays, in addition to the parent compound, were quantitated by MEKC in about 3 min using borate buffer and SDS.

Most of the recent antiepileptic drugs, such as gabapentin, felbamate, zonisamide, and lamotrigine, have not had commercial immunoassays developed. Gabapentin (neurotin), which is similar to the neurotransmitter gamma amino butyric acid, can be derivatized by incorporating fluorescamine into the deproteinization reagent. Separation was achieved within 12 min using UV detection at 200 nm with a sensitivity of 1 mg/L. Felbamate, a neutral compound, was analyzed by MEKC after addition of an internal standard and then directly injecting serum into the capillary. The assay was rapid (about 5 min), with sensitivity of 5 mg/L, with no interferences noted. Phenobarbital was also analyzed using the same method. In both cases CE was much faster than the HPLC method.

Zonisamide, a new antiepileptic drug, was determined in serum using (MEKC) with detection by diode array. A high correlation (r = 0.981) was found between the zonisamide levels in human serum and those obtained by HPLC. The serum levels of phenobarbital, phenytoin, and carbamazepine have also been measured using the same method.

Lamotrigine, another antiepileptic drug, is a basic compound. In general, basic compounds are difficult to analyze by either GC or HPLC, usually requiring derivatization. CE can analyze most basic drugs quite easily in pure aqueous solutions. Their analysis in serum, however, is more difficult than that of acidic compounds. Deproteinization by acetonitrile followed by the addition of acetic acid to lower the pH below the pKa of the compound being analyzed and also below the pH of the separation buffer was necessary in order to obtain a good separation.

Anti-arrhythmic

The majority of anti-arrhythmic drugs are basic compounds and many also act as antihypertensive agents. These compounds migrate rapidly and are seen in the first part of the electropherogram. However, they can be difficult to separate since they tend to bind to the capillary walls, making analysis and especially stacking difficult. Recently, we have shown that buffers containing amines and zwitterions are useful not only in analysis but also stacking of these compounds. The analysis of procainamide and N-acetylprocainamide is a good example of stacking of basic drugs on the capillary. In this method, which correlated well with immunoassay, about 10% of the capillary volume was injected with sample. Using the same method, urinary procainamide also has been analyzed by CE.

Lukkari et al. separated after urine extraction 10 β-adrenergic blockers, i.e., propranolol, oxyprenalol, and nadolol. CE also determined Amiodarone, a highly hydrophobic compound, in buffers with a high content of organic solvents. Using "Field Amplified Injection," the sensitivity for amiodarone analysis was increased by several orders of magnitude. The method compared well to HPLC. MEKC was also used by Evanson and Wikotorwicz to separate procainamide, N-acetylprocainamide, disopyramide, and chlorodisopyramide.

Analgesics

Many analgesics such as ibuprofen, salicylates, and acetaminophen are available without a prescription. Because of their wide therapeutic windows, routine monitoring of these drugs is not necessary. However, acetaminophen overdoses are occasionally encountered and in cases, careful monitoring of acetaminophen levels and half-life is very important. High doses near the toxic level of ibuprofen have also been advocated recently for the treatment of cystic fibrosis. Hence, monitoring the serum level is important. Many methods have been described for the analysis of these drugs in either tablet or pure form. We measured ibuprofen and ketoprofen in serum by CZE after acetonitrile deproteinization using borate buffers. Watzug and Lloyd and Kunkel described the direct serum analysis of acetaminophen and salicylic acid by MEKC using borate buffer containing SDS. Goto et al. measured salicylic acid in serum by CZE and found that the results compared quite well to fluorescence polarization immunoassay.

Antidepressants

Antidepressants, such as the tricyclics, trazdone, and Prozac, are commonly used to treat anxiety and depression. Since these basic, hydrophobic drugs are present in serum at low levels they are very difficult to measure regardless of methodology. In order to separate by HPLC the use of a welldeactivated column with a high plate number is important. Lomon et al. used CE to separate seven antidepressant drugs in aqueous media using a CAPSO buffer at pH 9.5. The zwitterionic buffer, CAPSO, along with methanol decreases the adsorption of these compounds to the capillary wall. We have also shown that amine-containing buffers are important for the stacking of these compounds in order to improve their detection. Additionally, Harrell et al. separated seven antidepressant drugs using a synthetic nonionic forming micelle polymer in about 15 min.

Anti-asthmatic

Theophylline, a drug used in the treatment of asthma, has a narrow therapeutic window. Because of this narrow window, it is important to know the serum concentration in order to determine whether it is in the therapeutic or toxic range. Additionally, theophylline and the closely related compound, caffeine, are frequently used to treat apnea in newborns. Like the antiepileptic drugs, these compounds have been analyzed by either MEKC or CZE. MEKC allows direct injection of serum, urine, or saliva in a borate buffer, pH 9.0, in the presence of SDS with separation in about 15 min. We obtained a good correlation (r = 0.98) to immunoassay when theophylline was measured by CZE in borate buffer, pH 8.5. Zhao et al. determined caffeine and its metabolites by MEKC, and Johansson et al. used CZE to measure theophylline in phosphate-borate buffers. Caffeine, dyphylline, theobrómine, and theophylline have also been separated by MEKC in borate buffer, pH 9.3 containing SDS and 30% acetonitrile.

Renal function and contrast agents

In clinical labs, renal function is routinely estimated by measuring the creatinine clearance. This test is convenient but it is known to be inaccurate especially when a significant loss (>50%) in renal function occurs. In research several iodinated compounds such as iothalamic acid and iohexol are used to provide a better measurement of renal clearance using either serum or urine. Iohexol was rapidly assayed (<5 min) by CZE after deproteinization of serum by acetonitrile. Values as low as 5 mg/L can be measured by this technique. Isovue, another candidate compound for the measurement of renal function, was also measured by CZE after acetonitrile deproteinization. Landers et al. used CE to quantitate iothalamic acid in serum and in a timed urine collection to measure the glomerular filtration rate.

CE and Immunoassay

Many drugs, such as tacrolimus and digoxin, remain far below the detection limits of CE or HPLC without extraction and subsequent concentration. In response to this limitation, Chen and Evangelista described a method that has potential for better sensitivity along with simultaneous detection of several drugs. This method is based on a combination of immunoassay, laser-induced fluorescence (LIF), and CE. In this system, fluorescent-labeled drug conjugates antibodies of known specificity and the unknown samples were mixed. After the reaction is completed, CE separates the free drug (including the fluorescent-labeled drug) from the bound. The quantity of drug in the unknown sample that can be estimated from a standard curve established using the same methodology. Cortisol, an endogenous substance and a drug, has also been quantitated using a similar approach.

Recently, Steinmann and Thormann described an assay using MEKC, LIF, and commercial Fluorescence Polarization Assay reagents to separate a variety of drugs. The free and bound tracers for the different drugs were separated in phosphate-borate buffer containing SDS. The feasibility of simultaneous determination of several drugs was also demonstrated. A similar method was also described for the analysis of digoxin using the commercial reagent from an enzyme immunoassay kit. Additionally, Chiem and Harrison described a microchip CE method to separate the reaction products of a reaction of an antibody and theophylline within approx 40 s. The buffer system consisted of tricine, pH 8.0, with 0.01% (w/v) Tween 20, and 40 mM NaCl, allowing adequate separation for theophylline and for the theophylline-antibody complex. Reproducibility of migration times was 1–1.5%.

Special Features of Analysis

In addition to measurement of the serum drug levels, other pharmacological parameters are important in TDM such as protein binding, half-life, ionization, and metabolism. The following represent some interesting studies related to TDM, which were performed by using CE.

Chiral separation

Although isomers have very close chemical structures, they can exhibit different biological effects or can be metabolized differently (86). These isomers can also show differential binding to serum proteins. Giacomini et al. have shown that the coadministration of racemic disoprymide affected the clearance of the d-isomer due to the more avid binding of its isomer to serum proteins. Also the S form of verapamil has less binding to serum proteins increasing its plasma clearance to twice that of the R form. Thus, several proteins, including those found in human serum, such as transferrin, have been utilized in CE for chiral separation of a variety of drugs.

Chiral separations have generated great interest in CE because of low cost, ease of analysis, speed, and the high resolution relative to HPLC. Unfortunately, most of the chiral separations described are performed on drugs to check for purity in pharmaceutical preparations. A few studies, however, have been performed on separations from biological samples. For example, Srinivassan and Bartlett described a stereoselective method for serum phenobarbital using cyclodextrin and solid phase extraction. Ohara et al. also described a method using CE to determine the enantioselective determination of the basic drug verapamil that was not bound to serum proteins. Nishi reviewed the separation of enantiomers of drugs by electrokinetic chromatography using chiral micelles and proteins. In addition, Fanali and Bojarski and Aboul-Enein reviewed the identification of chiral drugs by CE including those present in biological fluids.

D'Hulst and Verbeke and Altria et al. showed that a limit of detection of <1% and 0.1% of the total drug level, respectively, can be obtained for the minor enantiomer levels. Thus, CE offers a very rapid, low cost, and excellent separation for chiral separations, but the reproducibility falls short of that of HPLC.

Physico-chemical properties of drugs

The pKa of a compound or drug can also be measured using CE by measuring its mobility as a function of pH (98). Schmutz and Thormann (99) determined how the physical and chemical properties of 25 drugs would effect their analysis by MEKC. They found that compounds, which did not bind tightly to proteins in addition to those with a low pKa, dissociated easily from the bound proteins and migrated as sharp peaks.

Free drugs

Most drugs bind to serum proteins while the unbound fraction (free) of the drug is thought to be the active form. Thus, it is important to measure and understand the drug-protein interaction. This is especially important in such disorders as renal failure where the amount of the free drug changes as a result of uremia and binding protein concentrations.

The free, bound, percentage of binding, and the binding constant can be determined based on several well-established techniques such as dialysis, filtration, and size exclusion. CE can extend these techniques to measure free drugs. For example, several free drugs were measured after filtration through special membranes. The problem with this method of measurement is that free drugs are present at a much lower concentration than the total drug. Thus, in order to measure these low levels, concentration or stacking steps may be necessary. For example, in the analysis of phenytoin, acetonitrile is added to the filtrate to concentrate the drug on the capillary.

In addition to the previous techniques, CE based on changes in the electrophoretic mobility can measure drug binding. Kraak et al. described three different methods for measuring protein-drug binding by CE. The first is based on the Hummel-Dryer method in which the capillary is filled with a buffer containing the drug giving a large background signal. The sample, which contains the drug, protein, and buffer, is injected. The bound drug migrates differently from the free drug, producing a negative peak. The area of the negative peak is a measure of the bound drug. The second method is based on the vacancy method where as the capillary is filled with mixture of the buffer, the drug, and the protein. This also causes a large background signal. The sample that contains only the buffer is injected. Both the free and the bound drug migrate separately and each gives a negative peak. The third method depends on the frontal analysis. In this method the capillary is filled with the buffer. Different concentrations of the drug in the presence and absence of a fixed binding protein concentration are incubated at 25°C followed by injection of a large amount of sample (~5–7% of the capillary volume). The free drug, the complex and the protein gives each a frontal, plateau-shaped peak. The free-drug concentration can be calculated from the height of the frontal peak as follows:

$$E = (D/S) \times P$$

where D = Height free drug concentration, E = free drug concentration, S = concentration of the pure standard, and P = drug peak height in presence of the protein.

The concentration of the bound drug can be calculated by subtracting the free drug from the total. The percentage and the binding association constant can be also calculated from a Scatchard plot of this data. Kraak et al. concluded that the frontal analysis appeared to be the preferred method for drug binding. It is more reproducible and gives a smooth Scatchard curve compared to the other two techniques.

Binding of drugs to a specific carrier is also a promising approach to target drugs to specific organs. Protein binding can alter the metabolism or delivery of the drug to the target organ. Naproxen conjugated to albumin is an example of such drug targeting. Albrecht et al. have shown that naproxen, a nonsteriodal anti-inflammatory drug, can be determined in serum using MEKC as free, albumin conjugated, and lysine conjugated. Samples were injected and separated in a borate/phosphate buffer containing SDS with LIF detection. This method has also been extended to measurement of this drug in liver and kidney tissue.

In general, CE is a versatile analytical technique capable of analyzing a wide variety of drugs both charged and uncharged. CE is most useful in TDM to analyze new drugs rather than for those with established immunoassays. The cost of operation is much less than that of HPLC. In addition to analyzing a drug and its metabolites, CE can be used for analysis of the bound, free drugs, isomers, and measure the physicochemical properties.

As stated already, one of the main limitations of the CE is poor sensitivity. For the most part this can be overcome by preconcentration (either on or before the capillary) or by the use of special flow cells. Using these methods, sensitivities close to that of the HPLC can be obtained. In addition, several relatively simple methods for sample stacking on the capillary for CZE and MEKC have been described in the last few years. However, because of the need to measure drugs at lower and lower serum levels, there is still a need for further studies addressing new stacking methods, flow cells, and detectors (i.e., LIF).

Precision is the other area of CE that is still in need of improvement. By addition of multiple internal standards, using mobility data and a better understanding the sources of the variation, the precision of CE has become much better. Again the goal is to match or surpass the precision of HPLC. Although CE is faster than HPLC, shorter and narrower capillaries, (i.e., microchips) together with high voltage would further speed analysis.

Overall, analysis of drugs (especially newly developed drugs) by CE will keep on growing because of the continued need to monitor the serum levels of these new drugs.

6

ISOLATED ORGAN TECHNIQUES

The concept of organ perfusion for physiological and biochemical studies is not new. Early accounts of organ perfusion techniques in biochemical and physiological studies may be found in the descriptions of Baglioni and Muller. More detailed accounts of the historical development of organ perfusion techniques may be found in the works of Brodie and Embden and Glaussner. Systematic early developments in organ perfusion techniques have been reviewed by Skutual and Kapfhammer. Increasing interest in the application of perfusion techniques in biochemical and physiological investigations is apparent in the more recent works of Ross, Diczfalusy, and Ritchie and Hardcastle.

The rationale for experimental studies using perfused organs and for trying to improve the technology of organ perfusion lies in the following physiological and biochemical considerations. We recognize homeostasis to be the outcome of many simultaneously occurring, interacting complex processes. It is recognized that when many simultaneously occurring processes interact, they may collectively take on functional properties that cannot be perceived in any of the individual component processes. In endocrine and metabolic systems, a basic experimental question arises at the organ level: how does the organ's uptake or output of some toxic substance depend upon the composition of the arterial blood reaching the organ? The technique of organ perfusion can, if certain conditions are met, permit one to make controlled concentration changes in the perfusing blood, while observing the time course of the organs's response, in terms of its uptake or output of one or more substances. This kind of experimentation has several advantages. Mathematical models based on some convenient equations can be constructed relating the nature of toxic compound(s) and its concentration in blood. The nature of the substances produced as a result of the biotransformation can be investigated and related to the specific organ. The role of the specific organ in converting a substance into either more harmful or biochemically inert species can be effectively evaluated. Quantitative input on these pathways of biotransformation into the appropriate mathematical models can lead to our understanding and development of predictable values.

In the simplest terms, the essentials of perfusion techniques are: the desirability of separating individual organs from the whole animal to permit the study of one in the absence of complex interaction by others; the need for the tissue to be physiologically compatible to the *in vivo* situation; and the desire to simulate the natural circulation through an organ. In this regard, the composition of the medium changes constantly just as in the whole body, at least with respect to the experimental toxic agent, since not all substances reenter the perfusion medium, nor are all the substances entirely removed by the organ. Finally, an analytical study of the organ itself can be undertaken: artificial means of stimulating organ function may aid in magnifying the physiological role of or effect on the organ, thus enabling determination of such an interaction. Although use of the autologous whole blood would be considered ideal for homeostatic mechanisms, substitution of artificial medium is often necessary for technical reasons; an attempt is made to maintain the cell structure and function by following as many viability criteria as possible.

Choice of Donor Animal

A variety of factors may influence the choice of organ donor animals in perfused organ studies. Often, the nature of the particular problem being investigated might be the determining factor in choosing the experimental animal. Susceptibility or refractoriness to the toxic agent to be tested and the presence or absence of biotransformation pathways govern the selection of a particular species and often a particular strain. Other factors may influence the final selection of the experimental animal. Availability of pertinent background information in a particular animal model may compel the investigator in favor of that species in the interest of savings in time and resources. Availability, cost of animals, and maintenance or unique genetic characteristics may become important considerations. The rat has been most popular in this regard, as a donor for perfusion experiments. Thus heart, liver, lung, kidney, brain, and pancreas perfused preparations obtained from rat have been employed by many investigators for a variety of biochemical studies. Larger animals employed in perfusion experiments include the cat, the dog, the rabbit, and the monkey. Among the larger animals employed for perfusion experiments are calves, goats, pigs, and sheep.

All small animals have the disadvantage of small blood volume, thus limiting the volume of blood available, and small blood vessels, which pose difficulties in surgical procedures. In many instances, the experimenter might be interested in using autologous blood for perfusion, and small animals may not yield sufficient blood supply to prime the perfusion apparatus. The recent trend has been to utilize either diluted or reconstituted blood or completely artificial perfusion medium composed of natural or synthetic ingredients. Nevertheless, in a few instances, the necessity of using autologous whole blood as a perfusate essentially eliminates the use of small experimental animals in perfusion experiments. An additional factor to be considered might be the volume and the number of perfusate samples needed to carry out necessary analytical tests during the course of the experiment. These difficulties are clearly overcome by using larger experimental animals. Larger animals however, have the distinct disadvantage of increased cost of animals on the one hand, and requisite chemicals, equipment, space, and other supplies on the other. Use of expensive ability of valuable samples of newly synthesized or isolated test drugs may make it necessary to restrict perfusion experiments to organs from smaller animals.

Large or small, other considerations may also be important. Much fat, particularly in the abdominal area of larger animals or older small animals, will contribute to surgical difficulties. Presence or absence of some tissues, such as the gall bladder, which is absent in the rat but present in the rabbit, might be an additional consideration. For the purpose of acquainting oneself with the techniques of organ perfusion, size of the animal per se matters little. However, considerations of economy in space, equipment, smaller apparatus, and animal costs might make the choice of a smaller animal a prudent one. In view of these and other considerations discussed above, whenever, possible, we shall consider the rat as the animal of choice. However, it is important to bear in mind that most procedural and other technical considerations will remain the same with minor modifications when a particular perfusion technique is intended to be applied to a larger animal or to an animal of similar or smaller size.

In situ and Isolated Organ Perfusion Systems

Isolated organs perfusion may be defined as the maintenance of an organ in vascular isolation from the rest of the tissues and organs of the body by mechanically assisted circulation of a suitable fluid through its vascular bed. In most cases, a special apparatus is acquired, and each investigator has invariably adopted an individual approach to solving the technical problems associated with maintaining a particular organ in a viable condition for a particular toxicological investigation. The resulting scattered literature and many technical variations introduced in the techniques of organ perfusion have to a large degree contributed to the difficulty of a newcomer to the field of isolated organ perfusion to readily adopt the application of these techniques toward investigating the special problems of toxicology. Often, it is difficult to assess the merits of various available methods. Given the complexity of the problem, there is often a reluctance on the part of some toxicologists perfused organ studies, even in those areas of biochemical toxicology where these techniques may offer unique and definitive advantages over other *in vitro* or *in vivo* techniques. Establishment of a set of standards for each organ perfusion system by an internationally composed committee might alleviate many of the problems arising out of infinitely varied perfusion techniques and methodology introduced by individual investigators in a scattered body of diverse literature.

One rather obvious prerequisite for isolated organ perfusion studies is that the organ to be perfused should be capable of vascular isolation from the neighboring tissues, although physical isolation is not obligatory. A separate vascular bed is sufficient to ensure that only one tissue or organ is perfused in isolation. For instance, an organ may be perfused in isolation but may remain *in situ*, as in the case of the lung, liver, intestine, or kidney. A principal advantage of perfusing the organ *in situ* is the time saved in surgical removal of the organ, thus reducing the time of interrupted perfusion. An additional advantage is to reduce physical damage to the organ, which may be inflicted during surgical removal of the organ.

Alternatively, the organ to be perfused may be physically isolated from the animal, as in the case of lung, liver, kidney, heart, and intestine. The principal advantage in physically isolating an organ is the elimination of interactions between the organ being perfused and other tissues and organs present in the body. Although the vascular bed of the organ being perfused may be totally isolated, the endogenous substances being secreted may seep out of other tissues and organs and might come in physical contact with the organ being perfused, resulting in incontrollable or even unanticipated interactions. Similarly, the compound being studied in the perfused organ may be secreted and absorbed by other surrounding tissues and organs by physical contact and hence may introduce experimental errors in the quantitative and qualitative aspects of the disposition of the toxic chemical being studied.

Advantages of Isolated Perfusion Organ Techniques

Isolated perfusion organ preparations offer several advantages over experimentation with intact animals. Perfusion experiments lend themselves to a definitive evaluation of the role of a particular organ or tissue in the disposition of endogenous or exogenous chemicals. Although experimentation with whole animal preparations may provide clues implicating the possible role of a particular organ in regulating the levels of a test toxin or an endogenous substance in response to a toxin, decisive conclusions may not be feasible. Isolated perfusion studies provide opportunities to decisively ascertain or reject such possibilities. Unlike the *in vitro* homogenate preparations, intact organ perfusion studies allow the experimenter to retain the structural and functional integrity of the organ in question during such experiments. Unlike in the intact animal, perfusion experiments allow the experimenter to retain a control over several experimental parameters. For instance, the experimenter would retain control over perfusion pressure and blood flow, unlike in the intact animal, where these are likely to change during the course of an experiment, especially in response to the administration of the experimental toxic chemical. The concentrations of endogenous or exogenous stimulatory substances and other factors can be under experimental control in isolated perfused organ would lend itself to a broader range of concentrations of the experimental drug to be used in the study. That is, concentrations of drug at which the intact animal would not be expected to survive can be tested in isolated perfused organs. Determination of accurate and complete mass balance of the toxic chemical in question is possible throughout the perfusion experiment, since the compound must either be in the perfusate, in the tissue, or excreted via excretory fluids such as bile and urine. Binding of the test chemical to the glassware, tubing, and other components of the perfusion apparatus may occur, but this can be determined in appropriate blank experiments to derive appropriate correction factors, and often removal of such interfering factors is technically feasible. Another advantage of perfusion studies is the availability of larger size blood or perfusate samples, so that complete quantitative and quantitative analyses of minor and major biotransformation products of the test compound are feasible, since the volume of perfusate used in these experiments can be controlled. A further advantage of perfusion experiments in comparison with the whole animal experiments si the feasibility of tests with smaller quantities of toxic chemicals. This is particularly noteworthy, since limitations of either the availability of small quantities of the toxins or the cost of isotopically labeled newly synthesized compounds can be formidable.

Another advantage of perfused organ studies is the maintenance of appropriate membrane barriers, not only between vascular and parenchymal sides, but also between individual cells; hence the natural constraints of intact organs are retained throughout the experimental duration. Recent evidence has made it clear that one may not be able to predict the qualitative and quantitative aspects of biotransformation of a test drug by intact organ based only on the results of *in vitro* experiments with homogenate preparation. Factors governing the generation and availability of cofactors and transport of substrate to the site of biotransformation influence the final results in the intact perfused organ. These factors can remain operative in perfusion studies, unlike the other *in vitro* techniques, thus enabling realistic extrapolation of the results to *in vivo* situations. Finally, no matter how determined, experimental results have to be interpreted and extrapolated to the *in vivo* situation, where intact organs interact continuously, and such interpretation and extrapolation is made easier by use of intact perfused organs in toxicological investigations.

Limitations

The present-day state of the art allows maintenance of isolated perfused organ preparations with adequate physiological and biochemical integrity for only short periods of time. Clinically, recent advances have allowed the maintenance of the kidney for several days for later physical transplantation in patients. These procedures require subambient temperatures in order to preserve organ function. Such techniques are not generally useful in toxicological studies, since maintenance of the organ at optimal functional level is necessarily a prerequisite for most toxicological studies. Hence the principal limitation imposed by the isolated perfused organ preparations is the short duration of study. Critical and vital organs functions deteriorate in isolated perfused organs with time. For example, isolated perfused lung preparations can be maintained only for a maximum of 4 hr. Often, it is not possible to determine the effect of therapeutic agents on the lung tissue in such a short period of time. Similarly, isolated perfused liver preparations cannot be maintained for longer periods of time without compromising liver function. A practical consideration of interest in this connection may also be the level of expertise required in setting up the perfusion experiments. Setting up and conducting successful perfusion experiments requires specially trained personnel in all aspects of the surgical procedures as well as other technical aspects of associated instrumentation. Unavailability of such personnel imposes divesting valuable time of the investigator in training the necessary personnel.

Often, a principal arguments in favor of isolated perfused organ studies is the maintenance of natural membrane barriers, integrity of the intact cells, and the complex and dynamic interrelationship between individual and groups of cells. For certain types of studies, this very argument may represent a principal limitation. The very complexity of a whole organ deprives the toxicologist of access to individual reactions that occur in the intact organ. Compartments and permeability barriers may prevent substrates and test drugs from exerting effects that are known to be manifested when the particular toxic agent is allowed direct access to the enzyme or organelle of interest. *In vitro* experiments with homogenate preparations and tissue slice preparations would be the obvious choice of techniques when dissection of individual transport processes and biotransformation reactions is the principal objective. The size of a single experiment and time required to perform it may make organ perfusion a far less efficient use of time and resources than *in vitro* preparations that will demonstrate the same effects. Schimmel and Knobil have pointed out the greater efficiency of establishing an experimental fact with tissue slices than with isolated perfused organ. Finally, despite all the refined techniques of maintaining the organ *in vitro* in as near a normal state as possible, the resulting preparation may differ in some highly significant manner from the organ *in vivo*, limiting the interpretation of results obtained in the organ perfusion system.

The principal scope of this chapter will be to acquaint the reader with generalized methods for isolation and perfusion of certain selected organs from experimental animals. Accordingly, the following discussion represents simplified and often idealized procedures so that a relative novice could undertake application of perfusion techniques to toxicological investigations in his other laboratory. Sufficient references are included, however, to serve as focal points for the benefit of those who are already engaged in perfusion of isolated organs and seek advanced information. Thus although the principal emphasis is placed on the nut-and-bolt methodology, sufficient references are included to allow one to proceed with in-depth examination of a particular aspect of organ perfusion or application of perfused organ technique.

Thorough considerations of pumps and mechanical devices used in perfusion of organs, application and testing of pharmacokinetic concepts to isolated perfused organs, and the mathematical considerations of single-pass studies in isolated organs are available elsewhere. Similarly, use of radiolabeled microspheres to determine intraorgan and regional blood flows may also be considered in isolated perfused organ studies. Finally, excellent reviews on the application of perfusion techniques to biochemical studies, to the studies of reproductive endocrinology, and to the general consideration of perfusion techniques, especially in larger experimental animals, are available for those seeking additional and detailed considerations of organ perfusion techniques.

Methodology

Isolated Perfused Heart

Since Langendorff described a procedure for isolation and perfusion of dog or rabbit heart, heart has been the model for study of the effects of toxic agents on metabolism in muscle. A succession of investigators have demonstrated the stability and versatility of the preparation. The original method of Langendorff has survived with only minor modifications and remains the standard preparation upon which toxicological studies are performed.

Two procedures have been used for isolated perfused heart preparations. One uses the aortic perfusion described by Langendorff. The other method uses atrial perfusion, in which the left atrium is cannulated. The Langendorff preparation perfuses the muscle of both ventricles, while only the left ventricle produces any tension by contracting against the closed aortic valve. The atrial perfusion method gives a "working heart" preparation: this allows the left ventricle to fill, which results in the normal systolic and diastolic cycles. The perfusion described by Morgan et. al. and later improved by Neely et. al. provides for the "working heart" circulation. Several studies have compared the use of the aortic perfusion of Langendorff and the atrial perfusion of "working heart" preparation is the ease and accuracy with which myocardial performance can be quantified. In the Langendorff preparation, coronary flow and heart rate are the only available physical parameters of function. The "working heart," on the other hand, has aortic output as a quantifiable parameter of function, although this is dependent upon the heart achieving an aortic pressure of at least 100 cm of water. Anoxia, lack of substrate, poison, and drugs may all be qualitatively and quantitatively tested on this basis. Linearity of oxygen and substrate uptake is an additional means of assessing function in this preparation, and together with easily observed abnormalities of cardiac rhythm, which may also indicate failure of the preparation, the "working heart" preparation is easily and accurately assessed.

However, despite the completeness of description and advantages of the "working heart," investigators in this field have experienced many difficulties in establishing a viable "working heart" preparation for significant lengths of experimental time. Hence although quantitative differences do occur in many biochemical and functional measurements, the "working" and "nonworking" heart preparations are similar in many respects. No particular benefit has been incurred in these studies by the use of the elaborate and time consuming "working heart" preparation. Although in certain experimental protocols it may be necessary to utilize both preparations, it is doubtful if it will be necessary to carry out all toxicological tests on the heart in both Langendorff and "working heart" preparation. Since the former is so much simpler, its use will continue to be popular for some time to come.

Aortic perfusion of the heart

Apparatus

The heart is suspended in a water jacketed cylindrical chamber of 3 cm diameter and 20 cm long with a course sintered-glass filter disk sealed into the lower portion. The aortic cannula is mounted in a Teflon stopper, through which pass the gas inlet tube and an outlet vent for the excess gases. The inflowing gas is delivered by means of a fine plastic tube extending into a small pool of perfusion medium, which collects on the surface of the sintered-glass filter. After passing through the filter, medium is recirculated by a peristaltic pump. However, the wave form applied to the heart is considerably dampened by passing the perfusate first through a bubble trap containing 1 to 2 ml of air, so that the characteristics of the pump wave form may be eliminated.

Operating procedure

Rats weighing approximately 250 to 300 g can be used for obtaining isolated heart preparations. The donor animal is killed by decapitation. It may be desirable to heparinize the animal by administering heparin intraperitoneally (5 mg) 1 hr before decapitation to prevent formation

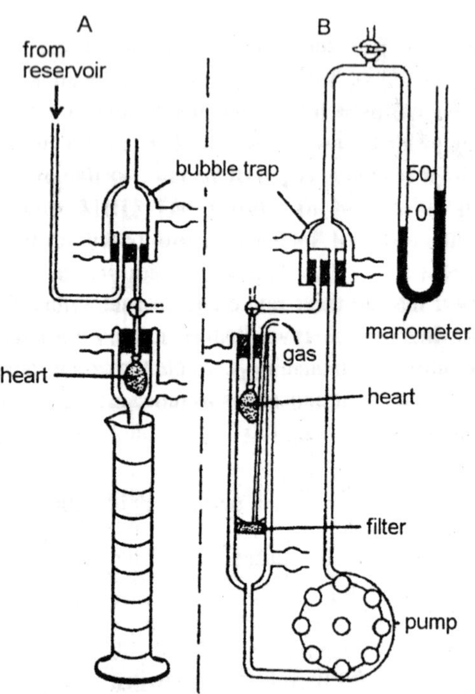

Fig. 6.1. Schematic diagram of "Langendorff" heart perfusion. A–Single-pass perfusion; B–Recirculating perfusion.

of large clots. Within 20 sec after decapitation, the thorax is widely opened by incisions to remove the anterior wall. The heart is removed immediately by means of a scissor cut across the great vessels about 5 mm from the heart. Earlier investigators allowed a 1 to 2 min cooling period by immersing the heart in ice cold Krebs-Ringer buffer solution. This is not necessarily desirable, and in fact, greater speed may help reduce the likelihood of anoxic damage to the heart. After blotting the heart with filter paper and weighing, a small glass cannula (or a polyethylene tubing, PE 200) can be inserted into the aorta with the tip of the cannula positioned just above the semilunar valves. The instantaneously beating heart is then perfused through the aortic cannula. The heart preparation thus established may be allowed to equilibrate for a period of 15 to 20 min by means of a setup in which the perfusate is allowed to recirculate. Oxygenation of the perfusate is accomplished by using a 95:5 mixture of oxygen and carbon dioxide, which is humidified by passing through water at 37°C before entering the apparatus to prevent loss of perfusate volume by evaporation.

Atrial perfusion of the working heart

Apparatus

The glass components of the working heart perfusion apparatus are a double jacketed oxygenator, a 100 cm bubble trap, a mixing column, connecting pieces, a bubble trap, a mixing column, connecting pieces, a bubble trap condensers, a 100 cm reservoir, a heart chamber, and a second bubble trap. The filter is a closed millipore system adapted from that used in ultrafiltration. For example, a millipore in-line filter holder may be used. Wherever possible, tubing components should be made up of glass using flexible tubings connections, with the exception of the compression tubing used in the roller pumps, where siliconized medical grade tubing may be used.

Operating procedure

A rat weighing approximately 250 g is lightly anesthetized with ether. Without preparation of the skin, the first incision is made with

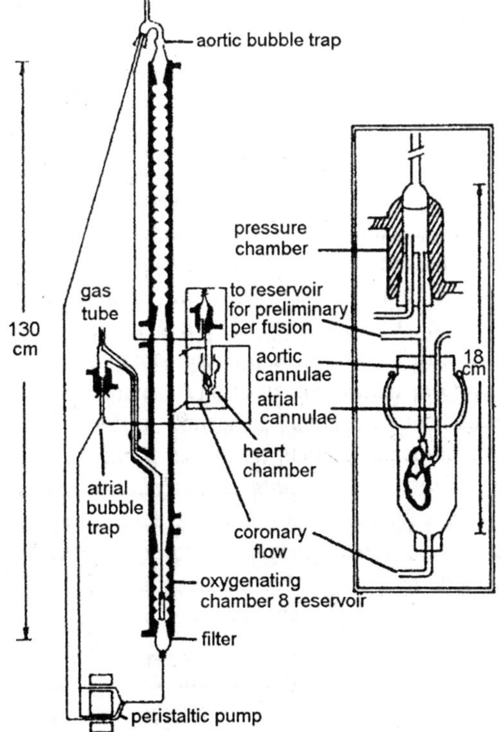

Fig. 6.2. Schematic illustration of a working rat heart preparation.

large pointed scissors around the lower margin of ribs. The first cut is made across the upper abdomen with care to injure the liver. This cut is extended laterally and for this purpose the rat may be held in the left hand. Then the point of the scissors is directed toward the head, and a single cut is made through the layers of the thorax, including the ribs up to the clavicle. Cuts are made on the left side and on the right side, producing a free flap of the anterior chest, which is removed with a cut transversely at the level of the second rib. At this time the heart is fully exposed. The heart is grasped firmly between the thumb and forefinger of the left hand and lifted, drawing it to the animal's right. This exposes the pulmonary veins and the site of entry into the left atrium. The point of the scissors is passed horizontally and behind the left atrium, the pulmonary veins, and the aortic arch. Before closing the blades to cut, the instrument is drawn well over the animal's left to leave the maximum length of pulmonary vein in continuity with the atrium. After cutting the pulmonary veins, the scissors are pointed downward and away from the operator, and the aorta is cut at about 1/2 cm from the ventricle. This length is adequate for cannulation. If the cut is made too near to the heart, a hole is made in the left atrium, rather than through the pulmonary veins, and this makes cannulation difficult.

The heart is thus removed and transferred rapidly to ice-cold Krebs-Ringer buffer, and aortic cannulation is carried out. The cannula is filled to the tip with oxygenated medium making sure to avoid entrapment of air bubbles. The aorta is grasped from opposite sides in two pairs of fine curved forceps and gently lifted over the straight cannula. The cannula may be retained by a single ligature around the aorta. It is important to watch that the tip of the cannula does not rest upon the aortic valve by being too far down the aorta. A flow of the medium at maximal rate is begun as soon as the ligature is tied, and this ends the unavoidable period of operative myocardial anoxia. The heart should begin to beat within 10 to 15 sec of starting the perfusion.

Atrial cannulation may be conducted at leisure since the heart is fully perfused via the aorta and is no longer at risk of anoxia. The atrial wall is grasped by forceps as it lies on either side of the cannula and by turning the wrist outward the wall is slightly averted. Then the atrium is drawn over the cannula itself The cannula is positioned and retained in this position by means of a ligature. The final step is to incise the right ventricle and its pulmonary trunk. This allows for the drainage of the medium accumulated in the right side of the heart from minor coronary veins; otherwise, such accumulation would result in poor cardiac function. The incision is made with pointed scissors through the base of the ventricle and at the origin of the pulmonary trunk.

Perfusion media

A variety of perfusion media with minor modifications have been used to perfuse isolated heart preparations. Use of whole blood, Krebs-Henseleit bicarbonate buffer medium, and Krebs-Ringer buffered solution have been reported for maintaining successful perfused heart preparations. Many advantages have been pointed out in arguing for the use of whole blood to perfuse isolated heart preparations. However, where this has been done, circulation of whole blood through the isolated heart was maintained by using support animals. In these preparations, the circulation from the isolated heart enters the circulation of the support animal via the right jugular venous cannula and exist the support animal via the left carotid artery. Although satisfactory preparations are obtained, such isolated preparations may not lend themselves to certain types of toxicological investigations. A principal limitation arises from the introduction of the support animal with the perfusion circuit. The support animal would clear the test chemical, making the correlation of effects of test toxins on cardiac function and evaluation of possible myocardial biotransformation difficult. Hence use of an artificial perfusate has been most popular in biochemical and toxicological investigations.

Various investigations have introduced minor variations in individual ion composition of the particular medium used in their own experimental setups. The medium of choice, however, seems to be the Krebs-Ringer bicarbonate buffer solution of the following composition: NaCl, 119 mM; KCl, 4.75 mM; $CaCl_2 \cdot 2H_2O$, 2.54 mM; KH_2PO_4, 1.19 mM; $MgSO_4 \cdot 7H_2O$, 1.19 mM; $NaHCO_3$, 25.0 mM; and dextrose, 5.5 mM. The solution may be sterilized by ultrafiltration to avoid microbial contamination. If autoclaving is used, addition of dextrose should be withheld until later. Equilibration with a mixture of 95:5 oxygen and carbon dioxide for at least 30 min before using the perfusate increases the viability of the perfused preparation as well as the buffering capacity of the perfusate during perfusion. The pH of the medium is adjusted to 7.4 by means of a dilute solution of NaOH.

Viability criteria

A number of functional, biochemical, and histological determinations have been used to insure the viability and validity of the perfused heart preparation. Physical measurements of cardiac function include the recordings of electrocardiogram of the left ventricular pressure, left ventricular end-diastolic pressure and perfusion pressure of isolated heart preparation. Other functional parameters that can be continuously recorded include the heart rate, isometric systolic tension, and coronary flow. These later investigators recently examined the effect of perfusion time on a number of these parameters. Changes in the heart rate were evident 15 min after the end of the initial equilibration period. However, after being perfused for as long as 4 hr, the heart rate was approximately 86% of the initial level, indicating the usefulness of the perfused heart preparation in toxicological studies. In contrast to the heart beat, coronary flow and isometric systolic tension appear to be more sensitive, as indicated by their decrease with perfusion time. A number of biochemical parameters can be examined in heart preparations as indices of viability. Glycogen concentration was not significantly decreased until 3 hr. But decreased to 33% of the zero time control values after 4 hr of perfusion. Likewise, adenosine-5′-triphosphate (ATP) concentrations remained quite stable for 3 hr, but significantly decreased in hearts perfused for 4 hr. Creatine phosphate concentrations showed the greatest change during the first hour of perfusion, when they diminished to 51% of the amount present at zero time in the control group. After perfusion for 4 hr, the creatine phosphate content of the tissue was 45% of the zero time control value. Histochemical evaluation of the heart preparations for viability can useful initially in establishing the perfusion methodology. Tissues fixed by classical histological methods can be examined for any evidence of inflammatory infiltrate, edema, or hemorrhage.

Applications

Although isolated perfused heart preparations have been used in a variety of ways to study the mechanisms and interaction of various drugs and hormones, and in biochemical investigations, these preparations are not generally applied to screen drugs or toxic chemicals for potential cardiotoxicity. However, recent effort has been directed toward using such preparations for toxicological investigations. For example, Autian has stressed the need for the development of reliable *in vitro* systems with which to screen large numbers of drugs and has emphasized the advantages of using isolated perfused heart preparations. Gad et al. used isolated perfused rat heart preparations to examine the inhibitory actions of the prooxidant butylated hydroxytoluene (BHT) on cardiac function. Cardiac contractility was depressed and leakage of creatine phosphate into the perfusate was found within 30 min of perfusion when BHT was included in the perfusion medium in concentrations ranging from 1 to 500 mg/liter. Thus these investigations provide direct evidence that BHT depressed contractility and causes cellular damage of isolated heart as measured by the leakage of creatine phosphate from the myocardium.

Drug effects on myocardial contractile function are obviously of considerable practical importance for the toxicologist. The basic mechanism of such actions must reside at some point in the metabolism of cardiac muscle. Interference in liberation of energy of the metabolic fuels utilized by the myocardial tissue may be implicated in many of the toxicological effects induced by drugs and other toxic chemicals. Anesthetic drugs that produce reversible depression of myocardial contractile function in a dose-dependent fashion have been shown to interfere with many of the mechanisms involving the generation and utilization of cellular energy in the heart tissue. Use of isolated perfused heart preparations would be avoid and useful technique in the toxicological investigations related to drug-induced heart diseases.

For many studies in toxicology, it will be necessary to determine the perfusate concentration of the experimental drugs with time. It will also be necessary to determine the appearance and disappearance kinetics of possible metabolites of the test toxin. As is true in the case of most perfused organ studies, these experiments can either be carried out employing recirculating perfusate or using a single-pass mode. In most experimental protocols, it will be prudent to determine in advance which mode of circulation would be utilized. It will also be necessary to determine the size of the perfusate sample desired in order to carry out the type of analyses intended and the time courses as well as the total duration of the experiment. Many enzymatic determinations can be carried out in the perfusate as well as in the heart tissue itself.

Isolated Perfused Liver

The isolated perfused liver preparation has enjoyed the longest standing sustained attention in terms of preserved isolated organs for biochemical, pharmacological, and toxicological studies. The view of Miller et al. concerning the perused liver is that functional performance of the liver cells is best studied in the isolated liver perfused with continuously oxygenated whole, homologous blood under closely approximated physiological conditions. Earlier attempts to obtain viable, perfused liver preparations were marked by many problems, and in most cases, the failure can be attributed to several factors; the use of aqueous perfusion media such as Ringer's solution in place of whole blood; lack of adequate filtering devices to remove tiny fibrin clots, which plug the hepatic circulatory system; the relative unavailability of effective, nontoxic anticoagulants such as heparin, which resulted in ominous failure to carry out perfusion for more than 1 to 2 hr when whole blood was used as the perfusate. In recent years, we have witnessed the increased use of isolated liver preparations in a variety of pharmacological and toxicological investigations. Much credit for developing and standardizing isolated perfused liver techniques belongs to miller et al. and Schimassek.

There are two sources of blood supply to the liver. The portal vein supplies 80% and the hepatic artery supplies 20% of the blood flow. Most workers have ignored the hepatic arterial supply in perfusing the rat liver. Although experiments confirm that the liver functions normally even in the absence of perfusion through the hepatic artery, techniques are now available which allow this very small blood vessel to be perfused at normal arterial pressure, either under hydrostatic conditions, or by direct pumping. By and large, the rat has been the choice for isolated perfused liver preparations, although livers from other experimental animals have been perfused for various investigations.

Apparatus

In the liver perfusion technique of Miller et al., the liver is perfused at a constant hydrostatic pressure using diluted rat blood as the perfusion medium, which passes through a glass multibulb oxygenator. The perfusate enters the portal vein via a filter, drains from the liver through the inferior vena cava either via an indwelling cannula or through a free cut of the vena cava, and collects into a bottom reservoir. From the reservoir, it is pumped to the top of the oxygenator and enters the oxygenator through a filter. The liver is removed from the animal after the cannulation procedure, and perfusion is conducted by connecting the portal cannula of the liver to the preprimed circulation of the apparatus housed in an enclosed liver chamber.

The apparatus designed by Miller has been almost universally adopted by workers using this technique, and it is also available commercially. The liver perfusion apparatus used in our laboratory is based on Miller's description. The perfusion chamber is kept warm by means of a heater-fan assembly, which is thermostatically controlled. The original description of Miller et al. used heating coil that traversed

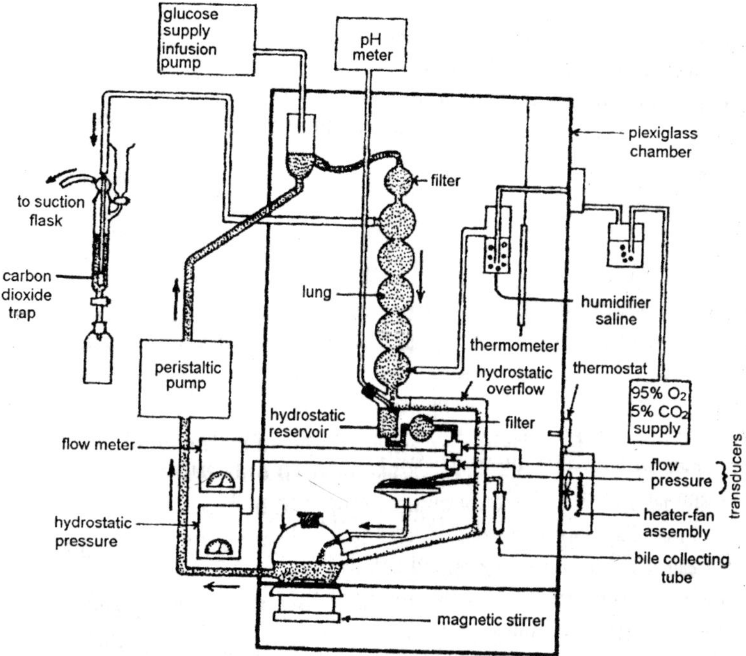

Fig. 6.3. Schematic illustration of a liver perfusion apparatus.

the inner surface of the chamber. Cleaning of the chamber becomes difficult with this arrangement. Hence the heating may be accomplished by installing a highly efficient heating coil inside a box, which would also house a fan. The glass multibulb oxygenator can be easily put together by connecting a series of 100 ml round bottom flasks. At the bottom of the multibulb glass oxygenator, in inlet is provided for oxygen supply, and at the top of the oxygenator, a side outlet is provided for the carbon dioxide to escape. The bottom reservoir is provided with a number of side arms and a principal opening at the top to connect the platform that supports the liver. A magnetic stirrer can be introduced into the bottom reservoir, and a magnetic stirring device can be placed below the reservoir under the chamber. The perfusate can be pumped by means of a peristaltic pump to avoid hemolysis of blood cells when either whole blood or diluted blood is used as the perfusate. A mixture of 95:5 oxygen and carbon dioxide is passed through a water trap in order to humidify the gas mixture. The expired gas escaping from the top of the multibulb glass lung is passed through a carbon dioxide trapping device. This is especially useful in studies in which either labeled carbon dioxide or other volatile metabolic products are expected to be formed. Efficient filtration of the blood perfusion medium is considered to be crucial for successful perfusion. Two disks of Lucite are compressed together to hold a disk of white silk (100 × 150 mesh per inch), and two such filters are introduced in the perfusate circulation to clear broken cells and any other debris in the perfusate.

Surgical procedure

Surgical removal of the liver from the rat can be performed under ether anesthesia. With the animal lying on its back, the limbs can be fixed in extension on a surgical board. The anterior abdomen is cleaned with 75% alcohol, and a ventrical longitudinal midline incision is made extending from the pubis to the upper chest. The common bile duct is cannulated with PE-10 tubing. The animal is heparinizing with 1,000 units of sodium heparin by injecting the solution into the inferior vena cava anterior to the renal vein Immediately after the injection, the vena cava is ligated anterior to the site of injection. The portal vein is then cannulated with a PE-240 cannula filled with the perfusate. An incision can be made in the thorax and the thoracic cavity exposed to facilitate cannulation of the thoracic vena cava, using a PE-240 cannula. A loose ligature is placed around the inferior vena cava, and the outflow cannula is inserted through the right atrium. The inferior vena cava is cut between the heart and the cannula. The liver is dissected out together with the diaphragm. Some investigators suggest an incision through the anterior diaphragm, leaving only a collar of the diaphragm attached to the inferior vena cava. The liver with or without the diaphragm is then lifted free of the abdomen together with its cannulae and transferred to a warm saline bath. Immersing the liver in the worm saline bath facilitates proper orientation of the lobes in addition to cleaning the blood clots and debris that may be on the surface of the liver. Removal of the liver and subsequent handling requires skill and should be accomplished with a minimum of handling of the organ itself. After ensuring that the lobes of the liver and properly oriented, the liver may be attached to the perfusion apparatus by connecting the portal cannula to the circulating perfusate. The liver is placed on the platform, making sure that the outflow cannula is let down through the central porthole of the platform extending into the neck of the bottom reservoir. Proper orientation of the common bile duct cannula should ensure unhindered bile flow.

An equilibration period of 30 min is generally sufficient to establish proper perfusion flow and for the liver to recover from the brief period of anoxia encountered during the surgical procedure. Glucose can be infused throughout the perfusion in order to replenish the glucose utilized by the liver. This procedure also allows replacing any fluid losses due to evaporation of the perfusate in the heated chamber.

Earlier investigators have used antibiotics in order to prevent bacterial growth in the perfusate during the course of the perfusion. In many toxicological studies, it may be important to keep the perfusion system free of drugs in view of the complexity of possible drug interactions. Most pieces of the perfusion apparatus can be autoclaved and sterilized. The perfusion chamber can be surface sterilized using 75% ethanol as well. For instance, the perfusion flow transducer, pressure transducer, pH probe, and polyethylene cannulae and filters can be surface sterilized using ethanol. Use of antibiotics has not been necessary under these conditions to obtain viable preparation up to 6 hr.

Perfusion media

Miller used a medium of fresh, heparinized rat blood usually diluted to a hematocrit of 25 to 40% with Ringer's solution. By far, the single most variation introduced in the liver perfusion system is due to the differences in the composition of perfusate used. Whole rat blood would be the ideal physiological perfusate to be used. Advantages of including whole blood are implicit in having hemoglobin and a natural oxygen carrier as well as natural protein and lipid composition of the blood to provide binding and carrier sites for experimental drugs. However, economic limitations make the use of whole rat blood as a perfusate impractical. Moreover, certain experimental protocols such as single-pass studies utilize large volumes of perfusate, and use of whole blood becomes exceedingly expensive and impractical. The following blood perfusate has the advantages of containing rat blood as well as being economical, since it is mixed with two parts of Krebs-Ringer bicarbonate buffered solution (pH 7.4). Krebs-Ringer bicarbonate solution includes the following in grams per liter: NaCl, 6.896; KCl, 0.354; $CaCl_2 \cdot 2H_2O$, 0.373; KH_2PO_4, 0.162; $NaHCO_3$, 2.1; $MgSO_4 \cdot 7H_2O$, 0.293; bovine serum albumin Cohn fraction V, 45.0; glucose, 0.901. The pH of the solution is adjusted to 7.4 with 1N NaOH solution. Freshly collected heparinized whole rat blood is mixed with this solution to obtain a 30% blood perfusate. A required volume of glucose solution (20% solution) is added to the perfusate to obtain a final glucose concentration of 3.2 g/liter.

Triner et. al demonstrated that isolated perfused liver preparations can be supported by using artificial oxygen carriers such as fluorocarbon emulsions emulsified in electrolyte buffer solution. The use of fluorocarbon emulsion in the perfusion of isolated organs would have a number of advantages over erythrocyte suspension. Avoidance of possible antigenicity from nonautologous erythrocytes and simpler, more standardized, and less expensive preparations of perfusion media are among these advantages. In experiments comparing the adequacy of fluorocarbon emulsions to replace erythrocytes in the perfusate, three kinds of fluorocarbons were evaluated. Urea nitrogen, glucose, sodium potassium, and alanine aminotransferase in the medium, and incorporation of ^{14}C-lysine into the circulating proteins were all found to be either normal or above normal as compared to perfusate containing erythrocytes when fluosol-43 was used as the fluorocarbon oxygen carrier. Using the fluorocarbon FC-47 emulsified in Krebs-Ringer bicarbonate buffer solution, Goodman et al. found that oxygen consumption, alanine gluconeogenesis, production of lactate and ketone bodies, and hepatic ATP concentrations were no different than when buffer or an erythrocyte suspended medium was used as perfusate. The cytosolic and mitochondrial redox states as indicated by the hepatic lactate:pyruvate and β-hydroxy butyrate:acetic acid ratios, respectively, were also the same whether the medium contained erythrocytes of FC-47.

Viability criteria

Certain viability criteria can be readily used in evaluating the perfused liver. For instance, bile flow can be used as a viability criterion. Here 1 to 1.5 μl/min/g of liver can be expected from a normal rat liver, which can change depending upon the experimental conditions. Bile flow can be expected to drop with the time of perfusion, since the endogenous bile acid pool would be depleted during bile collection. Another easily recognizable viability criterion is perfusion flow rate. At a hydrostatic pressure of 15 to 20 cm water, a flow rate of up to 60 ml/min can be obtained using diluted (30%) blood as perfusate. Even after allowing for lower viscosity of the perfusate, this flow rate would be judged to be beyond the normal physiological range. Hence the perfusion flow rate should be controlled by means of a suitable clamp placed between the portal cannula and the hydrostatic reservoir. Once a stable flow is attained, the flow rate through the liver can be used as a readily available criterion for evaluating the viability of the organ.

Another easily detectable criterion is visual examination of the liver. Inadequately perfused liver gives a reddish appearance, indicating anoxia, as well as a blotchy appearance on the surface of the liver. Quite often, if the liver is not secured on the platform, it may move in such a way as to impede proper, continuous, and uniform perfusion through the organ. The liver may move so that the flow out of the organ through the outflow cannula may be impeded, resulting in swelling of the liver. Visually, this can be easily recognized by the tensile and anoxic appearance of one or more lobes of the liver. Oxygen consumption by the liver can be used as another criterion for viability. For instance, Schimassek reported that oxygen consumption by the perfused liver was 2.2 mmoles/min/g of tissue after the 30 min equilibration period and this was maintained thereafter. Oxygen consumption can be measured by following the oxygen tension (PO_2) of the perfusate before it enters the liver and sampling the oxygen content of the perfusate after it effuses from the liver.

A number of biochemical parameters can be used for ascertaining viability of the perfused liver. Schimassek has shown conclusively that isolated perfused livers under standard conditions have concentrations of glycolytic intermediates, respiratory quotient, and adenine nucleotide levels very close to those fond in the liver fresh out of the animal. Such determinations in the isolated perfused liver preparation have allowed several investigators to determine normal conditions of perfusion. A variety of other biochemical parameters have also been determined in isolated perfused liver preparations to establish the physiological validity of using such a preparation. Miller et al determined incorporation of ^{14}C-lysine into hepatic proteins as a biochemical index of optimum macromolecular synthetic activity during perfusion. Bock et al., measured a number of biochemical parameters associated with microsomal mixed function oxidase (MFO) and the cytochrome P-450 system and found satisfactory preservation of the hepatic MFO system after a 4-hr perfusion when erythrocyte containing perfusate was used. Biliary excretion of sulfobromophthalein (BSP) and indocyanine green has also been useful as a measure of the functional status of the isolated perfused liver. The disadvantage of using these markers for functional status is that the same perfused livers cannot be used for toxicological investigations after establishing that these livers are indeed viable. These tests will be helpful in evaluating isolated perfused liver preparations, establishing the procedure, and subsequently, these tests will also be useful in evaluating the functional status of the liver preparations after treating them with an experimental toxic agent.

Although routine histological examination of perfused livers is not conducted, the technique may be useful in setting up a perfused preparation. Several authors have reported results of histological examinations of perfused livers, indicating the general usefulness of morphological examination in ascertaining the viability of perfused liver preparations. However, one should be aware that morphological examinations may be of limited usefulness, since cells that appear abnormal morphologically may exhibit normal cellular function, and conversely, normal appearing cells may retain abnormal cellular functions. Oomen and Chamalaun reported an excellent correlation between biochemical and histological parameters in their isolated perfused rat liver preparations.

Applications

Depending upon the experimental protocol, the isolated perfused liver preparation can be used in either a single-pass or in a recirculating mode. Many examples can be cited for the use of isolated perfused liver preparations in the evaluation of toxic responses to a variety of chemicals. It is instructive to consider only a few examples of the use of isolated perfused liver preparations in toxicological investigations. Rice et al. utilized isolated perfused rat liver preparations to determine the effect of carbon tetrachloride administered *in vivo* on the hemodynamics of the liver. Portal blood pressure and flow were recorded in perfused livers from either control or treated animals. The study concluded that although the primary lesion caused by carbon tetrachloride was hepatocellular damage, subsequent effects included increased vascular resistance and enhanced response to norepinephrine. Bullock et al utilized isolated perfused rat liver preparations to examine the effects of two fungal toxins, namely, sporidesmin and icterogenin, or the mechanisms of bile secretion. Electron microscopic examination of livers perfused with the two fungal toxins indicated that the cholestatic reaction was due to changes in canalicular membranes, which included extrusion of material into the canalicular lumen and aggregation of lysosomes in the cytoplasm. Abraham et al examined the effect of hyperoxia on lysosomal enzymes using perfused liver preparations.

Radwan and Henschler have utilized isolated liver preparations to study the uptake and metabolism of the hepatocarcinogen, vinyl chloride. Using erythrocyte suspended perfusion medium, they found that the solubility of vinyl chloride stayed constant at concentrations of 50 to 25.000 ppm. The amount metabolized as determined by the difference between vinyl chloride concentration before and after passage through the liver was found to stay constant at 14.6% over the above range of concentrations. Ethanol (12 mM) and pyrazole (200 μM) reduced the metabolism of vinyl chloride by 13 and 32%, respectively. Since metabolism of vinyl chloride was modified by prior exposure of the animals to inducing and inhibiting agents, it was concluded that vinyl chloride underwent a metabolic transformation via mixed function oxidation to reactive metabolites. The above study can be taken to represent how perfused liver preparation can be utilized to determine the effect of even volatile substances.

Recently, Nastainczyk and Ullrich have used isolated perfused rat liver preparations to examine the effect of hypoxia on the metabolism of halothane. The study concluded that halothane is biotransformed via reductive *in vivo* metabolism of halothane to reactive intermediates when the oxygen concentration of the perfusates drops below a critical level (about 50 mM). These authors utilized a whole organ spectrophotometry of isolated perfused livers to establish that a complex of macromolecules and halothane is formed under slightly hypoxic conditions, and that metyrapone, an inhibitor of MFO reactions, abolished the formation of this complex.

Use of isolated perfused liver preparations in the metabolism of toxic substances as well as the effect of the toxic substances on hepatic function are illustrated by a series of studies in which the hepatobiliary function was examined after the animals had been exposed to toxic chemicals. In these studies, the effect of exposure to chlorocarbon pesticides, mirex and chlordecone, was examined in isolated perfused liver preparations. Biliary excretion of an anionic model compound BSP and imipramine was examined. These studies also serve to illustrate the utility of isolated liver preparations in studying the biotransformation of chemicals. By assaying a series of perfusate samples as well as liver tissue at the end of a perfusion study, the metabolism of imipramine by control as well as treated livers was followed. Although both chlordecone and mirex were known to be inducers of hepatic mixed function oxidases, these experiments revealed that biliary excretion of endogenously formed metabolites of imipramine was suppressed by prior exposure to the above chlorocarbons. The pattern of imipramine metabolism indicated that the surpressed biliary excretory function was not related to alterations in metabolism of imipramine.

Other experiments, in which readily excretable polar metabolites of imipramine were introduced into the perfusate of control and treated liver preparations, indicated that biliary excretion of these metabolites was also hindered by prior exposure to mirex and chlordecone. Thus such experimental manipulations using isolated liver preparations were useful in evaluating the role of drug metabolism in biliary excretory function. Isolated liver preparations can also be utilized to examine the role of hepatic uptake and metabolism in the disposition of toxic chemical. Uptake, metabolism, and biliary excretion of polychlorinated biphenyls was examined using isolated perfused rat liver preparations. Similar preparations were also useful in discovering the inhibitory effect of mirex on biliary excretion of polar metabolites of monochlorobiphenyl.

Thurman et al. studied the kinetics of *p*-nitroanisole O-demethylation in hemoglobin-free perfused rat liver preparations. Using the isolated liver, these investigators were able to demonstrate that the rates of *p*-nitroanisole metabolism were linear for 30 min in normal livers, and that these rates were only linear for 1 to 2 min in phenobarbital-induced livers. This reduced rate of metabolism could be reversed by infusing additional glucose, suggesting an intimate relationship between drug and carbohydrate metabolism in the intact liver. Alteration in the rate of *p*-nitroanisole metabolism with various inducing agents of the MFO system produced parallel changes in rates of hepatic lactate production, reflecting the action of *p*-nitrophenol to uncouple oxidative phosphorylation. Thus these investigators were able to demonstrate that the reduction in the rate of *p*-nitroanisole metabolism in induced liver preparations was due to reduced availability of NADPH for MFO catalyzed substrate oxidation. Such experiments with intact liver preparations give us valuable insights into what might be occurring in terms of drug metabolism under *in vivo* conditions. These results serve to demonstrate that despite the induced status of the liver, enhanced drug metabolism may not necessarily be the end result, since other factors such as availability of cofactors might become limiting and hence change the quantitative aspects of drug metabolism.

Isolated Perfused Lung

The heart-lung preparation of Knowlton and Starling has been used extensively to study the respiratory functions of the lung in small and large animals. However, the refinement of the isolated perfused lung preparation technique has only been undertaken recently, after the nonrespiratory functions of the lungs were recognized. Popjack and Beeckman utilized a rabbit perfused lung preparation to examine the utilization of oxygen and substrate incorporation into phospholipids of the lung tissue. A number of investigators have since then refined the technique of perfusing lungs.

A variety of methods have been used to perfuse lungs from experimental animals. Leary and Ledingham described an *in situ* perfusion method with or without pulmonary ventilation. Similarly, Bakhle and coworkers described an isolated perfused lung preparation without ventilation of the lung during perfusion. Isolated perfused lungs can be ventilated either using negative or positive pressure. Pulsatile perfusion was utilized by Hauge, while hydrostatic pressure was used for perfusion by Levey and Gast. Gillis and Iwasawa have perfused right and left lungs of rabbits independently, while others have perfused right and left lungs as an intact organ.

An ideal perfused lung preparation is a totally isolated perfused lung preparation which can perform respiratory as well as nonrespiratory functions in total isolation. The isolated lung preparation has the advantage of being able to account for all the perfusion medium from the lung circulation at the end of perfusion experiments. Leary has pointed out that the *in situ* preparations result in some loss of perfusion medium through collateral vessels supplying the chest wall, and some fluid may be lost through exudation from the lung surface. Ventilation of the lung is essential for toxicological investigations in which maintaining physiological route of gas exchange is important. Ventilation is an integral part of lung function, and hence nonventilating lung preparations represent less than desirable conditions, irrespective of whether respiratory or nonrespiratory functions are being investigated. Retaining the ability of testing certain experimental drugs through the gaseous phase to simulate inhalational exposure would also be an additional advantage of maintaining a ventilating perfused lung preparation. Two types of isolated lung preparations will be described here, one that utilizes negative-pressure ventilation and one that utilizes positive-pressure ventilation.

Apparatus

The perfusion system developed by Niemeier and Bingham with small modifications and as is being presently used will be described. The apparatus consists of three main components. A combination of pumps for ventilation, a peristaltic pump to drive the perfusate, an assembly of tubing for carrying the perfusate to and from the lung, and an artificial thorax kept warm by heated, circulating water. The thorax is made up of double jacketed thick glass provided with an air-tight lid, which fits on the top. Perfusate flow to the lung is maintained

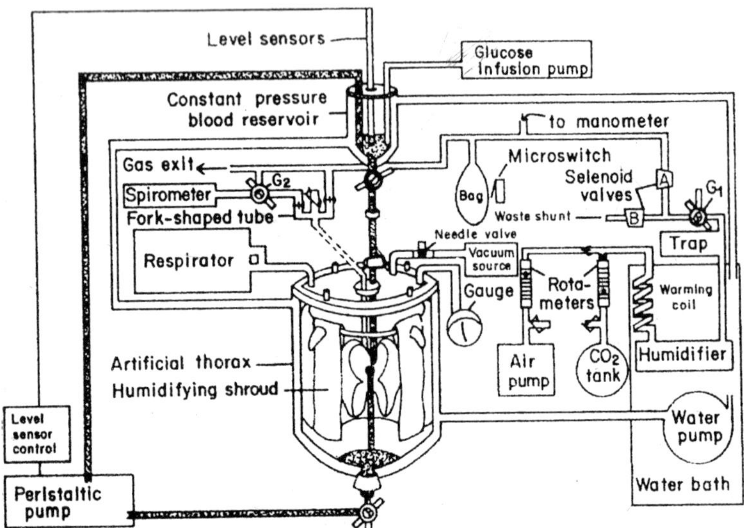

Fig. 6.4. Schematic illustration of an isolated perfused lung apparatus.

from the upper reservoir connected to the central porthole of the lid. The bottom of the reservoir has an opening through which the perfusate can be directed to the peristaltic pump. A small-animal respirator and a vacuum pump are connected to two of the portholes on the lid; these provide alternating negative pressure as a means of ventilating the perfused lung preparation. A magnehelic gauge or a simple manometer can be connected to another porthole on the lid in order to monitor the operating negative pressure in the thorax. At the center of the lid, there are two portholes, one for a tracheal cannula and the second for a pulmonary arterial cannula. The upper reservoir, which is also double jacketed, connects to the central pulmonary arterial cannula by means of a stopcock arrangement and via pressure and flow transducers. The tracheal cannula is connected to a source of a mixture of 95:5 O_2:CO_2 gas, which is filtered and humidified by bubbling through warm saline. By means of appropriate one-way valves, provisions are made for inspiration as well as expiration of the ventilating lung. A spirometer is connected to measure the inspiration volume.

The perfusate from the upper reservoir passes through the assembly of transducers into the lung via the pulmonary arterial cannula. The perfusate empties into the bottom of the reservoir and is led to a peristaletic pump, which delivers it to the upper reservoir. A level-sensor controlling device can be introduced at the upper reservoir in order to maintain a constant level of the perfusate in the reservoir to provide constant hydrostatic pressure. This automatic sensing device regulates the peristaltic pump in order to maintain a designated level of perfusate in the upper reservoir. An infusion pump can be used to infuse glucose in order to replace glucose utilized by the perfusing lung. In the upper reservoir, a pH probe can be installed to monitor the pH of the circulating perfusate. The water bath, equipped with a heater and a circulating water pump, provides a means for maintaining the thorax as well as the upper reservoir at physiological temperature (37°C).

Almost all components that come in direct contact with the perfusate are made up of glass with the exception of small pieces of medical grade silastic tubing used in the peristaltic pump, which requires a flexible tubing. The glass components as well as the flexible tubing of the apparatus are coated with Siliclad in order to avoid binding of experimental drugs to the tubing used in transporting the perfusate. The lid (thoracic roof) with a number of portholes is made up of Plexiglass fitted with a rubber "O" ring and sealed with silicone high vacuum grease, and the lid is held in place on the ground glass rim of the thorax by appropriate clamps. The small animal respirator is connected in reverse to the porthole on the lid for the purpose of creating alternating negative pressure in combination with the vacuum pump.

Prior to the surgical procedure to remove the lung, the apparatus should be thoroughly cleaned, assembled, and rinsed with physiological saline. A measured volume of perfusate can be introduced into the upper reservoir, and the entire perfusate line can be primed with the perfusate. Precaution is taken to avoid entrapment of any air emboli in the perfusate anywhere in the apparatus. The remaining perfusate can be introduced into the upper reservoir.

Surgical procedure and preparation of lung

Isolated perfused lung preparations can be obtained from almost any experimental animal. For a generalized description, the isolated perfused rabbit lung preparation will be used. The animal can be anesthetized using Nembutol (50 mg/kg), which is previously mixed with heparin (1,000 IU/kg), is injected into the marginal ear vein. Upon reaching a proper level of anesthesia, the animal can be bled by means of a cardiac puncture with an 18 gauge needle connected to a silicone tubing, which drain into a beaker held below the plane of the animal to facilitate flow by gravity procedures as well as decreasing the amount of blood remaining in the vasculature of the lung. The blood is collected in a heparinized container. This blood can also be used as a perfusate upon proper filtration. In carrying out cardiac puncture, care is taken to enter between the sixth and seventh rib next to the sternum so as not to damage the lungs.

A midline incision is made from the neck to the abdomen to expose the trachea and the rib cage. The liver is retracted and the sternum grasped by means of a curved hemostat. The sternum is lifted upward to facilitate inflation of the lungs, at which time the trachea can be clamped by means of a hemostat to entrap the proper amount of oxygen in the lungs. An incision in the diaphragm at the midline area will ensure cutting the diaphragm on both sides along the rib cage. The rib cage can be cut laterally on both sides, making sure that the lung tissue is detached from the roof of the rib cage. The lungs and heart are thus exposed through midline sternatomy, and the rib cage is retracted. The lungs and heart can be removed from the animal and transferred to a petri dish containing warm saline. All the subsequent operations can be carried out while the lungs rest in this petri dish.

The trachea is first cannulated using a PE-300 tubing (200 for the rat). At this time, the lungs can be ventilated artificially by means of a 100 cc syringe attached to the tracheal cannula by means of a silicone tubing. Alternatively, the tracheal cannula can be attached to a small animal ventilator so that the lungs can be ventilated during the subsequent cannulation procedure. The trachea, lungs, and heart are dissected free from their attachments and connective tissue and other extraneous material, taking care not to puncture the lungs, and then rinsed with warm physiological saline. The pericardium is removed and the pulmonary artery cannulated with a PE-300 cannula (3 mm i.d., 5 cm in length) prefilled with perfusate. During this procedure, care must be taken not to introduce air emboli in the vasculature or immediate interruption of flow will occur upon perfusion. The entire right ventricle and the right atrium together with most of the left ventricle (up to 0.5 cm) below the A-B septum are removed. The left atrium is cannulated by passing a PE-300 cannula (3 mm i.d., 6 cm in length, and curved) through the remaining left ventricle and bicuspid valves to the atrium. The cannula is secured with a ligature and the remaining tissue dissected free of the cannulated lung preparation. Throughout the procedure, a hemostat is retained on the pulmonary arterial cannula to avoid air bubbles entering the pulmonary artery. The cannulated lungs along with the hemostat can be weighed at this time after blotting dry with filter paper.

The lung preparation is now suspended in the artificial thorax by connecting the tracheal and pulmonary arterial cannulae to the respective tubings, which extend to the inside of the Plexiglass lid. It is also important to avoid entrapment of any air bubbles, especially when the arterial cannula is connected to the perfusion apparatus. Flow is resumed through the arterial cannula after the lid is closed, and the perfusate line from the pump is connected to the top of the upper reservoir. Perfusion can be established at this time very slowly, ensuring that no bubbles pass through into the pulmonary artery. The pumps can be activated to inflate the lung. The lungs are inflated by applying a negative pressure of 25 to 30 cm of water by activating the vacuum pump and increasing the vacuum. Once the collapsed lungs are inflated to a desired level, since the respirator is already turned on, the alternating negative-positive pressure will automatically ventilate the lung. In the rabbit, the frequency is kept at 50 respirations per min. In the rat, this can be maintained at approximately 60 per min. Once the ventilation cycle is initiated, the apparatus is automatic, and perfusion and ventilation can continue throughout the experimental duration. The perfusion flow rate will increase quickly upon inflation of the lung, and this may steadily increase until steady-state ventilation is established. If the automatic level sensor is in operation, this is of no consequence. However, if such an arrangement is not available, care must be exercised to maintain perfusate in the upper reservoir by manual control of the peristaltic pump. The lungs are usually allowed to equilibrate in the perfusion apparatus for a period of 15 to 20 min.

Positive ventilation procedure

The perfusion apparatus developed by O'Neil and Tierney can be used to illustrate perfusion of lungs from smaller animals and by using a positive ventilation procedure. The lungs are ventilated directly by means of an animal respirator, which is attached to the tracheal cannula. This procedure avoids the need for the additional vacuum pump required in the negative alternating pressure ventilation method. Two solenoid valves are used to direct gas flow during the respiratory cycle. A tidal volume of approximately 3.5 ml is obtained for the rat and is adjusted to provide a maximum transpulmonary pressure of 12 cm of water. The end expiratory pressure is set at 3.5 cm of water to keep the lung from collapsing during expiration. The rat lungs are perfused in this apparatus at a frequency of 13 per min. The procedure for isolation and cannulation of the lung is essentially the same as described for the rabbit lung preparation, with the exception of the smaller

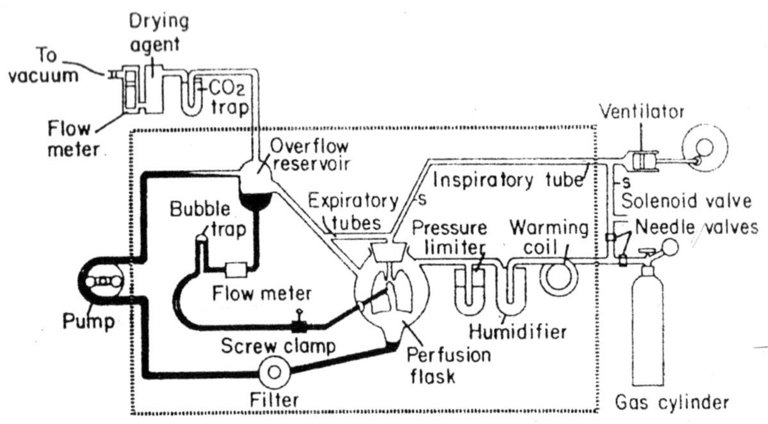

Fig. 6.5. Schematic diagram of the isolated perfused lung preparation.

diameter PE cannula. The procedure for maintaining the isolated perfused rat lung using positive ventilation has been described adequately.

Perfusion Media

Nicolaysen has studied the effect of perfusate composition on edema development and whole blood was found to be the most suitable perfusate. The perfusion procedure described by Niemeier and Bingham included the use of autologous whole blood as a perfusate. This was practical in the case of the rabbit, since 100 ml or more of whole blood can be obtained from a rabbit weighing 3 kg or more by cardiac puncture. Blood is collected in a heparinized container and filtered to remove any debris, dead cells, or small blood clots. The blood is heparinized once again prior to circulation in the apparatus in order to avoid any clotting. Using autologous whole blood si impractical, however, for perfusing rat lungs or lungs of other smaller animals. Blood may have to be collected from several animals in order to supply an adequate volume of perfusate for one perfusion experiment. Furthermore, for certain experimental protocols such as single-pass experiments, large volumes (several liters) of perfusate may be required. For these reasons, use of artificial perfusate has been most popular.

The most widely used lung perfusate is the one described by Junod, which has the following composition in mM concentration: NaCl, 118; KCl, 4.75; $CaCl_2$, 2.54; KH_2PO_4, 1.19; $MgSO_4$, 1.19; and $NaHCO_3$, 25. Bovine serum albumin is added at a concentration of 4.5 g/liter, and the final pH of the solution is adjusted to 7.4 with 1 N NaOH, so that the final Na^+ concentration of the standard medium would be 161 mM. The medium is equilibrated with a mixture of 95:5

oxygen and carbon dioxide prior to priming the apparatus. This perfusate has been used by a number of investigators; the standard perfusion medium is Krebs-Ringer bicarbonate buffer solution, described by Umbreit et al. containing 5 mM of glucose and 4.5% bovine serum albumin. Several advantages of using this artificial medium as a perfusate can be cited. First, in the one-pass type of experiments, large volumes of the perfusate are often used, and using whole blood as a perfusate becomes uneconomical. Second, manipulations of ionic changes in the perfusate can be introduced easily in an artificial medium. Introducing such changes in the perfusate is essential for studies aimed at mechanisms of pulmonary uptake of drugs. An additional advantage of artificial perfusate is the relative ease with which the test drug can be extracted and analyzed in the absence of erythrocytes and any interfering hemoglobin.

A combination of either autologous or mixed whole blood and the Krebs-Ringer bicarbonate buffered artificial medium as a perfusate can also be used in perfusing lung preparations. Such a preparation has the advantage of including the natural constituents of blood in order that natural binding sites can be provided for the test drug. Differences in the uptake of drugs by the lung have been found in either the whole blood or artificial medium when used as perfusate. Perfluorocarbons have not been used in the perfusate in isolated perfused lung preparations, although their successful usage in perfusing livers would suggest that fluorocarbon emulsions would also adequately support the isolated lung preparations. In the isolated lung preparations ventilated by positive pressure, Young also utilized Krebs-Ringer bicarbonate buffer solution containing glucose and bovine serum albumin, similar to the one described above. By and large, it appears that this erythrocyte-free medium has served as a widely used perfusate in maintaining preparations of isolated perfused lungs.

Viability criteria

Niemeier and Bingham determined a number of biochemical parameters in the circulating perfusate as well as in the lung to ascertain the viability of isolated perfused rabbit lung preparations. The concentrations of blood urea nitrogen (BUN), Ca^{2+}, albumin, total protein, and pyruvate in the perfusate, changed little throughout the perfusion. Inorganic phosphate, uric acid, lactic acid, and total bilirubin increased moderately during perfusion. Lactate dehydrogenase and SGOT activities, as well as plasma hemoglobin, increased markedly during the 3 hr perfusion. Hematocrit levels decreased slightly, which may have been a result of hemolysis, since autologous whole blood was used. In these experiments, sodium bicarbonate was added periodically to maintain the blood pH at 7.4, and additions of heparin and epinephrine were made in order to maintain proper perfusion flow rates. These additions might have contributed to the decrease in hematocrit. Glucose levels decreased (34.5 ± 4.1 mg/hr) during perfusion, necessitating the addition of glucose with an infusion pump at the rate of 30 mg/hr in 0.3 ml of water. Thus when glucose was replenished, concentration of glucose in the perfusate did not decrease significantly over a 3 hr period of perfusion. Cholesterol increased at a rate of approximately 11% per hr, but when α-tocopherol was added to the perfusate, cholesterol increased (53%/hr) markedly.

Lungs can be examined visually during perfusion for the appearance of translucent areas, which would indicate development of edema. Niemeier and Bingham found that the lungs gained weight on an average of 2.8% per hr over 3 hr of perfusion with autologous whole blood. Histopathological examination revealed no edema after 3 hr of perfusion, and the integrity of the pulmonary ultrastructure was well preserved.

Often, after prolonged perfusion of lungs, the lung preparations deteriorate, with the concomitant development of edematous areas characterized by a translucent appearance on the surface of the lung. After continued perfusion, the lung does not inflate and deflate with each respiratory cycle, and surfactant material might appear in the tracheal cannula. If the perfusion is continued after the lung appears to be edematous, large and copious flows of the surfactant material will continue to appear through the tracheal cannula. Maintenance of perfusate pH can be a problem, and Niemeier and Bingham were able to accomplish this by the addition of 1 mM sodium bicarbonate to the perfusate. However, they used room air mixed with 5% CO_2 is used for ventilating the isolated lungs, and the lungs are properly inflated, no problem is encountered in maintaining physiological pH of the perfusate. An additional criterion of viability of the lung preparation is the evaluation of drug metabolizing enzymes in the perfused lung. Various investigators have found that after 2 to 3 hr of perfusion, microsomal drug metabolizing activity of the lung remains unaltered, indicating satisfactory preservation of microsomal MFO activity of the perfused lung preparation. Levels of ATP were measured in rat lungs perfused for 90 min by a positive ventilation procedure and were found to be at or above the ATP levels in nonperfused lungs. By contrast, ATP content was decreased by slicing the lung.

Applications

Isolated perfused lung preparations have been used for a variety of studies including drug uptake, metabolism, and disposition of various pharmacological and toxicological agents. Rhoades has described a technique utilizing isolated perfused lungs ventilated by positive pressure for evaluating the effect of various gaseous environments on pulmonary biochemistry. Block and Cannon have investigated the effect of anoxia or hyperoxia on the ability of lungs to clear endogenous as well as exogenous chemicals. Use of isolated lung preparations has resulted in significant contributions to our understanding of the pulmonary role in uptake and metabolism of a variety of xenobiotics. Examples of toxicological investigations using isolated perfused lung preparations include studies on the pulmonary uptake and disposition of aldrin and dieldrin, uptake of the herbicide paraquat uptake and metabolism of trichloroethylene, and uptake and metabolism of benzo(a)-pyrene. Although this is by no means a survey of toxicological investigations utilizing isolated perfused lung preparations, these investigations do serve as examples of how useful isolated perfused lung preparations have been in determining the pulmonary contribution to the disposition of toxic chemicals.

Perfused lung preparations have been useful in demonstrating epoxidase activity in the lung tissue. Aldrin is a cyclodiene pesticide which is readily epoxidized to aldrin, and in the liver can be further metabolized by epoxide hydrase to dihydro diol metabolites. It was demonstrated that in the lung dieldrin could be readily epoxidized to dieldrin, which is a stable epoxide and can e quantitated as a measure of aldrin epoxidase activity. This represented the first direct demonstration of epoxidase capability of the lung tissue. Aldrin is thus metabolized to dieldrin irrespective of whether it enters via airways or through the vascular system, and the metabolites appear in the perfusate rather rapidly. In these studies, it was demonstrated that intact perfused lung preparations were able to turn over aldrin to dieldrin at a lesser rate than the *in vitro* incubations of lung homogenate preparations. These studies serve to illustrate the utility of perfusion intact organs in order to gain a realistic evaluation of the biochemical metabolic contribution by the organ to the metabolism and disposition of a test drug. Thus turnover of aldrin to dieldrin was four to seven times greater in *in vitro* preparations compared to *ex vivo* preparations using perfused intact lungs. Although the reason for such a discrepancy between *in vitro* and intact organ perfusion systems is incompletely understood, Itakura et al. have demonstrated that availability of necessary cofactors might be limiting in intact perfused lung preparations. They observed that demethylation of *p*-nitroanisole by the perfused rabbit lung preparations was limited by the availability of the cofactor NADPH, the generation of which could be stimulated by introducing glucose to the perfusion medium.

The study of Dolbey et al illustrates the utility of isolated perfused lung preparations in studying the uptake and disposition of gaseous toxic substances. They studied the uptake and metabolism of trichloroethylene in isolated perfused rat lung preparations by introducing trichloroethylene vapors through the trachea. Perfused rat lung preparations metabolized trichloroethylene to trichloethanol, and the guinea pig lungs were more active in the metabolism of trichloroethylene to the alcohol. In the future, it should be anticipated that more experimentation will be carried out utilizing isolated perfused lung preparations for such toxicological investigations.

The use of isolated perfused lung preparations for metabolism of carcinogenic chemicals such as benzo(a)pyrene can be cited as another example of the development of perfused lung preparations, aiding advancement in this area. Bingham et al. have studied the metabolism of benzo(a)pyrene and report the formation of several metabolites of this chemical, including the formation of carcinogenic reactive epoxide and dihydrodial metabolites in the lung. In addition to containing the necessary enzyme systems for carrying out oxidative metabolism of these toxic chemicals, the lungs contain enzyme systems which catalyze phase II reactions such as epoxide hydrase and glucuronyl transferase activities, as can be demonstrated by using intact perfused lung preparations. The use of isolated lung preparations in determining other physiological effects of toxic chemical mediated via the endogenous hormone system can be illustrated by the studies of Seiler et al. They examined the effect of certain anorectic agents, including chlorphentermine, on the clearance of 5-hydroxytryptamine (seotonin) and observed that the anorectic agents enhanced the vasoconstrictor effects of serotonin in pulmonary circulation. Another example of the use of isolated perfused lung preparations to evaluate the effect of foreign toxic chemicals on the role of pulmonary clearance of endogenous chemicals is represented in the studies of Gillis and Roth, in which they examined the turnover of endogenous hormones such as 5-hydroxytryptamine and norepinephrine.

Although the recirculation apparatus was illustrated above, simple modification allows one to perform experiments using single-pass perfusion system. A number of investigators have utilized single-pass perfusion to investigate the mechanisms of drug uptake and release from the lung. For example, Junod examined the mechanisms of pulmonary uptake of imipramine using a single-pass mode of perfusion. Likewise, single-pass kinetics were used to determine the uptake metabolism and release mechanism of aldrin and dieldrin in rabbit perfused lung preparations. Single-pass experiments can be expensive both in terms of materials (albumin used in preparing the perfusate) and the technical assistance required to conduct these experiments. An ideal single-pass experiment will require assistance of three individuals to work in swift coordination and usually involves analyzing a large number of samples. Hence the information to be gained from such experimental protocols should be weighed against the expense involved. Often equally valuable information may become available from recirculating perfusion experiments at a fraction of effort and resources expended.

Isolated Perfused Kidney Preparations

Although a number of methods for obtaining perfused kidney preparations from various mammalian species have been devised, use of isolated kidney preparations in toxicological studies has been infrequent. Most workers in this field have been concerned with the study of autoregulation, excretion, and reabsorption functions of the organ. Isolated perfused kidney preparations have been used in such studies from rat, dog, rabbit, pig, monkey and sheep, and man. Considerable variations has existed between different investigators in terms of specific techniques used for perfusing kidneys. The kidney may be perfused via the aorta or via the renal artery. Pulsatile or nonpulsatile perfusate flow can be used, and perfusion pressure may be exerted either with the pump or by means of a hydrostatic pressure head.

As in other perfused organ systems, the most important variable has been the perfusion medium, and a considerable range of varying compositions have now been tested. Argument persists in the literature relating to whether pulsatile flow is to be preferred as a simulation of the *in vivo* situation. A second principal problem has been the vasoconstriction and deterioration of the kidney preparations associated with the use of whole blood as a perfusion medium. By and large, to circumvent this problem, investigators have used either diluted blood, a reconstituted blood type of perfusate, or an erythrocyte-free medium containing various electrolytes, glucose, and albumin. Most investigators are content with the use of a Krebs-Ringer bicarbonate buffer solution containing albumin and glucose as a most satisfactory perfusate. As in the case of other organs, kidneys can also be perfused either *in situ* or can be perfused in total isolation in chambers that can be kept warm for normothermic perfusion. A further variation can be in the mode of perfusion; kidneys can be perfused either using recirculating perfusate or in a single-pass mode.

Apparatus

The apparatus used for perfusing kidney preparations is similar to the one described for perfusing liver. This includes the outer chamber used in perfusing the liver, which is fitted with the heater-fan assembly for maintaining the desired temperature inside the chamber. A multibulb-glass lung can be used to oxygenate the perfusate. Perfusate is led to a roller type or perstaltic pump and is transported to the top

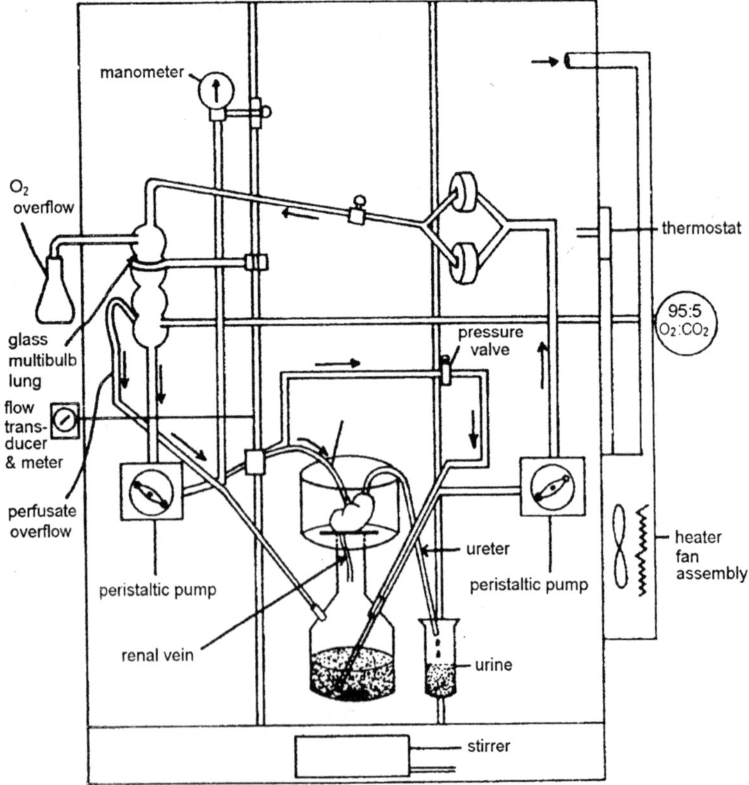

Fig. 6.6. Schematic illustration of an isolated perfused kidney apparatus.

of the oxygenator via a glass tubing. A filter placed between the lung and the glass tubing ensures trapping fat droplets and any other particulate material, including cell debris, from the perfusate before it enters the kidney. A major difference between the liver and kidney is the higher (120 cm) hydrostatic pressure used in perfusing the kidney. Oxygenated blood by means of glass tubing thence enters the renal arterial cannula. A set of perfusion pressure and flow transducers can be placed between the arterial cannula and the glass tubing in order to measure the perfusion pressure and flow rates. Similarly, electrodes can be placed before an after the kidney to monitor oxygen levels of the perfusate. A pH probe can be placed anywhere in the circulation to monitor pH continuously. The effusate from the kidney is guided back to the reservoir to complete one recirculation. An overflow arrangement from the hydrostatic reservoir to the central reservoir allows for maintenance of constant hydrostatic pressure. The kidney rests on a nylon mesh stretched over a ring approximately 7.5 cm in diameter. The stainless steel strip is mounted about 2.5 cm above the tray to support the arterial cannula. The temperature of the cabinet can be maintained at approximately 38°C so as to allow the kidney and the perfusate temperature to equilibrate at 37°C.

Most of the tubing used in the apparatus can be replaced by glass in order to minimize binding of test drugs to rubber or plastic tubings used in earlier perfusion setups. The arterial cannula is made up of glass tubing of 2.8 mm internal diameter (external diameter 3.5 mm) drawn to a taper of 1.3 mm external diameter and 1 mm internal diameter. It is bent to a right angle 1.5 cm from the tip and the short limb of the cannula has little or no taper. The tip of the cannula is beveled slightly to facilitate its insertion into the renal artery. The venous cannula is placed in the inferior vena cava and consists of a 3 cm long size PE-270 (2 mm i.d., 3 mm o.d.) cut off at an angle to form a sharp tip. With the cannula in position, the opening of the cannula lies opposite the right renal vein. It might be advantageous to prepare several cannulae of varying sizes since considerable variation in the renal artery can be seen from animal to animal. The renal arterial cannula should be filled with heparinized perfusate in order to facilitate avoiding air emboli during cannulation.

The surgical procedure for isolating and perfusing rat kidney will be described here, since this animal appears to be the most popular experimental animal for toxicological investigations. Kidneys can be surgically removed from rats weighing 300 to 400 g, preferably starved

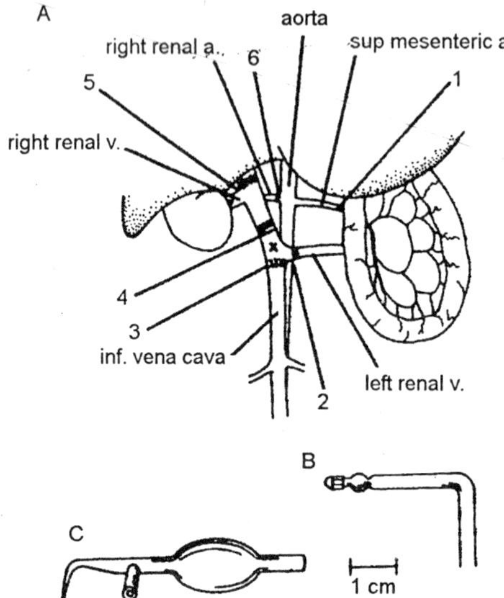

Fig. 6.7. A–Schematic drawing showing peripheral blood vessels in the upper abdomen of a rat with position of ligatures in preparation for cannulation of the kidney. B–Venous canula. C–Arterial cannula.

overnight to decrease rates of gluconeogenesis and possibly reduce perinephric fat. After anesthetizing the rat with an injection of pentobarbital (50 mg/kg), an abdominal incision is made in the midline and extended laterally. The intestines can be sweeped to the animal's left to facilitate the next steps. Because of the anatomical advantage of the mesenteric artery arising from the aorta at the same level as the renal artery, the right kidney is used for perfusion. This facilitates passing the cannula through the aorta into the renal artery without loss of much blood and interruption of blood flow to the kidney.

To expose the major abdominal vessels and the right kidney, fat and perivascular tissue are cleared away by teasing the tissues around the blood vessels. The adrenal branch of the right renal artery is ligated, and loose ligatures are placed around the vessels as follows: one on the inferior vena cava just distal tc the liver, one on the aorta above the mesenteric artery, two ligatures on the mesenteric artery near the aorta separated by 0.5 cm, three ligatures on the inferior vena cava, one between the right and left renal vein, one distal to the left renal vein and finally, one ligature further down on the inferior vena cava. Finally, a ligature is placed on the left renal vein. The ureter is cannulated by means of PE-10 tubing, and a ligature is placed around the ureter to hold the cannula in place.

The animal is heparinized by injecting approximately 200 units of heparin to the inferior vena cava, after which the opening in the wall of the vein is closed by means of a ligature passed over the point of the injecting needle. After typing the ligature on the left renal vein, the venous cannulus in inserted in the inferior vena cava and tied in place by means of the two upper ligatures on the inferior vena cava. The cannula should be turned such that the opening lies opposite the right renal vein. The other end of the cannula can be temporarily closed by a loose plug of tissue paper. The distal ligature on the mesenteric artery is tied, and the artery is grasped at its origin with fine curved forceps and an incision is made on the wall. The cannula filled with perfusion medium is inserted and passed to meet the forceps, which are then removed. The tip of the cannula is advanced into the aorta and then into the renal artery, which takes off on the opposite side of the aorta, allowing the perfusion medium to flow to the kidney. The cannula is tied in place by means of the anterior ligature on the renal artery and the ligature on the mesenteric artery as well.

With all the cannulae intact and in place, the kidney is surgically removed. The isolated kidney is transferred to the kidney platform in the perfusion chamber, and perfusion is resumed by connecting the arterial cannula to the perfusion flow of the preprimed apparatus. With practice, the total time required for the surgical procedure can be reduced to approximately 15 min, starting from the initial midline incision.

Perfusion media

As indicated earlier, the perfusion medium of choice appears to be a cell-free perfusion fluid with adequate buffering capacity, containing solutions of salts, glucose, and albumin. The perfusion medium described earlier for liver and lung, containing Krebs-Ringer bicarbonate buffer solution, appears to be quite satisfactory for perfusing kidney preparations. Earlier attempts to utilize blood as a natural perfusate have met with problems relating to vasoconstriction, whether the blood was defibrinated or heparinized. Another cause of impaired renal flow was found to be the embolization of fat droplets, especially at later stage of perfusion using whole blood as a perfusate. An additional disadvantage of using whole blood as a perfusate is the unavailability of a requisite volume of blood, especially in smaller experimental animals such as the rat. A volume of 100 ml of perfusate is often necessary to conduct an isolated perfused kidney experiment, and several animals would be required to obtain the requisite volume of blood for perfusing the rat kidney. In addition to the economic considerations, other problems may be encountered in mixing blood from several animals. One difficulty is the possibility of immunological interactions in blood pooled from several animals. Finally, in certain experiments, it is essential to have one-pass circulation through the kidney. This will require greater volumes of perfusate, and using blood would be impractical in such studies.

A major advance in the development of isolated perfused kidney preparations was made with the use of artificial, cell-free perfusion fluids such as buffered saline solutions supplemented with serum albumin or macromolecular plasma substitutes. A principal disadvantage of using a perfusion fluid devoid of red blood cells is the relatively high perfusate flow rates observed under these conditions and the relative anoxia due to the limitation of O_2 carrying capacity of the cell-free media. Second, absence of natural components of blood in perfusion medium devoid of whole blood may alter the disposition of the test chemical. Although Krebs-Ringer bicarbonate buffer solution containing glucose and albumin can be used for perfusing kidneys, investigators have found it necessary to dialyze the bovine serum albumin to obtain satisfactory kidney preparations perfusing for longer durations of time. Third, use of millipore filters in the circulation is necessary to filter out any cellular debris that may enter the circulation. Forth, higher flow rates are necessary to insure an adequate O_2 supply to the kidney when an artificial medium is used for perfusion.

In addition to the composition for artificial perfusate given above, Fonteles et al found that addition of glutathione (500 mg/liter) to the perfusate prevented depletion of endogenous cortical and medullary glutathione. Further, glutathione supplementation of the perfusate decreased renal vascular resistance and increased perfusate flow. Glutathione extraction studies revealed a progressive decrease in renal extraction with time, ranging from complete extraction at 10 min to a value of 38% at 60 min. Including glutathione in the perfusate might be especially relevant for toxicological investigations in view of the reports that may toxic agents deplete endogenous glutathione levels in various tissues.

Viability criteria

As indicated earlier, to date most of the isolated perfused kidney studies have dealt with the mechanism of autoregulation and physiological functions of the kidney. Because of such a background upon which perfused kidney preparations have been refined, techniques for evaluating adequacy and viability of the perfused kidney are abundantly available. Renal blood flow can be measured by placing a flow transducer prior to the kidney (flow transducer can also be placed after the perfusate exist can also be placed after the perfusate exist the kidney). Blood flow through the kidney can reach 6 to 7 ml/ min/g of tissue, depending on perfusion pressures varying from 90 to 130 mm of mercury. With the artificial perfusate, the perfusate flow through the kidney can reach as high as 30 to 60 ml/min/g of tissue. One problem associated with using perfusion flow rate as an index of viability is not knowing the intrarenal distribution of the flow. The regional distribution of the blood flow within the kidney can change markedly with artificial perfusion, with a string increase in flow to the medulla and inner cortex. This is especially important for any toxicological investigations, since blood flow through an organ can be either shunted or altered in other ways as a result of toxic action of a test drug. Radiolabeled microspheres (10-15 μm) introduced into the circulation of a perfused organ may be used to assess the regional distribution of flow through the organ.

Another criterion used for viability of perfused kidney preparations is the glomerular filtration rate (GFR). During the initial phase of perfusion, the GFR is at a lower limit to 50 ml/min/100 g) of the normal range. Better values have been obtained with difibrinated blood at 69 ml/min/100 g tissue. The GFR decreases progressively after 2 to 3 hr of perfusion. Often, when blood is used as a perfusate, this impairment has been attributed to the embolization of fat droplets in the glomeruli. In unsuccessful experiments, when the weight of the kidney increases, often it is due to retention of fluid in the tubules and interstitial edema.

Urine concentration and excretion of water are other criteria used for establishing the viability of perfused kidney preparations. During the first period of up to 1 hr, urine may reach an osmolality of 800 mosmoles, which is later reduced (60-150 mosmoles) due to increased urine flow. The water diuresis in the kidney preparation can be suppressed by administration of vasopressin in the perfusate. After 3 to 4 hr, the urine concentration approaches isotonicity. This pattern has been observed by several authors. When observed, loss of urine concentrating power is probably due to medullary edema and disturbances of deep cortical and medullary blood flows. Sodium excretion can also be used as an additional parameter of viability. In contrast to frequent statements in the literature, the fractional reabsorption of sodium can be normal in perfused kidney preparations. In Berndt's experiments, sodium excretion exceeded 0.4% of the filtered load after 2 hr of perfusion using the Krebs-Ringer bicarbonate buffer type of artificial medium. After prolonged perfusion, however, sodium rejection may develop unless the perfusate is replaced, and this may be due to accumulation of metabolic end products such as ammonia in the perfusate.

Acidification of urine is yet another functional viability criterion used for evaluating perfused kidney preparations. The loss of ability to excrete acidic urine represents a major functional abnormality of isolated kidney. An additional functional parameter that can be applied to perfused kidney preparations is the determination of insulin as well as *para*-aminohippurate (PAH) clearance values. A disadvantage of using these clearances as determinants of viability is that depending upon the experimental conditions, these tests may or may not be compatible with the original intended use of the perfused preparation. Hence many functional tests may have to be carried out infrequently rather than routinely as an internal check of the perfused preparation.

Finally, the kidney preparations can be sampled for electron microscopy as well as light microscopy, and morphological examinations can be used as determinants of functional abnormality. However, routine morphological examination at the light microscopical or ultrastructural level might not be practical for several reasons. Whether the preparation was viable cannot be determined until after the perfusion experiment. Facilities or expertise for routine morphological examination may not be available, and when available, might be prohibitively expensive for routine use in experimental work. Often, the validity of using morphological alterations as indicative of functional abnormality is questionable because other functional parameters might be optimal in spite of the morphological alterations at the cellular or subcellular level. Conversely, despite the normal morphological appearance, distinct functional aberrations may be observed. At least in part, such discrepancies can be explained on the basis of the relatively shorter time required for functional abnormality to be detected, while longer periods of time may be required for observed morphological alterations to develop and vice versa. At any rate, as has been pointed out earlier for the liver and lungs, morphological observation should be helpful initially in establishing a viable perfused kidney preparation in any laboratory. Second, it will be useful in examining effects of toxic chemicals on perfused kidney preparations.

Applications

Isolated perfused kidney preparations have not been utilized in pharmacological and toxicological investigations despite the availability of refined techniques for some time. The bulk of the isolated perfused kidney work can be seen in the physiological literature. One reason for this might be increased attention devoted to establishment of the physiological parameters such as GFR, autoregulation of blood flow through the kidney, absorption reabsorption mechanisms in the kidney tubules, and hormonal regulation of renal tubular functions. However, the utility of isolated perfused kidney preparations can be demonstrated by the nature of information which can be obtained using this technique. For instance, the control of the GFR by an endogenously released humoral factor was definitively demonstrated by using isolated kidney preparation. Using isolated erythrocyte-free, perfused rat kidney preparations, Schurek et al. have been able to demonstrate that sodium reabsorption can be increased by including glucose as the sole energy source for the kidney. The nature of glucose handling by the kidney has also been investigated using perfused kidney. Since the tubular transport maximum (t_m) for glucose is proportional to the GFR in perfused kidney preparations, it was concluded that the t_m for glucose is not controlled by extrarenal factors. Many physiological parameters of kidney function have been studied and understood, and in many cases, the renal control mechanisms have been confirmed by using isolated perfused kidney preparations.

The study of extraction of glutathione from the circulating perfusate by isolated perfused kidney preparations may be mentioned as an example of a biochemical study that can be useful in toxicological investigations. Including glutathione (GSH) in the circulating perfusate at a concentration of 500 mg/liter resulted in the preservation of cortical and medullary GSH. Perfusion without the addition of glutathione consistently resulted in depletion of tissue levels of this important tripeptide. In addition, including glutathione in the perfusate resulted in decreased renal vascular resistance and increased perfusion flow. Whether the increased perfusion flow is due to intrarenal alterations in flow patterns is unclear. It appears that glutathione storage in the kidney can level off, as indicated by the above study, in which complete extraction of added glutathione was seen at 10 min, and this uptake was reduced at 38% of administered glutathione at 60 min. In these studies, Fonteles et al. indicate a high affinity in the rabbit kidney for glutathione and a relatively large net reabsorption of this important tripeptide. In view of the many toxicological molecular events that are related to alterations in the endogenous pools of glutathione, this observation might be important in toxicological studies using isolated perfused kidney preparations.

Another example of using the isolated perfused kidney in toxicological investigations can be cited in the studies of Dovrak et al., in which they examined the effects of high doses of methylprednisolone on the isolated perfused dog kidney. They noted several histological changes in the kidneys perfused with methylprednisolone for 20 hr or longer. The primary changes consisted of necrosis of capillary loops, inclusion of eosinophilic material in Bowman's space, thickening of the basement membrane, and endothelial cell damage. Arterial changes consisted primarily of inclusion of afferent arterioles with dense eosinophilic material. Tubular changes consisted of inclusion of tubular lumens and damage to tubular epithelial cells. These studies demonstrate that administration of high doses of methylprednisolone can produce irreversible hemodynamic and histological changes in the kidney.

Summerfield et al. utilized isolated perfused kidney preparations to examine conjugating reactions involved in the elimination of certain bile acids in urine. These investigators, using isolated perfused rat kidney preparations, demonstrated that lithocholic and chenodeoxycholic acids can be metabolized by the perfused kidney to their monosulfate conjugates. The disulfate metabolites of the bile acids were not detected in the urine. These findings support the hypothesis that renal synthesis of monosulfate conjugates may account for at least some of the bile acid sulfates present in urine in the cholestatic syndrome in man. Moreover, these results suggest that in chemically induced hepatic injury, the kidney may be able to conjugate some of the bile acids. Furthermore, these studies demonstrate the presence of sufficient biochemical machinery within the renal tissue for conjugating endogenous substrates. These experiments also demonstrate the possibility of conjugation of foreign chemicals in the renal tissue, facilitating their elimination in urine.

As an example of another use of isolated perfused kidney in toxicological investigations, the study of Tark et al may be cited. These investigators examined the substrate metabolism in the isolated perfused dog kidney and established that free fatty acids and glucose serve as significant substrates for providing energy for sodium transport in the kidney. Second, their studies suggest that glucose may substitute for free fatty acids as an energy source at times when free fatty acids in the circulation are reduced. The effect of toxic chemicals in the renal circulation on substrate metabolism in the kidney can be examined using the methods described by Tark et al. Recently, Johannesen et al. utilized perfused kidney preparations to study the renal energy metabolism using the metabolic inhibitor 2,4-dinitrophenol.

Isolated Perfused Brain

The brain does not lend itself to simple and totally isolated perfusion, and all the preparations to date include more or less extraneural tissue. Perfusion has found little place in many of the biochemical and toxicological studies with brain tissue, since the technique presents great difficulty even when effort is not made to exclude extraneural tissue. In addition, the brain is heterogenous, and the contribution by both neuronal and nonneuronal tissue of the brain to drug uptake and turnover in perfusion causes difficulties in duplication of the results. The blood-brain barrier is one aspect of brain metabolism in particular that remains noticeably obscure and has been the subject of studies with perfused brain preparations. The heterogeneity of the preparation together with the many different neural tissues represented in the brain make perfusion a somewhat less valuable technique for toxicological investigations than other individual organs. Nevertheless, several investigators have been able to maintain a viable perfused brain preparation which can be utilized for drug metabolism and investigations on the effects of toxic chemicals that may adversely affect the central nervous system. The difficulties of maintaining an isolated perfused brain preparation, coupled with the readily available *in vitro* and *in vivo* techniques, have resulted in underutilization of perfused brain preparations for pharmacological and toxicological investigations.

Comparatively simple techniques of perfusing the rat brain will be described here. The "perfused rat head" preparation of Thompson et al. in which the entire head is perfused with no attempt to limit the circulation to the brain, will not be described here in detail. However, such a technique may be useful in some toxicological investigations and may be considered before setting up more difficult preparations. Far more elaborate and therefore technically more difficult is the preparation described by Andjus et al., which attempts to exclude the muscle of the head and neck from the perfusion circuit; this will be described because of the obvious superiority of the technique. The preparation is based upon the more elaborate perfusion technique developed in the cat by Geiger and Magnes, which may be consulted if larger animal models will be suitable, depending upon the particular need.

Apparatus

Figure shows the schematics of the equipment used for oxygenating the venous drainage from the brain and perfusion of the isolated rat brain described by Andjus et al. A bubble oxygenator and the reservoir are made from two disposable plastic drug administration sets combined and fitted with connector and plastic tube. A small volume of recirculating fluid pumped by a peristaltic pump is used to perfuse the brain. The perfused brain preparation is held in a funnel from which the effluent perfusate drips to the oxygenator and passes through a filter to complete one recirculation. If a single-pass circulation is desired, the perstaltic pump is disconnected, and a reservoir of perfusate is used at a height sufficient to provide satisfactory perfusion pressure and flows.

Surgical procedure

After the animal is anesthetized using a proper anesthetic agent, both common carotid arteries are exposed, and the trachea is intubated via a tracheostomy. The animal is heparinized by injecting 500 units of sodium heparin through the jugular vein, which is then ligated by means of a suture. The external carotid artery and the pterygopalatine

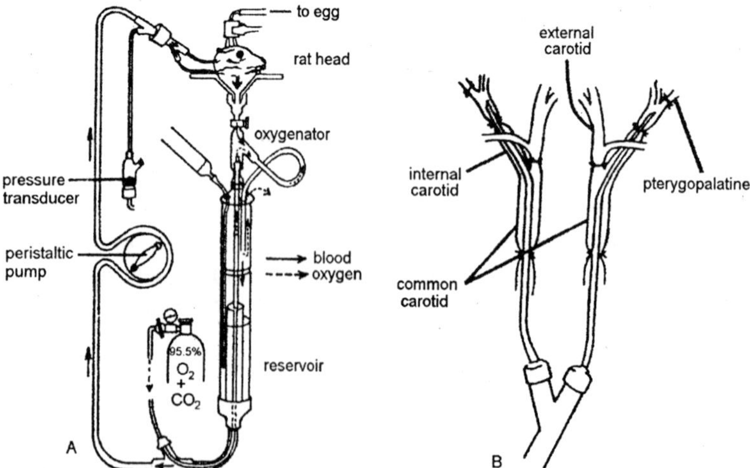

Fig. 6.8. A–Schematic illustration of the perfusion system for the isolated perfused rat brain preparation. B–This diagram show schematically the ration of the perfusion cannulae to the cannulated and adjacent arteries.

artery are ligated. In the rat, the pterygopalatine artery is a branch of internal carotid artery, which supplies blood to various extracranial structures. A plastic cannula filled with perfusion fluid is then instead into each common carotid, advanced into the internal carotid artery, and tied into position os that its tip is near the origin of the previously ligated pterygopalatine.

A slow perfusion is initiated, and then the skin, muscles of the head, face, and neck are removed, together with the mandible. A sturdy ligature is placed around the vertebral column, which is transected just below the ligature. The transected vertebral canal is packed with a cotton or tissue paper plug, and the canal is sealed with melted wax. The completed preparation consists of the skull and its contents with the upper cervical vertebrae and small remnants of muscle tissue attached. Toward the end of the surgical procedure, the perfusion flow is gradually increased. After severing the vertebral column, the perfusion flow rate is adjusted to a desired value (1.4 ml/min). The entire preparation and the apparatus can be housed in a heating chamber to facilitate maintaining proper temperature. The chamber used for liver preparation may be used for this purpose.

Thompson et al. have described a technique of *in situ* perfusion of the rat head. They used an apparatus reminiscent of that of Miller et al. The aortic arch of the rat is perfused, and the inferior vena cava is cannulated for the outflow. Recirculation of the perfusion medium made up of diluted rat blood maintains the preparation for up to 3 hr. The isolated perfused rat brain preparation described by Andjus et al. can be maintained for 2 hr with satisfactory CNS function. Geiger and Magnes have described an isolated perfused brain from the cat that is very similar to the preparation described above for the rat. This preparation of Geiger and Magnes has been used for various studies by subsequent investigators. For example, Barrett et al. used the preparation to evaluate the effect of a number of centrally acting drugs on cat brain. In addition, Otsuki et al. used the cat brain preparation to evaluate the suitability of using various perfusion media.

Perfusion media

Andjus et al. used pooled rat blood obtained from several rats as the perfusion medium. However, they found that when blood was used, it did not support the spontaneous electrical activity of the isolated brain. After several trails, they concluded that an artificial perfusion fluid similar to that described by Geiger should be used. The fluid portion of the artificial perfusate is Krebs-Ringer bicarbonate buffer solution, described earlier for perfusion of the liver, lung, and kidney. Bovine serum albumin is dissolved in distilled water and deionized by passing it through a column of Amberlite MB-3 before using it to mix with the Krebs-Ringer bicarbonate buffer solution. Erythrocytes obtained from dog blood were washed and used in this perfusion fluid. The cells are washed four times with cold, buffered (0.01 m, pH 7.4) isotonic sodium chloride solution and finally with isotonic Krebs-Ringer bicarbonate buffer solution prior to use. The final perfusate contains 7 to 8% bovine serum albumin, a hematocrit of 20 to 25%, and pH adjusted to 7.3. The perfusate is always best prepared freshly just prior to use. The glucose concentration of the blood for perfusion is adjusted to 200 mg% by adding a requisite volume of 5% glucose in normal saline solution.

The perfusate and the isolated brain preparation described by Andjus et al. remained at room temperature throughout the experiment. The room temperature throughout the experiment. The room temperature was between 23 and 27°C; the majority of perfusion experiments were conducted at 25°C. However, maintaining the entire perfusion at body temperature should be considered. This can be easily done by employing a heated chamber such as the one used for perfusing the liver. Total volume of perfusate is 100 ml, and perfusion is carried out to the constant arterial pressure of 100 to 120 mm of mercury. The perfusion rate is 3 to 5 ml per min and should be maintained at this rate throughout the experiment. The temperature of the brain can be maintained at 30°C or 37°C using a heated chamber as indicated above. Otsuki et al. compared a number of perfusion media using Krebs-Ringer bicarbonate buffer as the solution and using either low molecular weight (40,000) or high molecular weight (70,000) dextran as the substituent for bovine serum albumin. They also compared the effect of including a number of amino acids in the perfusion medium. Their study concluded that dextran could replace bovine serum albumin in the perfusion medium, and that the low molecular weight dextran was superior to high molecular weight dextran. Further, including glutamic acid in the perfusate along with low molecular weight dextran improved functional performance of the isolated perfused cat brain.

Viability criteria

Spontaneous electrical activity was recorded by Andjus et al. as a functional parameter of brain activity. The isolated rat brain preparation had spontaneous electroencephalographic (EEG) activity, which persisted as long as 5 hr with open circuit perfusion and about 2 hr when recirculating perfusion was conducted. Although the reason for the shorter period of viability in a recirculation is not well understood, it is possible that endogenous biochemical products of intermediary metabolism may accumulate in the recirculating perfusion, to the detriment of the perfused brain. Addition of pentylenetetrazol to the perfusing blood evoked characteristic EEG signs of convulsive activity either before or after spontaneous EEG activity had ceased. Otsuki et al. carried out a similar study using EEG measurements in comparing the suitability of altering perfusion medium to perfuse cat brain. Response to loud sounds can also be recorded by EEG recordings and can be used as a viability criterion. After perfusion for 5 hr, Andjus et al reported that the rat brain was nonresponsive to sound, indicating deterioration of the preparation. Thus although EEG recordings indicated viability of the rat brain preparations, response to loud nose was lost after 5 hr of perfusion, indicating that not all criteria may be satisfied, especially in a perfusion lasting for several hours.

An additional criterion for viability is the rate of glucose utilization by the isolated brain preparation. This can be measured as a decrease in the glucose concentration in the perfusing blood and should be linear during the first hour of the experiment; later it tends to decrease with the deterioration of the preparation. Lactate accumulates in the circulating perfusate, but the rate at which it accumulates does not appear to be directly related to glucose utilization. Otsuki et al also used rates of glucose of utilization as a measure of viability in evaluating the different perfusion media to support isolated perfused cat brain preparations.

Applications

Although the use of isolated perfused brain preparations for toxicological investigations has been infrequent, examples can be cited from the literature where isolated perfused brain preparations have been used for such studies. The principal reason for the relatively infrequent use of isolated perfused brain preparations seems to be a relatively slow development of the techniques. In a recent study, Hein et al investigated the effect of thiopental anesthesia on the energy metabolism of the isolated perfused rat brain. They perfused the rat brain in the presence or absence of 5 to 15 mM thiopental and investigated the turnover of glucose as well as measuring a number of indicators of the glycolytic pathway. They noted that glucose uptake by the brain preparation was elevated by inclusion of thiopental in the perfusate. However, the glycolytic pathway remained inhibited, indicating sensitivity of the glycolytic pathway to thiopental anesthetics. They also noted that this effect was not mediated via hindered uptake of glucose. Thus this report demonstrates the usefulness of the perfused brain preparation in studying intermediary metabolism of the brain as affected by the presence of toxic drugs or chemicals in the circulating perfusion. Similar preparations should be useful in studying the effect of centrally acting toxic chemicals such as industrial solvents and gaseous substances. Similar preparations should also be useful in evaluating the centrally acting neurotoxic chemicals. For example, Krieglstein and Stock have described the effect of chloral hydrate and trichloroethanol on cerebral intermediary metabolism.

The applicability of isolated rat brain preparations to study central neurological mechanisms can be illustrated by the study of Kilbinger and Krieglstein. They found that physostigmine caused a rise in the acetylcholine concentration of the isolated perfused rat brain, and the same effect occurred when using the rat brain *in vivo*. Oxotremorine, on the other hand, produced an increase in acetylcholine content in the brain *in vivo* but was ineffective in the isolated rat brain at the same dosage. These investigations were carried out both by recording EEG as well as determining perfusate and brain levels of acetylcholine. These studies suggest the feasibility of using brain preparations to evaluate the effect of toxic chemicals on alterations of endogenous neurohormones and neurotransmitters. In addition to the studies mentioned above, the technique of perfusion has also been used to aid histological fixation of brains from experimental animals. For this purpose, the arch of the aorta is perfused with a balanced salt solution followed by a fixative. A distinct advantage of the perfusion technique to fix the brain preparation for histological examination is the delivery of oxygen through the oxygenated perfusion medium to the brain in order to achieve better preservation of the tissue.

Although the isolated perfused brain preparations described to date include extramural tissue together with many different types of nerve centers represented within the brain itself, the perfusion technique should nevertheless be valuable in examining the specific effects of centrally active toxic chemicals. The state of the art in this area has developed to a degree at which the technique should prove extremely useful in toxicological investigations.

Isolated Perfused Intestines

Over the years, there have been several attempts to study the mammalian intestine as an isolated tissue sustained by a vascular perfusion. Mainly because of the nature of the tissue itself, there has been an ambiguity in the use of the term "perfusion" in the field of intestinal research. Intraluminal circulation of fluid for the purpose of studying the transport of small molecules across the intestinal mucosa has often been referred to as intestinal perfusion. A full range of experimental techniques are available for work with intestinal tissue, and the topic has been reviewed, including the technique of vascular perfusion. No single experimental technique will proved information about all phases of the absorptive processes involved in the removal of a substance from the lumen of the small intestine, its transport across the intestinal wall, and its entry into either blood or lymphatic circulation. Techniques such as intraluminal perfusion and everted sac are described by Wilson and Wiseman. This particular discussion will deal with the vascular perfusion of the small intestine.

Isolated vascular perfusion of intestine has not been prominent in gastrointestinal research because of the many problems encountered in sustaining a viable tissue. It is clear that vascular resistance, spasmodic bowel contractions, tissue edema, and progressive destruction of the mucosal epithelium were the principal problems encountered in earlier attempts to establish a perfused intestinal preparation. Second, since most investigators were concerned with the mechanisms of intestinal absorption and were dealing with the mucosal layer, these investigators found it convenient to use intraluminal perfusion with fluid containing the experimental drug to study the intestinal absorption. In addition to supplying the experimental drugs through the fluid, such a fluid could also carry the necessary O_2 for supporting the mucosal layer. However, arguments can be made for developing a viable, vascularly perfused intestinal preparation. The role played by other layers of the intestinal wall such as the muscle can be studied in a vascularly perfused intestinal preparation. Also, the disadvantages of everted gut preparation, in which only transport across the wall is studied rather than the transport into the blood circulation, are overcome by utilizing an isolated vascularly perfused preparation. Thus anatomically and functionally distinct compartments such as lumen, lymph, and bloodstream are kept separated and can be studied individually. These arguments and the need to separate intestinal tissue to describe those absorptive, distributive, and metabolic functions of the tissue fully well justify the development and use of the isolated vascularly perfused intestinal preparation.

As has been observed for other isolated perfused organs, intestine can be perfused either *in situ* or in complete isolation. In addition, the perfused preparation can be used either with an intraluminal flow maintained in the natural direction of peristalsis or without the intraluminal flow. If the intestine is perfused without the intraluminal flow, two dynamic compartments (perfusion fluid and lymph) can be sampled for an experimental test chemical in addition to the intestinal tissue itself. If intraluminal flow is maintained, however, three dynamic compartments (perfusion fluid, lymph, and intraluminal fluid) and the static compartment of intestine tissue can be sampled for an experimental test chemical. For most practical purposes, maintaining intraluminal flow would introduce another dynamic variable in the experimental condition, so that analysis and interpretation of the experimental results from analyzing all four compartments would be difficult if not impossible. The following description of an isolated perfused intestinal preparation is based on the procedure of Kavin et al, later improved by Windmueller et al.

Apparatus

An acrylic plastic box (75 cm high, 60 cm wide, 50 cm deep) houses the apparatus. Temperature in the chamber is maintained at 37 to 38°C by means of a heater and fan assembly, which is thermostatically controlled. The chamber is kept humidified by a small jet of steam blown inside the chamber. The acrylic plastic cyclical oxygenator-reservoir (7 cm diameter and 15 cm high) contains a thin acrylic disc with a gently sloping convex upper surface and serrated edges supported on three equidistant flanges about 3.7 cm from the top. The tip of the silastic tubing which carries venous and bypassed blood, rests on the disc so that the blood flows on the disc and spreads out to the serrated edges and finally down the inner wall of the cylinder as a thin film, thereby exposing a maximum surface area for oxygenation. A mixture of 95:5% O_2 and CO_2 is bubbled through distilled water and led into the gas inlet of the oxygenator-reservoir via the thin silastic tubing. At the bottom of the reservoir, an appropriate blood filter can be placed in order to filter out any broken cell debris, etc., before the blood circulation is pumped via a peristaltic pump to the animal. From the plastic filter, blood is led to a peristaltic pump via silicone tubing (4.6 mm o.d., 3.35 i.d.). Between the peristaltic pump and the animal, a hydrostatic reservoir is maintained in order to provide a constant perfusion pressure. A bypass flow from the hydrostatic reservoir to the central reservoir facilitates maintaining a constant hydrostatic head. Blood flow is determined by means of a transducer connected to the venal circuit by a three-way stopcock.

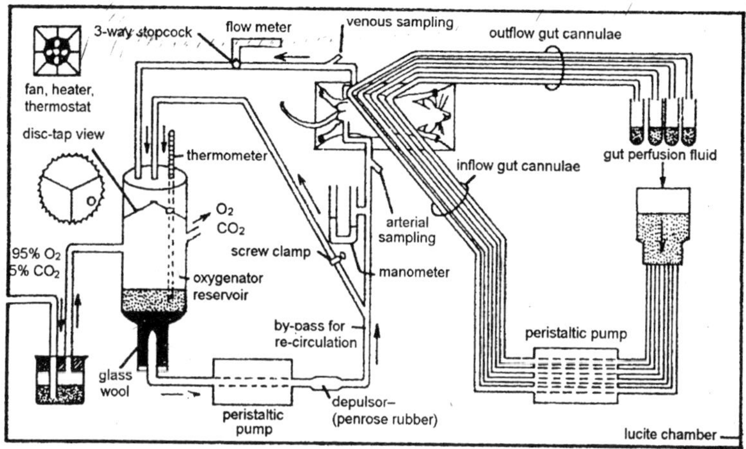

Fig. 6.9. Diagrammatic illustration of the apparatus for vascular perfusion of the small intestine.

Blood is sampled from the arterial and venous channel via polyethylene tubing, using Y connections near the arterial and venous cannulae. Thus blood is in contact with silastic tubing, a hydrostatic reservoir, and polyethylene connections. In the apparatus, most of the silicone tubing could be replaced by glass, and use of the silicone tubing should be restricted to glass tube connections and to the peristaltic pump. If intraluminal flow is desired in the experimental protocol, an infusion pump can be used to introduce a fluid either with or without the test chemical into the intestinal lumen. A peristaltic pump can be used for this purpose, giving a peristatic wave motion for the intraluminal flow. Fluid effusing out of the intestine can be collected as desired or recirculated after sampling.

Perfusion procedure

The rat is anesthetized with a mixture of ether and oxygen or intraperitoneal injection of pentobarbital (50 mg/kg). Through an L-shaped abdominal incision, the small intestine, cecum, and proximal large intestine are gently exteriorized and supported on a plastic platform, which is covered with gauze soaked in warm 0.9% NaCl. The intestine is covered with saline-soaked gauze in a plastic sheet and kept at 37°C by means of a heat lamp. Both ends of the intestine are ligated using an appropriate suture, proximally at the duodenum about 1.5 cm from the pylorus and distally near the midpoint of the descending colon. Included in the proximal ligature are the common bile duct and the mesentery between the duodenum and superior mesenteric vein. A PF-90 size cannula is placed in the duodenal lumen and secured by the same ligature, in those experiments in which intraluminal infusion is required.

Lymph is collected from a polyethylene cannula of 0.023 in i.d. and 0.0238 in o.d., secured with a ligature in the main intestinal lymph duct. Lose ties are placed around the superior mesenteric artery, about 5 mm from the aorta, and around superior mesenteric vein just below the junction with the pyloric and coronary veins. The mesenteric artery can be cannulated using a PE-50 cannula filled with perfusion fluid and connected to a syringe with perfusate at the other end. Insertion of the PE-50 cannula is facilitated by introducing the beveled end of the cannula via a V-shaped cut made in the mesenteric artery by means of fine scissors. After the cannula is secured by a ligature, flow of the perfusate can be started by disconnecting the syringe and connecting the cannula to the perfusate of the preprimed perfusate flow is essential since the isolated small intestinal loop has been ischemic through the surgical procedure. At this point, a flow of 8 to 9 ml/min would insure adequate O_2 supply to the tissue.

The rat is then exsanguinated by severing the left jugular vein and carotid artery. The superior mesenteric vein is cannulated by means of another PE-50 cannula in a manner analogous to the above procedure and secured by means of a suitable suture. The venous effluent is recycled through the perfusion apparatus to the oxygenator-reservoir. Once recirculation of the perfusate is established, arterial flow is increased until an arterial pressure of approximately 95 mm Hg is reached. The venous pressure is adjusted to 150 mm of water by an adjustable clamp on the outflow cannula. With experience, total surgical time can be minimized to 30 min or less.

Perfusion media

The semiartificial perfusion medium consists of the following: 80 to 120 ml fresh heparinized rat blood drawn by abdominal aortic puncture from ether-anesthetized animals. The blood is heparinized with 10,000 to 25,000 units of sodium heparin. Windmueller et al. used antibiotics in the blood (penicillin G, streptomycin, etc.), but often use of these compounds is undesirable, since they are likely to interfere with experimental test drug. If the perfusion chamber and all of the components of the apparatus are sterilized, use of antibiotics has not been necessary for isolation and perfusion of organs such as the lung and liver. Use of antibiotics should be avoided unless this becomes critical in a particular experimental protocol. Norepinephrine is used continuously at a rate of 1 to 2.2 ml/min as a 0.153 mg/ml solution in order to alleviate increased vascular resistance experienced by earlier investigators. A glucocorticoid (dexamethasone, 6×10^{-7} M) is added in a single dose as a solution (25 mg/ 100 ml) in the perfusate to the reservoir. A combination of the glucocorticoid and norepinephrine aids in maintaining the low vascular resistance and improved tissue preservation.

The perfusate described for other perfused organs containing Krebs-Ringer bicarbonate buffer solution with glucose and albumin can be used for perfusing intestinal preparations with satisfactory results. Kavin et al. utilized a similar perfusate with low molecular weight dextran instead of albumin in their perfusion fluid. Addition of norepinephrine and a glucocorticoid to this perfusate would make it comparable to Windmueller's preparation. The fluid for intraluminal flow is 0.9% saline containing glucose (220 mM) and sodium taurocholate (10 mM) infused at 2.6 ml/hr. Whether intraluminal flow is intended or not, use of the Krebs-Ringer bicarbonate buffer solution with glucose and albumin or low molecular weight dextran should be considered for toxicological investigations. The perfusion flow rate of 16 to 20 ml/min is obtained under these conditions at an arterial pressure of 95 mm Hg. *In vivo* flow rate was found to be 8 to 10 ml (160), approximately half of that observed with the heparinized blood as perfusate. This is an indication of low vascular resistance when the intestinal vasculature is isolated, and this resistance may persist during the remainder of the perfusion period.

Viability criteria

Histological examination of the intestine after 5 hr of perfusion indicated that the integrity of the vascularly perfused tissue was well preserved. Cross sections through the duodenum showed that the brush border of the intestinal wall and the base epithelium of the duodenum were all well preserved after 5 hr of perfusion. Additional parameters used for determining the viability of vascularly perfused intestinal preparations include the perfusion flow rate, uptake of glucose by the tissue, and production of lymph and continued satisfactory O_2 consumption. In general, the preparation can be maintained viable for at least 5 hr as indicated by its gross and microscopic appearance and by the continued O_2 consumption, peristaltic motility, water transport, and vascular responsiveness to norepinephrine. The perfused intestine is capable of glucose transport, and in most experiments, lymph flow continues without reduction for 5 hr. The rate of lymph flow is increased by infusing intraluminal fluid and by increasing venous pressure. An additional parameter used in evaluating the perfused intestinal preparation is fat transport and lipoprotein biosynthesis. Morphological examination of the intestinal tissue under light and electron microscopes can be useful in ascertaining viability.

Applications

The isolated vascularly perfused intestinal preparation has not been used in toxicological investigations. It is not readily apparent as to why this is so, but difficulties in developing the techniques for maintaining a viable perfused preparation and the requirement for a thoroughly elaborate set of equipment must have some influence on the use of this technique. The preparation should prove especially useful in studies relating to drug absorption and interaction of drugs as it relates to intestinal absorption and transport mechanisms. It might also be useful in evaluating the role of intestinal metabolism and overall disposition of various drugs and toxic chemicals. The preparation should prove useful in testing reported intestinal elimination of a number of chlorinated hydrocarbon compounds via the liminal surface. All of these aspects related to toxicology of a particular test drug. Finally, the effect of toxic chemicals on absorption of nutrients, generation and preservation of mucosal cell lining, and various drug metabolizing enzymes can also be evaluated using the perfused intestinal preparations. The effect of toxic chemicals on endogenous biochemical parameters related to the intermediary metabolism of the intestine itself can also be investigated.

Isolated Perfused Pancreas

The pancreas is a highly vascular endocrine organ in which the anatomy of the blood supply lends itself to isolated vascular perfusion. In comparison to the isolated islet incubation, pancreatic slices, tissue fragments, and the superfusion method of Burr et al., the isolated perfused pancreas is the most satisfactory and ideal approach to study the interrelationship between pancreatic and other hormones, as well as to study the effect of toxic chemicals on the pancreatic function. The method of perfusing the pancreas is to be preferred in comparison to all the other tissue preparations for these studies in view of the following advantages offered by the isolated perfused pancreas preparation. Superficial and deep islets are equally provided with oxygen, which is constantly replenished, and the substrates and the effectors arrive at the cell in a physiologically normal way. The islets remain in an anatomical relationship with other cells and tissues of the organ, including blood vessels and nerves. Only an extrinsic nerve control is lost, and many intrinsic factors that actively regulate the gland's function may be preserved in an isolated perfused pancreatic preparation. The maintenance of the tissue's cellular integrity can be confirmed at the end of the experiment by light and electron microscopical examination. There is a possibility of a control and experimental period of study in the same pancreas preparation. Such controls in other *in vivo* systems require multiple incubations.

Of greater significance might be the ability to maintain the exocrine secretions of the pancreas from getting back into contact with the islet cells, since the cannulation of the segment of duodenum into which the exocrine secretions drain allows the collection of these secretions separately. Thus the enzymes and other secretions produced are kept separate from the cells that produce them. Hence the well-known digestive effect of pancreatic enzymes on the pancreatic tissue would be avoided. Despite the overwhelming superiority of vascularly perfused pancreatic preparations, there has been a lag in the development of perfusion techniques with this endocrine tissue. This lag can be attributed to the technical difficulties encountered with surgical preparations and the heterogeneity of the tissue perfused in obtaining an isolated pancreatic preparation

The location of the pancreatic duct entering the duodenum might be of some significance, especially in studies related to exocrine function such as protein synthesis. The pancreatic ducts are multiple and their entry into the intestine is variable. Doerr and Becker illustrated the main pancreatic duct as emptying into the bile duct rather than into the duodenum in the rat. In the guinea pig and rabbit, the main pancreatic duct enters the duodenal tract. The general rule is: in carnivores, the ducts empty near or into the common bile duct, while in herbivores, they empty more distally into the duodenum.

A limited literature is available on technique of an isolated perfused pancreatic preparation. The principal descriptions are those of Grodsky et. al. Sussman et al. and Loubatieres et al. The following is a description of a combination of the better features of all these three perfusion preparations.

Apparatus

The apparatus used by Sussman et al. is quite adequate for perfusing an isolated pancreas and will be described here. The chamber of the perfusion apparatus is based upon the original description of that used by Miller et al. Perfusate is pumped from the reservoir through a

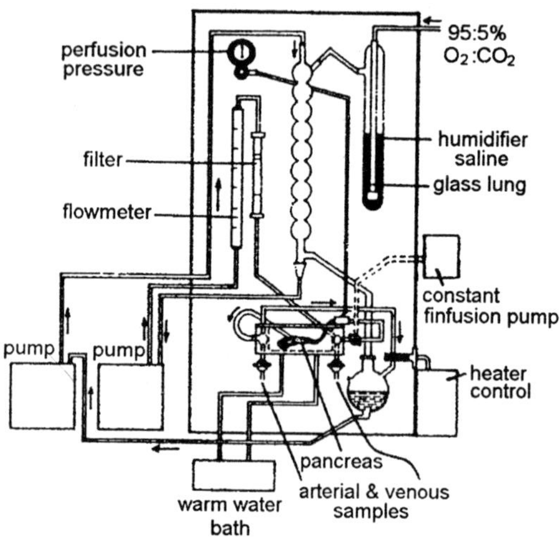

Fig. 6.10. Schematic illustration of the apparatus for perfusion of an isolated pancreas preparation.

silastic tubing to a multibulb glass lung for oxygenation. The perfusate is then pumped by means of a peristaltic pump through a flow transducer, and it then courses through a filter to the enclosed perfusion chamber. The perfusate enters the pancreatic circulation through the arterial cannula, and the pressure is measured in mm Hg using an aneroid manometer. The arterial blood may be sampled through a sideline arrangement fitted with a stopcock and venous blood through another similar arrangement. A mixture of O_2:CO_2 (95:5%) is directed to the lung after bubbling through a humidifier. The pancreas is kept moist using either the same solution used as perfusate or normal saline. The pancreas is perfused using Krebs-Ringer bicarbonate buffer solution (pH 7.4) containing glucose and albumin, as described for the liver, which is circulated through the glass lung for oxygenation. A pediatric plastic cannula (1.5 mm o.d.) is used to cannulate the arterial side with an attachment for measurement of intraluminal pressure. The venous cannula is a PE-tubing. For the duodenal cannula, an arrangement similar to the one described earlier in perfusion of the intestine would be adequate.

Surgical procedure

The animal may be starved overnight to facilitate the operation by depleting the omental fat. The animal is anesthetized by appropriate means (for example, 50 mg/kg pentobarbital, i.p.). A midline incision through the skin and linea alba and through the skin over the inferior thorax and a lateral incision are made as described for the surgical procedure to isolate the liver. The intestine is moved to the animal's left and covered with a wet saline gauze, and the aorta with the superior mesenteric branch is clearly made visible. The descending colon is easily identified as it remains attached to the lower posterior abdominal wall by a short mesentery. This fine layer of connective tissue is cut along the length of the colon in a plane in which no blood vessels are found, thereby mobilizing the lower gut, which will be later removed. By means of blunt end dissection scissors, the pancreas is separated from the overlying colon. The jejunum is ligated and severed just behind its pancreatic attachment. This ligature will be useful for orientation later. The distal jejunum has a copious blood supply, and its vessels are tied for the last half inch of the distal segment to facilitate its later removal.

At this time, the superior mesenteric vein which runs into the portal vein, can be seen over the surface of the pancreas. The superior mesenteric vein is tied just below the pancreas with double ligatures and cut between them. Any other attachments of the pancreas to the descending colon are ligated and cut. At this stage, the superior mesenteric artery and coeliac axis can be identified and should be preserved throughout the following dissection. The fine membrane covering the spleen and any other closely adherent tissue is carefully picked off with sharp forceps. The main splenic vessels, entering toward the upper pole, are tied twice and cut between the ligatures. A whole set of vessels curve through the mesenteric to cross between the pancreatic tail and the spleen. If tied together, the pedicles can bunch the vessels in the tail of the pancreas. It is better to tie each of them individually with additional investments of time. A marker thread may be left to denote the tail of the pancreas for relative ease in orienting upon its isolation.

The stomach is pulled downward, and the major left gastric artery, which runs into the upper and medial aspect of stomach near the esophagus, is tied. One ligature encloses both the vessels and esophagus, while the second and third include the vessel and esophagus separately higher up. Both the vessels and esophagus are cut between ligatures. Lifting the stomach to the right exposes vascular connections to the posterior wall. By means of a single distal tie these can be tied and cut. Finally, the pylorus is tied twice and cut between the ligatures, releasing the stomach, which can now be checked. At this stage the animal can be heparinized by means of an injection via inferior vena cava. The right renal pedicle (containing artery, vein, and ureter) is cleared with a blunt dissection, and a ligature is passed behind the artery and vein with curved forceps. Double ligatures allow the vessels to be cut and the kidney removed.

By careful dissection, the aorta is exposed at this level to clear it from the inferior vena cava between the left renal artery and superior mesenteric artery. A ligature passed behind the aorta at this level can now be tied. Three loose ligatures are passed around the portal vein as it leaves the pancreas for the liver. The uppermost ligatures should include all the structures of the portal tract (vein, hepatic artery, and bile duct), while the other two include only the vein. Cannulation is delayed until the aorta has been cleared along its length, preserving the seliac and mesenteric branches. This entails passing ligatures around and tying particularly the lumbar arteries. The aorta is free from the inferior vena cava from the level of the diaphragm to the ligature below the left renal artery. Loose ligatures are poisoned around the aorta just below the diaphragm. avoiding the origin of the seliac artery.

The portal vein can be cannulated in a retrograde manner by typing the uppermost ligatures first and making an incision in the arterial wall of the vein. The cannula (made from PE-140 to 200 size tubing) is filled with heparinized perfusion medium before insertion. When a flow through the portal cannula is assured, aortic cannulation is performed. The rat is turned around with the head toward the operator, and a midline incision through the edge. From the moment of entering the thorax, the anoxic phase begins and speed of surgical procedure is essential; this comes with practice. The thoracic walls may be spread apart by means of appropriate retractors, and the thoracic aorta is separated from behind the esophagus. The cannula is inserted and advanced until its tip just passes the diaphragm. The abdominal aortic ligature is tightened, and with the cannula in place, the flow should commense. The final step is to complete the isolation of the pancreatic circulation by tying the ligature that has already been prepared around the lower inferior vena cava.

Now the perfusing pancreas must be transported to the organ chamber. The inferior vena cava is cut distal to the last tied ligature, and removal of the cannulated pancreas should be possible by grasping the two cannulae and loop of the duodenum to lift the pancreas clear of the rat. The organ is oriented on the platform in the perfusion chamber by means of identifying ligatures placed during the preparation, and successful uniform perfusion is obtained if this step is carefully undertaken. There should be a flow of 2 ml/min with a perfusion pressure of about 30 mm of Hg. It may be wise to reject preparations if pressures above 80 mm Hg are obtained, since this usually results in further deterioration of the perfused pancreatic preparation. This entire surgical procedure takes roughly 60 to 75 min, assuming familiarity with surgical techniques.

In the method of Grodsky et. al. the perfusion of the pancreas is accompanied together with the stomach, spleen, and duodenum as a unit, which is removed from the rat through a ventrical abdominal incision and transferred to the warmed chamber. The seliac axis is cannulated for the inflow and the portal vein for the outflow. A peristaltic pump supplies the perfusion medium to the seliac axis at a pressure of 40 to 100 mg Hg, and the flow is adjusted to 10 ml/min. The principal disadvantage of Grodsky's procedure is that it involves perfusion of additional tissues so that ascribing a particular biochemical function to the pancreas would be more difficult when such a perfusion is used. The principal advantage is that the surgical procedure is much simpler.

Perfusion media

Grodsky et al. used whole rat blood mixed with an artificial medium as a perfusate, but they as well as other who utilized whole blood, encountered hemolysis of the red blood cells, which resulted in complications of perfusion. Hence the use of artificial medium has become more popular with the perfusion of the pancreas. The medium containing 4% dextran in Krebs-Henseleit medium prepared and gassed with a mixture of O_2:CO_2 (95:5%) is satisfactory. This is the standard medium mentioned in the subsequent work of Grodsky as well as many other investigators. Alternatively, 4% human serum albumin or bovine serum albumin can be used instead of dextran with no apparent difference in insulin production, medium flow, and rate of circulation of perfusion. The pH should be adjusted to 7.4, and the addition of sodium bicarbonate and adequate bubbling with the mixture (95:5%) of O_2:CO_2 ensures maintaining appropriate pH. Also, if the pH seems to fluctuate during the experiment, addition of sodium bicarbonate solution to the perfusate will be helpful in stabilizing the pH of the perfusing medium.

Khayambashi and Lyman used a medium containing fresh rat plasma diluted 1:1 with Ringer's saline or 0.9% saline with satisfactory results. Costiner et al. used dilution heparinized rat blood as perfusate to support satisfactory pancreatic function.

Viability criteria

Several parameters of physiological and biochemical function were reported by Grodsky et al. Histological examination at the end of the perfusion period indicated well-preserved granules diminished in number roughly in proportion to the measured release of insulin into the medium. Oxygen consumption by the perfused pancreas can be used as a comparatively rough indicator of viability. However, in the preparation of Grodsky et al., since other tissues are involved in the perfusion circulation, consumption of O_2 may not be an exclusive indicator of viability of the perfused pancreas. In the preparation of Sussman and Vaughan, since less peripheral tissue is involved, consumption of oxygen might represent a better viability criterion. In any case, production of insulin by preparation, consumption of glucose, and the analysis of exocrine secretion collected through the duodenal cannula can be used as adequate criteria for the viability of the perfused pancreas. The pH of the circulating perfusate can be monitored and adjusted if necessary by regulating the mixture of 95:5% O_2:CO_2 in oxygenating the perfusate. Second, the addition of appropriate amounts of sodium bicarbonate solution can be made to adjust the pH of the circulating perfusate.

Formation of amylase has been shown to be linear for 40 min in the preparation used by Khayambashi and Lyman, and such an assay for amylase might be a reasonable parameter for viability. However, they observed that the rate of amylase production fell beyond 40 min despite the linearity of the perfusion flow rate. This may be a reflection of the discharge of existing enzymes or the inability of the isolated perfused organ to synthesize enzymes. In the work of Khayambashi and Lyman, the composition of the perfusion medium was demonstrated to have a definite effect on the secretion of the amylase type of enzymes by the pancreas. Hence such a criterion may have to be established in conjunction with other parameters of the perfused preparation. Sampling of the tissue to demonstrate effects that may be reflected i the medium or related to a particular treatment of perfusion is clearly important in the assessment of the perfused organ. In this connection, it may be pointed out that the dendritic form of the rat pancreas lends itself to sampling by typing off a single arm of the pancreas with continuation of perfusion of the remaining tissue. However, if sampling of a portion of the organ is carried out, the biochemical study done with the same perfused organ may be compromised, especially with respect to later time points, since all of the organ would not be present at later time if such sampling is carried out and continued.

Applications

Use of the perfused pancreas has not been made in toxicological investigations. The development of very sensitive radioimmunoassay of insulin and glucagon in biological fluids has enabled the quantitative measurement of their secretion and has led to the use of pancreas perfusion techniques in such studies. Clearly, the perfused pancreas can be used to evaluate the effect of drug interactions affecting the pancreatic function. Drugs not having exclusive action on the pancreas may mutually interact within the body to produce an action on pancreatic secretory activity after exposure to agents such as ethanol and carbon tetrachloride. The mechanism of such enhanced pancreatic secretory activity has not been understood. Use of a perfused pancreatic preparation obtained from control and treated animals may be useful in the elucidation of the underlying mechanisms. Similarly, other examples can be cited where the perfused pancreas can be used to determine the effects of toxic agents.

7

Isolated Organelle Techniques

Cells are composed of a number of organelle compartments that play crucial roles in facilitating metabolic processes essential to cellular viability. The effects of many toxic agents on cells are mediated via damage to one or more of these specialized subcellular compartments. Specific organelle systems may become damaged to toxic agents due to a primary role in the metabolism of a particular toxicant, intracellular storage of toxicants, or an inherent sensitivity of some essential biochemical pathway in the organelle to perturbation. In terms of understanding the mechanisms of cellular toxicity, it is clear that evaluation of organelles as basic units of subcellular function may provide useful insights into the basic of toxicant action. It should be obvious that the ability to detect damage within particular organelle systems depends on the sensitivity and nature of the parameters measured.

The following discussion examines some of the current ultrastructural and biochemical methods available for evaluation of specific organelles and reviews some of the ways in which these techniques have aided understanding the mechanisms of toxicity.

Mitochondria

Mitochondria are essential organelles which play an important role in cell metabolism by mediating a number of metabolic functions. Enzymes involved in energy production, carbohydrate metabolism, heme biosynthesis, and the urea cycle are found in this organelle. It is also

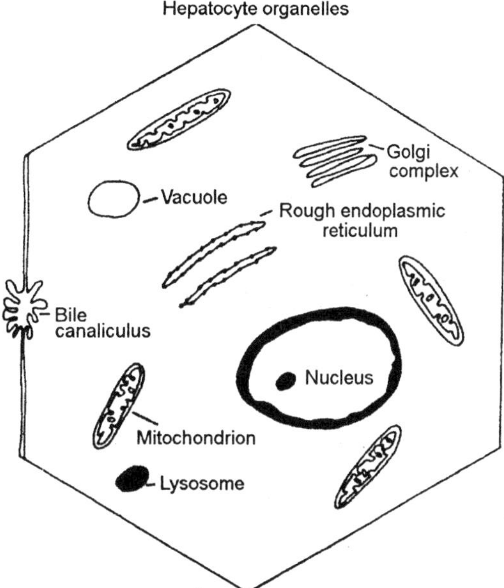

Fig. 7.1. Diagrammatic representation of a hepatocyte showing nucleus, mitochondria, lysosomes, endoplasmic reticulum and Golgi apparatus.

important to consider that these enzymes are not randomly distributed within the mitochondria but localized within specific subcompartments such as the other and membranes and matrix.

In terms of understanding the effects of toxicants on this organelle, it is important to understand the relationship between particular metabolic functions and the physical integrity of the mitochondrion as a structure because frequently *in vitro* biochemical perturbations result directly from structural damage. The following examination of ultrastructural and biochemical methods for mitochondrial evaluations will utilize examples of some well-known toxicants to illustrate how each technique aided in understanding the mechanisms of toxicity.

Ultrastructural Techniques

Fixation and embedding

Preservation of mitochondria within intact cells is routinely carried out by chemical fixation using glutaraldehyde or glutaraldehyde-formaldehyde based fixatives. Tissues may be either placed in these fixatives or perfused via the blood vasculature for optimal preservation of cellular structure. Electron density is imparted to the mitochondrial membranes by post fixation in a 1% solution of osmium tetroxide

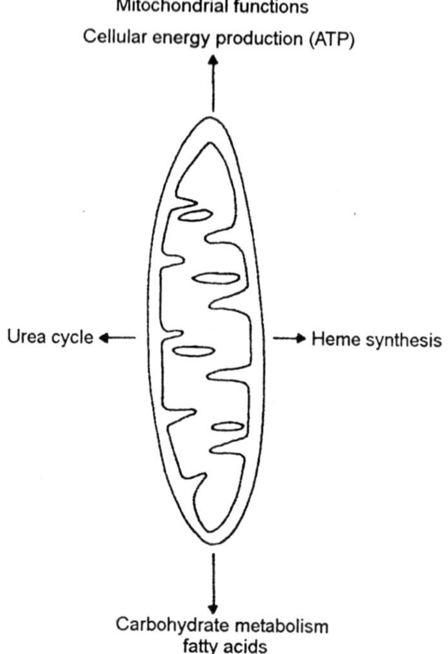

Fig. 7.2. A diagrammatic representation of a mitochondrion showing outer membrane, inner membrane with infoldings (cristae), and matrix.

(OsO_4) followed by dehydration in a graded series of alcohol from 70 to 100%. Dehydrated tissues are then placed in solutions of propylene oxide and embedded in plastic resins such as Epon. A stepwise routine procedure for fixation and embedding of tissues for electron microscopy is as follows:

1. Place tissue blocks (1 mm^3) in fixative (2%) glutaraldehyde, 2.6% formaldehyde in 0.07 M cacodylate buffer (pH 7.4) and 3% sucrose for 2 hr in a refrigerator.
2. Decant fixative and place blocks in above cacodylate buffer overnight in a refrigerator.
3. Post fix blocks in 1% OsO_4: (Caution: volatile toxicant) in 0.1M phosphate buffer (pH 7.4) for 2 hr and then decant in a fume hood.
4. Dehydrate tissue blocks in 70%, 90%, 95% (2 changes), and 100% alcohol at room temperature for 15 min at each step.
5. Decant final 100% alcohol solution and place blocks in 2 changes of propylene oxide.

6. Place blocks in 50:50 propylene oxide plastic resin mixture overnight to infiltrate tissue blocks.
7. Place tissue blocks in final plastic resin mixture and embedded in Teflon capsules.
8. Place in curing oven (60°C) to harden plastic before sectioning.

Ultrastructural morphometry

This technique, which is essentially an approach to quantitating the dimensions of organelle compartments within intact cells based on evaluation of their surface area in a large number of electron micrographs, has been extensively reviewed. The method may be readily employed to determine the overall volume of organelles such as mitochondria within cells (volume density) but determinations of mitochondrial membrane surface area (surface density) and numbers of mitochondria (numerical density) require the application of correction factors that have recently undergone revision. The specific steps in this technique, as well as equations necessary for evaluation of generated data, are given in an article by Weibel et al. and will not be repeated here.

Application of morphometry to evaluation of mitochondria following *in vivo* exposure to arsenate, cortisone, methyl mercury, and vitamin E deficiency has been successfully employed to document increases or decreases in this organelle system and the relationship of these effects to observed biochemical changes.

Ultrastructural evaluation of mitochondrial fractions

Evaluation of mitochondria from tissues following homogenization and isolation in sucrose by electron microscopy provides one method for evaluating the purity of the samples and degree of structural integrity. This technique also has been employed to examine changes in mitochondrial conformational behaviour during respiration following *in vitro* exposure to uncoupling agents such as dinitrophenol or *in vivo* following exposure to lead or arsenate.

The technique essentially involves utilizing the chemical fixation and embedding process described above to process pellets of mitochondria and other organelles. A more quantitative approach to evaluation of isolated organelles has been recently described by Deter.

Negative staining of isolated mitochondria

The technique of negative staining involves uranyl acetate, phosphotungstic acid, or ammonium molybdate, to stain the Formvar grid backing so that isolated organelles such as mitochondria stand out against the dark background. This method has proven extremely useful for high resolution microscopy studies of mitochondrial membrane preparations and has been used to evaluate changes in mitochondrial membranes following *in vitro* exposure to these organelles to uncoupling agents. A general flow sheet for this technique follows and a more complete discussion is given elsewhere.

Technique

1. Isolate mitochondria.
2. Final dilution of mitochondria to 60 mg/ml.
3. Pipet sample on the Formvar coated grids and allow to dry in covered dish.
4. Cover grids with a drop of negative stain (pH 7.4) at 1-2% concentration.
5. Blot excess stain from edge of grid with filter paper.
6. Examine sample with transmission electron microscope.

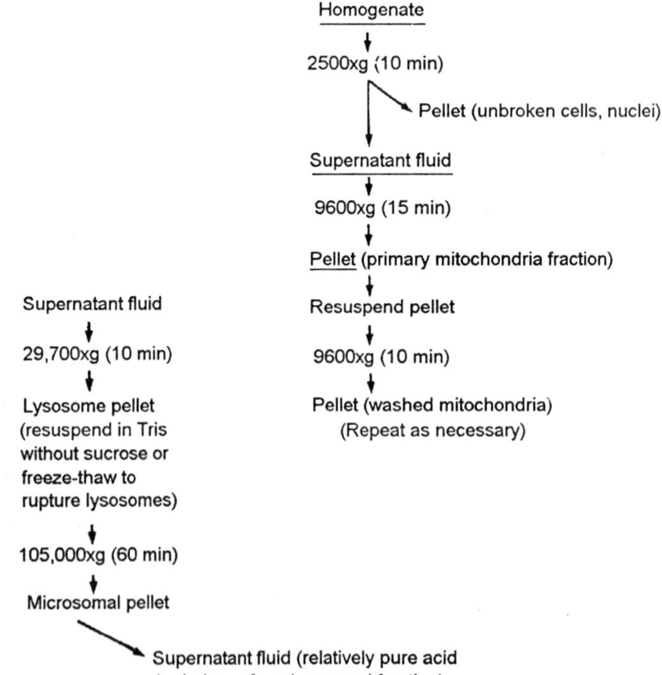

Fig. 7.3. Standard isolation procedure for mitochondria and other organelles such as lysosomes and microsomes by differential centrifugation in 0.25 M sucrose - 0.05 M Tris buffer (pH 7.4).

Scanning electron microscopy

Application of scanning electron microscopy (SEM) to evaluation of mitochondrial conformational behaviour or the conformational behaviour of the intact inner membrane (mitoplast) has been employed by Andrews and Hackenbrock to confirm finding obtained by transmission electron microscopy.

Technique

1. Mitochondrial or mitoplast sample (1-2 mg/ml) placed on Formvar coated grids and covered with 1 drop 2% glutaraldehyde in 0.1 M phosphate buffer (pH 7.4).
2. Grids placed in perforated vials and dehydrated in acetone followed by critical point drying.
3. Samples coated with 150 Å layer of palladium-gold in a vacuum evaporator.
4. Examine in a scanning electron microscope.

Freeze etch analysis

The technique of freeze-etching has been employed to study the three dimensional structure of mitochondrial membranes during different energy states and their relationship to localization of protein complexes within the membrane. This method essentially involves chemical fixation and rapid freezing of biological samples in Freon prior to fracturing in a freeze etch device. The fracture plane is thought to primarily cleave across the hydrophobic regions of the membranes, thereby exposing both inner and outer surfaces. The surfaces are then sputter-coated with metals such as platinum and carbon to form replicas that are floated off the tissue and collected on standard electron microscopy grids for evaluation in a transmission electron microscope. A detailed examination of the technique and known artifacts has been given elsewhere. To date, this technique has not been applied to evaluation of toxicant action on mitochondria.

Technique

1. Fixation of tissue in glutaraldehyde fixative described above.
2. Incubation of tissue in 10-20% glycerol until tissue is impregnated.
3. Place specimen on specimen carrier and immerse in Freon 22 cooled to −165°C with liquid nitrogen.
4. Place specimen in freeze-etch device and fracture with steel blade.
5. Etch cleaned surfaces of specimen by allowing ice to sublime from sample.

6. Shadow specimen surface with carbon-platinum to form replica and cover replica with carbon backing layer.
7. Remove specimen and replica from evaporator and place in an aqueous solution similar to original glycerol freezing solution to release replica from specimen surface.
8. Clean replica in 5% sodium hypochlorite solution.
9. Rinse replicas in several changes of water and mount on 150 mesh grids.

Biochemical Procedures

There are a variety of biochemical parameters that can be used to assess the effects of toxicants on mitochondrial function. In part, the effectiveness of these techniques depends on the procedures used to isolate mitochondria prior to evaluation. A relatively standard procedure essentially involves Tris (0.05 M)-sucrose (0.25 M) with subsequent pelleting of mitochondria by centrifugation. In addition to this basic procedure, resuspension and recentrifugation may be used to "wash" the mitochondria and to remove contamination by microsomes. In the process of reducing mitochondrial contamination, it should be noted that mitochondria from different tissues vary in their sensitivity to physical damage or chelating agents such as EDTA. This means that caution must be exercised in order to separate toxicant effects on these organelles from other effects derived from the isolation procedures. A more complete examination of problems encountered in the isolation of mitochondria and other organelles has been given by Deter.

In addition, mitochondria may be separated into the outer mitochondrial membrane and inner mitochondrial membrane and inner mitochondrial membrane plus matrix (mitoplast) by treatment with controlled digitionin digestion or use of a pressure cell with subsequent pelleting of membranes by centrifugation. This technique has been successfully used to identify the submitochondrial localization of a host of marker enzyme activities.

General mitochondrial isolation procedure

1. Homogenize tissues in 0.25 M sucrose mannitol in 0.07 M Tris-HCl Buffer (pH 7.4) at 1 g tissue 9 ml of Tris-sucrose. Agents such as EDTA may also be added to aid disruption of cells.
2. Place in centrifuge tubes and spin at 2,500 × g for 10 min to remove nuclei and unbroken cells.
3. Decant supernatant fluid into centrifuge tubes and spin at 10,000 × g for 10 min to form primary mitochondrial pellet.

4. Decant supernatant fluid and gently resuspend pellet in 10-ml Tris-sucrose for washing. Recentrifuge pellet and decant supernatant fluid. This washing cycle may be repeated a number of times depending on the tissue involved and degree of mitochondrial purity desired.
5. Resuspend final mitochondrial pellet (1 ml Tris-sucrose/1 g of original sample).

Separation of outer and Inner mitochondrial membrane

1. Washed mitochondria (30-60 mg protein/ml) are placed in a pre-cooled French pressure cell and subjected to 1,500 psi. Extruded material is taken up in an equal volume of double strength medium and centrifuged at 12,00 × g for 10 min.
2. The resultant pellet is resuspended in the previous volume and recentrifuged at 12,100 × g for 10 min.
3. Supernatant material from the above pellets is combined and centrifuged at 27,100 × g for 10 min.
4. Supernatant fluid from this pellet is centrifuged at 144,000 × g for 90 min to obtain the outer membrane (pellet) and intermembrane fraction (supernatant fluid).

Respiratory function

One of the primary functions of mitochondria within intact cells is the oxidation of substrates with subsequent generation of ATP. There are two major classes of oxidizable substrates that are capable of causing electron flow through the mitochondrial electron transport chain. The first of these involves those substrates (pyruvate, malate, and β-hydroxybutyrate) which use NAD as an acceptor of protons and is capable of generating 3 moles of ATP per molecule oxidized. Succinate is the other substrate type which generates 2 moles of ATP per molecule oxidized. Methods employed for evaluation of mitochondrial respiratory function include Warburg respirometry and the oxygen electrode; each measures oxygen consumption by mitochondria in the presence of oxidizable substrates. The advantage of the first type of measurement rests with its ability to measure oxygen consumption within intact tissue slices while the latter is capable of detecting changes in respiration during different states of respiration.

Technique (oxygen electrode)

1. Isolated mitochondria in tris-sucrose medium (10 to 20 mg/ml) are placed into a 1 to 3 ml oxygen electrode cell with stirrer containing a reaction mixture composed of: 40 mM Tris Cl (pH 7.5), 5 mM

K_2HPO_4, 5 mM $MgSO_4$ and 100 mm KCl with a to 2 mg mitochondrial protein per ml.

2. A stable recorder baseline is obtained initial state 4 respiration initiated by addition of succinate or NAD-linked substrates to yield a final concentration in the cell of 5 mM.
3. After 1 to 2 min of state 4 respiration, state 3 respiration is initiated by addition of 2 to 5 μmoles ADP.
4. Following complete utilization of the added ADP, a return to state 4 respiration will be observed.
5. Respiratory control ratios (RCR) are calculated by dividing the state 3 rate by the state 4 rate. ADP/O ratios are calculated by dividing the amount of ADP added by the calculated amount of oxygen consumed as described by Estabrook.

As an approach to the toxicity assessment of mitochondria, respiratory function is an essential index of mitochondrial function which is easily damaged by many toxic agents. Toxic trace metals such as arsenic lead mercury and cadmium inhibit mitochondrial respiration. For lead and arsenic, this inhibition is relatively specific for NAD-linked substrate such as pyruvate/malate. This process is thought to be due to inhibition of mitochondrial dehydrogenases for these substrates which are located in the mitochondrial matrix. In addition, alternation of mitochondrial conformational behaviour has been reported in relation to these phenomena indicating that the well-known energy-linked transformation of these organelles is also altered. Organic toxicants such as pesticides and others also damage mitochondrial respiratory function leading to diminished production of ATP.

Carbohydrate metabolism

Many of the enzymes involved in intermediary metabolism are localized in mitochondrial matrix. Dehydrogenases for pyruvate, malate, and glutamate are localized in this portion of the organelle. A typical assay procedure for malate dehydrogenase has been extensively described elsewhere. Toxicant damage to this aspect of mitochondrial function has been demonstrated for agents such as arsenic and methyl mercury.

Heme biosynthesis

Three of the key enzymes in the heme biosynthesis pathway are localized in the mitochondrion and associated with the inner mitochondrial membrane. Ferrochelatase and δ-aminolevulinic acid synthetase are highly sensitive to the action of toxic metals with resultant increases in the urinary excretion of porphyrin precursors that have proven to be useful biological indicators of toxicity. Assay procedures for these mitochondrial enzymes have also been extensively described and hence will not be described here.

Mitochondrial protein synthesis

Studies on the synthesis of mitochondrial proteins have been extensively reviewed and may be generally regarded as divisible into two categories; structural and enzymatic. Beattie showed that these two categories of proteins could be separated biochemically on the basis of solubility in dilute acetic acid into proteins synthesized within the mitochondria for structural purposes, and those enzymes synthesized outside the mitochondria in the endoplasmic reticulum with subsequent incorporation into the mitochondria.

Technique

Application of this technique to toxicology studies has shown that prolonged *in vivo* exposure of fetal rat liver mitochondria to methyl mercury produced preferential suppression of membrane but not enzymatic protein synthesis. In contrast, exposure of adult rats to arsenate produced and increased synthesis of both protein compartments and morphometric increases in the surface density of the inner mitochondrial membrane. The changes in protein synthesis were associated with increases in the specific activities of the mitochondrial marker enzymes monoamine oxidase cytochrome oxidase and Mg^{-2} ATPase.

Technique (mitochondrial protein biosynthesis)

1. Rat is given an intraperitoneal injection of ^{14}C leucine (20 μCi) and killed 10 min later.
2. Liver tissue is excised and mitochondria are isolated as described above.
3. Isolated mitochondria are placed in 1.4% acetic acid in capped ultracentrifuge tubes and shaken for 30 min in the cold (4°C).
4. Centrifuge tubes at 90,000 × g for 1 hr to pellet acid insoluble proteins. Rinse pellet with ice-cold water and suspend in 0.4 N NaOH followed by shaking at 37°C in an incubator until material is dissolved.
5. Pipet supernatant fluid into new centrifuge tubes and neutralize solution while shaking with 2 N NaOH.
6. Centrifuge solutions at 105,000 × g for 1 hr to pellet acid soluble proteins.

7. Wash pellet in ice-cold water and suspend in 0.4 N NaOH followed by shaking at 37°C in an incubator until material is dissolved.
8. Pipet 0.2 ml of each fraction into counting vials, add 20 ml of scintillation fluid, shake, and count in a liquid scintillation counter.

Conformational behaviour

The technique of following mitochondrial swelling and contraction by measurement of light scattering in a spectrophotometer was developed by Tedeschi and Harris. This method is based on the increased optical density of mitochondria in a contracted state and decreased density in a swollen or orthodox configuration due to cation influx. Agents such as arsenic and phosphate produce detectable alterations of mitochondrial swelling and contraction behaviour that can be detected by measurement of light scattering at 520 nm.

Technique

1. A solution of 0.12 M KCl in 0.02 M Tris-Cl (pH 7.4) is placed in spectrophotometer cuvettes and isolated mitochondria are added to a final concentration of 2 mg/ml.
2. Mitochondrial swelling is measured as a decrease in optical density at 520 nm with time.
3. Maximal swelling is usually achieved by 15 min with liver mitochondria.
4. Contraction of the mitochondria is initiated after about 15 min by addition of Mg^{+2}+ATP (5 mM) which produces a corresponding increase in the optical density of the sample to near its original reading.

Ion translocation by specific ion electrode

During mitochondrial respiration or changes in conformation, the transport of H^+, Na^+, K^+, or Ca^{+2} occurs. Movement of these cations between isolated mitochondria and the surrounding medium may be monitored by specific ion electrodes as described in a review by Pressman that contains specific details for application of this technique. Application of this approach to measuring mitochondrial membrane functionality following exposure to mercurials and lead have provided useful information about the nature of mercury-mitochondrial membrane interactions. Other studies have shown energy-dependent mitochondrial uptake of arsenic.

Lysosomes

Lysosomes are spherical structures which play a central role in the storage and catabolism of many substances. Biochemically, these organelles are characterized by the presence of several acid hydrolases. In terms of understanding the impact of toxicants on this organelle system, it is useful to discern the various categories of lysosomes by both ultrastructural and biochemical techniques.

Ultrastructural Techniques

Cytochemistry

Active lysosomes (secondary lysosomes) may be cytochemically distinguished from inactive (teleolysosomes) or autophagic vacuoles by the presence of acid phosphatase activity. This technique gives a clear demonstration of this enzyme activity provided development time of the reaction is carefully monitored to minimize spurious or nonspecific deposition of lead-phosphate reaction product.

Technique (histochemical determination of acid phosphatase)

1. Remove tissue under light ether anesthesia.
2. Cut into thick (2-3 mm) slices on plate of dental wax.
3. Fix at approximately 4°C for 2 to 3 hr in 2.5% glutaraldehyde in 0.1 M Na-cacodylate buffer containing 7.5% sucrose. Final pH 7.1 or standard glutoraldehyde-formaldehyde fixative described above.
4. Rinse slices in cold Na-cacohylate buffer, pH 7.4, containing 0.33 M sucrose.
5. Transfer pieces to stage of tissue chopper and cut 10 to 50 μ sections.
6. Collect in cold Na-cacodylate, pH 7.4, containing 0.33 M sucrose.
7. Rinse 20 min to 2 hr in two changes of sucrose buffer.
8. Warm Gomori medium to 60°C for one hr; cool to room temperature for 4 min, filter through 1 piece Whatman #1.
9. Incubate sections 15 min to 2 hr at 37°C in medium.
10. Rinse twice for one min in cold 0.05 M acetate buffer, pH 5.0, containing 7.5% sucrose and 4% formaldehyde.
11. For light microscopic monitoring of reaction development, expose sections to $(NH_4)_2S$ (2 drops of 45% $(NH_4)_2S$ in 10 ml H_2O.
12. Transfer to glass slides and mount in water soluble embedding medium.
13. For electron microscopy: post-fix for 30 to 60 min in 1% OsO_4 in acetate-veronal buffer, pH 7.4, containing 49 mg/ml sucrose.
14. Rapidly dehydrate starting with 7% ethanol.
15. Embed in plastic resin as described above.

Gomori medium

0.12 g Pb $(NO_3)_2$.

100 ml 0.05 M NaAc buffer, pH 5.0, containing 7.5% sucrose.

Add slowly with gentle mixing 10 ml of 3% sodium-β-glycero phosphate or cytidine monophosphate (CMP).

Gluteraldehyde fixative

0.1 M cacodylate buffer, pH 7.4, 97.5 ml, containing 7.5% sucrose.

Ultrapure glutaraldehyde (70%), 2.5 ml.

Buffer rinse

0.1 M cacodylate butter, pH 7.4, containing 0.33 M sucrose (11.2%).

Formaldehyde rinse

0.5 M acetate buffer, pH 5.0, 40 ml.

37% formaldehyde (formalin solution), 10 ml 7.5 g sucrose.

Acetate buffer

15 ml N HCl

50 ml N NaAc.

Adjust to pH 5.0; dilute to 1300 ml.

Localization of substances within lysosomes

There are several ultrastructural techniques available for demonstrating the presence of particular substances within lysosomes of intact cells. X-ray microanalysis has been used by several investigators to demonstrate the presence of toxic trace metals within lysosomes following *in vivo* exposure. This method essentially utilizes the focused electron beam of the electron microscope to displace orbital electrons from the atoms present in the sample with resultant generation of characteristic X-rays from within the sample that are separated by wavelength or energy dispersive techniques. Major problems with the technique for analysis of biological samples are related to extraction or translocation samples are related to extraction or translocation of elements during tissue processing, volatilization of elements by specimen heating, and detection of elements within biological thin sections due to insufficient excitation or low concentrations of the elements within the tissue.

Technique—X-ray microanalysis—thin sections (≤ 2500 Å)

1. Blocks of tissue embedded for electron microscopy as described above are sectioned at 250 Å or less using an ultramicrotome and placed on coated carbon-coated grids made of carbon, beryllium,

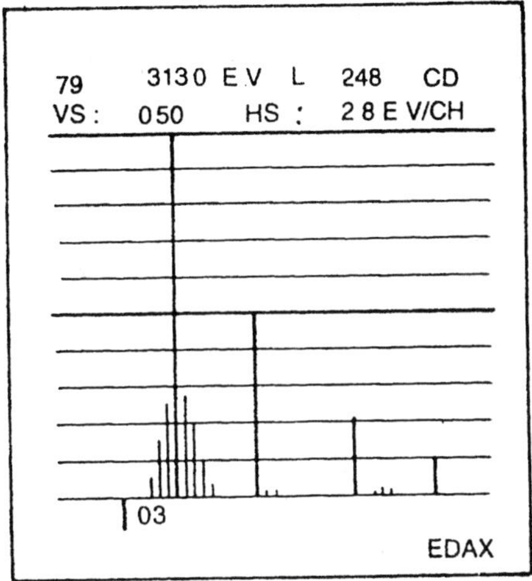

Fig. 7.4. Energy-dispersive X-ray spectrum from a renal proximal tubule lysosome of a rat injected with 0.6 mg/kg cadmium (Cd) as cadmium-metallothionein following background substraction.

or some other element with X-ray emission lines different from those in the sample to be analyzed.

2. Sample grid is placed in specimen holder of transmission or scanning electron microscope fitted with energy dispersive or wavelength dispersive spectrometers.
3. X-ray microanalysis of lysosomes or other organelles of interest is performed by condensing the electron beam onto the site to be analyzed and monitoring elemental X-rays generated.
4. Problems associated with extraction of elements from the tissue during fixation, dehydration, and embedding may be circumvented to some degree by use of cryosectioning of frozen samples and liquid nitrogen-cooled cold stages.
5. Vaporization of elements by specimen heating from the condensed electron beam may be dealt with to some degree by altering the accelerating voltage of the electron microscope and reducing counting times.
6. A more complete description of this technique and available instrumentation has been given elsewhere.

Ultrastructural autoradiography

Autoradiography of compounds labeled with ^{125}I or ^{3}H is another sensitive tool that requires great care in application due to translocation of label and insufficient grain development. This technique has been successfully applied to detection of proteins within lysosomes of intact cells to show uptake into this cellular compartment. At the light microscope level, lysosomal uptake of fluorescent dyes has been demonstrated by fluorescence microscopy. Histochemical staining methods have also been used to demonstrate lysosomal uptake of metals in cells of metal-exposed animals.

Ultrastructural morphometry

In terms of quantitating *in vivo* changes in the lysosomal compartment, ultrastructural morphometry has been employed to evaluate changes in the lysosome system with prolonged methyl mercury and age. Application of this method to lysosomes is subject to some of the same constraints and limitations noted previously for mitochondria.

Biochemical Methods

Changes in lysosomal sedimentation characteristics have been reported following loading with metals such as iron. This effect as well as alterations of lysosomal membrane stability should be carefully considered when evaluating lysosomes in toxicity studies. In addition, consideration should also be given to the distribution of lysosomes within different cell types within a given organ since not all cells will be equally affected.

Lysosomal protein degradation

Protein degradation by lysosomes has been monitored by following release of ^{125}I from labeled proteins following either *in vitro* or *in vivo* incubations. *In vitro* exposure of lysosomes to agents such as toxic metals or mycotoxins have been found to alter the ability of lysosomes to perform this basic function.

Marker enzyme assays

Measurement of the various acid hydrolase activities found in lysosomes is another means for assessing lysosome functionally. As noted in these assays are frequently performed on lysed lysosomes so that activities of the lysosomal enzymes may be more clearly separated from those present in the microsomal fraction. Marker enzymes frequently measured are the cathepsins A, B, C, and D, acid phosphatase, aryl sulfatase, glycosidases, and acid RNAase. Exposure of animals by intravenous injection of protein activates a number of the above enzymes in kidney lysosomes.

Technique—acid phosphatase assay

0.1 ml 0.04 M citrate buffer, pH 4.8.

0.1 ml p-nitrophenylphosphate 100 mg/25 ml (kept frozen).

0.1 ml enzyme extract.

Incubate at 37°C for various times.

Stop reaction by the addition of 5 ml of 0.2 M glycine, pH 10.4

Centrifuge in table top centrifuge for 5 min.

Read optical density at 405 nm.

Report specific activity in terms of nmoles/min/mg.

Prepare standard curve of OD_{405} versus nmoles p-nitrophenol/5.4 ml of reaction mixture.

Cathespin D assay

1. 1.0 ml of 0.2 M acetate, pH 4.5.
2. 0.5 ml of 2% hemoglobin.
3. Add 0.5 ml of enzyme solution.
4. Incubate at 37°C for one hr.
5. Stop reaction by adding 8 ml of 5% TCA.
6. Centrifuge at 1,400 rpm for 5 min.

Read at 280 nm.

Report specific activity as Δ OD_{280}/mg or protein.

RNAse assay

0.2 ml 0.03 acetate-0.15 M NaCl, pH 5.8.

0.1 ml homogenate

0.1 ml H_2O

0.2 ml 1% RNA.

The reaction mixture is shaken at 37°C for 20 min. After incubation the tubes are placed in ice and 0.9 ml of a mixture of 10 volumes of 76% ethanol in 1 N HCl and 1 volume of 0.75% uranyl acetate in 2.5 N $HC10_4$ is added to precipitate the protein and RNA. After allowing the mixture to stand for 10 min, they are centrifuged at 1,000 × g for 10 min. The absorbance of a 1:10 dilution of each supernatant is read at 260 nm. Specific activity reported as ΔOD_{260}/min/mg. Caution: The RNA is unstable and needs to be prepared just before use to prevent high reading in the blank.

β-glucuronidase assay using p-nitrophenyl-β-glucuronide as the substrate

0.1 ml 0.2 M acetate, pH 5.0.

0.6 ml of p-nitrophenyl β-D-glucuronide (15 mM).

0.2 ml of lysosomal protein.

Incubate at 37°C for 15 to 30 min.

Step the reaction by adding 3 ml of 0.2 M glycine, pH 10.4.

Centrifuge in table top centrifuge for 5 min.

Read at 405 nm.

Obtain nmoles of p-nitrophenol from standard curve.

Report activity in terms of nmoles/min/mg of protein.

Endoplasmic Reticulum

The endoplasmic reticulum is comprised of a complex pattern of membranes or cisternae that permeates the cytoplasmic matrix, and the centrifugal fraction containing fragmented endoplasmic reticulum is called the microsomal fraction. Two distinct forms of endoplasmic reticulum have been characterized by histological as well as biochemical and centrifugal techniques. The rough endoplasmic reticulum (RER) is a complex of granular basophilic membranes distinguished by extensive ribosomal units on the outer surface of the membrane. In mammals, the RER forms layered stacks of cisternae. The smooth endoplasmic reticulum (SER) is essentially a granular and forms a myriad of breaching interconnecting tubules extending to all areas of the cytoplasmic matrix. In general, protein synthesis occurs in the RER, whereas the SER functions in protein transport and glycogen storage. Both the RER and SER function in drug metabolism as evidenced by the detection of bioactivation/detoxification enzyme systems in both microsomal subfractions.

The heterogeneous microsomal fraction is commonly employed to assess the capacity of the endoplasmic reticulum to bioactivate and/or detoxify a variety of foreign chemicals, as well as some endogenous compounds such as the steroid hormones. The role that microsomal enzymes play in chemical toxicity is extremely difficult to evaluate since a single enzyme system might activate or deactivate a chemical depending on molecular structure of the chemical, animal age (state of development or differentiation), site of metabolism (as related to organ-specific toxicity), and interactions with other chemicals (potentiation or antagonism). To study microsomal metabolism of chemicals, standard techniques are employed to prepare heterogeneous microsomal fractions or to separate SER and RER. Much of the information presented in this section will deal with hepatic microsomal function because of the wealth of methodological information available for this tissue. However, the relative sparcity of time spent on extrahepatic tissues should not detract from the contribution of extrahepatic pathways to pharmacokinetics and toxic reactions.

Ultrastructural Methods

Ultrastructural morphometry

The surface area or more precisely the surface density (S_v) of smooth and rough endoplasmic reticulum may be estimated by application of morphometric techniques to intact cells. This approach has been used to quantitate changes in the endoplasmic reticulum of hepatocytes following exposure of rats to phenobarbital. Studies of this type provide useful *in situ* correlations with the biochemical evaluations of microsomal enzyme preparations described below, as well as a means for estimating membrane recoveries from intact cells.

Ultrastructural evaluation of microsomal fractions

Ultrastructural examination of microsomal fractions may be conducted to assess the purity of the preparations in a manner similar to that previously described for mitochondria. Fixation, dehydration, and embedding procedures for microsomal pellets are essentially similar to those used for other organelle fractions.

Biochemical Methods

Preparation of microsomes

Standard method. The most common method used to prepare microsomes from a variety of tissues involves tissue and cell disruption followed by differential centrifugation. A general procedure for rat liver is as follows:

1. Liver is removed, minced, and homogenized in 1.15% KCl buffered with 0.2 M N-2-hydroxyethypiperazine-N-2-ethane-sulfonic acid (HEPES), pH 7.5, at 5°C to make a 20% (w/v) mixture. Homogenization is accomplished by using six strokes in a motor-driven Potter-Elvehjem homogenizer.
2. Nuclei and cell debris are removed by centrifugation at 670 g for 10 min.
3. Mitochondria are removed by centrifugation of the 670 g supernatant fluid at 10,000 g for 15 min.
4. Microsomes are pelleted by centrifugation of the post-mitochondrial supernatant fluid at 105,000 g for 60 min, washed once with HEPES-KCl buffer, and finally resuspended in the buffer so that 1.0 ml of microsomal suspension contains materials from 0.5 g liver (wet wt). The 10,000 g pellet can be homogenized by hand and recentrifuged to avoid loss of microsomes in unbroken cells and sedimented microsomal vesicles.

There are some points that need to be considered when experimental protocols are being developed. For example, depending on the tissue, microsomal fragments may pellet with the nuclear or mitochondrial fraction. Although it appears that extramicrosomal drug metabolism does occur many researchers have mistakenly reported the subcellular distribution of microsomal enzymes because of tissue differences in fragmentation of the endoplasmic reticulum. Preliminary experimentation must therefore include a thorough examination of the effect of various disruption techniques (homogenization, sonication, etc.) on the disruption of the endoplasmic reticulum.

Calcium aggregation method. Recently, a new method was developed to prepare microsomes from rat liver that does not require ultracentrifugation. This procedure results in aggregation of microsomes following the addition of Ca^{2+} ions to the postmitochondrial supernatant fluid. In addition to eliminating the need for an ultracentrifuge, this method greatly reduces the time needed to prepare microsomes. The procedure is outlined as follows:

1. Liver is removed, minced, and homogenized in 10 mM Tris-HCl containing 250 mM sucrose, pH 7.4, to make a 20% (w/v) mixture. Homogenization is accomplished by using six strokes in a motor-driven Potter-Elvehjem homogenizer.
2. Nuclei and cell debris are removed by centrifugation at 670 g for 10 min.
3. Mitochondria are removed by centrifugation of the 670 g supernatant fluid at 10,000 g for 15 min.
4. Solid $CaCl_2$ is added to the postmitochondrial supernatant fluid to achieve a final concentration of 8 mM. The suspension is stirred and the microsomes pelleted by centrifugation at 25,000 g for 15 min.
5. The microsomal pellet is resuspended in 150 mM KCl–10 mM Tris HCl, pH 7.4, and centrifuged at 25,000 g for 15 min, which sediments the washed microsomal pellet.

Many studies have compared the activities of microsomal enzymes prepared by the two methods. In general, specific activities of rat liver microsomes were similar in preparations derived by either method. However, the calcium aggregation method cannot be applied to all tissues or species. Researchers have found markedly different enzyme activities in preparations derived by the two methods as function of species and tissue. These findings emphasize the need to determine whether the calcium aggregation method is a viable method before applying it to preparation of microsomes from a source other than rat liver.

Although many xenobiotics include the specific activity of microsomal enzymes, these chemicals do not generally cause great changes in total microsomal protein content. However, some changes do occur in the relative distribution of SER and RER, and significant changes also occur in SER:RER specific activity ratios of enzymes. For example, the potent inducing agent 2, 3, 7, 8-tetrachlorodibenzo-p-dioxin (TCDD) reduces the SER:RER activity ratio for aminopyrine demethylation, benzpyrene hydroxylation, p-nitrophenol glucuronidation, and microsomal protein. These biochemical and pharmacological changes are associated with concomitant alterations in the cellular distribution of SER and RER in hepatocytes following *in vivo* exposure to TCDD as well as to a wide range of organohalogens, some of which are hepatotoxins.

The following discontinuous sucrose gradient method is commonly used to isolate SER from RER in liver.

1. Liver is homogenized in 0-25 M sucrose to make a 20% (s/v) mixture.
2. The postmitochondrial supernatant fluid is prepared as described earlier in this section.
3. 2.0 ml of 1.3 M sucrose (not containing CsCl) is added to a centrifuge tube.
4. 0.5 ml of 0.6 M sucrose (also not containing CsCl) is layered on the heavy sucrose.
5. The postmitochondrial supernatant fluid is made 15 mM with respect to CsCl and 4.0 ml of the suspension layered above the 0.6 M sucrose. The three-layered system is then centrifuged at 105,000 g for 90 min. The RER is pelleted at the bottom of the centrifuge tube and the SER forms a band at the top of the 1.3 M sucrose.
6. The SER fraction can be aspirated off and pelleted by dilution with buffer and centrifugation at 105,500 g for 60 min.

Several other methods are available to further subfractionate SER and RER including rate-differential centrifugation and isopycnic density gradient centrifugation.

In vitro methods for evaluating microsomal function

Isolated organs

Although the use of isolated microsomes has many advantages in the characterization of individual enzyme systems and the quantitation of the response of these systems to inducers, inhibitors, or repressors, it is difficult to develop a good pharmacokinetic model using such preparations. Accordingly, many investigators have used isolated perfused organs to evaluate the complex interrelationship among heterogenous cell types, different metabolic pathways, variations in substrate concentrations, and time-course relationships. This system represents an open metabolic system capable of generating important information in "steady state" pharmacokinetics. Several organ systems have been used extensively including the liver, lung, intestine, kidney, and testes.

Isolated cells

The use of isolated hepatocytes as an experimental model to study drug biotransformations and toxicity has increased over the past few years. Isolated cells are often selected as an experimental model to study microsomal function because they provide a reasonable intermediate between perfused organ systems and preparation of subcellular organelles and reconstituted systems. Now that many of the technical problems have been resolved for the isolation and maintenance of isolated hepatocytes, it is possible to sue this system to investigate the activity and products of complex bioactivation/ detoxication enzyme systems and to also investigate, in a more precise way, organelle interactions that might qualitatively and/or quantitatively alter the metabolic capacity of microsomal enzyme systems. References are available that detail and summarize procedures for evaluating metabolism and toxicity in isolated cells. Of particular importance is the requirement that (a) the cells remain viable for a sufficient period of time to evaluate a biochemical or pharmacological parameter and (b) the isolated cells retain the characteristics and functions present *in vivo*. Cell viability is commonly determined by the trypan blue exclusion test or by leakage of cytosolic enzymes (indication of membrane dysfunction or damage) such as lactate dehydrogenase into the cell-free medium. Following the maintenance of isolated hepatocytes for relatively long periods of time (more than two days), liver cells have been reported to revert to a more fetal form. The relative contribution of fetal type cells can be monitored by biochemical indicators such as α-fetoprotein, alkaline phosphatase, and λ-glutamyl transpeptidase. Although most studies are conducted on liver cells, other organ systems can be investigated by analogous techniques.

Isolated cells, in general, seem to provide an excellent experimental model to study microsomal activation/deactivation of chemicals and the subsequent reactivity of metabolites to cellular macromolecules such as DNA, RNA, and protein, and thereby allow the investigator to gain insight into the mechanisms of toxicity of some carcinogens, mutagens, teratogens, and organ-specific toxins.

Microsomal Activation/Deactivation Systems

Microsomal Cytochromes

The endoplasmic reticulum contains a series of flavoproteins and cytochromes that function in electron transport, ultimately resulting in the activation and reduction of molecular oxygen. An enormous number of studies have focused on the behaviour and characterization of cytochrome P-450, a microsomal cytochrome, which functions in oxidative biotransformation reactions such as epoxide formation, hydroxylation of aromatics N-hydroxylation, C-hydroxylation, N-dealkylation, O-dealkylation of xenobiotics, and many endogenous compounds such as the steroid hormones and fatty acids. The enzymes catalyzing these reactions are cytochrome P-450 dependent and are collectively termed mixed-function oxidases (MFO). The function of the cytochrome P-450 system involves a series of sequential reactions:

(a) the formation of a substrate-ferric heme complex;

(b) flavoprotein NADPH-cytochrome P-450 reductase mediated reduction of this complex;

(c) formation of an oxycytochrome P-450 substrate complex following interaction of oxygen with reduced heme protein;

(d) activation of oxygen for interaction with the organic substrate; and

(e) dissociation of the less lipophilic product and regeneration of the ferric heme protein.

More detail on the nature and function of this system is available. The net effect of this series of coupled reactions is the generation of

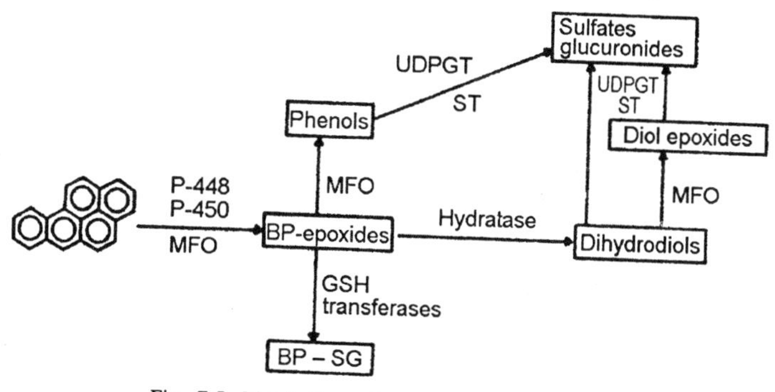

Fig. 7.5. Metabolic pathways for benzo(a)pyrene.

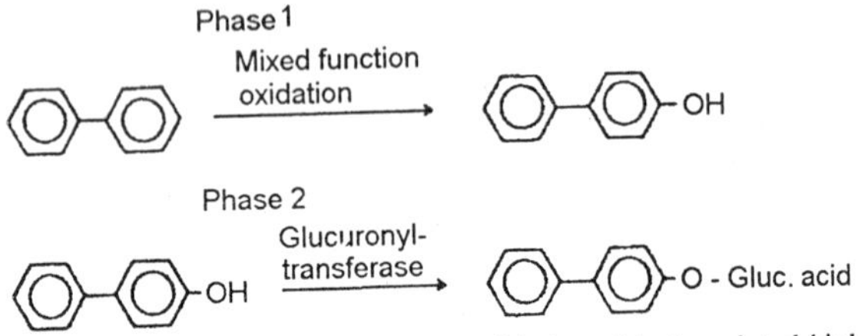

Phase 1
Mixed function oxidation

Phase 2
Glucuronyl-transferase

Fig. 7.6. Schematic representation of glucuronidation of hydroxylated biphenyl.

a metabolite less lipophilic than the parent compound and therefore more excretable. However, electrophilic, reactive, and highly toxic metabolites can also be formed by this system.

Determination of P-450 by difference spectra

The most common method of measuring cytochrome P-450 content of a microsomal preparation is by the appearance of an absorbance band at 450 nm for the CO adduct of the reduced cytochrome. The procedure is as follows:

1. The microsomal suspension is diluted with the homogenizing buffer to achieve a protein concentration of approximately 1.5 mg/ml.
2. Baseline of equal light absorbance is determined by placing equal volumes of diluted microsomal suspension into two cuvettes.
3. The sample cuvette is gently gassed with CO, and the spectrum is recorded that quantifies oxyhemoglobin contamination.
4. Sodium dithionite (about 1 mg solid) is added to the sample cuvette, and the difference spectrum of the CO adduct of the reduced cytochrome P-450 is recorded.
5. Sodium dithionite is added to the reference cuvette, and the difference spectrum on the CO complex of reduced cytochrome P-450 minus the spectral contribution of reduced cytochrome P-450 is recorded.
6. The change in absorbance at 450 nm relative to 490 nm is converted to cytochrome P-450 concentration using a millimolar extinction coefficient of 91.

Administration of many compounds such as phenobarbital to intact animals results in induced levels of cytochrome P-450. Exposure to another class of chemicals, such as the polycyclic hydrocarbon, results in induced levels of a closely related cytochrome, P448. This change in absorbance maximum can be detected by sophisticated double beam spectrophotometers. Lists of those chemicals that selectively induce P-450 (phenobarbital type) or p-448 (3-methylcholanthrene type) are provided elsewhere.

In addition to measurement of cytochrome P-450 content, difference spectra are also used to study substrate interactions with cytochrome P-450 and to investigate mechanisms of inhibition of mixed function oxidation reactions. Depending on the substrate, three types of spectral interactions can be detected *in vitro*. Type I spectral change characterized by a peak at 385 nm and a trough at 420 nm; Reverse-type I spectral change, which is the mirror image of the Type I spectral change; and Type II spectral change characterized by a broad trough between 390 and 410 nm and a peak between 425 and 435 nm.

Detection of hemoproteins by SDS gels

During recent years convincing evidence has accumulated to support the idea that microsomal cytochrome P-450 consists of multiple forms. Several hemoproteins have been detected using a variety of electrophoresis techniques. Analysis of hemoprotein profiles has provided considerable insight into the ability of chemicals to selectively induce or repress specific forms of microsomal hemoproteins.

Reconstituted and purified systems

The use of crude microsomal preparations allows only limited characterization of individual components in the complex sequence of reactions involved in cytochrome P-450 dependent oxidative reactions. To better understand the nature of this system, researchers have utilized a variety of techniques to purify individual components of the system and to reconstitute the electron transport chain. Prior to purification of the cytochrome P-448 system, animals are induced with 3-methycholanthrene or an appropriate P-448 inducer, whereas greater yields of P-450 can be obtained using phenobarbitaltreated rats. Using purification/reconstitution techniques, basic differences have been observed in microsomal hemoproteins of different species and from different tissues of the same species.

Synthesis/degradation of hemoproteins

One common method used to study the turnover characteristic of hepatic hemoproteins involves pulse-labeling of the heme moiety with ^{3}H-δ-aminolevulinic acid, partially purifying (removal of the other microsomal cytochrome, b_5) the CO-binding particles (P-450) and measuring synthesis/degradation characteristics of the cytochrome. These kinds of studies have identified a fastphase component and a slow-phase component of P-450, and each component exhibits selective responses to inducive or repressive agents and is age and sex-dependent.

Other methods

In addition to the methods described above, basic information on P-450-substrate interactions has been generated using ESR spectroscopy and immunochemical techniques.

Microsomal Enzymes

Cytochrome P-450 dependent enzymes

One of the most common assays is oxidative demethylation using aminopyrine, ethymorphine, or benzophetamine as the substrate. This method measures the production of formaldehyde which is an intermediate in oxidative demethylation reactions. The assay for aminopyrine as the substrate is conducted as follows:

1. Buffer (50 mM Tris-HCl, pH 7.5, 1.5 ml) is added to incubation tube.
2. Saturating levels of NADPH (3.1 mM) are added in 0.5 ml Tris buffer.
3. The incubation medium is made 20 mM with respect to $MgCl_2$.
4. Ammopyrine is added to achieve a substrate concentration of 2.5 mM.
5. After prewarming the incubation contents to 37°C, the reaction is initiated by adding approximately 0.5 to 1.5 mg of microsomal protein.
6. After a 10 min incubation, the reaction is stopped by adding 1.0 ml 10% trichloroacetic acid.
7. Protein is sedimented by low-speed centrifugation and two ml of supernatant fluid is added to one ml of NASH reagent (2 M ammonium acetate, 0.05M acetic acid, 0.02M acetylacetone).
8. The solution is heated for 8 min at 60°C, and the formaldehyde concentration is measured at 405 nm and read against a standard curve. Blank values are obtained by omitting microsomes from the incubation medium.

The reaction rate is linear with respect to time and microsomal protein under these incubation conditions, although each investigator should assess these parameters as part of preliminary investigations. Ethylmorphine and benzphetamine demethylation rates can be determined using the same method. A radiolabel assay has been devised for aminopyrine demethylation that can be used when increased sensitivity is required to detect low enzyme activity as a function of tissue, developmental stage, or toxic or disease state.

Cytochrome P-448 dependent enzymes

Aryl hydrocarbon hydroxylase (AHH) is an indicator of P-448 function. AHH is often used as an indicator of the capacity of biological system to form reactive electrophilic metabolites, that are frequently in the form of arene oxide intermediates produced in hydroxylation reactions. However, AHH assays often are a measure of total hydroxylated or polar metabolites and are not necessary indicative of metabolic activation. For example, polycyclic hydrocarbons such as benzo(a) pyrene produce large numbers of microsomal oxidative metabolites possessing widely different capacities for binding to cellular macromolecules in *in vitro* systems. Information on the rates of formation of specific active metabolites capable of eliciting biochemical lesions is needed to achieve a valid toxicokinetic evaluation. However, such a definitive evaluation is not feasible for each toxicant. Therefore, determinations of AHH activity by using benzpyrene, biphenyl, or another suitable substrate may provide approximate data on the capacity of some biological systems to activate some substrates (those activated by the microsomal monoxygense system). A general scheme illustrating benzo(a) pyrene metabolism is presented. AHH can be measured by a fluorometric method as described below:

1. Buffer (50 mM Tris-HCl, pH 7.5, 0.075 ml) is added to incubation vessel.
2. Benzpyrene suspension (0.25 ml 60 mM in 2.5% carboxymethyl-cellulose) is added.
3. Microsomes (0.25 ml) are added so that the final incubation medium contains approximately 1 mg protein per ml.
4. The reaction mixture is equilibrated at 37°C for 3 min and the reaction initiated by the addition of 0.25 ml NADPH solution to achieve a concentration of 3.1 mM in the incubation medium.
5. After 10 min the reaction is stopped by the addition of 2 ml ice-cold acetone.
6. Hexane is added (20 ml) to stoppered 45-ml shaking tubes.
7. The incubation mixtures are washed into the shaking tubes with water (three times with 0.5 ml)
8. The tubes are shaken for 10 min and can be stored overnight at 4°C or frozen.
9. The tubes are centrifuged for 15 min at 600 g.
10. The hexane layer (upper 15 ml) is transferred by pipette to a clean 45-ml shaking tube.

11. NaOH (5 ml, 0.1 M) is added and the tubes shaken for 10 min followed by centrifugation for 10 min.
12. Fluorescence of the aqueous layer is read (excitation 400 nm; emission 525 nm). Concentration of phenolic metabolites is determined using 3-hydroxybenzpyrene as the standard.

In addition to the fluorometric assay for AHH, a radioactive assay is available that uses ^{3}H-benzopyrene as the substrate. For those investigators who wish to avoid carcinogenic substrates, a direct fluorometric method with 7-ethoxyresorufin as the substrate is available. This assay method is an extremely good indicator of cytochrome P-448 levels. Another fluorometric method, that has the advantage of simultaneously measuring biphenyl-2-hydroxylase (P-448 dependent) and biphenyl-4-hydroxylase (P-450 dependent), is available. Epoxide hydrase is an important microsomal enzyme system that functions in the deactivation of reaction epoxides/arene oxides and can be measured by the method of Oesch.

Toxicant-receptor interactions

The findings that (a) some xenobiotics selectively induce cytochrome P-448 dependent enzymes; (b) precise structure-activity relationships can be described for selective induction; and (c) some inducers are extremely potent, suggested that polycyclic hydrocarbons such as 3-MC and TCDD may initiate their inductive actions by interaction with a cytosolic receptor protein in a manner analogous to steroid hormone action. Researchers have characterized such a receptor, which has a finite capacity, pronounced selectivity, high dissociation constant, and the ligand-receptor complex appears to undergo nuclear translocation. The receptor was characterized using high specific activity ^{3}H-TCDD.

Microsomal Conjugative Enzymes

On simplification, and depending on the chemical substrate, the drug biotransformation process may be divided into two parts; first an oxidative reaction, such as hydroxylation, that results in the formation of a free hydroxyl group; this is then rapidly conjugated with glucuronic acid, sulfate, or another conjugate as indicated. This series of reactions renders the molecule more polar and generally more excretable and less toxic. However, conjugation reactions may also function in the formation of reactive electrophilic intermediates.

UDP glucuronyltransferase

One of the more important and routinely measured conjugative enzymes is UDP glucuronyltransferase. This enzyme system appears to consists of multiple forms, and it functions in the metabolism/excretion of many endogenous compounds (i.e., steroid hormones) as well as xenobiotics. Recent evidence has demonstrated functional as well as biochemical heterogeneity (4) of UDP glucuronyltransferase. Depending on molecular structure, substrates appear to be conjugated either by Group I or Group II glucuronyltransferase. A general method to measure p-nitrophenol glucuronidation (Group I) is shown below:

1. Incubation medium contains 1.5 mM UDPGA (co-factor), 0.5 mM $MgCl_2$, 0.8 mM p-nitrophenol (substrate) in 1.4 ml 40 mM Tris-HCl, pH 7.5.
2. The incubation mixture is warmed at 37°C for 3 min.
3. Reaction is started by the addition of 0.25 to 1.0 mg Triton X-100 activated microsomes. Microsomal suspensions are activated prior to addition to the incubation medium by mixing 0.2 μl Triton X-100 per mg microsomal protein.
4. Reaction is stopped by the addition of 5.0 ml 0.2 M glycine buffer containing 0.15 M NaCl, pH 10.4.
5. p-Nitrophenol concentration is measured spectrophotometrically at 405 nm. Blank values are obtained by omitting UDPGA from the reaction medium.

Group II substrates can be measured by a rapid radiometric method. This procedure is especially useful for the study of steroid conjugation reactions.

The incubation system for glucuronidation measurements is added to liquid scintillation vials and consists of the following: 1.2 ml 75 mM Tris-HCl buffer (pH 7.4), 1.0 μmol UDPGA, 10.0 μmol unlabeled substrate in 50 μl methanol, and 1×10^5d.p.m labeled substrate in 50 μl methanol. This volume of methanol is used to insure substrate solubilization and has no apparent effect on glucuronyl-transferase activity. The incubation contents are warmed at 37°C for 3 min, and then 0.4 to 0.6 mg microsomal protein is added. The incubation period is approximately 10 min. The reaction is stopped by the addition of 10-ml nonaqueous scintillation fluid prepared by mixing 43-ml liquiflour L. toluene. Samples are capped, shaken for 10 sec on a vortex mixer, and radioactivity counted in the same vials in which the incubation reactions are performed. Addition of the toluene-based scintillation fluid results in a two-phase mixture (toluene on top and the aqueous fraction on the bottom). Unreacted substrate partitions into the toluene and this radio-activity is detected in a Packard Tri-Carb liquid scintillation counter equipped with an Automatic Quench Analyzer.

Glucuronides remain in the aqueous and, since ^{14}C and ^{3}H in a water medium do not scintillate, radioactivity associated with glucuronides is not detectable by liquid scintillation spectrometry. This phenomenon enables steroid glucuronidation rates to be measured by substrate disappearance. Blank values are obtained by omitting UDPGA from the reaction mediums. The incubation blanks represent 0% activity and correct for the amount of substrate remaining in the aqueous fraction (incubation medium). Glucuronides detected after addition of scintillation fluid to incubation medium reflect the amount of radioactivity detected after 100% glucuronidation of substrate. Enzyme activity using 300 nmol substrate in the incubation medium is expressed by the equation:

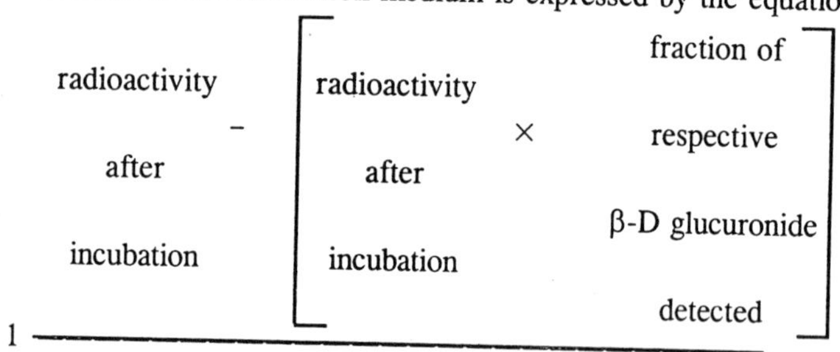

$$1 - \frac{\text{radioactivity after incubation} - \left[\text{radioactivity after incubation} \times \text{fraction of respective } \beta\text{-D glucuronide detected}\right]}{\text{radioactivity in blank}}$$

$$\times\ 300 \text{ nmol} = \text{nmol substrate conjugated}$$

This assay procedure is applicable to a wide range of substrates and enzyme reactions in which the polarity of the product is significantly different than the substrate.

Hydrolytic Enzymes

The endoplasmic reticulum also contain a variety of hydrolytic enzymes that exhibit a dual localization in that they are also active in lysosomes. These enzymes include β-glucuronidase (performs the reverse reaction of UDP glucuronidase by liberating the free aglycone from β-D-glucuronic acid conjugates), acid and alkaline phosphatase, and aryl sulfatase. The function of these microsomal enzymes is not clear, although they appear to play a role in the regulation of steroid metabolism and in some cases may represent structural proteins of the endoplasmic reticulum. Bacterial β-glucuronidase plays an important role in the absorption and toxicity of many chemicals including some carcinogens. One possible explanation for the dual localization of these enzyme systems is that they are synthesized in the RER, transported through the membranous cisternae of the SER and fragment of the SER are incorporated into lysosomes. Reviews describing the potential role of these lysosomal/microsomal systems are available. Hydrolytic enzymes such as β-glucuronidase can be detected by histochemical or biochemical methods. One simple method for measuring mammalian β-glucuronidase activity is as follows:

1. The incubation medium contains 1.0 mM substrate (β-D-glucuronide of p-nitrophenol, 4-methylumbelliferone, or phenolphthalein) in 50 mM acetate buffer, pH 4.5.
2. The incubation mixture is warmed for 3 min at 37°C.
3. Reaction is initiated by the addition of 1.0 mg microsomal protein.
4. After a 10 min incubation period, the reaction is stopped by the addition of 5 ml glycine buffer (see p-nitrophenol glucuronidation assay).
5. Protein is removed by low-speed centrifugation, and the formation of product is measured spectrophotometrically (p-nitrophenol, 405 nm, and methylumbelliferone, 365 nm).

Protein Synthesis

Although much of the pharmacological/toxicological research on microsomes focuses on their role in metabolic activation/deactivation reactions, the main function of this organelle involves protein synthesis. Increasingly, researchers are attempting to identify sensitive biochemical indicators of toxicity (usually proteins) that have predictive/diagnostic value and also provide insight into the mechanism of toxic actions of these chemicals. Although a survey of the genetics and molecular biology of protein synthesis is not in the scope of this chapter, there are some general useful methods that can be applied to investigations on the effects of chemicals on overall and/or specific protein synthesis. These methods involve injection of radiolabeled amino acids into intact animals (usually tail vein); the incorporation of radiolabel into specific organelles or specific proteins is then determined. Obviously, protein purification or immunochemical procedures must be undertaken to assess synthesis/degradation of individual proteins. When conducting such pulse-label experiments, it is essential that samples are taken over a wide range of sample periods so that meaningful and valid conclusions can be made concerning alterations either in synthetic or degradative phases for a particular protein. For example, if a toxic chemical selectively alters protein degradation and a pulse label is taken during the synthetic phase, the investigator could miss critical information. If possible, it is desirable to conduct pulse-label experiments with carbon rather than tritium in order to avoid nonspecific redistribution of label during homogenization and purification.

Another method, termed 2-dimensional gel electrophoresis, is being used to determine protein synthesis profiles. This procedure involves administration of high specific activity ^{35}S-methionine to intact animals or isolated cells, and the subsequent electrophoretic mapping of labeled proteins by SDS in one direction and isoelectric focusing in the second direction. This procedure as is now commonly used in studies investigating the role of specific protein synthesis in development and differentiation and can resolve as many as 1,000 proteins.

Phospholipids and Lipoproteins

Phospholipids and lipoproteins provide important permeability properties to membrane structures such as the endoplasmic reticulum. These membrane phospholipids and lipoproteins are synthesized on the endoplasmic reticulum and often play an integral role in enzyme activity by regulating the membrane environment of enzymes that are imbedded in the endoplasmic reticulum. The production of certain forms of lipoproteins seems to associate with specific toxic and disease states. For example, the relative amount of VLDL (very low density lipoproteins) produced by the liver appears to play a critical role in the development and susceptibility to cardiovascular disease.

Phospholipid and lipoprotein synthesis can be studied by measuring ^{32}P or ^{14}C incorporation into these compounds as outlined earlier in this section (protein synthesis).

8

Forensic Responses

Toxicants can affect any type of tissue in any organ. Different classes of toxicants affect various tissues to varying degrees and in a variety of ways, depending on the nature of the toxicant, the kind of receptor that it attacks, the nature of the binding of the toxicant to the receptor, and the routes, transport, and metabolism of the toxicant in the organism.

Before considering chemical classes of toxicants, it is useful to survey the major toxic responses and effects. It is obviously beyond the scope of a single chapter to discuss the whole broad array of toxic responses in all kinds of organisms. Instead, this chapter divides these responses on the basis of responses in the major tissues and organs of mammals, particularly humans. The systems considered are the respiratory system, skin, liver, blood and cardiovascular system, immune system, endocrine system, nervous system, reproductive system, and kidney and bladder. This order is somewhat parallel to the major pathways of exposure, transport, and elimination of toxicants in the human body. Toxicants can be inhaled through the respiratory system or absorbed through the skin. Those that are ingested through the digestive system normally pass through the liver. Systemic toxicants are carried by blood and through the lymph system to various organs and can affect the endocrine system, nervous system, and reproductive system. Finally, the kidney and urinary tract constitute the main route of elimination of the metabolites of systemic toxicants from the body.

A common result of exposure of tissue to toxicants is cell death. In *cell necrosis*, a cell dies, swells, and disintegrates. The cell membrane and membranes of cell organelles break up, and a large amount of cell debris is released at the site of cell death. These fragments induce inflammatory action of other cells, making the injury worse. In addition to a toxic effect that may have caused the cell death in the first place, secondary processes caused by the presence of soil debris make the injury much worse.

In contrast to cell necrosis, *apoptosis* is a process by which cells are systematically destroyed and removed. The nuclear body and organelles within the cell become enclosed in a membrane to form residues called *apoptotic bodies*. These are then said to be phagocytosed as they are enclosed within membranes and actively removed from the site of the injury. Apoptosis is an active process for eliminating dead cellular material.

Many of the detrimental effects of toxicants have been observed with pharmaceutical agents. These are often administered to millions of people so that even a miniscule fraction of subjects who have adverse reactions will be observed, medical supervision of subjects is usually rather thorough, and cause and effect is relatively easy to establish. On August 8, 2001, the U.S. Food and Drug Administration announced a voluntary recall of Bayer Pharmaceutical's cholesterol-lowering drug Baycol (also called Lipobay). Only recently approved and used by about 700,000 people in the U.S., Baycol was implicated in 52 deaths due to rhabdomyolysis. This acute and sometimes fatal disease is first manifested by pain in the muscles of the calves and lower back. The cells in muscles can break down, leading to symptoms of fever, fatigue, and nausea. As part of the muscle cell breakdown, phosphokinase and myoglobin are released into the bloodstream, eventually causing kidney failure. Virtually all of the fatalities occurred in patients who were simultaneously taking another cholesterol-lowering drug, gemfibrozil.

Baycol or Lipobay

Another even more widely used pharmaceutical that has been linked indirectly to numerous deaths is sildenafil citrate, marketed as the impotence drug Viagra. Used by millions during the few years since it was introduced, numerous deaths have been reported among men taking the drug along with nitroglycerin or nitrates administered for the treatment of heart disease. It is believed that the combination of these drugs with Viagra reduce blood flow through damaged coronary arteries, causing fatal heart attacks in some cases.

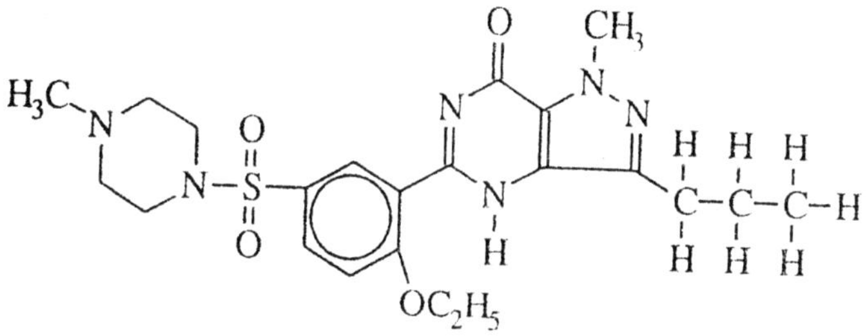

Sildenafil. The citrate salt is the drug Viagra, widely used to treat male sexual disfunction.

Respiratory System

In discussing toxic responses of the respiratory system, it is important to make a distinction between the respiratory system as an entryway for toxic substances, referred to as *inhalation toxicology*, and the respiratory system adversely affected by toxicants, referred to as *respiratory tract toxicology*. The term *pulmonary* refers to lungs. Generally, toxicants that adversely affect the respiratory system are those that have been inhaled, including such well-known substances as asbestos, chromate, and silica. However, it is possible for systemic poisons transported from elsewhere in the body to act as respiratory system toxicants. One interesting possibility that has been suggested is lung cancer caused by the diol epoxide of benzo(a)pyrene, which is formed by inhalation of benzo(a)pyrene, converted to the ultimate carcinogen in the liver, and transported back to the lung, where cancer develops.

The function of the respiratory system is to exchange gases with ambient air, taking oxygen from inhaled air into blood and releasing carbon dioxide from respiration back to air that is exhaled. Air enters through the nose and travels through the pharynx, trachea, and bronchi, reaching the small sacs in the lung called alveoli, where gas exchange with blood occurs. The alveoli have walls that are as thin as a single cell and highly susceptible to damage; they constitute the alveolar--capillary barrier across which gases are exchanged. A large variety of potentially toxic substances enter with incoming air, including air pollutant particles and gases, disease-causing bacteria and viruses, and airborne allergens, such as pollen. Volatile substances are expelled with exhaled air, and the respiratory tract has mechanisms to eliminate solid and liquid particles and residues from respiratory tract infections.

The respiratory tract may suffer from a variety of ailments that can result from exposure to toxicants. A common one of these is acute or chronic *bronchitis*, manifested by inflammation of the membrane lining of the bronchial tubes, which can be caused by toxicants or by infections. *Emphysema*, the bane of aging heavy smokers, is the result of abnormal enlargement and loss of elasticity of pulmonary air spaces, resulting in difficulty in breathing. Interstitial disorders, predominantly *pulmonary fibrosis*, in which excess fibrous connective tissues develop in the lungs can result from exposure to toxicants. Often indicative of acute lung injury, *pulmonary edema* is the accumulation of fluid in the lungs; in severe cases, the subject literally drowns from those fluids. And, of course, *lung cancer* is a major concern with exposure to some kinds of toxicants.

A common toxic effect to the lung is the result of *oxidative burden*. Oxidative burden occurs as the result of active oxidants, especially free radicals that are generated by a variety of toxic agents and the action of lung defense cells. Ozone, O_3, the air pollutant most commonly associated with photochemical smog, is a particularly active oxidant in polluted air, and smog contains other oxidants as well. NO_2, also associated with photochemical smog and polluted air, contributes to the oxidative burden. Much of the oxidative damage to lungs is probably done by free radicals, such as hydroxyl radical, HO·, and superoxide ion, $O\cdot^-$, which initiate and mediate oxidative chain reactions. Lungs of animals exposed to oxidants have shown elevated levels of enzymes that scavenge free radicals, providing evidence for their role in oxidative damage. There is evidence to suggest that lung cells damaged by toxicants release species that convert lung O_2 to reactive superoxide anion, $O\cdot_2^-$.

Lungs are subject to both acute and chronic injury from toxicants. A common manifestation of acute injury is pulmonary edema, in which liquid exudes into lung alveoli and other lung cavities, increasing the alveolar–capillary barrier and making breathing more difficult. Among the toxicants that cause pulmonary edema are ozone, phosgene ($COCl_2$), and perchloroethylene (C_2Cl_4). There are several major types of chronic lung disorders that can be caused by exposure to toxicants. A common symptom of chronic lung damage is chronic bronchitis. Among the toxicants that cause this condition are ammonia, arsenic, cotton dust (brown lung disease), and iron oxide from exposure to welding fumes.

Lung fibrosis occurs with a buildup of fibrous material inside lung cavities. The fibers are rich in collagen, the tough, fibrous protein that gives strength to bone and connective tissue. Chronic fibrosis can result from pulmonary exposure to aluminum dust, aluminum abrasives, chromium(VI), coal dust, kaolin clay dust, ozone, phosgene, silica, and finely divided mineral talc.

Snider et al. have defined emphysema as "a condition of the lung characterized by abnormal enlargement of the air spaces distal to the terminal bronchiole, accompanied by destruction of the walls without obvious fibrosis." Emphysema is characterized by enlarged lungs that do not expel air adequately and do not exchange gases well. Cigarette smoke is the overwhelming cause of emphysema. Inhalation of aluminum abrasives and cadmium oxide fumes can also cause emphysema.

Lung cancer is the best-known example of cancer caused by exposure to a toxicant, in this case cigarette smoke. As much as 90% of lung cancers are the result of exposure to tobacco smoke. The latency period for the development of lung cancer from this source is usually at least 20 years and may range up to 40 years or longer. Inhalation of other agents can cause lung cancer, although they are usually associated with synergistic effects from cigarette smoke. The most well established of these are asbestos and radon gas, a radioactive alpha particle emitter.

Skin

The pulmonary system and skin constitute the major routes of entry for xenobiotic materials into the body. The skin has a large surface area of up to two m^2 for adults. This large area, along with skin's external exposure, means that it is a common site of contact with toxic substances, especially in the workplace. It has been estimated that about one third of all reported occupational exposures to toxic substances is through skin, and much larger numbers that produce relatively minor symptoms remain unreported. Skin maladies constitute a large fraction of occupational and consumer problems with industrial chemicals and consumer products.

As with most organs, the structure of skin is relatively complicated. In addition to the layers, skin has a number of structures, including blood vessels, hair follicles, sweat glands and ducts, and sebacious glands that secrete oils, fat, and connective tissue. The two major layers of skin are the inner *dermis* and the outer *epidermis*. Skin cells are continually being generated and eventually end up in a much modified form on the surface layer, called the *stratum corneum*. The cells in this layer are not living and are continuously being shed. They consist mostly of *keratin*, a sulfur-containing protein that also constitutes nails and animal horns.

Although the stratum corneum acts as a simple physical barrier to outside influences, skin tissue as a whole is very active. It is crucial in maintaining the body's homeostasis, its essential steady-state environment. Skin maintains temperature and balance of electrolytes, the dissolved salts in internal body fluids. It is metabolically active and participates in hormonal and immune regulatory processes. More than serving as a passive barrier, it is proactive in response to xenobiotic insults and can be damaged in the defensive process by developing rashes and other symptoms.

Absorption through the skin, *percutaneous absorption*, is an important mechanism by which xenobiotic substances can enter the body. The surface stratum corneum layer is the main barrier to such absorption, and when it is shed or compromised, skin is much more susceptible to penetration by xenobiotic substances. A test for the ability of a hydrophobic xenobiotic substance to penetrate skin is to measure the partitioning of such a substance between water and powdered stratum corneum cells.

Modern medical science is taking advantage of skin permeability to chemicals by using it as a delivery system for some kinds of drugs. A single skin "patch" can deliver a drug at a uniform low rate for up to a week. The most long-standing transdermal drug delivery system is used to deliver nitroglycerin to blood for the relief of painful heart angina symptoms. Nitroglycerin is metabolized within minutes in the human body, so delivery through the gastrointestinal tract, where the substance first goes through the metabolically active liver, is relatively ineffective. Delivered transdermally, nitroglycerin enters the bloodstream directly and quickly reaches the heart, where its therapeutic effect is manifested. More recently, skin patches have been developed to deliver nicotine to relieve the cravings for this substance experienced by people trying to stop smoking. Estradiol, scopolamine, clonidine, and fetanyl have also been delivered by this means, and other drug delivery systems are under development.

In addition to serving as a physical barrier to the entry of xenobiotics, skin is active in metabolizing topically applied substances such as steroids and retinoids, primarily through the action of cytochrome P-450 enzymes. Active lipase, protease, glycosidase, and phosphatase enzymes have also been observed in skin. Skin contains some enzymes capable of catalyzing phase II conjugation reactions. In some cases, these metabolic processes detoxify xenobiotics. However, in other cases, they act in sensitization to make xenobiotics active in causing skin symptoms of poisoning.

Toxic Responses of Skin

The most common skin affliction resulting from exposure to toxic substances and the most common skin condition from occupational exposure is *contact dermatitis*, characterized by generally irritated, itching, and sometimes painful skin surface. Skin afflicted with contact dermatitis shows several symptoms. One of these is *erythema*, or redness. The skin surface may be subject to *scaling*, in which the surface flakes off. Thickening and hardening can occur, a condition clinically known as *induration*. Blistering, a condition called *vesiculation*, may also occur. Skin afflicted with contact dermatitis typically exhibits edema, with accumulation of fluid between skin cells. There are two general categories of contact dermatitis: irritant dermatitis and allergic contact dermatitis.

Irritant dermatitis does not involve an immune response and is typically caused by contact with corrosive substances that exhibit extremes of pH, oxidizing capability, dehydrating action, or tendency to dissolve skin lipids. In extreme cases of exposure, skin cells are destroyed and a permanent scar results. This condition is known as a *chemical burn*. Exposure to concentrated sulfuric acid, which exhibits extreme acidity, or to concentrated nitric acid, which denatures skin protein, can cause bad chemical burns. The strong oxidant action of 30% hydrogen peroxide likewise causes a chemical burn. Other chemicals causing chemical burns include ammonia, quicklime (CaO), chlorine, ethylene oxide, hydrogen halides, methyl bromide, nitrogen oxides, elemental white phosporous, phenol, alkali metal hydroxides (NaOH, KOH), and toluene diisocyanate.

Allergic contact dermatitis occurs when individuals become sensitized to a chemical by an initial exposure, after which subsequent exposures evoke a response characterized by skin dermatitis. Allergic contact dermatitis is a type IV hypersensitivity involving T cells and macrophages instead of antibodies. It is a delayed response, occurring one or two days after exposure, and often requires only very small quantities of allergen to cause it. Literally dozens of substances have been implicated as causative agents of contact dermatitis. Some of these are substances applied to skin directly as hygiene products. Included in this category are antibiotic bacitracin and neomycin, preservative benzalkonium chloride, therapeutic corticosteroids, and antiseptic dichlorophene. Among other substances causing allergic contact dermatitis are formaldehyde, abietic acid from plants, hydroquinone, acrylic monomers, triphenylmethane dyes, 2-mercapto-benzthiazole, *p*-phenylene diamine, tetramethylthiuram, 2,4-dinitro-chlorobenzene, pentaerythritol triacrylate, epoxy resins, dichromate salts, mercury, and nickel.

The effects of poison ivy constitute a type of allergic contact dermatitis with which people who spend time camping and in other outdoor pursuits may have an unfortunate familiarity. Poison ivy, poison oak, and poison sumac contain toxicodendron, in which the active antigen is pentadecylcatechol:

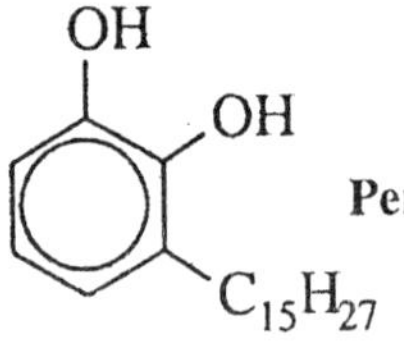

OH

OH

$C_{15}H_{27}$

Pentadecylcatechol

Urticaria, commonly known as hives, is a type I allergic reaction that results very rapidly from exposure to a toxicant to which the subject has become sensitized. It is characterized by the release of histamine from a type of white blood cell. Histamine causes many of the symptoms of allergic reaction, including tissue edema. In addition to edema, erythema, and accompanying raised welts on skin, urticaria is accompanied by severe itching. In severe cases, such as happen in some people as the result of bee or wasp stings, urticaria can result in systemic anaphylaxis, a potentially fatal allergic reaction.

Phototoxic Responses of Skin

Phototoxic responses of skin occur as the result of absorption of radiation, primarily sunlight and ultraviolet radiation in the UVB region of 290 to 320 nm. Because UVB radiation is vastly more effective in causing phototoxic symptoms than either UVA radiation (320 to 400 nm) or visible light (400 to 700 nm), reference will be made to it in discussions of phototoxicity. Photons of radiation are absorbed by functional groups called chromophores on biomolecules. The most significant chromophores in skin are molecules of DNA, which can be modified by absorbing photon energy. Also serving as chromophores in skin are amino acids and materials released by protein breakdown, including tryptophan and urocanic acid. The skin contains a protective pigment, *melanin*, synthesized from the amino acid tyrosine, that effectively absorbs UVB and protects people from the effects of sunlight. Levels of melanin differ widely in people, being high in darker-skinned individuals and very low in those with lighter skin. Production of melanin (suntan) can be promoted by exposure to natural or artificial sunlight.

The most common acute effect of exposure to toxic doses of UVB is erythema, commonly known as sunburn, the result of photooxidation processes in skin. Because of substances released from skin cells exposed to excessive UVB, systemic effects, including fever, chills, and a generally ill feeling, may result as well. Chronic symptoms of exposure to excessive UVB include changes in pigmentation, such as freckles, and general skin deterioration and wrinkling. Of greatest concern is the potential to form cancerous lesions. These include both basal and squamous cell carcinomas. The most serious such effect is the development of malignant melanoma, a particularly serious form of skin cancer.

Photosensitivity, or *porphyria*, is an abnormal sensitivity to ultraviolet radiation and visible light. A genetic predisposition to an inability to repair damage to skin from sunlight can cause photosensitivity, as can exposure to some chemicals, especially chlorinated aromatic compounds. These effects are tied with enzymatic malfunctions in the biosynthesis of heme, the protein molecule contained in blood hemoglobin. When this biosynthesis does not function properly, molecular fragments of heme (porphyrins) accumulate in skin, where they reach an excited state when exposed to light of 400 to 410 nm (the Soret band) and react with molecular O_2 to generate free radicals that are destructive to biomolecules in skin tissue.

Phototoxicity occurs when skin exposed to sunlight, especially in the UVA region of 320 to 400 nm, reddens and develops blisters as a consequence of the presence of certain chemical species. The phototoxic chemical species that result in such reactions are ones to which an individual is exposed either directly on the skin or systemically. These compounds absorb ultraviolet radiation and, like the porphyrins discussed above, enter excited states interacting with O_2 to generate destructive oxidant species and free radicals. Numerous chemical species, including furocoumarins, polycyclic aromatic hydrocarbons, tetracyclines, and sulfonamides, can be phototoxic.

Photoallergy is similar in symptoms and mechanism to allergic contact dermatitis discussed above, except that symptoms develop after exposure to sunlight. The subject develops an allergic response to light after sensitization with a chemical agent. This condition was observed in the mid- 1900s in individuals who had used soaps containing antibacterial agents, including tetrachlorosalicylanilide and tribrom osalicylanilide, which had to be taken from the personal care product market.

Damage to Skin Structure and Pigmentation

Defects in skin pigments can result from chemical exposure. *Hyperpigmentation* occurs from increased production and deposition of melanin. *Hypopigmentation* occurs with loss of skin pigments, giving it a white, albino appearance. Among the chemicals that cause hyper-pigmentation are volatile organics from coal tar, anthracene, mercury, lead, and hydroquinone. Hypopigmentation can result from exposure to hydroquinone and its derivatives, mercaptoamines, phenolic germicides, and butylated hydroxytoluene.

Acne, characterized by skin eruptions commonly known as blackheads or whiteheads plus a variety of pustules, cysts, and pits on the skin surface, can be caused by exposure to chemicals. The most notable kind of chemically induced acne is *chloracne*, resulting from exposure to chlorinated hydrocarbons. Of these, the most notorious is dioxin, 2,3,7,8-tetrachlorodibenzo-*p*-dioxin (TCDD):

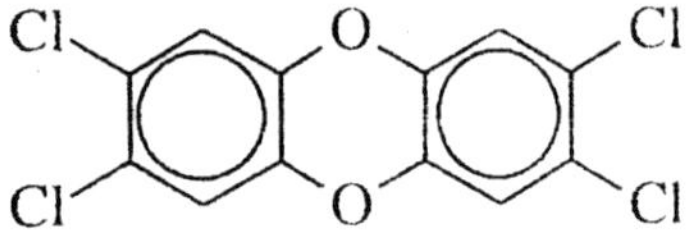

Cl O Cl

Cl O Cl

2,3,7,8-tetrachlorodibenzo-*p*-dioxin

In addition to lesions on the face, in severe cases chloracne is characterized by cysts and other manifestations of acne on the shoulders, back, and even genitalia.

Granulomatous inflammation occurs in cases where skin tissue builds up around the site of exposure to an irritant. Introduction of foreign materials such as talc or silica into skin can cause this condition. In some cases, it occurs in response to exposure to some metals, including beryllium and chromium.

Toxic epidermal necrolysis occurs when the skin epidermis is destroyed by the action of toxicants and becomes detached from the dermis. This condition severely disrupts the ability of skin to regulate the release of heat, fluids, and electrolytes. Metabolites of the anti-convulsive drug carbamazepine have been implicated in toxic epidermal necrolysis.

Skin Cancer

Skin cancer is the most common type of cancer. Damage to skin DNA from sunlight is the most common cause of skin cancer. This causes mutations that result in formation of cancer cells and that suppress the immune responses that normally prevent replication of such cells. The class of chemicals most commonly associated with causing skin cancer are the polycyclic aromatic hydrocarbons from sources such as coal tar. These can be metabolized to electrophilic substances that bind with DNA to initiate cancer. Arsenic in drinking water has been established as a cause of precancerous lesions, called arsenical keratoses, and squamous cell carcinoma of skin.

LIVER

The liver is often the first major metabolizing organ that an ingested toxicant encounters, and it has very high metabolic activity. The major function of the liver is to metabolize, store, and release nutrients, that is, to maintain nutrient homeostasis. When blood levels of nutrient molecules are high, the liver can convert them to glycogen and fats and store them. When blood levels of nutrients are low, the liver can convert some amino acids, pyruvate, and lactate to glucose, which is released to blood. It uses amino acids to synthesize proteins that are released to blood, including albumin, clotting factors, and transport proteins. The liver is the major site of fat metabolism and releases fat to blood as needed. It produces bile, which acts to emulsify fats in the small intestine.

Materials enter and leave the liver as blood in arteries and veins. Nutrients, drugs, and ingested xenobiotics absorbed from the small intestine go directly to the liver through the portal vein. The liver has another mechanism for excretion in the form of bile discharged back to the intestines. Bile discharge is a major route of elimination of xenobiotic compounds and their metabolites.

Insofar as toxicological chemistry is concerned, the major function of the liver is to metabolize xenobiotic substances through phase I and phase II reactions. Because of this function, the liver is a crucial organ in the study of toxicological chemistry. Since it processes xenobiotic chemicals, the liver is often the organ that is damaged by such chemicals and their metabolites. The livers of genetically susceptible individuals can be damaged by therapeutic doses of some drugs. Other xenobiotics ingested accidentally can damage the liver.

Toxic effects to the liver are studied under the topic of *hepatotoxicity*, and substances that are toxic to the liver are called *hepatotoxins*. Much is known about hepatotoxicity from the many cases of liver toxicity that are a manifestation of chronic alcoholism. Liver injury from excessive alcohol ingestion initially hampers the ability of the organ to remove lipids, resulting in their accumulation in the liver (fatty liver). The liver eventually loses its ability to perform its metabolic functions and accumulates scar tissue, a condition known as cirrhosis. Inability to synthesize clotting factors can cause fatal hemorrhage in the liver.

A wide range of substances can cause hepatotoxicity. Even an essential vitamin, vitamin A, is hepatotoxic in overdoses, a fact that should be kept in mind by health food fans who drink large amounts of carrot juice. Other hepatotoxins include toxins in hormones, tea (germander), and drinking water infested with the photosynthetic cyanobacteria *Microcystis aeruginosa*. Each year people are killed by eating toxic mushrooms, especially the appropriately named "death cap" mushroom, *Amanita phalloides*. This fungus produces a mycotoxin consisting of seven amino acid residues, a heptapeptide called *phalloidin*.

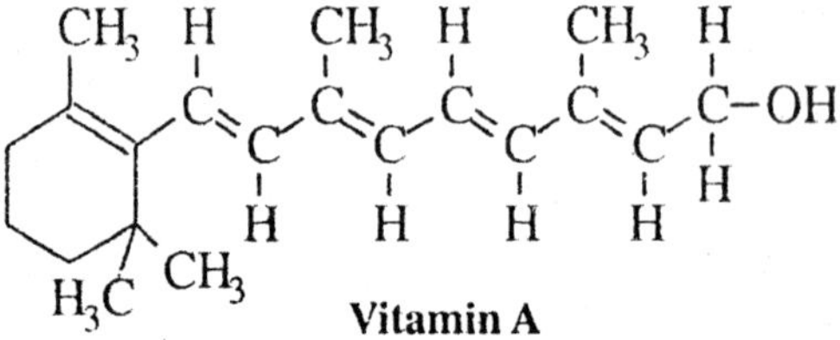

CH_3 H CH_3 H CH_3 H

C–OH

H H H H H

H_3C CH_3

Vitamin A

A great deal of information about hepatotoxicity has resulted from observed effects of pharmaceuticals, a number of which have been discontinued because of their damaging effects to the liver. An example of such a hepatotoxic compound tested as a pharmaceutical is fialuridine, which was tested during the mid-1990s as a treatment for viral chronic hepatitis B, a liver disease. Seven of 13 patients in the test developed debilitating hepatotoxicity with severe jaundice, along with lactic acidosis due to accumulation of lactic acid, a metabolic intermediate. The seven patients were given liver transplants, but five of them died.

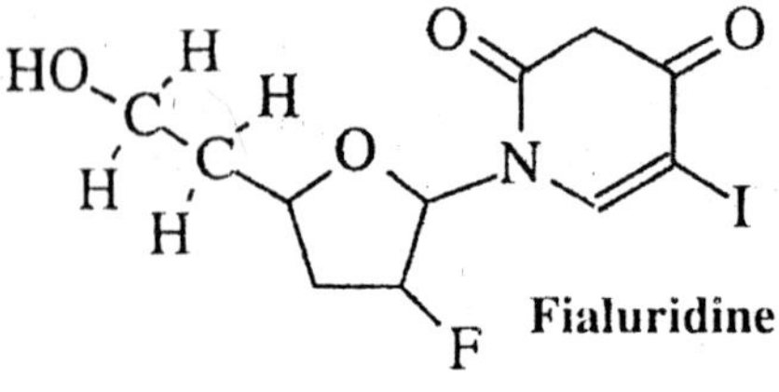

HO H O O

C H

H C O N

H I

F

Fialuridine

Steatosis, commonly known as fatty liver, is a condition in which lipids accumulate in the liver in excess of about 5%. It may result from toxicants that cause an increase in lipid synthesis, a decrease in lipid metabolism, or a decrease in the secretion of lipids as lipoproteins. An example of a substance that causes steatosis is valproic acid, once used as an anticonvulsant:

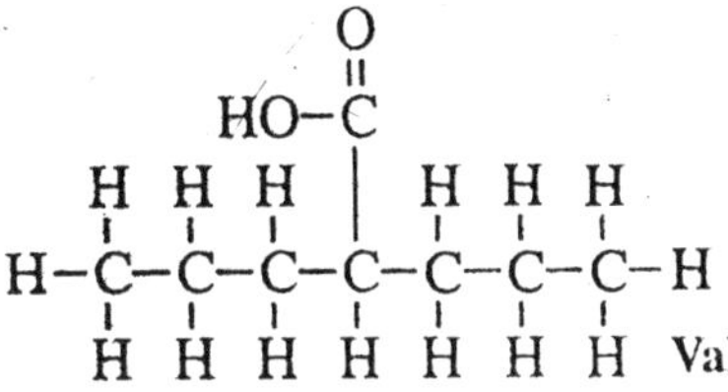

```
            O
            ‖
         HO-C
  H  H  H   |   H  H  H
  |  |  |   |   |  |  |
H-C--C--C---C---C--C--C-H
  |  |  |   |   |  |  |
  H  H  H   H   H  H  H
```

Valproic acid, 2-propylpentanoic acid

Other than ethanol, the xenobiotic chemical best known to cause steatosis is carbon tetrachloride, CCl_4. This compound was once widely used in industry as a solvent, and even in consumer items as a stain remover. It is converted by enzymatic action in the liver to $Cl_3C\cdot$ radical, then by reaction with O_2 to $Cl_3COO\cdot$ radical, which reacts with unsaturated lipids in the liver to cause fatty liver.

The general term hepatitis is used to describe conditions under which the liver becomes inflamed when liver cells that are damaged by a toxic substance, a substance that causes an immune response, or disease die, and their remnants are released to liver tissue. A number of toxicants can cause liver cell death. This is most damaging when it occurs through necrosis of liver cells, in which they rupture and leave remnants in the vicinity, which can lead to inflammation and other adverse effects. Dimethylformamide is a xenobiotic industrial chemical known to cause liver cell death.

A more orderly type of cell death is apoptosis, in which the cells become encapsulated and are systematically removed from the organ. This essential housekeeping function is accomplished in the iiver by special cells called *Kupffer* cells. These cells perform *phagocytosis*, in which a solid particle, such as a cell remnant or other foreign matter in the liver, becomes encapsulated in a plasma membrane and incorporated into the Kupffer cell, which is then eliminated.

Reduced bile output can result in an accumulation of bilirubin, a dark-colored pigment produced by the breakdown of blood heme. When this product is not discharged at a sufficient rate with bile, it accumulates in skin and eyes, giving the characteristic sickly color of jaundice. Impaired production and excretion of bile is known as *canalicular choleostasis*. It can be caused by a number of xenobiotic substances, such as chlorpromazine. Reduced bile output can also result from damage to bile ducts. Methylene dianiline used in epoxy resins is known to harm bile ducts.

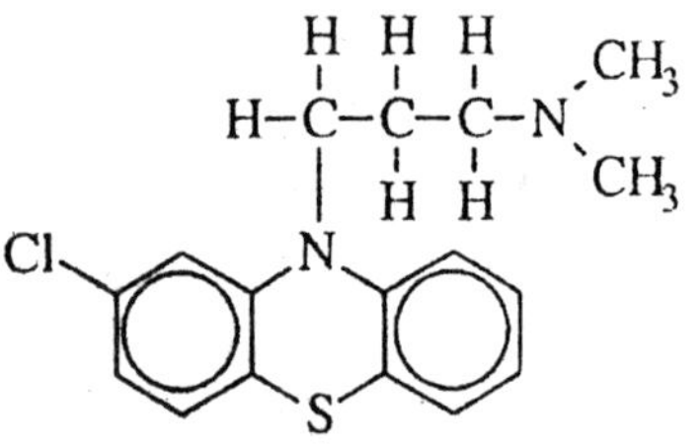

Chlorpromazine 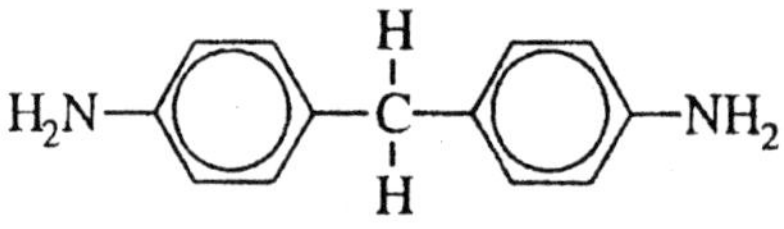 **Methylene dianiline**

Cirrhosis, which was mentioned in connection with chronic alcoholism above, is an often fatal end result of liver damage. It is often the result of repeated exposure to toxic agents, such as occurs with alcohol imbibed by heavy drinkers. Cirrhosis is characterized by deposition and buildup of fibrous collagen tissue, which replaces active liver cells and eventually forms barriers in the liver that prevent it from functioning.

Liver tumors have been directly attributed to exposure to some toxicants. Androgens (associated with male sex hormones), aflatoxins, arsenic, and thorium dioxide (administered as a suspension to many patients between 1920 and 1950 as a radioactive contrast agent for diagnostic purposes) are known to cause liver cancer.

Arguably the most clearly documented human carcinogen is vinyl chloride, which has been shown to cause a type of liver tumor called *hemangiosarcoma*, which is virtually unobserved except in workers heavily exposed to vinyl chloride. Up until about 1970, workers were exposed to high levels of up to several parts per thousand in air in the polyvinylchloride manufacturing industry. Poisoning was so common that reference was even made to "*vinyl chloride disease*," characterized by damage to skin, bones, and liver. It is believed that hemangiosarcoma resulted from the action of the metabolically produced reactive epoxide generated by enzymatic oxidation of vinyl chloride in the liver:

Blood and the Cardiovascular System

Blood is a fluid tissue in which particles, the *formed elements*, are suspended in a circulating fluid medium. When blood is centrifuged, the formed elements, which constitute around 40% of the volume, settle out; the liquid that is left is the *plasma*. The study of blood is called *hematology*.

In considering toxic responses of the blood, it is useful to consider more than just the blood fluid. So consideration is given as well to the bone marrow, where red blood cells are produced; the *spleen*, which is a reservoir for blood cells and which breaks down old red blood cells; and reticuloendothelial tissue, which produces macrophages capable of engulfing and digesting small foreign particles, such as microorganisms. In addition, consideration should be given to *lymph*, a fluid largely derived from blood that accumulates in spaces outside of blood vessels.

The system that circulates blood is the *cardiovascular system*, consists of two major components: the muscular part of the heart, called the *myocardium*, and the network of *blood vessels* composed of arteries, veins, and capillaries. Blood circulation is the body's transportation system that supplies tissues with the oxygen, nutrients and their metabolites, and hormones that they need for their function. Blood carries carbon dioxide, encapsulated dead cell matter, and other wastes away from tissues. Circulating blood is crucial to maintaining body homeostasis, with temperature, pH, and other crucial parameters kept within the narrow ranges required for good health. A number of toxicants have adverse effects on the cardiovascular system.

The toxicological chemistry aspects of blood and the cardiovascular system are very important. Systemic poisons and their metabolites are carried to receptors in the body through this system. It carries phase I and phase II reaction products to the kidney and bladder for elimination. Toxicants can bind to blood proteins. Analysis of blood for toxicants and their metabolites is a common way of determining exposure to toxic substances and generally the most accurate means for evaluating systemic exposure.

Blood

The formed elements of blood are red blood cells, platelets, and leukocytes. Red blood cells, or *erythrocytes*, are flexible biconcave disk-shaped bodies whose main function is to carry oxygen to tissue bound to the *hemoglobin* that they contain. They are generated in the marrow of various bones by the action of *stem cells*. The hormone *erythropoietin* stimulates erythrocyte production in response to tissue needs for oxygen. Marrow stem cells also produce *platelets*, tiny cell fragments that contain the biochemicals necessary for blood clotting. The third kind of formed elements consists of *leukocytes*, which are defensive white blood cells. Blood plasma is a straw-colored liquid laden with a variety of salts, nutrients, dissolved gases, and biomolecules, especially proteins. The major ionic component of blood is sodium chloride as Na^+ and Cl^- ions. Nutrients that circulate in blood include glucose (blood sugar), various amino acids, lipids, lactic acid, and cholesterol. An important glycoprotein (protein bound with carbohydrate) in blood is transferrin, which transports nutrient iron absorbed by the intestine to the liver, spleen, and bone marrow, where it is required to make hemoglobin. Plasma is very similar to other tissue fluids, with which it readily undergoes interchange, except that it has much more protein. When blood is caused to clot before separating out the formed elements, the pale yellow liquid remaining is a fraction of blood plasma called *blood serum*.

The key biochemical species in erythrocytes is *hemoglobin*, a high-molecular-mass protein containing iron for which the formula is $C_{3032}H_{4816}O_{780}N_{780}S_8Fe_4$. The key functionalities on each hemoglobin molecule are four *heme* groups in which iron(II) is bound with four N atoms. These groups bind with oxygen and carry it to tissues as the blood erythrocytes circulate.

Hypoxia

Hypoxia is the general term given to tissue deprivation of oxygen. Toxicants can cause hypoxia by several mechanisms. There are several categories of hypoxia. *Stagnant hypoxia* is a lowered flow of blood, which can result from reduced pumping efficiency of the heart or *vasodilation*, in which the walls of blood vessels are caused to relax, lowering blood pressure and flow. When blood flow is normal, hypoxia can also occur if there is a reduced capacity of the blood to carry oxygen, a condition called *anemic hypoxia*. *Histotoxic hypoxia* occurs when oxygen is delivered normally to tissue, but the tissue has a reduced ability to utilize oxygen.

A common cause of anemic hypoxia is competitive binding on the heme sites for oxygen, usually the result of exposure to carbon monoxide, CO. Carbon monoxide has a greater affinity for the iron(II) on heme sites than does molecular oxygen, forming a stable complex called *carboxyhemoglobin* in preference to the oxygen-bound *oxyhemoglobin*.

The other major cause of anemic hypoxia from chemical exposure is *methemoglobinemia*, in which the iron(II) in hemoglobin is oxidized to iron(III). The methemoglobin product is a dark-colored substance in which the iron does not preferentially bind molecular oxygen, binding with OH^- or Cl^- ions instead, so methemoglobin does not carry oxygen and the poisoning victim may die of oxygen deprivation. Nitrite ion, NO_2^-, aniline, and nitrobenzene are toxicants that can cause methemoglobinemia. Hypoxia can be the long-term result of reduction of blood cell formation in bone marrow. Some toxicants reduce the production of both erythrocytes and leukocytes in marrow, resulting in a condition called *aplastic anemia*. Exposure to benzene can cause this condition. The major biochemical effect of toxic lead is interference with the process by which heme is synthesized.

Though not strictly a blood malady, histotoxic hypoxia deprives tissue of oxygen, even when it is delivered by blood, by preventing its utilization. The most common toxicant that causes histotoxic hypoxia is hydrogen cyanide, which binds strongly to the iron(III) form of the endogenous cytochrome species involved in molecular oxygen utilization, so that it cannot be reduced back to iron(II) in the electron transfer processes involved with O_2 utilization in tissue. Interestingly, an antidote to cyanide poisoning (if given rapidly in those cases where the victim survives long enough) is to administer nitrite compounds that form methemoglobin that has iron(III) capable of binding competitively for the cyanide. Hydrogen sulfide, H_2S, causes histotoxic hypoxia by a mechanism similar to that of hydrogen cyanide.

Leukocytes and Leukemia

Leukocytes are much more complex than erythrocytes and perform an entirely different function. Although they are present in blood and carried by blood flow, they perform their activities largely outside the bloodstream. Their main activity is in defending the body against foreign bodies and agents such as pathogenic microorganisms. In defense against foreign bodies such as bacterial cells, leukocytes perform phagocytosis, in which they envelop the object, resulting in its eventual elim-ination. To defend against foreign agents, such as toxicants attached to blood proteins, leukocytes generate antibodies.

Uncontrolled production of leukocytes is a form of cancer called *leukemia*. Although toxicants are suspected of causing some cases of leukemia, the evidence for such cases is not very strong. However, benzene exposure is now regarded as a cause of this kind of cancer.

Cardiotoxicants

Circulation of blood occurs by the action of a beating heart and is also influenced by conditions in the remainder of the vascular system. Heartbeat involves both electrical (nerve impulse) and mechanical (heart muscle contraction and relaxation) events. Some toxicants can adversely affect these finely coordinated actions. Adverse effects such as *bradycardia* (decreased pulse rate), *tachycardia* (increased rate), and *arrhythmia* (irregular pulse) can result.

A number of pharmaceutical agents have shown toxic side effects involving the heart. These effects usually occur as the result of overdoses or in subjects with preexisting heart conditions. Some common antibiotics used to combat bacterial infections have shown a depressant effect on heart function. Antineoplastic agents used for cancer chemotherapy have caused cases of cardiotoxicity. Widely used 5-fluoruoracil has caused a variety of cardiac symptoms, including severe hypotension (low blood pressure). As might be expected from their potential to affect nerve impulses involved with the function of the cardiovascular system, drugs that act on the central nervous system may be cardiotoxic, causing symptoms such as reduced cardiac output and arrhythmia. Such drugs have included antidepressants such as imiprimine, antipsychotic agents, and general anesthetic. High systemic levels of local anesthetics such as lidocaine can cause cardiac irregularities because of their action in blocking nerve axon conduction. Synthetic catecholamines used to treat respiratory and cardiovascular disorders have caused toxic cardiac symptoms, including heart cell necrosis (cell death).

Some biochemical natural products have caused cardiotoxicity. Synthetic estrogens and progestins have been linked to cardiovascular disorders in women taking them for contraceptive purposes. Various animal and insect venoms and plant alkaloids may have adverse cardiovascular effects. There is some evidence to suggest that anabolic steroids, commonly linked to scandals involving athletes who take them to enhance performance, have caused cardiovascular disorders. (Though not a natural product, another performance-enhancing substance, Viagra, which is used to treat erectile dysfunction in men, has been suspected of contributing to cardiovascular problems, including heart attacks.)

A number of industrial chemicals have been linked to cardiotoxicity. Aldehydes and primary alcohols that can be metabolically oxidized to aldehydes have exhibited cardiodepressant effects. Acute exposure to ethanol has caused arrhythmia. Isopropyl alcohol (2-propanol), a widely used industrial chemical and personal care product, may cause cardiovascular depression and excessively rapid heartbeat. Some halogenated hydrocarbons, including chloroform, ethyl bromide, and trichlorofluoromethane, have been implicated in cardiovascular disorders, including arrhythmia.

Vascular Toxicants

A number of toxicants have effects on the arteries, veins, and capillaries comprising the vascular system. An important factor in vascular toxicity is that toxic substances are transported by blood, which means that they contact the cells making up the structure of the vascular system, which may be adversely affected as a consequence. It is likely that a significant fraction of organ toxicities are actually the result of damage to blood vessels in the organs.

Adverse toxic effects on the vascular system can be manifested in a number of ways, generally falling into the classes of degenerative and inflammatory effects. Deteriorated blood vessel walls may hemorrhage or leak fluid, causing edema. Damage to blood vessels in the lungs by agents such as hydrogen fluoride, nitric oxide, and ozone can cause the fluid accumulation known as pulmonary edema. A common toxic effect is abnormal thickening of arterial walls accompanied by loss of elasticity, a condition called *arteriosclerosis*. Another common effect is *atherosclerosis*, a form of arteriosclerosis in which the inner lining of artery walls becomes covered with plaque produced by the deposition of fatty substances. Cholesterol, carbon monoxide, dinitrotoluenes, polycyclic aromatic hydrocarbons, and amino acid homocysteine have been implicated as causes of atherosclerosis.

The number of substances that have been implicated for potential vascular toxic effects is too great to discuss in any detail here. Of such substances, one of the most well documented is tobacco smoke, which has been shown to contribute to arterial degeneration leading to myocardial infarction (heart attack). Acrolein, an ingredient of tobacco smoke and engine exhausts, is biochemically very active by virtue of its aldehyde group in close proximity to a carbon–carbon double bond and is thought to be involved in damage to vascular cells. Allylamine is a reactive, unsaturated amine that has been implicated in arterial hypertrophy (enlargement), hemorrhage of lung alveoli, and pulmo-nary (lung) edema, probably associated with damage to blood vessels. These toxic effects are believed to be the result of metabolic conversion of allylamine to acrolein.

$$\mathrm{H_2C{=}CH{-}C({=}O){-}H}$$

Acrolein

$$\mathrm{H_2C{=}CH{-}CH_2{-}NH_2}$$

Allylamine

Arsenic has been implicated as a cause of arteriosclerosis. Blackfoot disease, a malady suffered in areas of Taiwan having high soil and water levels of arsenic, is a very severe form of arterio-sclerosis. Dilation of arteries and capillaries is a symptom of acute arsenic poisoning.

Immune System

The *immune system* is the body's defense against biological systems that would harm it. The most obvious of these consist of *infectious agents*, such as viruses or bacteria. Also included are *neoplastic cells*, which give rise to cancerous tissue. The immune system produces *immunoglobin*, a substance consisting of proteins bound to carbohydrates. This material functions as *antibodies* against *immunogen* or *antigen* macromolecules of polysaccharides, nucleic acids, or proteins characteristic of invasive foreign virus, bacteria, or other biological materials. The cells that the immune system uses to provide protection are called *leukocytes*.

The immune system response to toxicants is called *immunogenesis* and can occur in several ways. *Immunosuppression* occurs when the body's natural defense mechanisms are impaired by agents such as toxicants. Radiation and drugs such as chemotherapeutic agents, anticonvulsants, and corticosteroids can have immunosuppressive effects. Immunosuppressants are deliberately used to prevent rejection of transplanted organs. In some cases, toxicants adversely alter the mechanisms by which the immune system defends the body against pathogens and neoplastic cells. Another effect of toxicants on the immune system occurs through the loss of its ability to control proliferation of cells, resulting in leukemia or lymphoma.

Foreign agents can cause the immune system to overreact with an extreme, self-destructive response, called *allergy* or *hypersensitivity*, that can be quite severe or even fatal. *Chemical allergy* occurs after the subject has been exposed to a substance and developed a sensitivity to it. Allergic reactions develop to large molecules, much larger than those of common synthetic substances. Therefore, chemical allergy develops after the foreign agents or their metabolites, called *haptens*, become associated with large molecules endogenous to the body. Among the many substances that cause allergy are metals (beryllium, chromium, nickel), penicillin, formaldehyde, pesticides, food additives, resins, and plasticizers. Allergic reactions may range from minor skin irritation to rapidly fatal anaphylactic shock. Allergies are most commonly expressed in humans by skin conditions, such as dermatitis, and by conjunctivitis of the eye. A particular concern is potentially fatal chemically induced asthma manifested by severe bronchiolar constriction.

Uncontrolled proliferation is another immune system disfunction that can occur. It may be manifested by lymphoma, leukemia, or related conditions.

In some cases, xenobiotic compounds adversely alter *host defense mechanisms*. This may reduce the body's ability to resist pathogenic bacteria or viruses or to combat neoplasia (tumor tissue).

Autoimmunity develops as a condition in which the body develops an allergic response to its own biomolecules. What essentially occurs is that to a degree it loses the ability to distinguish foreign antigens from its own antigens. Several important diseases are caused by autoimmune response, including rheumatoid arthritis and systemic lupus erythematosus. Binding of xenobiotic molecules to body proteins can induce autoimmunity. Chemicals that have been so implicated include heavy metals, hydrazine, epoxy resins, and chlorinated ethylene compounds.

A variety of chemical and therapeutic agents are known to cause allergic reactions in susceptible individuals. Several prominent examples of these are the following:

1. Formaldehyde, used in a large number of consumer products, resins, and wood products. This agent causes type I hypersensitivity manifested by respiratory symptoms, including rhinitis, bronchial asthma, and asthmatic bronchitis.
2. Trimellitic anhydride, used in chemical synthesis. Type II hypersensitivity manifested by adverse effects on blood, including hemolytic anemia and bone marrow depression, may be caused by exposure to trimellitic anhydride. This agent may also cause type III hypersensitivity, resulting from deposition of antigen–antibody complexes in tissue and causing symptoms such as rheumatoid disease or pneumonitis.
3. A variety of agents, including antibiotic penicillin, beryllium, mercaptobenzothiazole, phthalic anhydride, and dichromate salts, cause type IV allergic reactions, one common symptom of which is contact dermatitis.
4. Immunosuppression can result from exposure to a number of agents, including ozone, benzene, asbestos, silica, nitrogen mustards, and several metals.

Effects on the immune system are gaining increasing recognition as factors in toxicology and in evaluating the toxicity of various substances. There are numerous ways of evaluating potential effects on the immune system. The most modern methods are reproducible and sensitive and have been standardized and validated. One is a two-tier method that makes use of numerous tests made directly on the test organism and on samples taken from it. The first tier consists of relatively simple tests, such as measurements of body mass, blood count, examination of tissue (histology), and ability to form antibodies. The second tier consists of more sophisticated tests, such as the *Streptococcus challenge*, that measure host resistance. Bone marrow evaluations are also employed as second-tier tests.

Endocrine System

Whereas nerve signals represent an almost instantaneous response to stimuli and conditions affecting an organism, *hormones* are chemical messengers that take longer to deliver and act and are involved in long-term regulation of an organism's functions. They are crucial to the maintenance of homeostasis. Hormones are produced largely by special glands called *endocrine glands*, as well as by some tissues that are not part of such glands. Hormones are secreted by *endocrine cells*, enter the bloodstream, and are carried to *target cells*, where they have some sort of effect. Binding of hormone molecules to target cells can cause developmental, physiological, or behavioral responses.

The endocrine glands and the hormones that they produce are essential in determining development, growth, reproduction, and behavior of organisms. In humans they regulate many crucial metabolic and biochemical functions, including blood glucose levels, blood pressure, brain function, and nervous system response. These systems are obviously of crucial importance in maintaining human health and well-being, and any toxicological threats to their function are potentially quite serious.

Toxicants can affect the endocrine system in several ways. Those that impair the function of specific endocrine glands lower or stop the production of essential hormones. Carcinogens that harm endocrine glands would clearly have such an effect. Excessive stimulation of endocrine glands by exposure to toxicants has the potential to result in overproduction of hormones with detrimental effects.

Many chemicals are suspected of being *endocrine disruptors*. Such substances mimic the action of natural hormones, tricking the body into thinking that they are hormonal. In so doing, they may cause excessive action of the natural hormones or may act in an improper manner, thus having some sort of toxic effect. The greatest concern with endocrine disruptors is with reproductive effects and sexual development. But there is also concern that they may increase risk of some kinds of cancer, vascular disease, and diabetes.

Endocrine disruptors may act by binding to hormone receptors, such as steroid receptors, thereby preventing an endogenous hormone from binding with and activating the receptor. Or the disruptor may bind with a receptor and mimic the action of an endogenous hormone, excessively or inappropriately. Whereas natural hormones are released as needed by carefully choreographed action of the endocrine glands, a hormone-mimicking substance is introduced by exposure through food or other sources. Another potential mode of action of endocrine disruptors is that they bind to a receptor without blocking binding of the endogenous hormone, but prevent the activated receptor from properly triggering the signals by which it turns on hormone-responsive genes.

A number of compounds have been implicated as endocrine disruptors. They include 2,3,7,8-tetrachlorodibenzo-*p*-dioxin, polychlorinated biphenyls (PCBs), and some phenolic compounds, including nonylphenol and bisphenol-A:

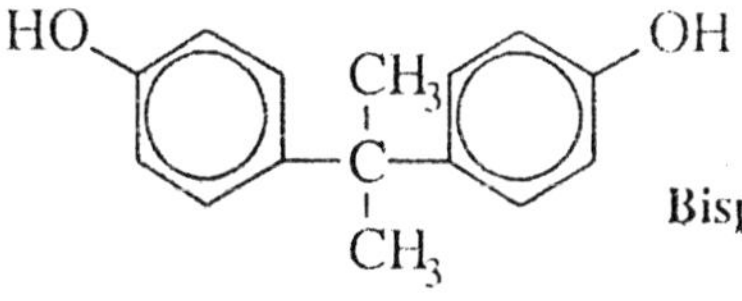

HO, OH, CH_3, C, CH_3

Bisphenol-A

Nervous System

The nervous system consists of the brain, spinal cord, and peripheral nerves. Whereas the hormones generated by the endocrine system discussed in the preceding section direct longer-term activities of the body, the nervous system sends impulses very rapidly to direct movement and response of the body. At intervals that are generally of slightly less than 1 sec, a sequence of nerve impulses directs the heart to beat from before birth to death, 24 h each day, 7 days of the week. If just a few of these impulses fail, life ends.

The nervous system is toxicologically important because of potential damage from *neurotoxins* that attack it. Beyond that, much of what is known about the nervous system has been the result of exposure to neurotoxins known to selectively attack certain kinds of cells or inhibit certain processes in the nervous system.

In humans and other more developed animals, most nerve cells are located in the *brain* and in the *spinal cord*, which together make up the *central nervous system*. The brain acts to process and integrate information. It is composed of several parts, the "thinking" portion of which is composed of two hemispheres at the top and front of the brain, called the *cerebrum*. This part of the brain is covered with a thin layer of gray matter called the *cerebral cortex*. Information is received to the brain from remote parts of the body, and impulses in turn are transmitted back through special cells called *neurons*. The system of neurons that links the central nervous system with other parts of the body constitutes the *peripheral nervous system*. A single neuron can encompass a very long distance, such as that from the spinal column to the toes. Neurons generally consist of four regions. The neuron cell nucleus and most cell organelles are contained in a compact *cell body*. Attached to the cell body are long, branched structures called *dendrites*, a name derived from the Greek *dendron* for tree. Dendrites carry information to the cell body. One of the dendrites that is normally the longest is the *axon*, which carries information away from the cell body. Axons are interfaced with a target cell, which may be a gland or muscle cell or another neuron. At this interface, the axon is divided into a number of nerve endings, which constitute an *axon terminal*. The interface of an axon terminal with a target cell constitutes a *synapse*, consisting of a specialized membrane of the axon next to a specialized plasma membrane of the target cell and separated by a distance of only about 25 nm, a gap called the *synaptic cleft*. When a nerve impulse is transmitted by the axon, it releases *neurotransmitters* that diffuse across the synaptic cleft, and then bind to receptors on the target cell plasma membrane. There are a number of different neurotransmitters, including acetylcholine, norepinephrine, dopamine, histamine, serotonin, γ-aminobutyric acid, and glutamate (a cause of adverse reactions in some people sensitive to monosodium glutamate added to food).

There is not space here to explain the process of nerve impulse transmission. It is an electrical process and involves pumping of Na^+ and K^+ ions across barriers. It should be noted that there are cells other than neurons in the nervous system, of which the most abundant are *glial cells*.

An important characteristic of the brain that largely determines its susceptibility to toxicants is the *blood-brain barrier*, which restricts transfer of substances between the blood and brain tissue. Brain cells have very tight junctions between each other, such that toxicants and their metaboliltes must move across cell membranes either by active transport processes or by virtue of their lipophilicity.

Brain function is dependent upon ready availability of energy by aerobic metabolism. This energy is provided by *aerobic glycolysis*, the breakdown of glucose blood sugar to pyruvic acid with O_2 as an electron acceptor. Therefore, brain cells and other nerve cells are highly susceptible to interruptions in the supply of either O_2 or blood glucose.

Neurotoxins may selectively attack neurons or even specific kinds of neurons. This can cause injury to the neurons. In severe cases, the neuron cells are killed, leading to irreversible loss of the neuron and associated dentrites, axons, and the insulating *myelin* sheathing around the axons.

The effects of neurotoxins may be manifested in a number of ways, divided broadly into two categories: encephelopathy and peripheral neuropathy. *Encephelopathy* refers to brain disorders, many of which may be caused by neurotoxins. It may entail cerebral edema (accumulation of fluid in the brain), degeneration and loss of brain neurons, and necrosis of the cerebral cortex. Symptoms of encephelopathy include loss of coordination (ataxia), convulsions, seizures, cerebral palsy (partial paralysis and tremors), and coma. Neurotoxins can cause symptoms of Parkinson's disease, which include rigidity, a shuffling mode of walking, and tremor of the hands and fingers. Psychological symptoms, such as shyness, uncontrolled anger, and extreme anxiety, may be symptomatic of damage by neurotoxins to brain tissue. Another effect of neurotoxins can be the development of dementia, characterized by loss of memory, impaired reasoning ability, and usually disturbed behavior.

As its name implies, *peripheral neuropathy* refers to damage to nerves outside the central nervous system. It is especially evident as damage to the motor nerves involved with voluntary muscle movement. Victims of peripheral neuropathy often have problems with movement and are afflicted with symptoms such as "foot drag" or "Jake leg," a malady that got its name from toxic effects of contaminated Jamaican ginger.

Maladies caused by the effects of substances that attack neurons are said to cause *neuronopathies* of various kinds. A number of toxicants cause neuronopathic symptoms. Metals that cause encephelopathy include aluminum, bismuth, lead, and arsenic (a metalloid). Arsenic causes peripheral neuropathy, bismuth causes emotional disturbances, lead causes learning deficits in children, manganese causes emotional disturbances and symptoms of Parkinson's disease, and thallium causes emotional disturbances, ataxia, and peripheral neuropathy. Elemental mercury inhaled as the vapor can result in a variety of psychological symptoms, including emotional disturbances, fatigue, and tremor. Methylated mercury compounds are highly neurotoxic, causing ataxia and paresthesia (abnormal tingling and pricking sensations, "pins and needles"). Carbon monoxide poisoning may result in loss of neurons in

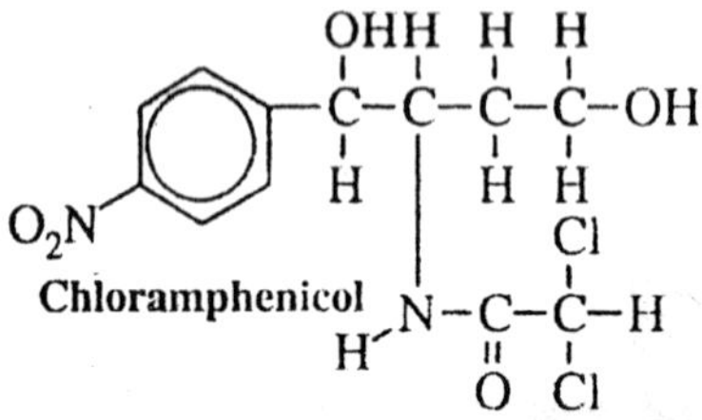

Chloramphenicol 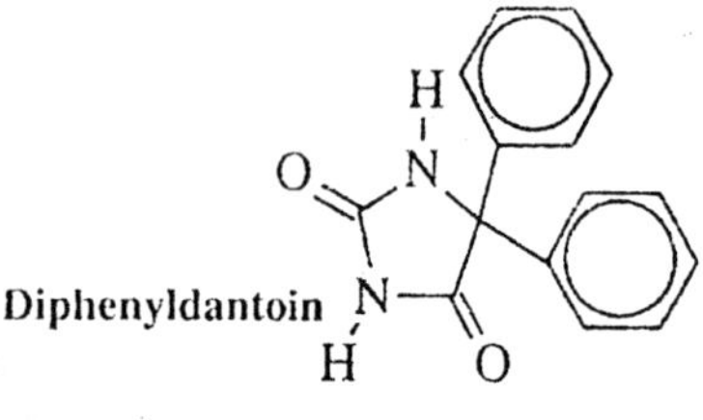 **Diphenyldantoin**

the cortex and symptoms of encephelopathy and parkinsonism. The second most common symptom of carbon tetrachloride poisoning after liver damage is encephelopathy. Victims who survive cyanide poisoning may suffer delayed parkinsonism. Antibiotic chloramphenicol has produced peripheral neuropathy, and pharmaceutical diphenylhydantoin has caused ataxia, dizziness, and nystagmus (involuntary, rapid, lateral eye movement) because of damage to cerebellum cells. Methyl bromide acts as a neurotoxin causing peripheral neuropathy and impairment of speech and vision.

The neuronopathic symptoms described above are caused by substances that attack and destroy the cell bodies of neurons. Another class of toxic effects occurs as the result of deterioration of nerve axons and its surrounding myelin. Symptoms resulting from this effect are called *axonopathies*. A classic toxicant cause of axonopathies is that of γ-diketones, most commonly 2,5-hexanedione:

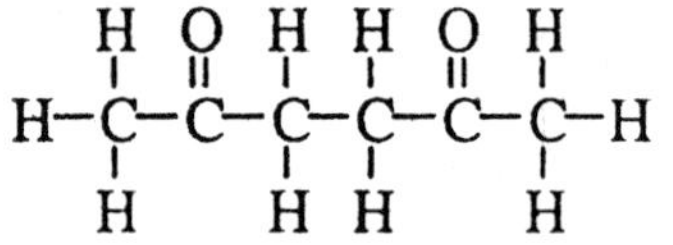

```
   H  O  H  H  O  H
   |  ‖  |  |  ‖  |
H—C—C—C—C—C—C—H   2,5-hexanedione
   |     |  |     |
   H     H  H     H
```

Substances that can be metabolized to γ-diketones, such as *n*-hexane, which is metabolized to 2,5-hexanedione, cause the same disorders. Examples of the many other substances known to cause axonopathies are colchicine, disulfiram, hydralazine, misonidazole, and insecticidal pyrethroids. Peripheral neuropathy is the most common kind of axonopathic disorder. However, other symptoms may be observed. Numerous cases of manic psychoses were produced in workers exposed to carbon disulfide, CS_2, in the viscose rayon and vulcan rubber industries.

Some neurotoxic effects are caused by attack on and disintegration of the myelin insulation around axons. A substance that was found to have such an effect is hexachlorophene, used until the early 1970s as an antibacterial agent for bathing babies. Disorders caused by damage to myelin are called *myelinopathies*.

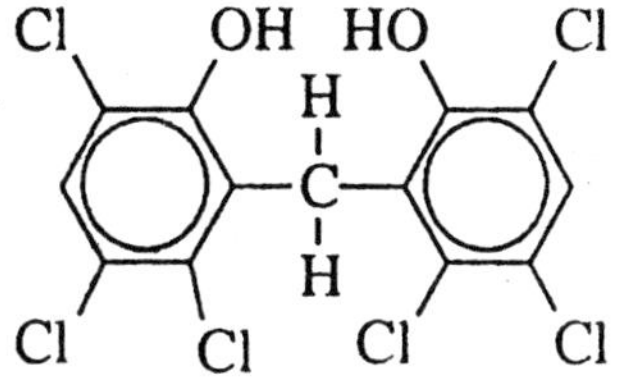

Hexachlorophene

Some neurotoxins do not alter nerve cell structure, but interfere with *neurotransmission*, the transmission of nerve impulses. In some cases, pharmaceutical agents are administered to interfere with nerve impulses in beneficial ways in the practice of *neuropharmacology*.

One of the most common substances known to interfere with neurotransmission is *nicotine*. Neurotoxic effects from nicotine have occurred in children who have ingested nicotine, people who have accidentally ingested nicotine-based insecticides, and even workers who have absorbed nicotine through the skin from handling wet tobacco leaves. The first symptoms of nicotine intoxication include accelerated heart rate, perspiration, and nausea. Later, the heart may slow to such an extent that blood pressure becomes too low. The subject may become drowsy and confused and lapse into a coma. Death occurs from respiratory muscle paralysis.

A particularly devastating substance that affects neurotransmission is the illicit drug cocaine, which blocks catecholamine uptake at nerve terminals. Addictive cocaine is particularly dangerous because it can cross the blood–brain barrier readily.

Some amino acids are called *excitatory amino acids* because of their ability to excite neurotransmission. The most publicized disorder caused by excitatory amino acids is the "Chinese restaurant syndrome," manifested by a burning sensation of the skin, particularly on the face, neck, and chest. This can be caused by ingestion of monosodium glutamate, which is widely used to season some kinds of oriental food.

Reproductive System

Humans reproduce sexually to produce young that are born live. Sexual reproduction occurs when two *gametes*, *sperm* from males and *eggs* from females, each carrying a single set of chromosomes, unite in a process called *fertilization*. The fertilized egg, called a *zygote*, contains two sets of chromosomes, one from each of the gametes. The zygote begins the process of division and cell differentiation that results in an individual capable of living outside the womb at birth. The whole process is rather complicated and can be affected in many stages by toxic substances. Therefore, one of the primary concerns in toxicology is the influence of toxicants on the reproductive system.

The glands that produce sperm are the *testes*. Prior to copulation, the sperm are stored and undergo further development in the epididymis, located on the testicles. For delivery, sperm are incorporated into seminal fluid produced by seminal vesicles, the prostate gland, and the bulbourethral gland, and ejaculated through the urethra of the penis. The process of forming sperm and other male sexual functions and characteristics are promoted by *testosterone*, the male sex hormone.

Whereas healthy males can produce sperm at any time, the production of fertilizable eggs by females is rather complicated. It involves the *ovarian* cycle of normally around 28 days. During the first half of the cycle usually one egg is produced and expelled from the ovary in a process called *ovulation*. If the egg is not fertilized and implanted in the uterus, the endometrium lining the uterus breaks down and is expelled through the vagina, a process called menstruation that occurs during the second half of the ovarian cycle. The egg produced by the ovary moves slowly toward the uterus through *oviducts* (fallopian tubes). The uterus is connected to the vagina, through which sperm enters by an opening called the *cervix*. Fertilization occurs in the upper region of the oviducts. In successful pregnancies, the zygote formed by the merging of the egg and sperm begins to divide in the oviduct, forming a *blastocyst* that becomes implanted in the endometrium wall of the uterus.

Several hormones are involved in the ovulation process. These include gonadotropin-releasing hormone from the hypothalamus, lutenizing hormone and follicle-stimulating hormone from the anterior pituitary, and estrogen from the ovaries. If the blastocyst becomes implanted in the endometrium, a layer of cells covering it begin to secrete *human chorionic gonadotropin*, produced only by pregnant females and used as the basis for pregnancy testing. These tissues also produce high levels of estrogen and progesterone that prevent the pituitary from generating gonadotropins, thus stopping ovulation and menstruation during pregnancy. Synthetic analogs of estrogen and progesterone in oral contraceptives act to prevent ovulation but not the uterine cycle of menstruation.

Various toxicants are toxic to sperm or adversely affect semen quality. Common parameters for detecting damage to sperm include sperm production, numbers, transit time, and mobility. The ultimate measure of sperm quality is the ability to produce pregnancy resulting

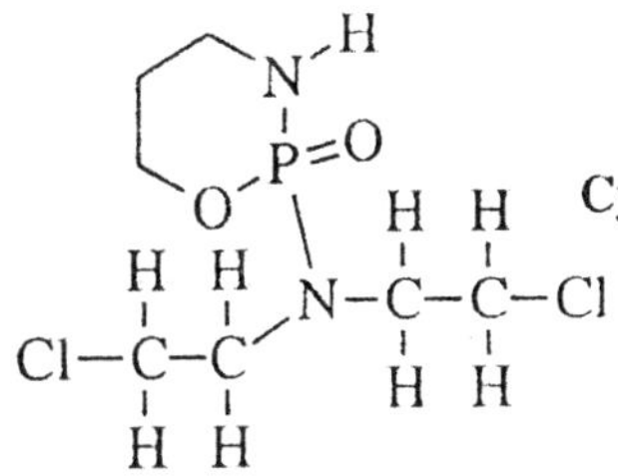

Cyclophosphamide

in normal offspring. Toxicants may interfere with the process of sperm development. In rodents, these include heavy metals (cadmium), hormones (estrogen), herbicides (linuron), industrial chemicals (dimethyl formamide), and pharmaceuticals, such as antihypertensive reserpine. Prominent among pharmaceuticals that are spermatotoxic are anti-metabolites, such as cyclophosphamide, used in cancer chemotherapy. The cottonseed pigment gossypol adversely affects sperm, as does antifungal benomyl.

Some toxicants are known to affect the female reproductive system and processes. Exposure to the alkylating agents cyclophosphamide and vincristine can lead to loss of female sexual function. Cyclophosphamide may attack and damage the oocytes, cells that lead to egg formation. Pharmaceutical busulfan damages ovaries. The 7,8-diol-9,10-epoxide of benzo(a)pyrene, as well as some other metabolites of polycyclic aromatic hydrocarbons, can be toxic to oocytes.

Prominent among toxicants that adversely affect both male and female reproductive systems are endocrine disruptors. Toxicants that mimic the actions of sex hormones are *agonists*, and those that prevent hormonal action or bind competitively to hormone receptor sites are *antagonists*. Male patients treated with cimetidine for peptic ulcers have exhibited low sperm counts and abnormal breast enlargement, a condition called *gynecomastia*. Gynecomastia has also been caused in men working in oral contraceptive production. Ketoconozole inhibits the enzymes required to produce hormones involved in sperm production and can immobilize sperm in seminal fluid.

Because of the complex hormonal cycle experienced by women, it is more difficult to study the effects of endocrine-disrupting toxicants in females. Estrogen-mimicking compounds have the potential to disrupt female hormonal cycles, causing adverse reproductive effects. The classic and tragic case of estrogen-disrupting toxicants is that of diethylstilbestrol, given to pregnant women in the 1950s to prevent miscarriages. Female children of these women developed vaginal cancer after reaching puberty. It is believed that the toxic agent responsible

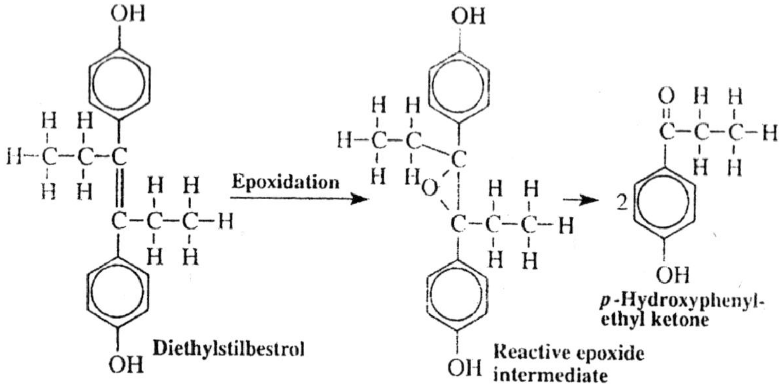

Diethylstilbestrol —Epoxidation→ Reactive epoxide intermediate → 2 *p*-Hydroxyphenyl-ethyl ketone

for the effect is a reactive epoxide intermediate in the metabolism of estradiol that binds with the receptor for the sex steroid estradiol.

The possibility that high estrogen levels may be linked to breast cancer has led to concern that estrogen-mimicking chemicals might also increase the likelihood of breast cancer. Among the possibilities are polychlorinated biphenyls and DDT. Elevated blood serum levels of the DDT metabolite DDE have shown a positive correlation with breast cancer incidence.

Developmental Toxicology and Teratology

Developmental toxicology deals with the effects of toxic substances on development of an organism from conception to birth. Toxic substances may interfere with embryo growth, homeostatis, differentiation, and development of physical and behavioral characteristics.

Much of developmental toxicology deals with *teratology*, the branch of embryology pertaining to abnormal development and birth defects due to exposure to toxicants called *teratogens*. Teratogens can act in a number of ways. Many of their effects are due to harmful alterations of DNA, the expression of genes from DNA, and the processes by which DNA generates RNA in protein synthesis. Teratogens can alter chromosomes, leading to defects. Enzymatic processes can be altered. Other teratogenic effects include oxidative stress, interference with the normal processes of programmed cell death, and alterations in cell membranes.

Teratology is the science of birth defects caused by radiation, viruses, and chemicals, including drugs. Xenobiotic chemical species that cause birth defects are called *teratogens*. Teratogens affect developing embryos adversely, often with remarkable specificity in regard to effect and stage of embryo development when exposed. A teratogen may cause a specific effect when exposure occurs on a definite number of days after conception; if exposure occurs only a few days sooner or later, no effect, or an entirely different one, may be observed. Although mutations in germ cells (egg or sperm cells) may cause birth defects (e.g., Down's syndrome), teratology usually deals with defects arising from damage to embryonic or fetal cells.

The biochemical aspects of teratology are not particularly well understood. Several kinds of biochemical mechanisms are probably involved. One such mechanism is interference with DNA synthesis, which alters the function of nucleic acids in cell replications, resulting in effects that are expressed as birth defects. Exposure to teratogenic xenobiotic substances may result in either an absence or excess of chromosomes. Enzyme inhibition by xenobiotics can result in birth defects. Xenobiotics that deprive the fetus of essential substrates (for example, vitamins), that interfere with energy supply, or that alter the permeability of the placental membrane may all cause birth defects.

Thalidomide

Perhaps the most notorious teratogen is thalidomide, a sedative-hypnotic drug used in Europe and Japan in 1960 and 1961. Some infants born to women who had taken thalidomide from days 35 through 50 of their pregnancies were born suffering from amelia or phocomelia, the absence or severe shortening, respectively, of the limbs. About 10,000 children were affected. The biochemical action of thalidomide leading to teratogenesis is not well understood. Possibilities include adverse modification of DNA and interference with the metabolism of folic acid or glutamic acid.

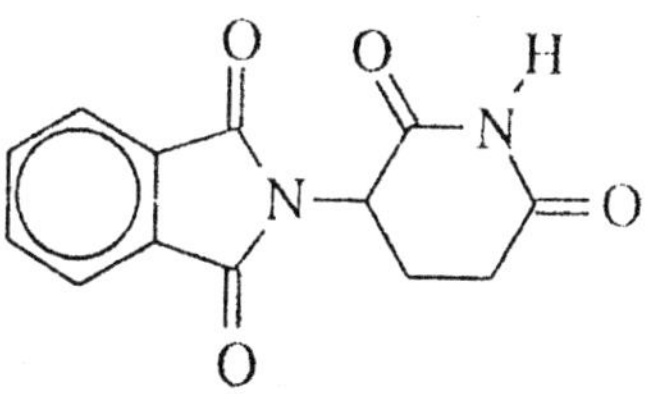

O O H N N =O O

Thalidomide

Accutane

In 1988, the U.S. Food and Drug Administration estimated that *Accutane*, used as an antiacne medication, may have been reponsible for approximately 1000 birth defects in children born to women taking the drug during the period of 1982 to 1986. The chemical name for Accutane is isoretinoin, and it is chemically related to retinoic acid, vitamin A, which likewise is teratogenic at excessive levels. Exposure of the fetus to Accutane over a period of only several days can result

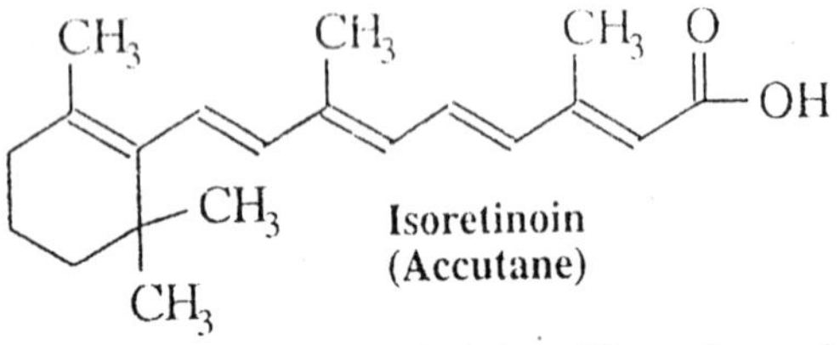

Isoretinoin
(Accutane)

in birth defects such as severe facial malformations, heart defects, thymus defects, and mental retardation.

Fetal Alcohol Syndrome

One of the more common and devastating teratogenic effects is *fetal alcohol syndrome*, which can afflict offspring of women who have regularly and heavily ingested alcohol during pregnancy. This syndrome is most visibly manifested by abnormal facial features, including a very thin upper lip, an upturned nose, and a broadened nasal bridge. The brain is affected and may be smaller than normal, resulting in mental retardation.

Kidney and Bladder

The kidney and bladder are very important in toxicology because they are the main route of elimination of hydrophilic toxicant metabolites and because damage to them in the form of impaired kidney function or bladder cancer is one of the major adverse effects of toxicants. The kidney plays a key role in maintaining body homeostasis. The basic unit of the kidney, through which the organ performs its crucial blood filtration action, is the *nephron*. As the main organ through which fluid is lost from the body, it is vital in the maintenance of extracellular fluid volume. It acts to maintain the critical electrolyte balance in the blood and other parts of the body. It also maintains acid–base balance. It is in a sense the main "filtering" organ for the body's blood, removing wastes and toxicants from blood and discharging them through the bladder with urine while conserving essential ions, amino acids, and glucose. Another crucial function of the kidney is production of the active dihydroxy form from vitamin D_3, crucial in regulating the absorption of calcium from the intestines and deposition of calcium in bones. The kidney produces essential hormones, including renin and erythropoietin.

Though only about 1% of body mass, the kidney receives about one fourth of the heart output of blood. This high level of blood combined with the kidney's ability to concentrate substances in the kidney tubular fluid, from which most of the water and sodium removed by the kidney are returned to the blood, often means that the kidney is exposed to especially high levels of toxicants. Such concentrations have been known to cause deposition of substances such as sulfonamides and oxalates in the kidney, resulting in cell necrosis. Fortunately, the kidney has a good ability to compensate for damage.

Toxic effects to the kidney may be manifested by acute and chronic *renal failure*. Many substances are known to be *nephrotoxic*. Included among such substances are therapeutic agents. Some of these include organic mercury compounds administered as diuretics to increase urine output, anti-infective agents such as sulfonamides and vancomycin, antineoplastic (cancer therapeutic) adriamycin and mitomycin C, immunosuppressive cyclosporin A, analgesic and anti-inflammatory acetaminophen, and enflurane and lithium used to treat disorders of the central nervous system. A number of substances to which environmental and occupational exposure may occur have also been implicated in kidney damage. Some metals, including cadmium, lead, mercury, nickel, and chromium, are nephrotoxic. Some substances derived from bacteria (mycotoxins) and plants (especially alkaloids) are nephrotoxic. These include aflatoxin B, citrinin, pyrrolizidine alkaloids, and rubratoxin B. Nephrotoxic halogenated hydrocarbons include bromobenzene, chloroform, carbon tetrachloride, and tetrafluoroethylene, which is transported to the kidney as the cysteine S-conjugate. Ethylene glycol and diethylene glycol harm kidneys because of their bioconversion to oxalates that clog kidney tubules. Herbicidal paraquat, diquat, and 2,4,5-trichlorophenoxyacetate also have toxic effects on the kidney.

9

INHALATION TOXICOLOGY

The fact that we breathe to survive underlies the importance of evaluating the effects of airborne materials in living systems. The respiratory system is in continuous contact with the external environment while conducting its primary functions: the uptake of atmospheric oxygen and the waste disposal of carbon dioxide. As these vital processes are being conducted by the respiratory system, other materials may enter the body via the lungs. Exposure to airborne materials is inevitable in all living situations and accounts for most respiratory illness.

The lungs are a unique link between the body's blood supply and the external environment. All of the cardiac output travels through the lungs with each cycle through the body. Materials entering the lungs thus have ready access to the internal milieu of the body and may produce rapid biologic responses. Furthermore, materials which can inflict direct injury to lung tissue can lead to permanent respiratory malfunction causing a complete spectrum of pathologic changes up to and including death.

ANATOMY AND FUNCTION OF THE RESPIRATORY TRACT

To understand inhalation toxicology, a brief discussion of the anatomy, function, and physiology of the mammalian respiratory system is necessary. This system can be considered as three components; the nasopharyngeal, tracheobronchial, and the pulmonary. The nasopharyngeal structure includes the turbinates, epiglottis, glottis, pharynx, and larynx, and serves as the entry for inspired air. The walls of the upper pharynx are supported by bone that makes them immovable and incapable of collapse. Stacks of cartilage lined with mucous membranes constitute the nasal turbinates. At this level, nasal hair and impaction in the turbinates serves to remove large-sized particles from inspired air.

The tracheobronchial component is composed of branching ducts, beginning with the trachea and ending in the terminal bronchioles, and serves as delivery ducts for inspired air. Surfaces of this section are covered with mucous-secreting globlet cells and ciliated columnar cells, which form a mucociliary blanket to assist in removal of particulate matter. This mucociliary escalator serves to move inspired particulate material from the bronchi and trachea up to the back of the mouth cavity, where the material may be collected and subsequently swallowed or expectorated. Furthermore, the branching ducts serve to condition inspired air by warming it to body temperature and saturating it with water vapor (the dense vascular plexus in the turbinate area is the primary site of humidification and thermal regulation of incoming air).

The pulmonary component of the respiratory system is composed of alveolar ducts and spongelike tissue with small unit structures, the alveoli. These alveoli function like small balloons to bring inspired air into intimate contact with circulating blood and lymph. The alveolar wall is very thin, composed of an inner fluid and surfactant layer, basement membranes, and alveolar and capillary tissues which separate external air from internal blood and lymph. Oxygen diffuses from the inspired air in the lung through the alveolar-capillary membrane. After dissolving in the plasma, oxygen then diffuses into the red blood cell where, bound to hemoglobin, it can be transported to tissues. Metabolic waste carbon dioxide diffuses from the red blood cells and plasma through the alveolar membrane and is ultimately expired.

A number of simple definitions are worth presenting to describe the physiology of the respiratory tract. Tidal volume, about 500 ml for man in the resting state, is the volume of air inspired and expired with each breath. Respiratory rate is the number of breaths per minute, about 12 a minute at rest, and the product of respiratory rate and tidal volume equals the respiratory minute volume. In the lung, there is a dead space, about 150 to 200 ml in man, which is occupied by gas but does not exchange with blood in the pulmonary vessels. Alveolar ventilation, the, is the tidal volume minus the respiratory dead space. An index of pulmonary function frequently measured clinically is the vital capacity, the greatest amount of air that can be expired after a maximal inspiratory effect.

At the anatomical level, gas exchange can be looked at from the external environment to the body—handled by the lungs. The blood serves as the internal exchanger, and cell membranes act at the cellular level with mitochondria serving the function at the subcellular level.

Oxygen transport is dependent on red blood cell hemoglobin and is quantitatively described by the sigmoid-shaped oxygen-hemoglobin dissociation curve, which relates percentage saturation of the O_2-carrying power of hemoglobin to the PO_2. Two conditions that affect the O_2-hemoglobin dissociation curve are pH and temperature. A rise in temperature or a fall in pH shifts the curve such that hemoglobin binds less oxygen at any given PO_2. The pH of blood falls as its CO_2 content increases, so that when the PCO_2 rises, the O_2 carrying capacity is decreased.

Carbon dioxide is transported in blood and plasma as dissolved CO_2 (7%), H_2CO_2 (negligible), carbamino bound (30%), and HCO_3^- (63%). When dissolved in the red blood cell, carbonic anhydrase converts CO_2 to bicarbonate according to the following chemical equilibrium:

$$CO_2 + H_2O \rightleftharpoons H_2CO_3 \rightleftharpoons HCO_3^- + H^+$$

The Henderson-Hasselbach equation, pH = pKa + log $[HCO_3^-]/[H_2CO_3]$, describes the reaction involved in maintaining blood pH at 7.4. Disturbances in acid-base equilibrium produce states of metabolic or respiratory acidosis or alkalosis.

The importance of unimpaired oxygen transport can be measured in its fundamental uses in the body for substrate oxidation and in biosynthetic reactions. The production of energy via oxidative metabolism consumes approximately 70% of the available oxygen. This occurs only in the mitochondria at extremely low oxygen tensions. Oxygen is also the obligatory oxidant for a wide variety of biosynthetic reactions. These reactions, accounting for approximately 30% of oxygen consumption, occur in the cytoplasm and microsomes of the cell.

Many chemicals interfere with oxygen uptake and carbon dioxide disposal. Materials such as N_2, N_2O, H_2, He, and other physiologically inert gases that decrease available oxygen in the air are known as simple asphyxiants. Serious adverse effects result when the available oxygen concentration in air is less than 10%. Carbon monoxide and cyanide are two examples of chemical asphyxiants which prevent the body from properly utilizing oxygen. Carbon monoxide has a great affinity for hemoglobin, hence reducing its oxygen-carrying capacity. Additionally, the oxygen-carrying capacity. Additionally, the oxyhemoglobin dissociation curves is altered to decrease hemoglobin saturation levels. Clinical signs include headache, nausea, fatigue, and delerium. Upon postmortem examination, congestion of major organs with microscopic hemorrhages and necrotic areas throughout the body are seen. The danger of carbon monoxide lies in the relatively small difference between effect and no-effect levels; concentrations of 0.04% (v/v) produce no measurable changes, while 0.35% for 1 hr is lethal to man.

Another chemical asphyxiant is cyanide ion, which acts by combining or interfering with tissue enzymes containing cytochrome oxidase. Normal detoxification of cyanide occurs by combining sulfur through the action of rhodanase to yield thiocyanate ion. Signs of cyanide poisoning include rapid changes in respiration, blood pressure, and heart rate, followed by convulsion and coma.

Pulmonary Deposition and Clearance

Inspired air may contain toxic materials in many forms—gases, vapors, aerosols, and dusts. Gases and vapors dissolve throughout the respiratory tract, those of high water solubility being removed predominantly by the upper respiratory tract, whereas less soluble materials may deposit more heavily in the alveolar spaces.

The predominant factor affecting deposition of airborne particulates is the size of the particle. The motion of particles that results in their deposition is related to their size, density, and shape. Three independent mechanisms may be distinguished:

1. *Sedimentation*. Particles suspended in a gas slowly sediment under the influence of gravity. The speed at which the particle falls is proportional tot he density of the particle and the square of its diameter.
2. *Diffusion*. Surroundings gas molecules bombard airborne particles, inducing random movement and resulting in transfer from one region

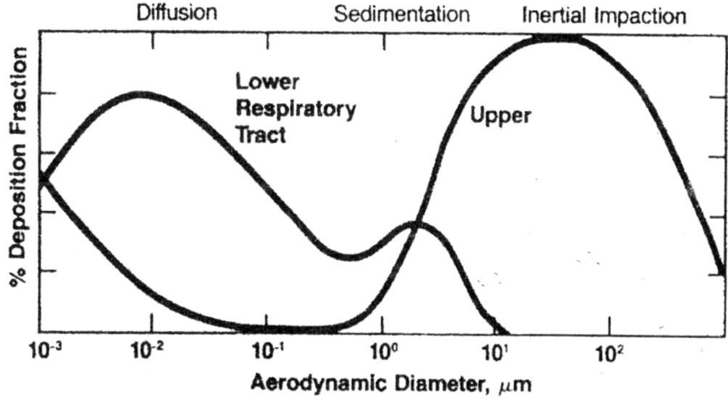

Fig. 9.1. Particle deposition in the respiratory tract.

of a gas volume to another. This property is inversely proportional to particle diameter but is independent of its density.

3. *Inertia*. If the direction of airflow changes, then the inertia of any suspended particle will cause it to continue in the original direction for a certain distance, then respond to the change. This is dependent on the velocity and angle of change in airstream direction, which, in turn, is dependent on particle density and diameter squared.

The branching pattern of the bronchial area has two features that influence the nature of lung airflow and particle deposition. First, the diameter of the airways becomes progressively smaller with each successive division: in man major bronchi have diameters of 1 cm while bronchioles and a alveolar ducts are 1 mm. Thus the chances of a particle depositing in a given time due to diffusion or sedimentation are much higher in a small airway, since it has a greater chance of contacting the boundary wall. The probability of deposition by these two mechanisms increases as the particle descends further into the lung. Second, since the total number of airways increases with each division, although the airway openings are small, the number of such airways is so great that the cross-sectional area is large. A given volume of air thus moves more and more slowly as it penetrates the deep lung. Casarett summarized deposition by particle size and considered particles from 5 to 30 μm to be deposited primarily in the nasopharyngeal region by inertial impacting, particles from 1 to 5 μm to be deposited in the trachea, bronchus, or bronchiolar regions by sedimentation, and particles less than 1 μm to be deposited in the alveolar region by diffusion.

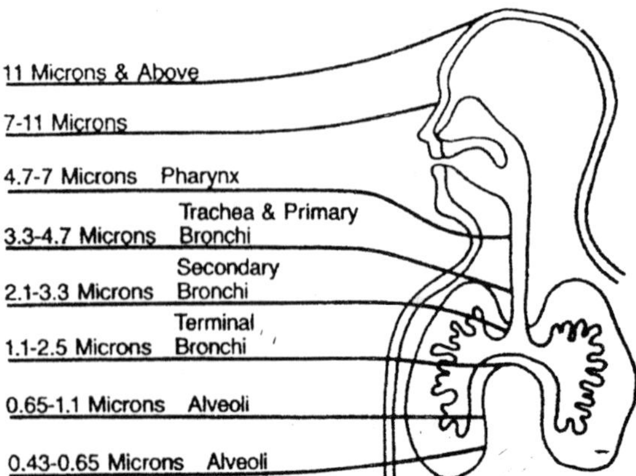

Fig. 9.2. Regional deposition of inhaled aerosols as a function of particle size.

Particle clearance relates directly to the site of deposition. The first level of clearance is at the nasopharyngeal areas. Coarse hairs in the nose filter out larger particles. Another portion of the larger particles is prevented from entering the lung by impaction and collection in the nasal turbinate area. Irritation of the nasal epithelium evoking the sneeze reflex is another common mechanism for removal of particulates from the body.

At the tracheobronchial level, irritation of the epithelial lining and other similar stimuli leading to the cough results in removal of particulate from the larger airways. Cilia, located from the lower pharynx to the terminal bronchioles, beat approximately 1,300 times per minute in man. Over these cilia is a 5 μm thick mucous blanket that moves upward at 18 mm/min. This mechanism allows for clearance of deposited particles. However, agents such as SO_2 can produce an increase in mucous secretion, which slows down ciliary movement, and hence, clearance. Also, the mucous layer itself can dissolve some substances, allowing them to become absorbed into the system.

Alveolar clearance occurs primarily by alveolar macrophage activity. Phagocytosis or fluid suction may bring the engulfed particles to the terminal bronchioles to be cleared via the ciliary escalator. Particles may also be transported to satellite lymph nodes which, originating at the level of the respiratory bronchiole, drain the lung. Particles may be sequestered within the alveoli as part of the condition known as pneumoconiosis. The particles may also be dissolved and transferred in solution to the blood or be bound to tissue substance in the lung.

The clearance rate of inhaled insoluble particles follows one or more experimental patterns. Casarett refers to four phases of clearance, the first reflecting clearance of material deposited in the upper respiratory tract. This phase includes particles deposited in the nasopharyngeal region and is constant and rapid, with half-times of 12 to 24 hr. Phase II is variable, reflecting clearance rates of material deposited in lung parenchyma. The mode of clearance here is primarily phagocytosis by alveolar macrophages. These phagocytized particles migrate to the ciliated epithelium or to the lymphatic system within the duration of this phase represented by a half-time ranging from 2 to 6 weeks. For some materials, a phase III is observed in which the same processes as phase II are operative, but the rate is much slower, with a half-time of many months. During this time, the action of body fluids leads to some solubilization of sequestered materials. It is felt that even the least soluble material shows gradual solubilization, and this process seems to be a reasonable explanation for the major clearance in phase IV, which has half-time values of months to years.

A special note on the role of the alveolar macrophage is in order. The relative toxicity of a compound may alter the ability of the macrophage to participate in the clearance process. Clearly, a cytotoxic material, when phagocytized, may be able to damage or destroy this cell. Silicon dioxide produces a cytotoxic response that results in a collection of particles in a given area; these become less subject to removal and the mass increases with death of cells to become the beginning of the silicotic nodule. This cytotoxic response to foreign materials has been suggested as a possible screen to predict long-term lung reaction.

Macrophages participate in pathological processes that can be classified as fibrogenic reactions (to inhaled dusts such as silica and asbestos), granulomatous reactions (to inhaled organic materials), or reactions of unknown etiology leading to emphysema. The hallmark of the macrophage is its capacity for phagocytosis. Associated bactericidal activity, which is also important, is impaired by silica, cigarette smoke, and/or other pollutants. This phagocytic capacity also accounts for the macrophage being a prime target for inhaled toxic particles. The cytotoxic action of silica results from interaction with membrane phospholipids. Asbestos is less cytotoxic, but induces secretion of hydrolytic enzymes, which may in part explain the observed granulomatous response of the pleura to injected asbestos. This release of hydrolase is also seen following beryllium exposure and may contribute to the pathogenesis of emphysema. In summary, the clearance patter observed is dictated by the type of particle, its size, the distribution, and the physiologic condition of the pulmonary tissue.

Experimental Inhalation Toxicology

The range of toxic effects to be measured includes irritation of the respiratory tract, changes in behavior, illness, pathological change to vital organs or tissues, metabolic disturbances, carcinogenicity, and even death. Protocols to measure the effect of chemical and physical agents following inhalation need careful design. Inhalation exposures are more complex than other modes of administration because of the equipment requirements and difficulty in measurement of applied dose; that is, relating the quantity of material inhaled to that retained. The dosage depends on the physical and chemical properties of the material, the physiologic condition of the animal, and natural deposition/clearance mechanisms. One must also consider that inhalation exposures often result in simultaneous exposure via the skin and gastrointestinal tract.

Animal Model

Since inhalation studies are designed to determine effects that can be extrapolated to man, the ideal subject would be man. It is obvious that testing of human volunteers can be considered only where the toxicologic hazard is already well established. In this regard, accidental human exposure cases should be given consideration, and all attempts to qualitate and quantitate effects or lack of effects from such situations should be encouraged. When extrapolating from experimental animal data to man, factors that need to be considered include the comparative anatomy of the respiratory tract, presence or absence of concurrent diseases or infections, and similarities of the physical, biochemical, and physiological responses. Against this background, selection of the test species is more often based on more practical criteria such as the size and availability of the test animal, the number of animal needed to separate chemically induced change from background rates, and the expense in procuring, handling, and maintaining these potentially large numbers of animals for long periods of time, up to and including the total lifetime of the particular species.

While the choice is never obvious, a compromise for general screening purposes is to use multiple species. This approach has been followed in the testing of radionuclides, uranium compounds, ozone and nitrogen oxides, sulfur oxides, polychlorinated biphenyls, chlorinated hydrocarbons, and organofluorides. For studies in pulmonary carcinogenesis, two species, the hamster and the rat, have been used extensively. Although great differences among rat strains do exist, the rat lung is highly susceptible to respiratory infections. On the other hand, the lung of the hamster is relatively clean, and the incidence of infection is quite low. The mouse is also frequently used as the second species, to the rat, in lifetime carcinogenic bioassays. In the selection of an appropriate animal species, one must consider the background information available on the various species: what, if any, unique functional or structural characteristics the species has which make it a good animal mode, what the anticipated response might be to enable the investigator to employ the correct number of animals and the proper study duration, and finally, appropriate controls. The use of rodents predominates, because their smaller size allows testing of large groups of animals, their relatively short lifetime allows for testing over the entire life-span, a large body of data already exist on these species, and finally, the relatively low cost of acquisition and upkeep.

Study Types

Studies can be described as either acute, subacute, or chronic. While the test duration to meet these classes can not be exactly defined, acute studies generally involve single exposures and measure responses to rather high concentrations, while chronic studies may last the entire lifespan of an animal and would involve multiple exposure at low concentrations. Acute studies are useful to determine the approximate range of toxicity of a chemical. Such data can be used primarily to establish exposure levels for repeated-dose inhalation studies. The clinical signs evoked often allow determination of the nature of the toxic effect. The two numerical values obtained are the ALC (approximate lethal concentration), which is defined as the lowest concentration at which mortality is observed, and the LC_{50}. The LC_{50} is defined as the calculated concentration which kills 50% of the animals within a prescribed time period. Generally, the time period post-exposure is fixed at 14 days, and the exposure is fixed at 14 days, and the exposure duration is 4 to 6 hr.

Subacute studies generally precede lifetime studies and are generally run to elucidate a target organ and to get a preliminary idea of cumulative toxicity potential. Our practice is to expose groups of animals, generally male rats, to graded levels of the toxic dose (1/5, 1/15, and 1/50 the ALC or the LC_{50} depending on the steepness of the mortality-response line), 6 hr per day, 5 days per week, for 2 weeks. *In vivo* observations are conducted daily, both during and following the actual exposure period, and body weights are taken daily. Following the tenth exposure, blood samples are collected for hematologic and clinical blood chemistry analysis, and an overnight urine sample (collected between the nine and tenth exposures) is analyzed. One-half of the rats from each group are then sacrificed and given a complete gross and microscopic pathologic evaluation. Organ weights are taken for the lungs, heart, thymus, spleen, liver, kidneys, testes, and any other organs that appear unusual upon gross examination. The remaining one-half of each group are allowed a 14-day recovery period and then are sacrificed for pathologic evaluation after complete hematologic, clinical blood chemistry, and urine analytical determinations. A variation of this to determine the target organs or target system has been proposed by Calandra and Fancher. An increasing dose regimen is followed until severe biologic effects are observed, providing information concerning minimal symptomatic and minimal toxic doses, major symptoms of intoxication, duration of action, tolerance development or cumulative toxicity, and major organs affected.

Chronic studies are conducted to determine effects of long-term exposures at levels at which acute toxicity is not obvious. We note here again the importance of parallel nonexposed control groups in order to separate background effects from chemically-induced effects. Chronic exposure patterns generally follow those encountered in the workplace, animals exposed 6 hr a day, 5 days a week, for their lifetimes. For environmental agents, continuous exposures of 23 hr per day (allowing 1 hr to feed the animals and clean their chambers) for 7 days per week are conducted. In both situations, each dose group is maintained on a fixed concentration (which is not reflective of the real situation, in which workplace chemical and environmental pollution levels fluctuate widely over any given time period). The choice of intermittent or continuous exposure depends upon the chemical being tested and the situation. Investigators measuring effects of airborne chemicals in confined spaces like a submarine would choose continuous exposures, while evaluation of materials in industrial atmospheres would likely use intermittent exposures.

Drew and Laskin pointed out practical advantages for intermittent exposures that seem relevant. Contaminant generation and maintenance systems are simpler because they operate only 6 or 7 hr a day. Since chambers operate for 6 or 7 hr, more animals can be exposed in a cage. Finally, there is no need to provide food and water during the exposure.

Basic Needs

The special mechanical features for inhalation exposures dictate specifically constructed facilities. Floor space should allow access to all sides of the chamber. Large constant supplies of fresh/filtered air need to be available with controls for both temperature and humidity (fast-reacting feedback systems or continuous monitoring equipment).

Chambers have been designed in many different shapes including cubes, spheres, and circular chambers with an elliptical cross-section. An early chamber design, the Rochester chamber, has a hexagonal cross-section with a pyramidal top and bottom. Stainless steel with glass in Lucite windows are the most commonly used structural materials.

Smaller chambers are frequently used, especially for the acute portions of toxicologic evaluations. The most common is the cylindrical glass battery jar, size ranging from 10 to 50 liters, mounted horizontally or vertically inside a laboratory fume hood. These studies may also be conducted in a 100-liter portable "Rochester" type chamber, which can be placed inside large walk-in hoods during operation. The number of animals needed for the particular bioassay, the amount of test chemical available, and the putative toxicity should help the investigator decide on the chamber type most appropriate for his particular experiment.

The design needs to ensure a uniform concentration of the test material and be large enough to handle adequate number of animals. It is essential that the structural components be nonreactive. Access to the chamber should be convenient with ample provision for viewing windows on all sides of the chamber. An adequate number of monitoring ports need be available to measure chemical concentrations, chamber pressure, temperature, and humidity.

Accurate regulation of airflow to the chamber is mandatory. The large 4.5 m^3 exposure chambers at Du Pont have a positive displacement exhaust pump for each set of 4 chambers. Another practice is to supply an excess of filtered air and tap off the common supply for each chamber. Airflows as low as 10 air changes an hour generally allow adequate thermal regulation, although higher flow rates are frequently used. The total animal volume should not exceed 5% of the total chamber volume, which conforms to thermal requirements and keeps animal surface effects from drastically affecting chamber concentration.

Intake air should be filtered by absolute filters and charcoal prior to entering the chamber and the test agent needs to be removed from exhaust air. For existing materials, common gaseous air pollutants may require only dilution, while scrubbers, charcoal absorbers, filters, electrostatic precipitators, cyclones, or combinations of these may be needed to remove other test agents.

With all chemicals, safety precautions must be taken to protect personnel and the surroundings. Chambers are operated at slightly negative pressure to minimize the chance of external contamination. Situations sometimes exist where double containment maybe appropriate.

Head-only Exposure

All of the preceding chamber designs are used for whole-body exposures. In the chambers, animals are either placed inside containment baskets or placed on racks designed to support animal cages. It is important that the exposure cages be made of nonreactive, mesh materials on all sides to allow proper aerodynamic mixing within the chamber. However, when skin absorption characteristics or unwanted ingestion of the test agent may present problems in interpretation of inhalation (versus dermal or oral) exposures, a system in which only the head or the nose of the animal is exposed may be used. (This is also used to measure the inhalation hazard of materials in short supply.)

The basic design consists in placing the animal in a cylindrical restrainer allowing protrusion of the head. This unit is then mounted into ports situated either radially along a cylindrical exposure tube or at the end of a vertically-placed bell jar. A light coating of silicone grease is used to seal the animal-containing cylinder to the exposure chamber. For larger animals, head-only exposure techniques would involve restraining the animal, such as slings for dogs or chairs for primates, followed by positioning in the exposure chamber such that only the head extends into the chamber. Head-only or nose-only exposures are then a function of the amount of the animal allowed to protrude from the restraining cylinder into the exposure chamber. For certain species, notably the dog and the monkey, investigators have been successful using fitted face masks.

The major disadvantages of the head- or nose-only exposure systems are the relatively few animals can be exposed simultaneously, the animals need to be restrained, adding possible stress-induced changes to those being measured, exposures here are generally limited to short periods of time (although certain investigators have used this technique for extended exposure periods), and thermal changes may occur when animals cannot normally dissipate body heat when contained inside tubes. Sachsse et. al. have recommended that pesticides and formulations in which aerosols need to be generated should be tested head-only to avoid oral and percutaneous exposures. For volatile liquids or gases, whole-body exposures, in which precipitation in animal fur and oral uptake are of minor importance, should be used.

A major limitation of most whole-body exposures is that there are no measurements of the inhaled doses. The exposed animals breathe *ad libitum* with breathing rates and tidal volumes that vary with time and from one individual to another. In many cases, small animals react to agents by altering the normal breathing patterns and/or by burying their noses into their own fur, thereby reducing the inhaled concentration by filtration. This factor may be minimal, as Ulrich and Marold found pulmonary deposition of aerosols in individual and group-caged rats to be essentially identical.

Animals can be exposed by feeding the material directly into the nasal airways. This allows the material to go directly to the animal to be breathed via the normal physiological route without significant deposition on any other body surface, the flow in and out can be readily monitored, and rigid confinement is generally not needed.

The many factors influencing the amount of compound inhaled by a test animal makes it extremely difficult to accurately predict the inhaled dose for an individual animal. This is particularly a problem in pharmacokinetic and toxicokinetic studies, where a quantitative dose is essential. To overcome this problem, several inhalation systems have been designed to expose a single animal to a known amount of compound. One such system fits a rat with a face mask to expose only the nose and mouth area. As the rat breathes, air is drawn into the generating impinger, where it mixes with test vapors and is subsequently inhaled. Two one-way valves prevent mixing of the inspired and expired air, and any vapor not inhaled collects in an expired air trap. Since the rat forces air through the system, it is important that the valves and the trap not impede the normal respiration. To quantitate the dose, it is necessary to establish a generation curve for each chemical. This is accomplished by attaching a rodent ventilator to the apparatus and measuring the amounts generated at various flow rates. Since flow rate and compound generated are linear, exposure is proportional to the respiratory rate. The retained dose can be calculated by substracting the quantity of expired vapor from the quantity generated.

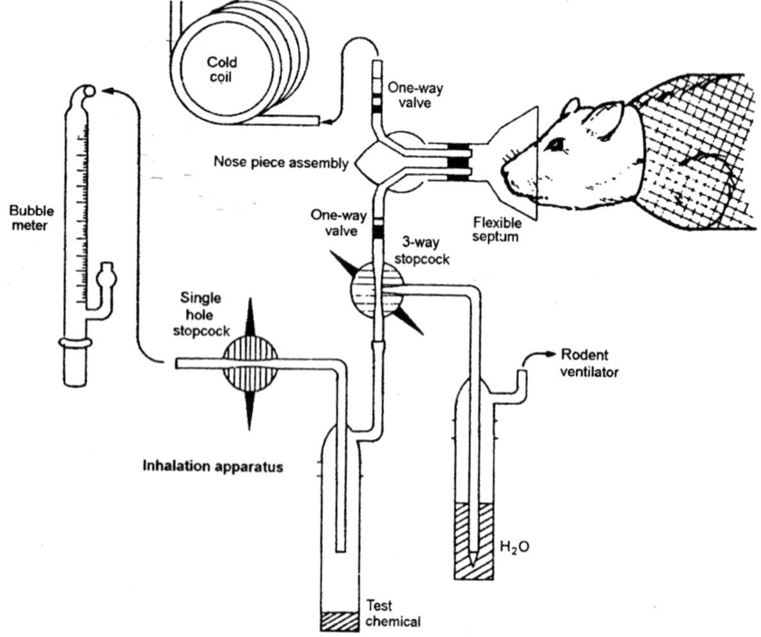

Fig. 9.3. Inhalation apparatus for quantitative measurement of retained dose.

Such a quantitative inhalation apparatus offers several advantages over conventional chamber systems for certain types of studies. The apparatus itself is small, inexpensive, and easily set up in any laboratory. Since approximately 70% of the vapors generated are inhaled by the rat, little test material is wasted, making this particularly useful in cases where radiolabeled compounds are expensive.

This system was used to study the disposition of inhaled ^{14}C-hexamethyl-phosphoramide, while a similar system was used for the inhalation of ^{14}C-chlordane and ^{14}C-heptachlor. In each study, the short exposure times, approximately 15 min, made possible a direct comparison between the inhaled and oral disposition of the compounds. The face mask exposure eliminated whole-body exposure, and the manner of quantitating the exposure allowed compensation for differences in rat respiratory rates to allow exposure to desired amounts of test compound.

It may be necessary to conduct brief or instantaneous exposure to airborne materials. Such would be the case with emergency exposure limits, or when small sample quantities of materials must be pre-equilibriated prior to exposure. Sliding airlock mechanisms have been used for this purpose. One simple design is a drop-away headspace compartment. Here animals are restrained and placed in slots which

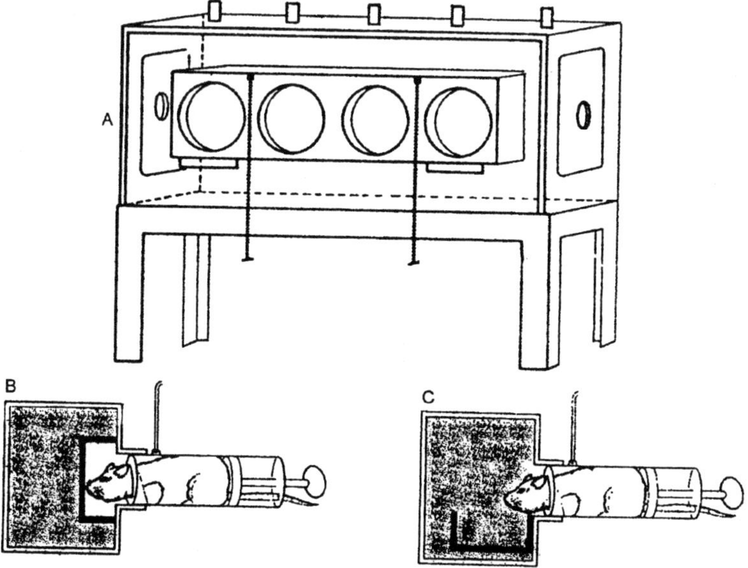

Fig. 9.4. Airlock exposure chamber for "instantaneous" exposure.

allow their heads to protrude into the exposure chamber. Prior to exposure, a headspace compartment is held in place over the head, allowing circulation of fresh air to the animals. Atmospheres are premixed to the desired concentration and the headspace dropped away to expose instantaneously. Such a design is inexpensive and simple to construct.

This apparatus was used to compare irritating and lethal concentrations of stannic chloride. Stannic chloride reacts with moisture in air to form an irritant smoke which has been proposed to test respirator fit on workers. In rats given a 1-min exposure (similar to the duration of an actual fit), marked respiratory irritation and no mortality were observed. At a 10-min exposure interval, respiratory irritation and mortality occurred—more importantly, in overlapping concentration ranges. On this basis, it was decided that an insufficient safety margin existed for general use of stannic chloride irritant smoke to test respirator fit on workers.

Chamber Operation

A well-handled exposure chamber should provide even distribution of the test material resulting in uniform exposure to all animals. Furthermore, atmospheric conditions should remain normal and constant, oxygen concentration approximately 20 to 21%, temperature 72 to 75°F, humidity approximately 50%, with no buildup of vapors from excreta. Two operations modes, static and dynamic, are described.

The static mode is an atmosphere produced by adding a finite amount of the test agent to a closed exposure atmosphere. The major advantage of this is that exposures can be conducted using relatively small amounts of material. Disadvantages are that oxygen concentration, temperature, vapors from excreta, and concentrations of the test agent vary markedly with time. These factors limit the practical duration of static exposures to the short term, perhaps up to 1 hr.

In dynamic operation, the atmosphere is continuously being generated in a flow-through manner. An equilibrium is set up between material being generated and dilution air flow to yield a steadily flowing and constant concentration atmosphere, which may then be passed directly into the exposure chamber. This mode is generally considered superior to the static exposure, allowing greater control of concentrations for indefinite time periods. The time to attain the desired atmospheric concentration is generally exponential in character and is approximated by the equation $C = (w/b)\ [1 - \exp(bt/a)]$, where C is chamber concentration, w is the weight of the agent introduced per

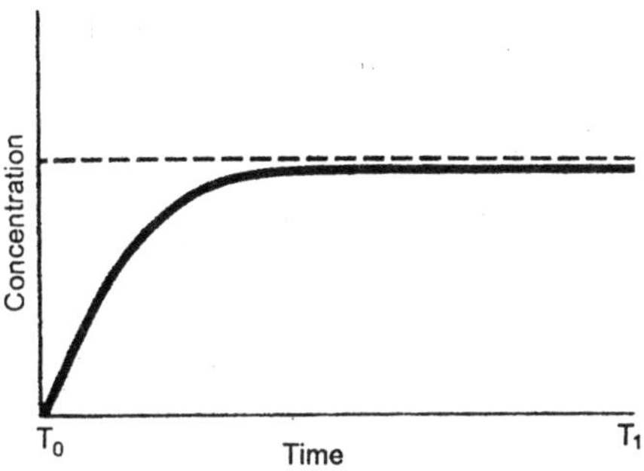

Fig. 9.5. Exponential concentration chamber buildup.

unit time, *b* is the total air flow rate through the chamber, *t* is the time, and *a* is the chamber volume. From this equation, the time to reach 99% (or any other percentage) of the desired concentration can be calculated by $t\% = k \times a/b$, where *k* is constant for any desired $t\%$. Once an exposure is terminated, the concentration will decay exponentially—as it built up. Adequate distribution and general satisfactory performance can be expected with gases with flow rates of 0.1 to 0.2 chamber volumes a minute, for vapors of volatile compounds with 0.2 to 0.5 chamber volumes a minute, and for light aerosols with 0.5 to 0.7 volumes. For dusts and dense aerosols, the flow rate may need to be 0.7 to 1.0 chamber volumes per min.

Dose Administered

Estimation of the dose of toxic agent administered is easiest and most accurate for injection techniques (subcutaneous, intraperitoneal, intravenous), easy and reasonably accurate for oral techniques, less easy and accurate for dermal applications, and most difficult and least accurate for inhalation studies. With inhalation exposures, dose is considered administered if the agent enters and remains in the respiratory tract regardless of absorption since, strictly speaking, the lumina of the alveoli are outside the body and transfer across the alveolar membrane would need to occur to bring the agent into the body. When considering inhalation dose, two problems arise: the animals are exposed as a group, not individually, and they are exposed to an atmospheric concentration of the agent, not given a discrete, measured amount. Thus the actual dose an animal receives is related to the atmospheric concentration, the individual animal respiratory physiology, the duration of exposure, and other factors. Generally, dosage in inhalation studies is expressed as the concentration of the exposure atmosphere and the duration of that exposure: "rats were exposed to *X* ppm of chemical *Y* for 6 hr a day, 5 days a week, for 2 week." For gases and vapors, the concentration may be expressed as percent, parts per million, or parts per billion. For dusts, aerosols (and gases and vapors), concentrations are generally expressed in terms of milligrams per liter or per cubic meter.

Magnitude of exposure to a toxic gas or vapor is often expressed as the product of the concentration (*C*) and the duration of exposure (time, *T*), or *CT*. This product estimates the total amount of agent delivered to the lungs over the exposure period, assuming that the breathing volume remains constant. Haber found the relationship between concentration, time, and animal death to be a constant and the postulate, now known as "Haber's Law," states that the product of the concentration and time of exposure required to produce a specific physiologic effect is equal to a constant, $CT = K$. The specific physiologic effect can be other than death, which in itself may be the end result of a series of differing responses. Two qualifications should be made. There are short (but finite) periods of time during which the physiologic endpoint may not be attained (mortality in 1/10, 1, 10 min, etc., may not be produced at attainable concentrations), and the concept of safe exposure limits for prolonged or repeated exposures would have no meaning if this were valid for an infinite time of exposure. At "no-observable effect" levels, the *CT* product depends on the duration of exposure and therefore, is not constant.

Rinehart and Hatch found that this relationship holds with phosgene in the rat. Low-level exposures equal to or less than 100 ppm·min caused increased resistance to breathing and poorer distribution of air within the lungs. Smith et. al. showed that the lethal effects of perfluoroisobutylene, plotted as *CT*, produced a rectangular hyperbola with exposure times from 0.25 to 10 min, and did allow the establishment of emergency exposure conditions. Kelly et. al. demonstrated that the lethality of the hydrolysis products of titanium tetrachloride, a chemical intermediate in pigment manufacture, expressed as a function of times ranging from 2 to 240 min, was approximately constant, with the LC_{50} at 2 min being 108 mg/liter, and at 240 min being 0.46 mg/liter.

The two deviations from Haber's Law bear restating. When *t* is short, the *C* required to produce the response may be larger, which may reflect changes in breathing patterns at high concentrations where, rather than time, duration of exposure may be better expressed in terms of tidal volume. When *t* is very long, the plot becomes parallel to the time axis representing a threshold, and below this point, exposures, no matter how long, will not produce the response.

Atmosphere Generation

Gases are the simplest atmosphere to generate. They can be metered by flowmeters, syringe drive, or some other suitable technique into a calibrated dilution air stream, allowed to mix, then introduced directly into the exposure chamber. A number of flow dilution devices are available, Saltzman describes an asbestos-plugged capillary tube receiving a constant pressure of contaminant gas which ensures a constant flow. The pressure is regulated by the height of a dip tube immersed in either oil or water.

Vapors of either liquid or solid compounds can be heated by a furnace (care needs to be taken to prevent chemical conversion) or a flask equipped with a heating mantle, and the vapors generated can be passed into the exposure chamber in either nitrogen or house-line air. Another technique, depending on physical properties such as viscosity and chemical purity, is to use an infusion pump to syringe-drive the liquid test material onto a heated surface. The resulting vaporized components are then carried via nitrogen or air into the test chamber. Other liquid materials may be vaporized in a fritted-glass bubbler prior to being carried by air or nitrogen into the exposure chamber. In all the above, the saturated airstream can be diluted with filtered air to the desired concentration.

The generation of particulate materials in a uniform manner is more difficult than vapor generation; these materials may be generated from a dry powder or from a liquid. The resultant particles vary from homogeneous to those varying greatly in size. Dispersions of liquids in air possess a size between colloidal and macroscopic and are called aerosols. Examples occurring in industrial processes include dusts, fumes, smokes, mists, clouds, and fogs. These various forms are distinguished by the physical properties, particle-size range, and source.

The physiologic effect of airborne particles is closely related to their chemical and physical properties. Since these properties are related to particle size, the significance to inhalation toxicology is great. Small particles are generally more active than large particles, and the resulting biologic effects are greatly influenced by the particles of a given size retained by the test species. Models for the study of particle retention and elimination in the lung have been developed. Factors influencing deposition are indicated in general terms with no sharp demarcation between them. The term "aerodynamic diameter"

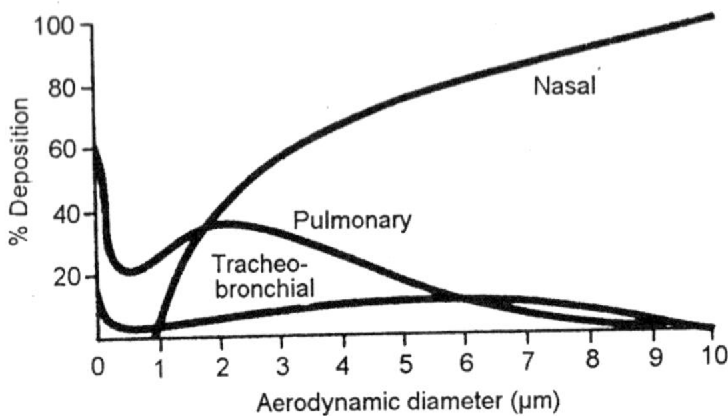

Fig. 9.6. Particle size-deposition probabilities for particles of varying sizes.

describes the behavior of a unit density sphere in air. A particle exhibiting the same aerodynamic motion will be assigned that aerodynamic size regardless of actual size and shape. A detailed discussed of lung particle retention and deposition is given by Morrow.

The special need in toxicologic studies to express aerosol concentrations both in terms of quantity and in terms of particle size should be stated. Size distribution should be given in terms of mass rather than size frequency for each size class. When particles are classified on the basis of their airborne behavior, the aerodynamic mass median diameter, referring to the size of a unit density sphere having the same settling velocity as the particle in question, is used.

The generation of aerosols using dry dispersion techniques presents problems that are unique to each dust being studied. The need in toxicologic testing is for the particle size distribution to remain constant over long periods of time. The powder being tested needs to be dispersed into unitary particles rather than agglomerates. This requires a means of continuously metering a powder into the generator at a constant rate and a means of dispersing the powder. That most materials contain particles of irregular size and shape means that monodisperse conditions are rarely met and that in the generating system, the particle size distribution will differ from that in the original powder.

Simple dust metering systems use gravity feed to loose powder into an air stream, usually assisted by agitators or vibrators. An improvement of this is a turntable dust feed, where the powder is gently and continuously packed into grooves on a rotating disc. The material is removed from the groove at a constant rate by an air ejector. Systems such as volume feeders deliver specific amounts to a reservoir prior to generation. The Wright dust feed uses a scraping mechanism to remove a finely ground powder from the surface of a packed cylinder.

The dispersion of powder is accomplished by supplying sufficient energy, usually as a high velocity airstream, to a relatively small volume of the bulk powder to separate the particles by overcoming their own attraction forces. Hydrophobic materials such as talc are more easily dispersed than hydrophilic materials like limestone or quartz. Dry powders are considerably easier to disperse than humidified ones. The metered powder may be dispersed and agglomerates broken up directly by a turbulent air jet, or the dust-laden airstream can be passed through an impactor or fluidized bed. Elutriators, used to prevent escape of large agglomerates, are useful in dispersion. The importance of clean, dry air to generate particles needs to be stressed by noting that extremely dry air (relative humidity less than 5%) can cause strong electrostatic forces among particles, reducing their dispersibility.

Willeke et. al. describe fluidized-bed aerosol generators that are capable of a very stable output of particles from 0.5 to 30 μm size. This generator uses a fluidized bed of glass or metallic beads (100-200 μm) into which the powder is directly added. The mechanism of dispersion involves the deposition of the particles onto the beads and their subsequent reentering into the airstream following the action of both impaction, as the beads collide with one another, and aerodynamic turbulence. The entire system also acts as an elutriator, preventing large particles and agglomerates from leaving the system. This means of generation can only be used for dry, nonadhering powders, but does produce electrically charged aerosols, which need to be neutralized upon leaving the fluidized bed.

The NBS Dust Generator is suitable for studies where high flow rates are required. In this system, the dust flows from a hopper (200-1,200 cm^2) with the aid of a vibrator into spaces of a metering gear. A spreader plate removes excess material as the gear turns at a given constant speed. Dust is pulled from the gears by a compressed air ejector, positioned to effectively removed the material from the gears. A plate can be fitted at the ejection output to remove large particles.

Atmosphere Analysis

The analysis of the generated atmosphere is a critical part of the experiment. In order to elucidate the effects produced by an agent in a biologic system, the quantitative aspects of exactly what produced the observed change or lack of change is most important. The collection of gases and vapors for chemical analysis using gas chromatography, liquid chromatography, spectrophotometry, or other analytical tools generally is fairly simple. The collection of appropriate samples of particulate material becomes more involved and will be discussed below. In all cases, the distribution of the chemical within the chamber needs to be established by analysis throughout the interior, generally by using a three-dimensional grid and sampling enough locations and intervals to assure the homogeneity desired. Following this, the operation of the chamber with animals (and excreta collecting pans where used) need to be verified.

The number of sampling intervals over a given test period needed to characterize the particular exposure will depend on the type of material and the homogeneity of the dispersed material. In all of our studies of a subacute or chronic basis, each chamber is monitored at least every 1/2 hr. Some materials may be tested at low concentrations requiring collection of larger amounts of test atmospheres for accurate chemical analysis; in these cases, the sampling intervals may need to be extended. Continuous on-line monitoring equipment is available and is a valuable time-saving tool in long-term inhalation testing. Again, from the original chamber concentration profiles, the exact sampling locations can be determined, but should always be collected in the animal breathing zone.

The collection and measurement of dust particles present a number of problems to an investigator. Dusts may be characterized by first collecting, then later measuring the samples, or by measuring samples during collection. Samples may be collected or measured using several methods, including sedimentation, filtration, centrifugation, impaction, thermal or electrostatic precipitation, or by optics. The choice of method will depend on many factors in addition to particle size. Most particulate samples are present as mixtures varying in chemical and physical properties as well as particle size and may be dispersed in a matrix that would interfere with the measurement. Particles can be measured most simply by weighing, by chemical analysis specific for the test agent, or by optical (or electron microscopy).

Impaction is probably most widely used to collect and classify particles. The principle behind this method is that when a moving particles hits an object, because of the initial change, the particle will impinge on the object. Aerosols are forced at high velocity through an orific allowing the aerosol to impinge on a flat surface, which diverts the air while collecting the particle. The size of the particle collected depends on the particle change in inertia. Cascade or multistage impactors function by setting up a series of chambers with progressively smaller orifices to collect and characterize impacted particles. The suitability of a given impactor for sampling depends upon the impactor fiber rate, the aerosol concentration, and the amount of sample required. Multijet impactor is mandatory and that impactor-given-sized particle is low, can be used along with adhesive-coated collection surfaces. Glass-fiber filter papers are effective in preventing deflection, but do modify cutoff characteristics. A multiple, rather than a single, cascade impactor approach is preferred when the aerosol size range is side (size 0.1-30 μm). Rao stressed several operational points; for example, that careful calibration of the impactor is mandatory and that impactor-stage loading affects performance. The lading of the first stage and the final filter and the wall losses reflect the quality of sampling. Pre-cutter should be used where excessive first-stage loading occurs. Excessive loading of the last stage and wall losses indicate excessive particle bounce.

Stoke's law states that the velocity of a particle is directly proportional to gravity, particle density, and the square of the particle radius. If the density is known as the velocity can be measured, the particle size can be calculated. Sedimentation techniques, depend upon gravitational forces, are often used to collect particles. Collection devices here are often quite simple, such as dust jars and sedimentation foils. The latter consist of aluminum or other films coated with an adhesive upon which settled particles may be captured. This method is still used to measure ambient air pollution, but for the most part has been replaced by other methods in toxicologic evaluations.

Filtration operates by interception, initial impaction, and Brownian diffusion (gravitation settling and electrostatic charges may also be involved). Fiber filters may consist of cellulose, glass, asbestos, wool, and synthetic organic polymers. The diameter of the fiber can be controlled to allow particle sizing. However, particles entrapped here may be difficult to remove for subsequent use. Membrane filters are formed of cellulose, cellulose diacetate, polyvinyl chloride, and acrylonitrile polymers with pore diameters from 0.01 to 10 μm. Membrane filters allow for easy removal of the trapped particle, but have a disadvantage in that there may be a rather high pressure drop in the collection system.

Centrifugation allows separation of particles as small as 0.05 μm in diameter, since centrifugal acceleration can exceed gravitation by many times. Centrifugal classifiers force the particles to flow in a spiral motion with movement toward the outer surface occurring at a rate dependent on size, shape, and density of the particles and on the angular velocity of the dispersant gas stream. Particles having the same shape and density will deposit at a given distance along the centrifuge surface, allowing separation and subsequent measurement according to size.

Thermal precipitators operate on the principle that a particle in a temperature gradient will move towards the coolest region; therefore, if particles are forced between two surface, one cooler than the other, the particle will move to the cooler surface. This technique is most frequently used to measure air pollutants requiring long-term collection of particulate.

The electric charge properties of particles can be used for separation and measurement. Whitby and Clark described an instrument in which entering particles are given a unipolar negative charge and then are drawn to a positively charged collector rod for classification according to their electrical mobility. By varying the collector rod voltage, the size distribution of particles can be calculated. The major limitation of this technique is that, at low ranges of particle size, collection is not efficient because so few particles in that region are charged. A piezoelectric microbalance gives the mass of the particle by measuring the change in frequency of the piezoelectric crystal produced by deposition of the particle on the crystal. This has been used in conjunction with a multistage impactor, each stage having a separate piezoelectric crystal.

Continuous monitoring of particles may be obtained using beta radiation attenuation (radiometric) systems. When beta particles impinge on matter, they are absorbed, scattered, or transmitted. The reduction in the incident beam intensity is known as beta radiation attenuation. This is a function of the beta particle energy, mass concentration of the matter in the radiation path, and the electron density of the matter. The system requires an extractive system to collect the particulate sample, since both gases and particulate will attenuate beta radiation. Filters are generally employed, which may lead to errors due to loss of sample in the probe, varying filter thicknesses, flow-measurement difficulties, changes in filter efficiency, statistic of radiation counting, and deviation from the Beer-Lambert law for attenuation. A research prototype for size distribution studies is currently available and shows promise as a useful tool.

An attractive way of measuring particulate size on a continuous basis is either by light scattering or by light extinction. These devices give rapid and precise data, but are very sensitive and are often difficult to control in exposure situations with rather large atmospheric particle concentrations. The total amount of light scattered by each particle increases with increasing particle size. Using a photoelectric counter with a pulse-height discriminator, size distribution can be measured as well as number concentrations when calibrated against a known standard. The usual light-scattering devices are suitable for measuring particles 1 μm or larger, perhaps being sensitive to 0.3 μm. To measure particles in the respirable range, instruments which measure the polarization of scattered light can be employed.

The laser allows a monochromatic light source for use in single-particle aerosol spectrometers. With polystyrene latex beads of sizes to 0.2 μm, excellent resolution with He-Ne laser light was obtained. The applicability of particle size measurements using laser spectroscopy was reviewed by Hinds and Reist who, using computer simulation, concluded that particle 0.03 ´m could be measured where the concentration is 10^6 cm^{-3} or greater and as small as 0.2 μm in diameter for concentrations as low as 10^2 particles cm^{-3}. Although not widely used, holography provides a method of storing the size, shape, and relative positions of particles in a hologram for a dynamic three-dimensional distribution of particles. This method provides a deep field for analysis and is able to handle rapidly moving particles in a dynamic exposure situation, but is limited to relatively large particles of approximately 10 μm.

Light extinction, the difference between the amount of incident and transmitted light, can be used to measure dilute aerosols. The principle here follows the Lambert-Beer law, which relates the incident and transmitted intensities of a beam of light passing through an aerosol to the concentrations of the particles and their sizes.

Quantitation of collected particles can be accomplished by weighing, chemical analysis, optical microscopy, and electron microscopy in modes involving transmittance, scan, or microprobe. With a single particulate as the variable, the simplest operation is weighing which, after selection of the method giving the desired precision and accuracy, gives the percentage by weight of a size fraction(s) separated. Chemical analyses can be conducted using classical reaction methods or by ultraviolet, visible, infrared Raman, X-ray photoelectron, microwave, Mossbauer, electron paramagnetic resonance, microwave and mass spectroscopy, nuclear magnetic resonance, gas chromatography with and without mass spectroscopy, ion exchange and thin layer chromatography, gel permeation chromatography, and X-ray diffraction.

The optical microscope may be preferred when only small samples in the range of 0.2 to 0.5 μm are available. Size distribution measurements here are tedious, but some automation, including flying spot counters, and operating in conjunction with a computer, may relieve this problem. Quantitative image analysis using a number of currently available microscopic systems has been thoroughly reviewed. The optical microscope also allows determination of particle shape which, for some applications, may allow identification of chemical composition. Care must be exercised in the preparation of particle-containing microscope slides to prevent artifact. Particles generally are dispersed in liquid (that selection by trial and error), covered with a slide glass, and observed visually.

Transmission èlectron microscopy has a much greater resolving power, to 3.5 Å with magnification from 100 to 250,000 ×. A beam of electrons is focused by either magnetic or electrostatic forces on particles mounted on a thin membrane supported by a wire screen. Hall describes determination of particle size and shape obtained by shadowing of the mounted specimen.

Scanning electron microscopy focuses electrons onto a very narrow portion of the viewing field and scans the field. The incident electron beam knocks electrons from the surface, those emitted producing a magnified picture of the particle surface in a cathode ray tube. The resolving power is approximately 15 Å, but the instrument accurately reveals particle shape and especially surface features. An advantage here is since the particle surface is scanned, the mounting needs are less critical. Byers et al. describe the application of computerized methods for particle size characterization of atmospheric aerosols.

Pulmonary Function Studies

Measurements to detect functional deficits in lung performance may be useful in determining the time of onset of early function loss resulting from potentially toxic materials. A battery of lung function tests directed toward specific aspects of function is used to determine the extent or magnitude of functional deficits. A key to this approach is the understanding of baseline values or means to allow interpretation of responses as indicative of either lung disease or damage. Pulmonary function testing primarily involves measurements of gas exchange in the living animal.

Various aspects of gas exchange in the lung include ventilation, diffusion, and perfusion. Ventilation is the movement of gases from external airway openings to the alveolar area, involving bulk flow in the upper airways and diffusion in the terminal segments. Diffusion acts via a simple concentration gradient and is the mechanism for gas exchange between the alveoli and capillaries. Blood moving through the lung brings gases in contact with limiting membranes by perfusion.

A few pieces of specialized equipment are basic to experimental determination of pulmonary function. The nonrebreathing valve, with the subject attached to the outlet by mouthpiece, mask, or tracheal catheter, is a means of separating inspired and expired gases. A pneumotachograph, composed of a fixed resistance, such as a screen or series of plates in a tube, allows measurement of gas flow rate. The pressure difference in the tube is measured by a differential pressure transducer with the amplified signal proportional to the flow rate. This is the most commonly used method for measuring breathing patterns and lung mechanics.

Volume changes during breathing are measured by a spirometer. The Tissot type consists of a cylinder sealed at one end, which slides inside a cylinder filled with water. Gas passes through the central core into the space inside the cylinder, which displaces a counterbalanced pen to record volume changes on a revolving drum. Wedge spirometers are simply bellows with a recording pen on one side. The plethysmograph measures breathing volumes and flow indirectly.. The test animal is placed inside a sealed chamber with a breathing part. Inspiration, and increase in lung volume, compresses the air and causes a pressure rise which, through a transducer, is calibrated to known volumes. A second type operates on volume changes and measures the air passing into or out of a second opening in the chamber with the end of a flow- or volume-measuring device.

Intrapleural pressure, needed to determine lung mechanics, can be measured directly by a catheter passed through the thoracic wall or can be estimated by measuring esophageal pressure. Air-filled, balloon-tipped catheters or saline-filled, open-tipped catheters are frequently used. Transpulmonary pressure measures the difference between the pressure above and that at the airway opening. With these tools, a number of important lung physiologic determinations can be made.

Lung volumes are measured by spirometery in humans and by plethysmography or by direct injection or withdrawal of gas by syringe in animals. Functional residual capacity and volume are measured indirectly by gas dilution or barometric techniques. Gas dilution may be done by washout of nitrogen from the lung into a collection device or by equilibration of tracer gas between the lung and a standaredized container. Barometric measurements operate by compressing gas in the thorax to measure the resulting pressure and volume changes. In laboratory animals, vital capacity is determined by inflating or injecting anesthetized subjects using standardized pressure limits and measuring volume changes by either plethysmography or a pneumotrachography.

Dynamic lung compliance, measured at several respiratory frequencies, can indicate uneven ventilation in the lung or the presence of terminal airway disease, Pulmonary resistance measured in this manner reflects primarily upper airway resistance when bulk gas flow conduction predominates.

Forced vital capacity in animals, where voluntary breathing maneuvers are not possible, can be measured indirectly by forcing volume changes. A whole-body respirator can produce pressure changes around the animal body with flows measured by a pneumotachograph. Volume plotted against time will indicate, when compared to either the norm or the pre-exposure readings, whether the change is obstructive (causing delay in lung emptying with no reduction in volume) or restrictive (causing reduction in volume without prolonging expiration, as in fibrosis). Plotting volume against flow helps differentiate between upper and lower airway obstruction or constriction. Normal curves peak rapidly at high flow rates, reflecting the effect applied, followed by a tapering off with a slope dependent on flow limitation in terminal airways. Restriction of flow in the upper or large airway produces a lower peak flow but does have the normal slope. If smaller airways are restricted, the flow peaks rapidly (perhaps lower), with the subsequent slope having a convex shape.

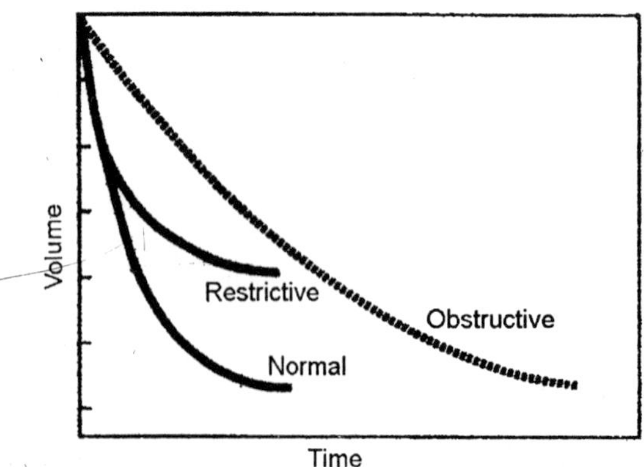

Fig. 9.7. Lung function, forced vital capacity measurement to indicate compromised lung function: volume-time curves.

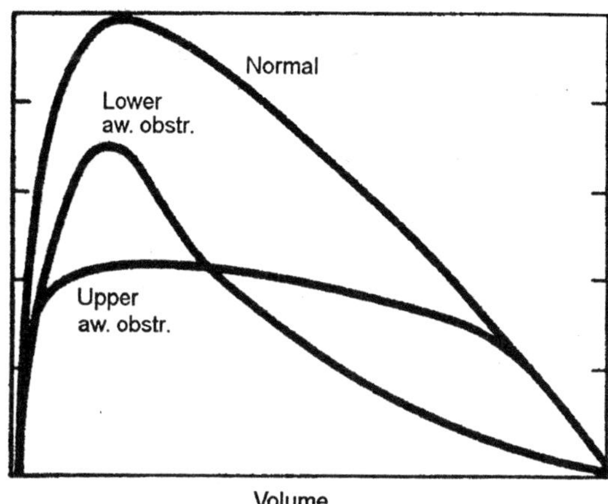

Fig. 9.8. Lung function, forced vital capacity measurement to indicate compromised lung function, lower vs. upper airway obstruction: flow-volume curves.

Distribution of gas within the lung should be uniform, but defects can result in mismatched ventilation and perfusion, impairing gas exchange efficiencies. The single-breath inert gas (nitrogen) washout test plots the concentration of the expired test gas against lung volume to measure lung ventilation. In animals, the breathing movements may be forced with a whole-body respirator or a syringe-tracheal catheter system. Multiple-breath testing can also measure the uniformity of gas distribution and mixing within the lung.

Diffusion across the alveolar-capillary membranes is reflected by the magnitude of the pressure difference across the membrane. Alveolar gas tensions are measured by a rapid gas analyzer at the mouth during spontaneous breathing. This is often very difficult in rodents, since the tidal volume is too small. Capillary gas tensions are estimated by measuring gas tensions in arterial blood by blood-gas electrodes. Again, these are easily obtained from dogs and rabbits (larger animals) but not from smaller rodents. Carbon monoxide diffusing capacity can be applied to small animals as well as large. The animal breathes a trace amount of CO in air, often with trace amounts of inert gases such as helium or argon added, and the volume of CO absorbed per unit time and the alveolar P_{CO} are measured or calculated. Diffusing capacity serves as a relatively sensitive index of gas exchange efficiency in diseases in which inflammation, edema, or fibrosis occur at the alveolar level. In these situations, it is often the most sensitive test of abnormality that can be used without stress or forced breathing maneuvers.

Mauderly and Tesarek describe the application of the nonrebreathing valve with the hamster and measured respiratory frequency, tidal and minute volume, oxygen uptake, carbon dioxide output, respiratory exchange rates, and ventilatory equivalents. The whole-body plethysmographic technique is described by Palecek using the rat to monitor tidal volumes, frequency, carbon monoxide response curves, and interpulmonary pressures. Lewis et. al describe the use of the dog to measure effects of automobile exhaust and include a rather complete battery of pulmonary function tests.

Recently, several new techniques have been developed to assess pulmonary function in rodents. It is now possible to assess the elastic properties of pulmonary tissue, diffusion capacity, and ventilation distribution aspects of the lung. Dynamic flow-volume parameters, blood-gas relationships, and various static volume divisions of the lung also can be measured in approximately 1 hr on anesthetized rodents. With precautions taken to minimize trauma, these measurements may be repeated serially. The assessment of pulmonary function is a useful approach to the study of toxic lung injury and the development of models of lung disease. However, the sensitivity of functional versus classical pathological evaluation in the basic respiratory physiologic phenomena in rodents is not completely understood. They are perhaps of greatest value in following the temporal development of disease in individual animals and as part of a comprehensive diagnostic procedure that includes pathologic observations.

Casto and Drew have developed a series of tests in the rat to evaluate pulmonary function which include measurement of spontaneous breathing parameters (tidal volume, transpulmonary pressure, pulmonary resistance, dynamic compliance), elasticity by quasi-static compliance, diffusion by carbon monoxide diffusion capacity, ventilation (multibreath nitrogen washout, maximal expiratory flow volume), blood gases, and division of lung volumes.

Upper Respiratory Tract Irritation

A specialized test that may be useful for detection of compounds which are irritating to the respiratory tract has been described. The basic design employs a whole-body cuff to transform changes in thoracic cavity volume into tracings that can be used to determine changes in respiratory rate and depth. The screening method for irritants is based upon the reflex-induced decrease in respiratory rate of animals, usually mice or rats, which may occur during inhalation exposure to chemical irritants. Animals are placed in small cylindrical tubes with the head protruding through a rubber dam. The animal is restrained at the back by a plastic plate. The neck fitting forms a relatively airtight seal which, with appropriate attachments, allows the unit to be used as a body plethysmograph. The animal in the tube is then connect to the exposure chamber with the animal head protruding through a hole in the side wall of the cylindrical exposure chamber. Following a period of time in which the animal is acclimatized, the animal can be instantaneously exposed to equilibrated atmospheres, and the change in respiratory rate as a function of chemical concentration can be determined. Each animal is exposed to the given concentration for approximately 10 to 15 min to get an accurate measure of respiratory rate change. This method allows determination of the irritating effects of substances to the upper respiratory tract in a manner that is simple and reproducible. Dose-response curve and minimum effective dose levels can be determined. The method is sensitive and does detect irritating effects at concentrations where no associated pathological modifications occur.

10

FORENSIC NEUROTOXICANTS

Most toxicants owe their toxicities to effects on the nervous system. Certain neurological and mental disorders induced by most poisons can be related to specific defects in synaptic mechanisms. For example, the organophosphate and carbamate insecticides (inhibitors of acetylcholinesterase) are believed to act at cholinergic synapses by reducing the rate of breakdown of acetylcholine. The neurotoxicity (e.g., hyperexcitability, tremor, and convulsions) induced by chlorinated hydrocarbons has been demonstrated to be related to the alteration of functional states of neurotransmitters.

Barchas et. al. have recently described the events of neurochemical function in terms of the neurotransmitters, which actually "convey information between adjacent nerve cells," and the neuromodulators, which act to "amplify or dampen neuronal activity." All of these substances have been termed neuroregulators in that they "play a key role in communication among nerve cells." As in the case of mediating hormone activities, the cyclic nucleotide, cyclic AMP and cyclic GMP, serve as second messengers in the central nervous system in that they "help to translate neurotransmitter or neuromodulator signals into metabolic events." Evidence abounds for expanding the second messenger concept to include mediation of neuroregulator effects.

Due to the development of highly sensitive and specific procedures for estimation of tissue concentrations of neuroregulators and cyclic nucleotides and the activities of their synthetic and catabolic enzymes, assays of neurotransmitters, neuromodulators, and cyclic nucleotides have played key roles in neurochemical investigations of brain functions. This chapter describes some of the techniques available for measuring the endogenous concentrations of biogenic amines, acetylcholine and γ-aminobutyric acid; the turnover rates of these neuroregulators; and the activities of enzymes involved in their biosynthetic and degradative pathways. Methods for determining endogenous levels of cyclic AMP and cyclic GMP and activities of the enzymes primarily responsible for the synthesis and breakdown of these cyclic nucleotides are also described. We have not attempted to be inclusive, but rather to select representative methods. The inescapable fact is that many excellent procedures have been omitted, since all methods currently available could not be listed, much less be selected for detailed description.

METHODS FOR NEUROTRANSMITTERS

Content

The biogenic amines, dopamine (DA), norepinephrine (NE), and serotonin (5-HT), have played an important role as neurotransmitters in neurochemical investigations of brain functions. There are numerous combined methods available for two or more of the biogenic amines. Examples of such methods are those used to determine DA and NE; 5-HT and 5-hydroxy-3-indoleacetic acid (5-HIAA) NE and 5-HT; NE, DA and 5-HT homovanillic acid and 5-HIAA, and NE, normetanephrine, DA. 3-methoxytyramine, and 5-HT. We have chosen to describe three of these methods in some detail.

Method for the Determination of 5-HT and 5-HIAA

Reagents

N-butanol is acidified by adding 0.85 ml concentrated HCl to 1 liter of n-butanol. Ortho-phthaldialdehyde (OPT) 0.004% w/v in 10 N HCl, 0.1% w/v OPT in methanol are prepared immediately before use.

Procedure

Whole brain or cortex is homogenized 10 volumes of cold acidified n-butanol. All other areas (weighing less than 300 mg) are homogenized in 3 ml of acidified n-butanol. After centrifugation for 5 min at 3,00 rpm (IEC Model E), 2.5 ml of the supernatant fluid are pipetted into a 25 ml glass-stoppered tube and shaken mechanically for 5 min with 5 ml n-heptane and 0.4 ml 0.1 N HCl containing 0.1% L-cysteine. The phases are separated by centrifugation as before, and 5 ml of the organic phase are retained for the 5-HIAA determination.

To determine 5-HT, 0.1 ml samples of the aqueous phase are pipetted into 12 × 125 mm test tubes, and 0.6 ml of 0.004% OPT in 10 N HCl are added to each tube. After mixing and heating in a boiling water bath for 15 min, the tubes are cooled in a water bath.

Contents of the tubes are transferred to micro-cuvettes, and fluorescence is measured using a spectrophotofluorometer. Activation and emission fluorescent wavelengths are 360 and 470 nm, respectively. Standards are prepared as 60 μg/ml solutions in deionized water (stored at -25°C), diluted 1:100 for use with 0.1 HCl containing 0.1% cysteine, and 0.1 ml or the OPT solution with 0.1 ml HCl-cysteine solution only. This reagent blank gives the same reading as tissue blanks prepared by reacting 0.1 ml of the aqueous phase with 10 N HCl.

To determine 5-HIAA, the 5 ml of the organic phase remaining after the extraction of 5-HT are pipetted into a 25 ml glass-stoppered tube containing 0.6 ml of 0.5 M phosphate buffer (pH 7.0) and shaken mechanically for 10 min. After centrifuging for 3 min at 3,000 rpm, two 0.2 ml portions of the aqueous phase are pipetted into two test tubes, A and B. To A is added 0.02 ml of 1% cysteine solution and to B, 0.02 ml 0.02% sodium periodate solution. Then 0.4 ml of concentrated HCl is added to both A and B. After this 0.02 ml of OPT solution (0.1% in methanol) OPT solutions are added to tube B. Both tubes are then placed in a boiling water both for 10 min, cooled in water, and read at activation and emission fluorescence wavelengths of 360 and 470 nm, respectively. The reading obtained for tube B (blank) is subtracted from that of tube A (test). Standards are prepared as 15 μg/ml solutions (stored at -25°C) and are diluted 1:100 in the pH 7.0 phosphate buffer for use, 0.2 ml being added to tubes A and B.

Simultaneous Spectrophotofluorometric Determinations of NE, DA, 5-HT and 5-HIAA

Reagents

Analytical grade reagents and glass distilled water are used. Standards: 100 μg per ml of the free bases or acids of 1-noradrenaline bitartrate, dopamin hydrochloride, serotonin creatinine sulfate, and 5-hydroxy-3-indoleacetic acid are prepared with 0.01 N HCl. These solutions are diluted to 2 μg/ml for use in the assay. Acidified-butanol, 0.1 M EDTA1 M Na acetate (pH 7.0), alkaline-sulphite, and 0.1 N iodine are prepared as described by Chang. Borate buffer, 0.35 M, (pH 11.0), and batches of alumina are prepared as described by Ansell and Beeson $NaHCO_3$ (0.33 N) is prepared in glass distilled water. Ortho-phthalidialdehyde (10 mg per 100 ml) is prepared in 10 N HCl.

Procedure

Brain samples are homogenized in 10 volumes of cold, acidified butanol; for samples weighing less than 280 mg, the weight is made up to 280 mg with distilled water before homogenization in 2.8 ml of butanol. The homogenates are centrifuged for 5 min at 800 × g. A 2.5 ml portion of the supernatant fluid is transferred to a 13-ml glass-stoppered centrifuge tube containing 2.5 ml of distilled water and 5.0 ml of heptane. The tubes are shaken for 5 min and centrifuged at 800 × g for 5 min; 6.0 ml of the organic phase are transferred to a clean 13-ml glass-stoppered centrifuge tube and refrigerated for later determination of 5-HIAA. Also, 2.5 ml of the aqueous phase are transferred to a screw-capped test tube containing 200 mg of alumina; 1.0 ml of 2.0 M Na-acetate is added and the tubes are gently shaken for 10 min and centrifuged for 5 min at 800 × g. From the aqueous phase, 3.0 ml are transferred to a clean screw-capped test tube and refrigerated for subsequent determination of 5-HT. The remaining aqueous phase is aspirated from the alumina. The alumina is then washed by shaking with 2.0 ml of distilled water for 5 min and centrifuging for 5 min at 800 × g. The aqueous phase is discarded and 2.0 ml of 0.1 N acetic acid are added to the alumina. The tubes are gently shaken for 10 min and centrifuged at 800 × g for 5 min; 1.0 ml of the aqueous phase is transferred to a small test tube (13 × 75 mm) for fluorescent assay of NE and DA, essentially as described by Chang. The fluorescence is read in as Amino-Bowman spectrophotofluorometer with activation and emission wavelengths set at 385 and 485 nm, respectively, for NE, and at 320 and 370 nm, respectively, for DA.

To extract 5-HIAA, 0.4 ml of 0.033 N $NaHCO^3$ is added to the tube containing the organic phase obtained from the initial transfer step. The tubes are gently shaken for 5 min and centrifuged for 5 min at 800 × g; 0.3 ml of the aqueous phase is transferred to a test tube, and 0.7 ml of the *o*-phthaldialdehyde reagent is added. The tube contents are mixed and then heated in a boiling water bath for 10 min. After cooling in cold tap water, the fluorescence is read with the activation and emission wavelengths set at 360 and 470 nm, respectively.

To extract, 5-HT, 3.0 g of NaCl, 1.0 ml of 0.35 M borate buffer (pH 11.0), and 6.0 ml of n-butanol and added to the aqueous phase transferred after the initial shake with alumina. The tubes are shaken for 10 min and centrifuged for 5 min at 800 × g; 5.0 ml of the organic phase are transferred to a centrifuge tube containing 0.5 ml of N HCl and 6.0 ml of heptane. The tubes are shaken for 5 min of the *o*-phthaldialdehyde added. The tube contents are mixed and then heated in boiling water for 10 min. After cooling, fluorescence is measured with the activation and emission wavelengths set at 360 and 470 nm, respectively. Internal standards are prepared by adding known amounts of each standard to a homogenate pool and running these in parallel with the tissue samples. The pool without added standards serves as a blank for the standards. Calculations of amine levels are based on the standard values by using a method similar to that of Ansell and Beeson.

Simultaneous Determination of NE, Normetanephrine (NM), DA, 3-methoxyryramine (3-MT), and 5-HT

Reagents

For standards, NE, DA-HCl, DL-normetanephrine HCl, 3-methoxytyramine HCl, and 5-HT creatinine sulfate are used. Standard stock solutions of these amines are prepared in 0.001 N HCl except for 5-HT creatinine sulfate, which is dissolved in water. The concentrations of the amines are expressed in terms of bases. Water is distilled and further purified by being run through an ion exchange deionizer.

Preparation of columns

Woelm aluminum oxide, active W-200 neutral, is used without prior acid washing or heat activation. Amberlite CG-50, type 2, 200 to 400 mesh is washed by cycling through the acid and sodium forms with 2 N HCl and 2 N NaOH, and finally with water. The resin is equilibrated with 0.1 M NaH_2PO_4-K_2PO_4 buffer (pH 6.1) and stored as a suspension in the same buffer. The concentration of the resin slurry will correspond to about 90 mg dry resin.

Columns are constructed from Pyrex glass tubing of 0.6 cm in diameter and 9 cm in length. One end of the tube is narrowed to form a tip of conical shape, and the other end is connected by fusion to a tubing of 1.7 cm in diameter and 5 cm in length which serves as a reservoir.

The apparatus for the double column procedure is composed of two column racks made of transparent plastic. The two racks are of the same size, each superimposable on the other. The heights of the racks are adjusted so that the tips of the upper columns will come just to the reservoirs of the lower columns. Using this apparatus, effluents from the upper columns (aluminim oxide column) can flow directly into the lower ones (Amberlite CG-50 column).

Preparation of tissue extracts

Tissue samples (up to 0.3 g) are homogenized in 3 ml of cold 0.4 N perchloric acid (PCA) by use of a Polytron homogenize. The homogenates are centrifuged at 15,000 × g at 25°C for 15 min in a refrigerated centrifuge. From the resultant supernatant fluids, 2.5-ml aliquots are taken and adjusted to pH 7.5-8.5 with 0.4 M K_2CO_3 while cooling in an ice bath. The precipitated $KCIO_4$ is removed by centrifugation at 0°C and the clear supernatant fluid is placed on the doubled columns of aluminum oxide and Amberlite CG-50 for isolating the amines, as described below.

Double column procedure

The tips of the columns are plugged with small pledgets of cotton wool. Tightness of each plug is controlled so as to permit a solution to flow through the aluminum oxide column at the rate of 0.3-0.5 ml. min and through the Amberlite CG-50 column at the rate of 0.1-0.3 ml/min. The cclumns for aluminum oxide are filled with water to expel the air trapped around the cotton plugs and packed with about 150 mg aluminum oxide. Into the column for Amberlite CG-50 is poured 1 ml of the resin slurry prepared above, which forms a resin bed of about 0.35 ml. The columns are placed in a cold room (0-5°C) and washed twice by filling the reservoirs with water. After the columns have been drained, the aluminum oxide columns are superimposed on the Amberlite CG-50 columns each on each by use of the column racks described above. The pH-adjusted supernatants of PCA extracts prepared above are put on the upper aluminium oxide columns. When the level of the sample solution has dropped just to the surface of the resin in the lower columns, 7 ml of cold water are poured into the reservoirs of the cold water poured into the reservoirs of the upper columns for wash. After the columns have been drained, the two column racks are separated, and another 7 ml of cold water are passed through both sets of columns. After complete draining of wash water, NE and DA are eluted from the aluminum oxide columns with 3 ml of cold 0.2 N HCl and NM, 3-MT, and 5-HT from the Amberlite CG-50 columns with 3 ml of cold 0.5 NHCl.

Fluorometric assays

NE. A 1 ml aliquot of the acid eluate from an aluminum oxide column is mixed with 1 ml of 0.2 M phosphate buffer, pH 6.3. The mixture is adjusted to pH 6.3 with 0.5 N NaOH and diluted to a volume of 2.5 ml with water. The volume of 0.5 N NaOH necessary for the pH adjustment does not vary with different column eluates. The mixture is immersed in an ice bath, and 0.1 ml of 0.1 N I_2-NaI is added. This is left for 20 min at 0-4°C to oxidize NE to the intermediates of trihydroxyindole. The oxidation reaction is stopped by adding 0.5 ml of chilled alkaline sulfite solution (500 mg Na_2SO_3 and

200 mg EDTA-Na2 in 20 ml of 2.5 N NaOH), which is prepared just prior to use. The mixture is left for 10 min at room temperature for tautomerization, followed by addition of 1 ml of 2.5 N acetic acid containing 0.01% cysteine HCl. The reaction mixture is allowed to stand for 60 min at room temperature before measurements at activation (380 nm) and emission (480 nm) wavelengths are made. An unoxidized tissue blank is prepared by reversing the order of addition of the iodine and sulfite reagents.

DA. To a 1 ml aliquot of the acid column eluate, 0.1 ml of 2% EDTA-Na2 and 0.1 ml of 0.8% potassium ferricyanide are added. To this mixture, 0.5 ml of freshly prepared 1.6% Na_2SO_3 in 1 N NaOH is added, followed 6 min later by additional of 1 ml of 2.5 N acetic acid. All of the above reactions are conducted at room temperature. The reaction mixture is then heated at 75°C for 20 min and cooled in an ice bath. The fluorescence is measured at 0°C using 330 nm activation and 370 nm emission wavelengths. Unoxidized tissue blanks are prepared as follows: 0.1 ml EDTA-Na_2 and 0.1 ml potassium ferricyanide reagents are mixed in a test tube, followed by 0.5 ml of the alkaline sulfite reagent. Six minutes later, 1 ml of 2.5 N acetic acid is added for acidification. Finally, 1 ml of the sample column eluate is added and the tube is treated thereafter in parallel with the test samples.

NM and 3-MT. A. 1 ml aliquot of the eluate from the Amberlite CG-50 column is mixed with 1 ml of 0.1 M pyro-phosphate buffer, pH 8.4. The mixture is adjusted to pH 8.4 with 0.6 NaOH and diluted to a volume of 2.5 ml with water. After the mixture is chilled in an ice bath, 0.1 ml of 2×10^{-4}M alcoholic iodine is added to the mixture for oxidation to occur. After 8 min, 0.5 ml of alkaline sulfite reagent is added and the mixture is allowed to stand for 10 min at room temperature for tautomerization, as described for the NE assay. After being acidified with 1 ml of 2.5 N acetic acid, the reaction mixture is left at room temperature for 60 min. The NM fluorescence is measured at activation/emission wavelengths of 380/480 nm, respectively. After the fluorescence measurements, the mixture is returned to the original test tube and heated at 75°C for 20 min. The tube is then cooled in an ice bath, and the 3-MT fluorescence is read at 0°C, using wavelengths of 330 and 370 nm. An unoxidized tissue blank is prepared as described above for the NE assay.

5-HT. A 1 ml aliquot of the column eluate is placed in a Pyrex glass test tube with a stopper, to which 0.3 ml of 1% cysteine HCl and 1.5 ml of *o*-phthaldialdehyde (OPT) reagent (10 mg% in conc. HCl) is added with mixing. The tube is stoppered and heated for 10 min at 75°C. After the contents of the tube returns to ambient temperature, the fluorescence is measured at 355 and 480 nm. The tissue blank is prepared as follows: 1 ml of the sample eluate is oxidized with 0.02 ml of 0.1 N ethanolic iodine for 15 min at room temperature to destroy 5-HT. This is followed by the addition of 0.3 ml of 1% cysteine HCl to reduce the residual iodine. OPT reagent is added. This blank is then treated in parallel with the test samples.

Turnover

Nonisotopic methods are considered to be most popular in measurements of turnover rates because of their low costs and simplicity. 5-HT turnover is generally considered to equal its rate of synthesis. The following assumptions are made for the estimation of 5-HT turnover: (a) 5-HT is formed by synthesis and lost by metabolism; (b) the rates of 5-HT synthesis and degradation are equal; (c) the turnover rates of tryptophan and 5-HT are constant; and (d) 5-HIAA is removed from brain by an acid transport process.

The nonisotopic method of Tozer et. al. will be described here. This method is based on the assumption that 5-HT is converted solely to 5-HIAA and that 5-HT is the only precursor of the acid. Accordingly, the following reactions may be written:

$$\text{synthesis} \rightarrow \text{5-HT} \xrightarrow{k_1} \text{5-HIAA}$$

$$\text{5-HIAA} \xrightarrow{k_2} \text{elimination}$$

If the rate of conversion of 5-HT to 5-HIAA is proportional to the level of 5-HT, the rates of 5-HT synthesis and catabolism are the same and are equal to k_1 (5-HT)$_0$, where (5-HT)$_0$ is the normal molar concentration of the amine, and k_1 is the rate constant of 5-HT efflux. Therefore, the rate of 5-HT synthesis also equals the rate of 5-HIAA loss, k_2 (5-HIAA)$_0$, where (5-HIAA)$_0$ is the normal molar concentration of the acid, and k_2 is the rate constant of 5-HIAA loss. Hence

$$k_1(\text{5-HT})_0 = k_2(\text{5-HIAA})_0 \qquad ...(1)$$

After the inactivation of monoamine oxidase, 5-HIAA is no longer produced and its level declines. If the rate of decline is proportional to concentration, that is, [–d(5-HIAA)/dt] = k_2(5-HIAA), then the decline of the level with time is exponential, as seen from integration of the equation: (5-HIAA)$_t$ = (5-HIAA)$_0e^{k2t}$=(5-HIAA)$_0 10^{k2t/23}$, where (5-HIAA)$_0$ is the initial level, and (5-HIAA)$_t$ is the level at time t. A plot of $\log_{10}$(5-HIAA)$_t$ versus time yields a straight line, the slope of which is 1/23 times the rate constant k_2 of 5-HIAA efflux. From Eq. (1), the product of k_2 and $(5\text{-HIAA})_0$ yields the rate of 5-HT efflux, which, in turn, is equal to the rate of 5-HT synthesis.

Animals are killed at various intervals after intraperitoneal injection of pargyline, 75 mg/kg. As the animals are killed, the brains are removed as rapidly as possible and stored in a freezer. Brain 5-HT and 5-HIAA levels are determined as described above. The values for the brain 5-HIAA levels are logarithmically transformed so that calculations of linearity of regression, standard error of the regression coefficients, and significance of differences between regression coefficients may be performed. The values for 5-HT are statistically analyzed in the same manner as those of 5-HIAA, but without the logarithmic transformation.

Catecholamine turnovers are assayed according to Brodie et al. The method of Brodie et al. is based on the assumption that brain levels of catecholamines disappear at an exponential rate after blockade of NE synthesis using α-methyltyrosine, an inhibitor of tyrosine hydroxylase.

The rate of NE synthesis (K) can be expressed as

$$K = k\,(NE)_0 \qquad \ldots(2)$$

where k is the rate constant of NE efflux, and $(NE)_0$ is the normal amine concentration. After blockade of synthesis, the concentration of NE declines at a rate that is proportional to concentration i.e.

$$-d(NE)/dt = k\,(NE)$$

Integrating this expression yields

$$(NE) = (NE)_0 e^{-kt}$$

and converting to $\log_{10}$ gives

$$\log (NE) = \log (NE)_0 - 0.434\,kt$$

where $(NE)_0$ is the initial level and (NE) the level at time t. A plot of log (NE) versus time yields a straight line, the slope of which is 0.434 times k, the rate constant of NE efflux. Substituting in Eq. (2), the product of k and $(NE)_0$ will give the rate of NE efflux, which is equal to the rate of NE synthesis.

Levo-α-methyltyrosine is dissolved in a small amount of 4 N NaOH, and the solution is adjusted with 4 N HCl to a pH of 9 and diluted with water to form a 2% solution. The amino acid (200 mg/kg) is injected i.v. via the tail vein. At various times, the animals are sacrificed. Both DA and NE are assayed as described above. The volume for the tissue levels of NE and DA are logarithmically transformed for calculations of linearity of regression, standard error of the regression coefficients, and significance of differences between regression coefficients.

Isotopic methods used to determine the turnover rate of 5-HT are based on measurements of radiolabeled 5-HT synthesized from radiolabeled tryptophan. Examples of such methods include constant i.v. infusion of high specific activity of L-tryptophan and correlation of the change of specific activity in plasma tryptophan and brain 5-HT with time; injection of labeled tryptophan intraventricularly; and administration of a MAO inhibitor (pargyline) followed by L-^{3}H-tryptophan and measurement of the amount of ^{3}H-5-HT synthesis. Neff et al. developed a procedure to measure the rates of synthesis of DA, NE, and 5-HT *in vivo* in the same group of animals after a pulse injection of tracer doses of radioactive tyrosine and tryptophan.

Related Enzymes

Enzymes involved in the biosynthesis of the biogenic amines (tyrosine hydroxylase, dopamine-β-hydroxylase, and tryptophan hydroxylase), as well as one involved in their destruction (monoamine oxidase), are often assayed in order to obtain additional (and sometimes essential) information.

Tyrosine hydroxylase (TH). Three main methods are being used for the determination of TH activity. The first method was introduced by Nagatsu et al. and is based on the conversion of labeled tyrosine to dopa; the dopa formed is then adsorbed onto alumina and eluted with acid. The radioactivity is then determined using techniques of liquid scintillation spectrophotometry. The second method was introduced by Nagatsu et al. and by Pomerantz and is based on the release of tritiated water from 3,5-^{3}H-tyrosine. The third method is based on the coupled decarboxylation of the dopa formed from L-1-^{14}C-tyrosine. The following two procedures are often used for determining TH activity in small tissue samples of different regions of the central nervous system.

The Dopa method as modified by Coyle

Preparation of tissue. Using a smooth glass homogenizer with a tightly fitting Teflon pestle, brain tissue is homogenized in 10 volumes (w/v) of ice-cold 0.05 M Tris-HCl buffer, pH 6.0, containing 0.2% Triton X-100 (v/v). The homogenates are centrifuged at 10,000 × g for 10 min, and the supernatant fluid is decanted for assay.

Purification of L-3H-tyrosine. Side chain (2, 3)-labeled L-^{3}H-tyrosine (specific activity, 13.5 mCi/mmole) is purified as follows: 1

mCi is diluted to 5 ml with 0.2 N sodium acetate buffer, pH 8.6. and stirred with 400 mg alumina. The alumina suspension is poured over a column of 400 mg of activated alumina and washed with 5 ml of water. The total effluent is titrated to pH 3 with 1 N HCl and applied to a Dowex-50 H+ column (0.5 × 3 cm). The column is washed with 100 ml of water followed by 2 ml of 2N HCl. The tyrosine is then eluted with 20 ml of 2 N HCl. The eluate is evaporated to dryness in a flash evaporator, and the purified L-3H-tyrosine is redissolved in 10 ml of absolute ethanol and stored until use at –20°C.

Immediately prior to an experiment, a portion of the ethanol solution of L-^{3}H-tyrosine is dried under a stream of nitrogen and redissolved in 0.2 N sodium acetate buffer, pH 8.6. After addition of approximately 1 mg of alumina, the suspension is mixed on a vortex mixture. It is then centrifuged at 6,000 × g for 10 min and a portion of the supernatant is mixed with an equal volume of a solution of 4 nM L-tyrosine in 0.2 N sodium acetate buffer, pH 8.6. ^{14}C-dopa (specific activity, 52 mCi/mmole), to be used as internal standard, is purified by chromatography over alumina and stored until use in 0.2 N HCl at –20°C.

Assay procedure. Fifty μl of the supernatant of the brain homogenate are added to 15 ml glass-stoppered centrifuged tubes containing the following reaction mixture: 10 μl of 1 M KPO_4 buffer (pH 5.5), 10 μl of sheep liver dihydropteridine reductase, 1,100 units of catalase in 10 μl of glass-distilled water, 5 μl of 0.01 M TPNH and 5 μl of 6.4 mM 2-amino-4-hydroxy-6, 7-dimethyltereahydropteridine. Blanks consisting of supernatant fluid heated to 95°C for 5 min are run in all experiments, as well as internal standards consisting of 15,000 cpm of ^{14}C-dopa in place of L-^{3}H-tyrosine. The reaction is initiated by the addition of 10 μl of 2.0 mM L-^{3}H-tyrosine, and is incubated for 10-60 min at 37°C in room air. The reaction is terminated by the addition of 6 ml of 0.4 N perchloric acid containing 6 μg of carrier L-dopa.

The perchlorate-inactivated incubation mixture is centrifuged at 1,000 × g for 10 min. The resulting supernatant is added to a 20-ml beaker containing 30 mg sodium bisulfate, 5 ml of 2% EDTA (w/v), 1.5 ml of 0.35 M KH_2PO_4, and 200 mg alumina. The mixture is stirred and titrated to pH 8.6 with 1 N NaOH. The suspension is then poured over columns containing 200 mg of activated alumina and washed with 20 ml of glass-distilled water. The ^{3}H-dopa is eluted with 2.5 ml of 0.2 N acetic acid, and the total eluate is collected in counting vials containing 15 ml of Triton phosphor. Radioactivity is determined in a liquid scintillation counter.

Coupled decarboxylation of dopa formed from 1-^{14}C-L-tyrosine

This assay is based on the differential affinity of aromatic L-amino acid decarboxylase for L-tyrosine and L-dopa. By starting with carboxyl labeled tyrosine as substrate, carboxyl labeled dopa is formed as product. An excess amount of decarboxylase is added to the tyrosine hydroxylase reaction medium, and the radioactive CO_2 preferentially liberated from the dopa formed during the tyrosine hydroxylase catalyzed reaction is collected and measured. Crude brain enzyme is prepared as a 1:10 homogenate in glass-distilled water. The assay medium contains (in a total volume of 0.5 ml): 10 μmoles of sodium acetate buffer, pH 6.1; 0.5 μmole of ferrous sulfate; 1 μmole of $DMPH_4$; 20 μmoles of 2-mercaptoethanol; 1 μmole of sodium phosphate; 7.5 units of hog kidney aromatic L-amino acid decarboxylase; 5 nmoles pyridoxal phosphate; brain homogenate; and 0.05 μmole 1-^{14}C-L-tyrosine (10 μCi/μmole, 1.1 × 106 dpm). The reaction is carried out with shaking for various time intervals at 37°C in a 10-ml Erlenmeyer flask, which is covered by a rubber injection vial cap. A plastic vial is suspended from the rubber injection stopper and contains a folded paper wick and 0.2 ml NCS solubilizer to trap $^{14}CO_2$ formed in the decarboxylation step of the assay. The reaction is stopped by injection of 0.5 ml 10% TCA. Following the injection of TCA to terminate the reaction, acidified medium is shaken at 37°C for an additional 2 hr to recover all $^{14}CO_2$. The plastic vials are removed, wiped with absorbent tissue, placed in 15 ml of scintillation fluid (0.5 g of dimethyl POPOP and 4.0 g PPO per liter of toluene), and counted by liquid scintillation spectrometry.

Dopamine-β-hydroxylase (DβH). DβH is the enzyme that catalyzes the β-hydroxylation of DA in the biosynthesis of NE. The early assay procedures have measured the β-hydroxylated products formed from either DA or tyramine. When DA is used as the substrate, the NE formed may be measured either flurometically or chromatographically. If tyramine is the substrate, the resulting β-hydroxylated product octopamine, can proceed to periodate cleavage, forming p-hydroxybenzaldehyde, which can be measured either spectrophotometrically or radiometrically.

A relatively sensitive and rapid procedure for the determination of DβH activity was later developed by Molinoff et al. The assay involves coupled enzymatic reactions in which the β-hydroxylated product of the DβH reaction is made radioactive by the transfer of a ^{14}C-methyl group from S-adenosylmethionine methyl-^{14}C (^{14}C-SAM). The latter reaction is catalyzed by phenylethanolamine-N-methyltransferase (PNMT), an enzyme with high specificity for β-hydroxylated amines. The final reaction product is separated from the radioactive S-adenosylmethionine by solvent extraction, and its radioactivity is determined. The reaction sequence utilized in this assay when phenylethylamine is the substrate is shown as follows:

$$\text{phenylethylamine} \xrightarrow{D\beta H} \text{phenylethanolamine}$$

$$\xrightarrow[{}^{14}\text{C-SAM}]{\text{PNMT}} {}^{14}\text{C - N - methyl phenylethanolamine}$$

When tyramine is used as the substrate, the tyramine is converted to octopamine, which yields N-methyl octopamine (synephrine) in the presence of PNMT.

DβH assay. Tissues to be used for the DβH assay are weighed and then homogenized in 25 volumes of 0.005 M Tris buffer, pH 7.5, containing 0.1% Triton X-100. Homogenates are centrifuged at 10,000 × g for 10 min, and the liquid layer is removed by aspiration. Supernatant fluid, 200 μl, is added to a 15-ml glass-stoppered centrifuge tube containing the following reaction mixture: 25 μl of 0.048 Mascorbic acid, pH 6; 25 μl of 0.5 M sodium fumarate, pH 6; 20 μl of 0.006 M of the monoamine oxidase inhibitor, pargyline; 1,500 units of catalase in 10 μl of 0.005 Tris buffer, pH 7.4; 10 μl of 0.03 M phenylethylamine; 10 μl of 1.0 M Tris buffer at pH 6; and 10 μl of 9.7×10^{-5} M $CuSO_4$. The reaction mixture (total volume 310 μl) is incubated at 37°C for 20 min. The DβH portion of the assay is ten stopped, and the PNMT reaction initiated by adding to each tube 100 μl of a mixture of 10 μl of purified PNMT, 10 μl of ^{14}C-SAM (1 μmole) and 80 μl of 1.0 M Tris buffer, pH 8.6. The PNMT reaction is allowed to proceed for 30 min at 37°C and then is terminated by the addition of 0.5 ml of borate buffer, pH 10. The ^{14}C-N-methyl phenylethanolamine is extracted into 6 ml of toluene containing 3% isoamyl alcohol by vigorous shaking on a Vortex mixer for 15 sec. After centrifugation at low speed, 4 ml of the organic phase are transferred to a counting vial containing 10 ml of phosphor for determination of radioactivity in a liquid scintillation counter. Blanks consisting of tissue homogenates heated to 95°C for 5 min are run in all experiments, as are internal standards consisting of the reaction mixture and 100 ng of phenylethnolamine. The internal standard is used in the calculation of absolute amounts of DβH activity and correct for any inhibition of PNMT. When tyramine is used as the substrate, the assay is carried out in a similar way, except that 10 μl of 0.03 M tyramine is used as substrate and 40 ng of octopamine HCl are used as the internal standard. After the reaction is stopped with borate buffer, the ^{14}C-N-methyloctopamine formed is extracted into a mixture of toluene and isoamyl alcohol, 3:2 (v/v). After centrifugation, a 4 ml sample of the organic phase is transferred to a counting vial containing an additional 2 ml of tolueneisoamyl alcohol, 3:2. The sample is then dried in a chromatography oven at 80°C. This drying step is necessary to remove volatile radioactive contaminants, which are extracted into the toluene-isoamyl alcohol. After drying, the residue is dissolved in 1 ml of ethanol, and after the addition of 10 ml of phosphor, radioactivity is determined in a liquid scintillation counter.

Tryptophan hydroxylase. Tryptophan hydroxylase occurs in extremely small amounts in most tissues; therefore, its assay requires sensitive radiometric procedures. The following reasons also make the assay of tryptophan hydroxylase difficult: nonenzymatic hydroxylation of tryptophan occurs unless precautions are taken; when radioactive tryptophan is used as a substrate, it is difficult to separate and assay the product 5-HTP; and when the reaction proceeds to 5-HT, the risk of tryptophan decarboxylation to tryptamine and the contamination of 5-HT may be present. There are at least three major procedures which are currently being used. Two are described briefly and one is outlined in considerable detail.

1. Assay using DL-5-^{3}H-tryptophan as a substrate. The assay is based on the intramolecular migration of tritium during enzymatic tryptophan hydroxylation, when 5-^{3}H-tryptophan is converted to 5-(4-^{3}H)-hydroxytryptophan. The tritium atom in the 4-position of the 5-hydroxyindole exchanges readily with H_2O under acidic conditions. Renson, Lovenberg et al. and Gal and Millard have used this assay successfully.
2. Direct measurement of 5-HTP by the method of Freedman et al. In this method, L-tryptophan is incubated with tissue preparations in the presence of an aromatic amino acid decarboxylase inhibitor. The product 5-HTP is then directly assayed by a fluorometric method. The method appears to work well with partially purified and rather active enzyme preparations. However, it may be difficult to use with crude brain preparations.
3. Incubation of tissue with carboxyl-labeled ^{14}C-tryptophan. This method was first described by Ichiyama et al. After tryptophan

hydroxylation has occurred, aromatic amino acid decarboxylase is added, and then labeled $^{14}CO_2$ produced from the decarboxylation of 5-HTP is trapped and counted. This method has been successfully employed by Ichiyama et al. Deguchi and Barchas, and by Knapp and Mandell. The procedure is described in some detail below.

Preparation of enzyme. Brain tissue (usually brain stem) is homogenized with an appropriate volume of medium in a Potter-Elvehjem type homogenizer with a Teflon pestle. All subsequent operations are carried out at 4°C. The crude mitochondrial fraction is prepared from the 10% homogenate in 0.32 sucrose. The particulate fraction is pelleted by centrifugation for 20 min at 12,000 × g and suspended in 0.32 m sucrose to make 3 ml of suspension from 1 g of the starting tissue by the use of the homogenizer. Approximately 1 g of the starting tissue yields about 30 mg of protein in the crude mitochondrial fraction. The supernatant fraction is obtained from the 33% homogenate of the brain stem in 0.02 M Trisacetate, pH 8.1, containing 10^{-3} M dithiothreitol by centrifugation for 30 min at 105,000 × g. Usually, 1 g of the starting tissue yields 1.8 ml of the supernatant fluid containing approximately 15 mg of protein per ml.

Assay procedure. Tryptophan hydroxylase is assayed by measuring the ratio of $^{14}CO_2$ formation from the substrate, L-tryptophan-(side chain 1-^{14}C). Two standard assay systems are used. The first assay system is used for the homogenate or crude mitochondrial fraction. The reaction mixture (0.5 ml) contains 50 μmoles of tris-acetate (pH 8.1), 125 μmoles of sucrose, 30 to 60 nmoles of L-tryptophan-^{14}C (approximately 100,000 cpm), and 0.15 ml of the enzyme preparation. The second assay system is used for the soluble tryptophan hydroxylase. The reaction mixture (0.5 ml) contains 50 μmoles of Tris-acetate buffer, (pH 8.1), 0.3 μmole of 2-amino-4-hydroxy-6, 7-demethyl-5, 6, 7, 8-tetrahydropteridine, 1.2 μmoles of dithiothreitol, 100 nmoles of pyridoxal phosphate, 10 nmoles of ferrous ammonium sulfate, L-tryptophan-^{14}C as in the first assay system, 30 μg of catalase, 5 to 10 units of aromatic L-amino acid decarboxylase, and 0.1 ml of the enzyme. The reaction is carried out for 60 min at 37°C in a test tube (diameter 1.6 cm, length 10 cm), which is connected, via thick rubber tubbing, to a counting vial. The vial contains a filter paper strip, which is immersed in 0.3 ml of a 20% solution of 2-phenylethylamine in methanol. At the end of the incubation period, 0.8 ml of 4% perchloric acid containing 2 × 10^{-3} M triton is injected through the rubber tube. The acidified reaction mixture is incubated for an additional 3 hr at 37°C with gentle shaking or allowed to stand for 12 hr at 4°C. To each vial, 10 ml of scintillation solution consisting of 2.5 g PPO and 150 mg of POPOP in 1 liter of toluene are added. Radioactivity is determined in a liquid scintillation spectrometer. In all experiments, a blank incubation is carried out, which contains all the ingredients listed above except that the enzyme preparation has been boiled for 5 min. The nonenzymatic evolution of $^{14}CO_2$ is subtracted from the value for the experimental incubations. The amount of CO_2 formed is calculated from the specific activity of the 1 carbon atom, which is expected to be the same as that of the L-tryptophan (side chain 1-^{14}C) used as substrate.

Monoamine oxidase. The enzymatic oxidation of amines is associated with the uptake of oxygen and the production of ammonia, hydrogen peroxide, and the corresponding oxidation production products of the amine. All of these parameters and the disappearance of substrate have been used as a basis for assaying these enzymes. Greater sensitivity in assaying amine oxidases has been obtained, based either on the reaction of *o*-dianisidine with evolved hydrogen peroxide, or on the extraction of oxidation products of specific substrates and their determination by fluorometric or radiometric procedures. A fluorescence assay procedure developed by Synder and Hendley is similar in sensitivity to the radiometric assays, and permits the use of multiple substrates and continuous monitoring. Their procedure is described here.

The tissues are homogenized in 5 to 20 volumes of ice-cold 0.1 M Na-K phosphate buffer in a motor-driven glass homogenizer. Aliquots of whole homogenate are taken for monoamine oxidase assay. The assay mixture contains, in final volume of 3 ml: 0.1 M Na-K phosphate buffer, pH 7.8; 0.04 mg of horseradish peroxidase (Calbiochem); 1 to 2 units of tissue enzyme preparation; 0.25 mg of homovanillic acid; and appropriate amine substrate. Before the addition of homovanillic acid and substrate, the reaction vessels (tubes) are preincubated for 10 min to remove endogenous substrates of H_2O_2-producing enzymes. Preincubation is performed in a Dubnoff metabolic shaker at 37°C. This procedure will lower tissue blanks between 15 and 45%. After preincubation, homovanillic acid and substrate are added and the tubes are incubated for 60 min at 37°C with shaking. The reaction is terminated by chilling the tubes to 4°C. Fluorescence intensity is measured in a spectrophotofluorometer (Amino-Bowman) at an activation wavelength of 315 nm and an emission wavelength of 425 nm. The tubes are then centrifuged in the cold for 20 min at 12,000 × g before fluorescence measurements are made on the supernatant fraction. Under these conditions, sampling of aliquots at 10-min intervals showed that enzyme activity is linear for 90 min.

Blanks containing tissue enzyme but no added substrate are subtracted for calculation of enzyme activity. A calibration curve is determined in each experiment by adding increasing amounts of freshly prepared standard hydrogen peroxide solution, 1 mM to a cuvette containing (in 2 ml): 0.1 M Na-K phosphate buffer, pH 7.8; horseradish peroxidase, 0.04 mg; and homovanillic acid, 0.25 mg. The exact molarity of the stock H_2O_2 solution is determined by titration with $KMnO_4$. The resultant fluorescence readings are used to calculate equivalent millimicromoles of substrate oxidized per hour. Fluorescence readings equivalent to twice the blank reading are obtained with 1 nmole of hydrogen peroxide.

Acetylcholine

Content

Bioassay procedures were once the only methods sensitive enough to be useful in determinations of acetylcholine. The sensitive (2.0-20.0 pmoles/ml) bioassay methods are those using the guinea pig ileum and the dorsal muscle of the leech. A recent method using the guinea pig ileum assay has sensitivity in the 0.01-0.1 pmole range.

Fluorometric, polarographic, enzymatic radiochemical, and gas chromatographic methods for estimation of acetylcholine have all been described. Fluorometric determination of the NADPH produced by coupled reactions has been used by Cooper, O'Neill and Sakamoto, and Browning. The sensitivity of these methods is in the range of 200 to 2,000 pmoles. Fellman has measured fluorescence of the salicyl hydrazone formed from acetylcholine. The sensitivity of this method is also in the range of 200 to 2,000 pmoles.

Two different reaction sequences have been utilized in the enzymatic radiochemical assays. One is the quantitative acetylation of acetylcholine by means of (acetyl-^{14}C)-acetyl-CoA and choline acetyltransferase. The sensitivity of this assay is in the range of 50 to 2,000 pmoles. The other procedure involves hydrolysis of acetylcholine followed by quantitative phosphorylation of the liberated choline using γ-32P-ATP and choline kinase. This method, as described by Goldberg and McCaman, is about 10 times more sensitive than the assay procedure using choline acetyltransferase. Since choline is a ubiquitous constituent of nervous tissues, arrangements must be made to remove it prior to the assay of acetylcholine in both of the above methods.

Gas chromatographic determination of acetylcholine involves the conversion of the ester to a volatile compound. N-demethylation with sodium benzene thiolate or via pyrolysis has been used to produce dimethylaminoethyl acetate from acetylcholine. The sensitivity of the procedure is dependent on the means of detection. With flame ionization detectors, the sensitivity of the demethylation technique is 50-10,000 pmoles; that of the pyrolysis technique is 200-10,000 pmoles. By using a mass spectrometer as a selective detector for the gas chromatogram, it is possible to identify fragments specifically originating from less than 1 pmole of acetylcholine. Use of the mass spectrometer in conjunction with the gas chromatogram has been made to provide a definitive identification of acetylcholine in rat brain, since this increases the already considerable specificity of the demethylation method. We have chosen to describe, in detail, an enzymatic assay and a gas chromatographic assay.

Enzymatic Assay of Goldberg and McCaman for Choline and Acetylcholine

Tissue preparation

Animals are decapitated and the brains are removed, weighed, and homogenized in 1 ml of cold 1 N formic acid/acetone (FA/A; 85, v/v) per 150 mg of brain. This procedure is usually completed in less than 1 min. The samples are centrifuged in the cold at 1,000 × g for min. Portions of the FA/A supernatant fluid are placed in conical shaped glass microtubes and lyophilized for approximately 30 min, yielding residue 1. Lyophilization is accomplished in a vacuum centrifuge. Residue 1 is resuspended in 30 μl of 10 mM sodium phosphate buffer (pH 6.6). Then 50 μl of 3-heptanone containing tetraphenylboron (5 mg/ml) are added, and the samples are mixed and centrifuged (1,000 × g for 5 min). A measured portion (40 μl) of the heptanone layer is placed in a fresh microtube containing 40 μl of 0.4 N HCl. After vigorous mixing and brief centrifugation (to break the emulsion), the entire organic phase is aspirated and discarded. A measured amount (30 μl) of the acid phase is transferred to a plastic microtube and lyophilized. The tube is dried within 90 min, yielding residue 2.

Choline assay

A 10 μl sample of cold (0-2°C) preincubated buffer-substrate is added to each tube containing the final residue (residue 2). The buffer-substrate consists of 1 mM ATP, 20 μM ^{32}P-ATP and 5 mM $MgCl_2$ in a 50 mM sodium phosphate buffer, pH 8.0. An amount of choline kinase is added (approximately 5 μg/μl of buffer-substrate), which will convert one-half of the choline to phosphorylcholine in less than 3 min. The samples are incubated at 38°C for tubes are returned to an ice-water bath, 15 μl of 0.3 M barium acetate are added, and the tube contents are mixed. The samples are centrifuged in the cold at 600 × g for 10 min. A measured aliquot (15 μl) is then transferred, in 400 μl of water, to the top of a microcolumn of Bio-Rad AG 1 × 8 (200-400 mesh, formate form) resin. The resin bed (5 × 20 mm) is prepared in a Pasteur pipette. The 32P-phosphorylcholine is washed through the column with the 400 μl of water containing the sample aliquot. This is followed by three 400 μl rinses of 75 mM ammonium acetate adjusted to pH 9.5-10 with ammonium hydroxide. All washing are eluted directly into scintillation vials. Then 15 ml of Aquasol are added, vial contents are mixed, and the radioactivity determined. Choline standards are routinely added to samples and carried through the entire procedure (internal standards). Results are calculated on the basis of these standards.

Acetylcholine (ACh) assay

Cold (0-2°C) incubation medium (10 μl) is added to each tube containing the final residue (residue 2). The incubation medium consists of 50 mm sodium phosphate buffer (pH 8.0), 1 mM ATP, 5 mM $MgCl_2$, and choline kinase (ATP: choline phosphotransferase; EC 2.7.1.32) in a final concentration of approximately 2 mg/ml of incubation medium. The actual quantity (in mg of protein) of the kinase varies in proportion to the specific activity of the preparation. Sufficient enzyme is added such that one-half of the choline will be converted to phosphorylcholine in approximately 2 min under the conditions of the a assay. The samples are incubated for 15 min at 38°C (first stage of the assay). Under these conditions, all the choline, as well as other potentially interfering substances, is phosphorylated, while the ACH remains unchanged. At the end of this incubation, the samples are returned to an ice water bath, and 2 μl of a second incubation medium containing 0.4 μCi ATP-(γ-^{32}P) (approx. 20 μM) and 0.01 unit of eel acetylcholinesterase (sufficient to hydrolyze 50% of the Ach in 0.1 min) in 50 mM sodium phosphate buffer (pH 8.0) are added and gently mixed. After incubating for an additional 15 min at 38°C (second stage of the assay), the samples are returned to an ice bath and 10 μl of 0.3 M barium acetate are added with thorough mixing. After centrifugation in the cold at 1,000 × g for 15 min, a 15 μl portion of the supernatant fluid is added to a microcolumn of Bio-Rad AG 1 ×

8 resin. The resin bed (5 × 20 mm) is prepared in a Pasteur pipette. The ^{32}P-phosphorylcholine is eluted from the column directly into a counting vial with 400 μl of water, followed by three rinses of 400 μl of 75 mM ammonium formate. Aquasol (12 ml), is added to the eluate (total volume of 1.6 ml) in each vial, and the radioactivity is measured in a liquid scintillation spectrometer. An ACh standard (usually 100 pmoles) is routinely added to the formic acid-acetone solution and carried through the entire procedure. The results are calculated on the basis of this "internal" standard. ACh standards are added to extra blanks and carried through the procedure to the residue 2 step ("external-internal" standards), or added to clean tubes just prior to the first stage of the ACh assay.

Gas Chromatographic Method of Jenden et al.

The principle for this determination of ACh and other choline esters is based on prior N-demethylation with Na-benzenethiolate.

Purification of solvents

Glass-distilled water is used and is boiled before use. Butanone is purified and dried by slow distillation from a Linde, Type 4A Molecular Sieve, using a 60-cm glass helix fractionating column. Chloroform (J.T. Baker, Spectroquality) is shaken with an equal volume of 2N NH_4OH until both phases are clear (2-4 hr), washed twice with 2N H_2SO_4 and three times with glass distilled water. It is stored with 1% absolute ethanol in a dark bottle. Pentane (M.C.B.-Spectroquality) is treated like chloroform, above, and is stored in pure form. All organic solvents are stored in tinted, ground-glass-stoppered vessels and kept in a cool, dark place.

Preparation of sodium benzenethiolate

Thiophenol (83 g, 0.75 mole) and 20 g (0.50 mole) of sodium hydroxide are warmed in 100 ml of anhydrous ethanol until solution occurs. Toluene (700 ml) is added, and the mixture is distilled slowly at atmospheric pressure; the product is crystallized out as the ethanol and water are distilled. An additional 600 ml of toluene are added in aliquots of 100 ml to volume of the boiling mixture at 500 to 600 ml. The product is then filtered under dry nitrogen and washed with boiling toluene.

The step that follow are necessary to obtain a quantitative yield of dimethylaminoethyl acetate from ACh at high dilutions. The product from the above reaction is added to 200 ml of absolute ethanol and 5 ml of ethyl acetate, shaken in an atmosphere of nitrogen until dissolved, and allowed to stand at room temperature for 60 hr. It is then filtered and the solvents are removed by distillation as before. The benzenethiolate salt is recovered by filtration under dry nitrogen and washed with boiling toluene. It is immediately placed in a vented desiccator over P_2O_5 together with 100-200 g of dry ice and left for 65 hr. The product is then rapidly transferred to individually sealed vials for storage. For the demethylation reaction, a solution containing 6 mg/ml (50 mM) sodium benzenethiolate in butanone is freshly prepared each day and stored under nitrogen until used.

Preparation of hexyldimethylamine (HDA)

Bromohexane (0.2 mole) is added slowly to a 25% methanolic solution of dimethylamine (0.4 mole) at 0°C; the mixture is allowed to warm spontaneously to 35°C, and is left at room temperature for 60 hr. After boiling for 30 min, 250 ml of water and 8 g of NaOH are added. The solution is extracted twice with 50 ml of diethyl ether and is dried with anhydrous $MgSO_4$. The product is precipitated as the hydrochloride by adding excess of dry ethereal hydrogen chloride followed by recrystallization from ethanol/ethyl acetate. The melting point of the product is 169-171°C.

Procedure for demethylation reaction

The sample to be tested containing 0.5 to 25 nmoles of ACh and a precisely known amount (e.g., 10 nmoles) of hexyldimethylamine hydrochlorides is placed in a conical centrifuge tube fitted with a Teflon-lined screw cap and evaporated to dryness. The sodium benzenethiolate reagent (0.5 ml) is added, and air is displaced from the remainder of the tube with a gentle stream of dry nitrogen. The tube is thin tightly capped and placed in a water bath at 80°C for 30 min, with shaking at 5-min intervals.

Procedure for extraction of dimethylaminoethyl acetate

The following procedure removes excess benzenethiolate and undesired reaction products, and concentrates dimethylaminoethyl acetate into a minimum volume, while retaining a high consistent yield.

Following completion of the demethylation reaction, the tube is cooled and opened. After adding 0.1 ml of aqueous citric acid (0.5 M) and 2 ml of pentane, the contents are shaken vigorously and centrifuged to achieve complete separation of phases. The upper organic layer is discarded and the aqueous phase is washed twice with 1 ml of pentane; the remaining traces of pentane are removed by evaporation with a gentle stream of dry nitrogen. To the aqueous residue, 50 μl of chloroform and 0.1 ml of ammonium citrate (2M) in ammonium hydroxide (7.5 M) are added, shaken vigorously, and centrifuged. An aliquot (approximately 5 μl) of the lower (organic) phase is injected into the gas chromatograph.

Gas chromatography

An F and M 5750A dual-column gas chromatograph equipped with flame ionization detectors is employed, using a silanized glass column (6 ft × 1/4 in) containing 80/120 mesh Polypak 1 (F & M), coated with 1% (w/w) phenyldiethanolamine succinate (PDEAS). Injections are made with a Hamilton No 701-N 10-μl syringe. Chromatographic runs are performed isothermally, and the column temperature is maintained at 180°C. Injection port and flame detector temperatures are 204° and 200°C, respectively, Nitrogen is used as carrier gas, at a rate of 45 ml/min (80 psi). Air flow is maintained at 280 ml/min (30 psi), and hydrogen at 30 ml/min (26 psi). Each gas is passed through special drying tubes containing Molecular Sieve before coming in contact with each other and with the chromatographic apparatus. Peaks are recorded on a Varian Associates Recorder, Model G-2000.

Turnover

The simultaneous measurement of endogenous ACh and a precursor is required for the estimation of steady state turnover of ACh *in vivo*. Schuberth et al. and Haubrich et al. injected radiolabeled ACh in the brain at various times following injection. Hanin et al. have estimated ACh turnover in rat salivary glands by a radio-gas chromatographic method. Jenden et al. have coupled gas chromatography and mass spectrometry to estimate the turnover of ACh in brain in vivo following a pulse i.v. injection of choline, using discrete deuterium-labeled variants of choline and ACh as tracer and internal standards.

Tritum-labeled (Me-^{3}H) choline (100 μCi, 0.5 μmoles) is injected i.v. via the mouse tail vein. Special efforts are made to standardize the injection procedure. The brains are chiselled out and ground to a fine powder in a mortar containing liquid nitrogen. The brain powder is then transferred to tared centrifuged tubes containing 2 ml ice-cold 7% TCA and 4 μmoles each of unlabeled choline and ACh chloride. After thorough mixing, the tubes are weighed and left in the refrigerator for 30 min, after which they are centrifuged at 12,000 × g for 5 min. Each pellet is then suspended in 1 ml ice-cold 7% TCA, without added carrier, and centrifuged. Supernatants resulting from both centrifugations are combined and, after portions have been taken for assay of total radioactivity, they are extracted six times with 3 ml portions of ether (pH then being adjusted to 4). After the removal of TCA, 2 ml of a freshly prepared saturated aqueous solution of ammonium reineckate are added. The precipitate formed is isolated by centrifugation, dissolved in 0.5 ml acetone-water (1:1, v/v), and applied to an anion exchange column (Dowex 2-X8 in chloride form, 70 × 8 mm). The column is eluted with acetone-water 1:1 and the first 6 ml of the eluate collected. The eluate is evaporated to dryness *in vacuo* and dissolved in 0.1 ml of water. The radioactive components in 10 μl of the solutions are then separated by high voltage electrophoresis in 0.2 M acetate buffer at pH 4.6. The choline and ACh spots are visualized by iodine vapour and cut out. The paper strips are combusted in oxygen flasks, which are then cooled to -10°C, and 14 ml of scintillation solution (dioxane-naphthalene-PPO-POPOP) are subsequently added. The radioactivity is measured in a liquid scintillation counter. The radioactivity can also be separated by paper chromatography in n-butanol-ethanol-water (5:1:4). Contrary to paper electrophoresis, ACh in this system moves in front of choline. Good agreement between the two systems is found regarding the amount of labeled choline and ACh in the brain extracts.

Related Enzymes

Choline Acetyltransferase (CHAc)

The radiochemical procedures are the most useful assays for CHAc. In general, the enzyme in homogenates is released by treatment with detergent or ether and incubated with 0.1 mM (acetyl-^{14}C) acetyl-CoA, 10 mM choline, 300 mM NaCl, EDTA, pH 7.4 phosphate buffer, and 0.1 mM eserine to prevent the hydrolysis of the ester by cholinesterases. The thiol groups of the enzyme are best protected by NaCN or thioglycolate; cysteine is inhibitory because it is acetylated by acetyl-CoA. Separation of the radioactive ACh formed can be achieved by precipitation of the reineckate salt, by passage over ion exchange resins, or by liquid-phase cation exchange using tetraphenylboron in an organic solvent.

The last method is very convenient and is the most sensitive, being capable of the determination of the choline acetyltransferase in 50 μg of brain. The methods is described below.

Chemicals

Sodium (1-^{14}C) acetate (specific activity, 52 mCi mmole) is used. The radioactive acetate is dissolved in water and stored frozen. Acetone-dried pigeon liver is extracted with 20 mM $KHCO_3$, and the clear supernatant is gel-filtered on a column (10 ml) of Sephadex G-25 (coarse grade) equilibrated with 20 mM sodium phosphate buffer, pH 7.4.

Enzyme preparations

Homogenates (5%, w/v) of brain are prepared in 1 mM EDTA buffer, pH 7.0 in a Potter-Elvehjem homogenizer. The clearance between pestle and wall is 0.2 mm, and the pestle is rotated at 1440 rmp. To release full enzyme activity, samples are treated with 0.5% Triton X-100. The homogenates are diluted with 1 mM EDTA to a final concentration of 5 μg wet weight of tissue/μl.

Standard assay procedure for ChAc

The incubation volume in the macro procedure is 1 ml, and it is 2 μl in the micro procedure. When the incubation volume is μl, 10 μl of cyclohexane are added as a cover to prevent evaporation. The presence of cyclohexane does not affect the enzyme activity or the extraction procedures. The incubation temperature is 37°C for both procedures, which are described below.

Macro procedure

This procedure is generally used when reaction volumes are larger than 50 μl. The incubation mixture contains 5 mM sodium (1-^{14}C) acetate (10^6 cpm), 12.5 mM choline, 300 mM NaCl, 50 mM NaF, 10 mM sodium phosphate buffer (pH 7.4), 0.05 mM CoA, 10 mM ATP, 0.1 mM eserine salicylate, 0.5 mM KBH_4, 2.5 mM $MgCl_2$ and extract from 12 mg of acetone-dried pigeon liver. The incubation is carried out in 10 ml centrifuge tubes with ground-glass stoppers. The mixture is incubated for 10 min to form acetyl-CoA, and the reaction is started by addition of enzyme. The reaction is terminated by adding 7 ml of an ACh chloride solution (0.5 mg/7 ml), followed immediately by 1 ml of butyl ethyl ketone containing 25 mg of sodium tetraphenylboron. After being shaken gently for 4 min, the tubes are centrifuged at 3,000 × g for 4 min in a swinging bucket rotor to separate the aqueous and organic phases. After gently string the ketone layer, proteins soon separate out as a flat layer at the interface between the two phases. When more than 10 mg of brain homogenate are used, it is advisable to extract with 2 ml of ketone. The ketone layer, containing acetylcholine, is transferred by a Pasteur pipette to another tube and is washed once with 4 ml of 10 mM sodium phosphate buffer, pH 7.4 containing 2 mg of sodium tetraphenylboron. After recentrifugation, a sample of the ketone layer (usually 0.5 ml) is transferred to a scintillation vial containing 2 ml of acetonitrile and 10 ml of toluene scintillation mixture. The radioactivity is determined in a liquid scintillation spectrometer.

Micro procedure based on (1-^{14}C) acetate

This procedure is used for reaction volumes less than 50 μl. The incubation mixture contains 2 mM sodium (1-^{14}C) acetate, extract from 2.5 μg of acetone-dried pigeon liver /μl of incubation mixture, and other components as described above for the "macro procedure." The incubation mixture (100 μl) is preincubated the enzyme preparation. After incubation, the tube is transferred to a 10-ml centrifuge tube containing 7 ml of 10 mM sodium phosphate buffer (pH 7.5) and 0.25 mg of ACh chloride. The phosphate buffer solution is flushed into the conical micro tube three times using a Pasteur pipette. This washes the contents of the micro tube into the large tube. The ACh is extracted with 1 ml of butyl ethyl ketone containing 15 ml of tetraphenylboron. The ketone layer is isolated by centrifugation, transferred to a new tube, and washed with 4 ml of 10 mM sodium phosphate buffer containing 2 mg of sodium tetraphenylboron. After recentrifugation, the radioactivity of the ketone layer is determined as described above.

Acetylcholinesterase (AChE)

A wide variety of methods are available for the determination of AChE. The hydrolysis of the ester is accompanied by the release of one equivalent of acid. This can be measured by Warburg manometry as CO_2 liberated from a bicarbonate buffer by the acid or determined titrimetrically with an automated pH-stat. Radiochemical assays, in which the ^{14}C-acetic acid produced by hydrolysis of acetyl-1-^{14}C-ACh is measured, also have been used. The most commonly used method is that of Ellman et. al. The method involves the formation of the coloured 5-thio-2-nitrobenzoate anion by the reaction of thiocholine with 5,5'-dithiobis-2-nitrobenzoic acid. This method is described below.

Solution

Phosphate buffer, 0.1 M, pH 8.0; acetylthiocholine iodine, 0.075 M (21.67 mg/ml; this substrate solution is used successfully for 10-15 days if kept refrigerated); 5,5'-dithiobis-2-nitrobenzoic acid (DTNB), 0.01 M, 39.6 mg are dissolved in 10 ml pH 7.0 phosphate buffer (0.1 M) and 15 mg of sodium bicarbonate are added (this reagent is made up in buffer of pH 7, in which it is more stable than in that of pH 8).

Tissue preparations

The tissue is homogenized (approximately 20 mg of tissue per ml of phosphate buffer) (pH 8.0, 0.1 M) in a Potter-Elvehjem homogenizer.

Assay procedure

An aliquot of the homogenate (0.4 ml) is added to a cuvette containing 2.6 ml of phosphate buffer (pH 8.0, 0.1 M). DTNB reagent (100 μl) is added to the photocell. The absorbance is measured at 412 mμ: when this has stopped increasing, the photometer slit is opened so that the absorbance is set to zero. Substrate (20 μl) is added and changes in absorbance are recorded, from which the change in absorbance per minute is calculated. The rates are calculated as follows:

$$R = \frac{\Delta A}{1.36 \times 10^4} \times \frac{1}{(400/3120)C_0}$$

$$= 5.74 \times 10^{-4} \frac{\Delta A}{C_0}$$

where R is the rate, in moles substrate hydrolyzed per minute per gram of tissue, DA is the change in absorbance per minute, and C_0 is the original concentration of tissue (mg/ml).

GAMMA-AMINOBUTYRIC ACID (GABA)

Content

Tissue levels of GABA and glutamate have been measured by various techniques such as ion exchange chromatography, paper chromatography-fluorometry, ligand-exchange chromatography, and most commonly, by an enzymatic-fluorometric technique or by a dansylation technique. More sensitive methods, e.g., radioreceptor assay and mass fragmentography, have been available recently. The most common method of enzymatic-fluorometry, the recently developed radioreceptor assay and mass fragmentography will be described here.

Enzymatic-fluorometry of Graham and Aprison

Preparation of brain extract

The animals are decapitated and the brains are removed immediately and frozen in crushed dry ice. About 0.5 g of brain is weighed and homogenized in 3 ml of precooled 75% ethanol in a Nalgene centrifuge tube using a Polytron. The homogenizer shaft is rinsed with 1 ml of 75% ethanol; then the Polytron is turned on for an additional 5 sec to spin out the rinsings to centrifuge tube. Homogenates are left at room temperature for several hours or are placed in a refrigerator overnight. After the homogenate is centrifuged at 20,000 × g for 30 min, the supernatant is dried under an airstream and the resuspended in exactly 10 ml of water and shaken at room temperature for 30 min. The slightly cloudy suspension is then recentrifuged in an ultracentrifuge at 100,000 × g for 30 min. The clear supernatant is carefully transferred to a storage tube using a Pasteur pipette. This supernatant is used for GABA and glutamate assay. The GABA assay is described below.

Reagents

Sodium pyrophosphate buffer, pH 8.1 (0.2 m), is prepared by dissolving 8.92 g of $Na_4P_2O_7 \cdot 10\ H_2O$ in 90 ml of water. The pH is adjusted to 8.1 with 3N HCl, and water is added to bring the volume to 100 ml. The solution is treated with 10 g Norit A (charcoal) and then filtered to remove fluorescent background. The α-ketoglutaric acid (α-KG) solution contains 4.6 mg α-KG in 2 ml of Na pyrophosphate buffer. The 2-mercaptoethanol solution is prepared by diluting 50 μl of 2-mercaptoethanol to a final volume of 7 ml with water. The NADP solution consists of 6 mg NADP in 5 ml of Na pyrophosphate buffer. The GABA stock standard is made by dissolving 10.3 mg of GABA in 100 ml water (1 mM) GABA is a partially purified cell-free preparation from *Pseudomonous fluorescence containing* GABA-α-ketoglutarate transaminase and succinic semialdehyde dehydrogenase. The reaction mixture consists of the following: 5 ml of the NADP solution, 0.6 ml of the α-KG solution, 0.3 ml of the 2-mercaptoethanol solution, and 0.2 ml of GABAse. For sample blanks, 0.2 ml of water is used to replace the 0.2 ml of GABAse.

Assay procedure

Using an Eppendorf pipette, 50 μl of brain extract are transferred to each of two 13 × 100 mm test tubes (one is used as sample blank in order to measure background fluorescence due to tissue extract itself). Na pyrophosphate buffer (50 μl) is added to each tube, and the tubes are placed in ice water. The appropriate reaction mixture, i.e., with or without GABAse, is added to each tube. Contents of tubes are mixed using a Vortex mixer, and each tube is covered with paraffin. Incubation is then carried out at 37°C for 50 min with constant shaking. Tubes are then placed into ice water, followed by incubation at 60°C for 30 min to stop the reaction. Tubes are allowed to stand for 10 min at room temperature. Then 1 ml of water is added and the contents are mixed well. Fluorescence is measured at the excitation and emission wavelengths of 350 and 460 nm, respectively.

Standard curve

In addition to experimental samples, a standard curve should be prepared for each assay. Dilutions from the 1 mm GABA stock solution serve as standard curve solutions (e.g., 0.02, 0.04, 0.06, and 0.1 mM).

Radioreceptor Assay of Enna and Snyder

This assay is based on the principle that the amount of ^{3}H-GABA bound to synaptosomal membrane fragments, in the presence of added GABA, is proportional to the logarithm of the added GABA.

Preparation of synaptic membranes

Crude synaptic membranes are isolated from rat brains. Male Sprague Dawley rats (150-200 g) are decapitated, and the brains are removed rapidly and homogenized in 15 volumes of ice-cold 0.32 m sucrose in a Potter Elvehjem glass homogenizer fitted with a Teflon pestle. The homogenate is centrifuged at 100 × g for 10 min. The pellet is discarded and the supernatant fluid is centrifuged at 20,000 × ft. for 20 min. The crude mitochondrial pellet is resuspended in distilled water and dispersed using a Brinkmann Polytron PT-10 homogenizer for 30 sec. The suspension is centrifuged at 8,000 × g for 20 min. The supernatant is collected and the pellet, a bilayer with a soft, buffy uppercoat, is rinsed carefully with the supernatant fluid to collect the upper layer. The combined supernatant fractions are then centrifuged at 48,000 × g for 20 min. The final crude synaptic membrane pellets are resuspended in water and centrifuged at 48,000 × g for 20 min and then stored at -30°C for at least 18 hr. Prior to use, the frozen pellets are resuspended in water, maintained at 25°C for 20 min, centrifuged at 48,000 × g for 10 min and then suspended in the buffer for GABA binding assay. The ^{3}H-GABA binding capacity of frozen pellets remains intact for at least 90 days under these conditions. Storing frozen tissues enhances GABA postsynaptic receptor binding and markedly lowers sodium dependent GABA binding, which is unrelated to receptor sites.

GABA assay procedure

Animals are decapitated and the brains are rapidly removed (less than 30 sec) and placed into a beaker of methanol precooled to approximately -80°C on dry ice-acetone. The brain tissue is dispersed with a Polytron in 20 volumes of ice-cold distilled water and the homogenate is centrifuged at 48,000 × g at 4°C for 10 min. For routine assays, a fraction of the supernatant is removed and diluted to the equivalent of 120 volumes with ice-cold distilled water. Twenty-μl aliquots of this solution are placed, in triplicate, into 16 ml Sorvall centrifuge tubes containing 1 ml of cold distilled water. To each tube is added 1 ml (0.7-1.2 mg protein) of the crude synaptic membrane suspended in 0.1 M Tris citrate buffer (pH 7.1 at 4°C) and 2 μl of a

^{3}H-GABA solution which, in the 2 μl incubation mixture, yields 25 nM ^{3}H-GABA (500,000 cpm). After mixing, the samples are incubated at 4°C for min, and the reaction is terminated by centrifugation at 48,000 × g for 10 min at 4°C. After centrifugation, the supernatant fluid is decanted, and the pellet is rinsed rapidly and superficially with 5 ml, then 10 ml of ice-cold distilled water. Bound radioactivity is extracted into counting vials containing 1 ml of Protocol. Ten ml of toluene phosphor are added and radioactivity is assayed by liquid scintillation spectrometry. Total specific ^{3}H-GABA binding is obtained by subtracting from the total bound radioactivity, the amount displaced by 2 μmol/2 ml of GABA.

Standard curves are determined routinely by placing 20 μl aliquots of various appropriate concentrations of unlabeled GABA into the incubation mixture and calculating the per cent displacement of ^{3}H-GABA by each concentration relative to the blank value. For internal standards, 0.2 or 0.4 nmol of unlabeled GABA is added to the incubation mixture along with the tissue extract.

To determine per cent recovery, brains from four rats are removed and frozen in the usual fashion. Each frozen brain is placed into a centrifuge tube and, prior to the addition of 20 volumes of ice-cold water, 20 μl of an aqueous solution containing 0.01 nmoles ^{3}H-GABA (0.1 μCi) are placed in each tube. After the addition of cold water, the brain is homogenized with a Polytron for 1 min and the homogenate centrifuged for 10 min at 48,000 × g at 4°C. After centrifugation, recovery is determined by analyzing 20 μl aliquots of the aqueous supernatant for ^{3}H-GABA by liquid scintillation spectrometry.

Mass Fragmentographic Method of Bertilson and Costa

Reagents and reference compounds

The following compounds are commercially available pentafluoropropionic anhydride and 1, 1, 1, 3, 3, 3-hexafluoroisopropanol (HFIP) from Pierce L-glutamic acid and 5-amino-n-valeric acid (AVA) hydrochloride from K & K Labs GABA from Calbiochem L-2, 3, 3, 4, 4-2H5 glutamic acid (glutamic acid-d_5) from Merck, Sharp and Dohme deuterium chloride (20% in deuterium oxide; 100.0 atom %D) and deuterium oxide (99.7 atom %D) from Aldrich.

4,4-$^2H_2$-Glutamin acid (glutamic acid-d_2) and γ-amino 2,2-$^2H_2$-butyric acid (GABA-d_2) are synthesized by heating glutamic acid and GABA (200 mg of each), respectively at 130°C in sealed tubes with 1 ml of 8% deuterium chloride in deuterium oxide. The solutions are reacted for three 12-days periods. After each period, the solvent is evaporated by a stream of nitrogen gas and replaced by a fresh deuterium chloride solution. After the last heating period, the crystals obtained are dissolved in protium water to replace active deuterium atoms with protium via exchange. When the water is evaporated, white crystals of glutamic acid-d_2 are obtained.

Tissue preparation

Rats (about 150 g) are killed by exposing their heads for 2.2 to 2.5 sec to a focused high-intensity microwave beam as described by Guidotti et al. The brains are dissected out and immediately frozen in dry ice. The tissue can also prepared as previously mentioned when high-intensity microwave is not available. The tissue is homogenized in glass homogenizer tubes in 80% aqueous ethanol containing the internal standards for the quantitations. Whole cerebells are homogenized in 500 μl of a solution containing 380 and 750 nmoles/ml of glutamic acid-d_5 and AVA, respectively.

After homogenization, the tubes are centrifuged at 12,000 $\times$ g for 5 min at −2°C. The supernatant (only 50 μl from the whole cerebellum) is transferred to glass vials and evaporated to dryness under a stream of nitrogen. Fifty μl of HFIP and 100 μl of PFPA are then added, and the vials are sealed, heated for 1 hr at 60°C and stored at 4°C. Just before the mass fragmentographic analysis, the reaction mixture is evaporated to dryness. The residue is dissolved in 10 to 100 μl of ethyl acetate, and 1 to 3 μl are injected into the gas chromatograph mass spectrometer.

Gas chromatography-mass spectrometry

An LKB 9,000 gas chromatograph-mass spectrometer with a multiple ion detector is used. The separations are made on a 2.5 m $\times$ 3 mm i.d. silaconized glass column packed with 3% OV-17 on Gas-Chrom Q, 100-120 mesh, maintained at a temperature of 115°C. The temperature of the flash heater is 200°C and the ion source is kept at 270°C. The flow-rate of the helium carrier gas is 25 ml/min. The ionizing potential and trap current are 80 eV and 60 μA, respectively. When mass spectra of reference compounds are recorded, the column temperature is 90°C.

Turnover

It is generally accepted that both GABA and glutamate play an important role in intermediary metabolism in addition to their postulated roles as neurotransmitters. Furthermore, neither glutamic acid nor

GABA crosses the blood-brain barrier. Therefore, radioactive precursors of the tricarboxylic acid cycle have been used previously to label glutamic acid in brain. The labeling of the glutamic acid that functions as a GABA precursor is, however, complicated by the presence of different pools of glutamic acid in glial cells. In contrast, glucose preferentially labels a large pool of glutamate, which is associated with neuronal structures. In 1977, Bertilsson et al. selected ^{13}C-glucose as a precursor for glutamic acid and measured the incorporation of this stable isotope into glutamic acid and GABA. They have further estimated the turnover rate of GABA after constant rate i.v. infusion of ^{13}C-glucose.

Animal treatments

Rats weighing 100 to 110 g are infused intravenously at a constant rate (0.10 ml/min) with ^{13}C-D-glucose. The labeled glucose is dissolved in saline (155 mM NaCl) and infused into the tail vein at a rate of 50 μmol-kg body weight/min for 10 min. Labeling by constant rate infusion is necessary to obtain a sufficient enrichment in the variant atomic species incorporated into glutamic acid and GABA at steady state. After the end of infusion, the rats are killed at 0, 2, 3.5, 5, 7, 10, 15, 25, 40, 70, and 100 min by exposing their heads for 2.2 sec to a focused high intensity microwave beam as described by Guidotti et al. Rats infused intravenously with saline are used as controls. The brains are dissected from the skull and frozen on dry ice. On the average, the sample analyzed contains 40 to 80 μg protein, depending on the tissue. The ^{13}C enrichments of endogenous glutamic acid and GABA are measured in tissue by mass fragmentography.

Analytical procedure

Tissues are homogenized in 1 ml glass homogenizers with a solution of 100 μl of 80% aqueous ethanol containing the internal standards. This internal standard solution contains glutamic acid-d_5 and AVA hydrochloride in concentrations of 42 and 84 nmol/ml, respectively. After homogenization, the tubes are centrifuged at 12,000 × g for 5 min at –2°C. The supernatants are transferred to glass vials and evaporated to dryness under a stream of nitrogen. Fifty μl of HFIP and 100 μl of PFPA are added. The vijals are sealed, heated for 1 hr at 60°C, and then stored at 4°C. During this reaction, the pentafluoropropionyl amide hexafluoropropyl esters of GABA, glutamic acid, and then internal standards are formed. Before measurement, the reagents are evaporated, and the residue is dissolved in 20 μl of ethyl acetate. A small aliquot (1 to 3 μl) of this solution is injected into a gas chromatograph-mass spectrometer. Separations are made on a column (3% OV-17 on Gas-chrom Q) maintained at 95°C. By using the multiple ion detector, the following fragments are analyzed: m/e 398 from endogenous glutamic acid, m/e 400 from ^{13}C glutamic acid, m/e 403 from glutamic acid d_5, m/e 399 from endogenous GABA, m/e 401 from ^{13}C-GABA, and m/e 413 from AVA. Standard curves for the quantitation of endogenous glutamic acid and GABA are prepared by analyzing a series of standard solutions containing various amounts of the natural forms of GABA and glutamic acid and constant amounts of the respective internal standards. The ratios of the ion currents generated by the characteristic ions monitored for glutamic acid/glutamic acid-d_5 and GABA/AVA are plotted against the various amounts of the natural compounds added to each tube. Pilot experiments carried out by these investigators have shown that after infusion with uniformly labeled ^{13}C-glucose, the maximal enrichment of ^{13}C occurs in two of the carbon atoms of glutamic acid and GABA. Therefore, the peak height ratios of the m/e values, 400/398 and 401/399, measure the incorporation of ^{13}C into glutamic acid and GABA, respectively.

Calculation of GABA turnover rates

The finite differences of Neff et al. have been used to calculate the turnover rates of GABA in substantia nigra, globus pallidus, N. caudatus, and N. accumbens. This equation refers to a kinetic situation where a precursor A (glutamic acid) is metabolized to the product B (GABA) in an open compartment system. The data obtained in their experiments indicate that recycling of ^{13}C may occur. This may present a problem in applying the principle of steady-state kinetics to GABA turnover rate measurements. Assuming that this perturbation is not important during the first 7 min of glucose infusion, Eq. (3) has been used to obtain an approximation of GABA turnover:

$$k_B = \frac{2[S_B(t_2) - S_B(t_1)]}{(t_2 - t_1)[S_A(t_2) - S_B(t_1) - S_B(t_2)]} \qquad ...(3)$$

The fractional rate constant (k_B) for GABA efflux is calculated for (t_2-t_1) = 1 min. The experimental values, S_A and S_B are the per cent enrichment of ^{13}C in glutamic acid and GABA, respectively. The values of the rate constant (k_B) obtained between 1 and 7 min after the cessation of ^{13}C-glucose infusion are averaged and used in the steady state equation to calculate turnover rate:

$$TR_B = k_B(B) \qquad ...(4)$$

where TR_B is the turnover rate of GABA, and (B) is the steady state concentration of GABA.

Related Enzymes

The method developed by Roberts and Simonsen is generally used by investigators. This method is routinely used in our laboratory with minor modification.

The activity of GAD is determined by measuring the $^{14}CO_2$ formation from uniformly labeled ^{14}C-L-glutamic acid. Brain (0.5 g) is homogenized with a glass homogenizer immediately in 5 ml of ice-cold 0.1 M potassium buffer, pH 6.5, containing 0.03% reduced glutathione (GSH) at 4°C. Each assay mixture (total volume = 1.0 ml) in a 18 × 150 mm test tube contains 100 μmoles of potassium phosphate buffer, pH 6.5, 100 μmoles L-glutamate (0.9 μCi), 4 mmoles GSH and 1 μmole pyridoxyl-5-phosphate. Into a plastic vial hanging from a test tube, 0.2 ml of 1 M hymine hydroxide solution in methanol is placed. The reaction is started by injecting 2.5 mg brain homogenate protein into the test tube. After 30 min of incubation at 37°C, 0.2 ml of 4 N H_2SO_4 is injected to stop the reaction and to release CO_2. After shaking another 90 min, the contents of the plastic vials are transferred to liquid scintillation counting vials which contain 10 ml Aquasol. The enzyme activity in μmoles glutamate decarboxylated/30 min/100 mg of protein of brain homogenate is calculated from the $^{14}CO_2$ liberated from ^{14}C-L-glutamate. The protein content of brain homogenate is determined by the method of Lowry et al. with crystalline bovine serum albumin as a standard.

γ-Aminobutyric-2-ketoglutarate Transaminase (GABA-T)

The isotopic assay of Waksman and Roberts is useful for measuring low activities of GABA-T because of the sensitivity of the method.

The activity of GABA-T is measured by the formation of labeled glutamate from 5-^{14}C-α-ketoglutarate and nonradioactive GABA. Animals are killed by decapitation and whole brains or discrete brain areas are removed rapidly and placed in glass homogenizers containing precooled 0.01 M phosphate buffer (pH 7.2) with 1.5 μg/ml each of pyridoxal-5-phosphate and reduced GSH. Each assay mixture (total volume of 1.0 ml) in a round bottom, capped, centrifuged tube, contains 15 μmoles of 5-^{14}C-α-ketoglutarate (0.1 μCi), 15 μg each of pyridoxal-5-phosphate and GSH, and 40 μmoles of borate buffer (pH 8.2). The assay is started by the addition of homogenate containing 2 mg protein. Incubations are performed in a Dubnoff metabolic shaker at 37°C for 30 min. Blanks are run in which GABA is omitted. After the reaction is stopped by addition of one drop of concentrated HCl and heating at 100°C for 3 min, the pH of the reaction mixture is adjusted to between

3 and 4. The mixture is then transferred onto a 1 × 8 cm column of AG 50W-4X in the H^+ form. The uncreated α-ketoglutarate is washed out with 30 ml of water, and the labeled glutamic acid formed is eluted with 25 ml of 2 N NH_4OH. After the eluate is evaporated to dryness under an airstream, 1.5 ml of 1 M hyamine hydroxide in methanol is added. One ml of this final solution is pipetted into a liquid scintillation counting vial containing 10 ml of Aquasol.

The spectrophotometric method of Schousboe et. al. is useful for routine and rapid assay of GABA-T

The GABA-T reaction is performed in a 100 mm Tris-HCl buffer, pH 8.0, containing 20 μM pyridoxal-5-phosphate, 100 μM AET (2-aminoethylisothiouronium bromide hydrobromide), 50 mM GABA and 10 mM α-ketoglutaric acid. This buffer plus enzyme is incubated in a water bath shaking for 30 min at 37°C. Under the above conditions, the reaction is linear with time for 1 hr. The reaction is terminated by the addition of aminooxyacetic acid to a final concentration of 100 μM, and the tubes are immediately transferred to an ice bath. Blanks run either without enzyme or in the presence of 100 μM aminooxyacetic acid give comparable low values in the subsequent determination of glutamate.

The glutamate formed in the transaminase reaction is determined in aliquots of the reaction mixture using glutamate dehydrogenase and acetylpyridine-NAD^+ to catalyze the oxidation of glutamate to α-ketoglutarate. The increase in optical density at 363 nm attributable to acetylpyridine-NADH is measured. The buffer for this reaction contains: 10 mm Tris HCl, pH 8.0, 25 mM hydrazine, 1 mm aminooxyacetic acid, 750 μM acetylpyridine NAD^+, and glutamate dehydrogenase (1.3 units/ml). The reaction is carried out at room temperature for 90 min. Acetylpyridine-NAD^+ is used instead of NAD^+, since it increases the equilibrium constant of the reaction by a factor of 100, and the reduced form has a 50% higher extinction coefficient than does NADH. Aminooxyacetic acid and hydrazine, which are carbonyl-trapping agents, are included to trap the α-ketoglutarate formed, thus ensuring completion of the reaction. Under these conditions, the conversion of glutamate to α-ketoglutarate is in excess of 95%.

The enzyme activity is expressed as units/ml of enzyme solution, and specific activities are units/mg of protein. One unit is defined as that activity catalyzing the formation of 1 μmole of glutamate/min at 39°C.

Methods for Cyclic Nucleotides

Adenyl Cyclase

Adenyl cyclase is the enzyme that catalyzes the formation of cyclic 3',5'-adenosine monophosphate (cyclic AMP) from its precursor nucleotide, adenosine triphosphate (ATP). It is assayed *in vitro* by methods based on measuring the rate of formation of radioactivity (^{14}C, 3H, or ^{32}P)-labeled cyclic AMP from the corresponding radioactively labeled substrate, i.e. ^{14}C, ^{3}H- or ^{32}P-ATP. The major problem inherent in the assay is that of obtaining efficient separation of the radiolabeled cyclic AMP from radioactive substrate and other radioactive contaminants. Since usually less than 0.05% of the substrate is converted to cyclic AMP, the sensitivity of the assay is directly proportional to and dependent upon the efficiency of such separation.

General Procedure

The tissue to be used (e.g., brain) is homogenized. Aliquots of the whole homogenate may be used in the assay, or subcellular fractions obtained through centrifugations may be used.

The reaction mixture contains radiolabeled ATP, magnesium, the required cofactor for adenyl cyclase activity, and nonradioactive cyclic AMP as "carrier," or theophylline. The "carrier" cyclic AMP prevents the destruction on newly formed labeled cyclic AMP by "trapping" it without interfering with its production. The use of theophylline is an alternate way to prevent the destruction of newly formed radioactive cyclic AMP, since it inhibits cyclic nucleotide phosphodiesterase. An aliquot of homogenate containing approximately 100 μg of protein is added to the above reaction mixture, the total reaction volume being very small, and incubation is carried out at 30°C for 10 to 15 min. The reaction is stopped by immersing the reaction vessel in boiling water.

The procedures of isolating radioactive cyclic AMP that have been used with success are:

1. Adsorption onto and elution from Dowex ion exchange columns, followed by addition of zinc sulfate and barium hydroxide solutions to the eluate to precipitate the remaining ATP and any residual trace contaminants. After centrifugation, aliquots of the supernatant are prepared for liquid scintillation counting of the radioactive cyclic AMP.
2. Adsorption onto and subsequent elution from columns containing neutral aluminum oxide followed by liquid scintillation counting of aliquots of the eluate.

3. Sequential chromatography on columns of Dowex cation exchange resin and aluminum oxide followed by liquid scintillation counting of aliquots of the final eluate.

The recovery of cyclic AMP can be determined either from measuring the O.D. (260 mμ) of the final purified eluate or by using a "marker" of cyclic AMP, cyclic AMP labeled with a radionuclide different from the label of the substrate. For example, if ^{32}P-ATP is used as the substrate, the "marker" would be ^{3}H-cyclic AMP. A typical assay for brain adenyl cyclase is described in some detail below.

Brain tissue homogenized gently in 10 volumes of 0.32 M sucrose. The crude homogenate is centrifuged at 3,000 × g for 10 min. The supernatant is then recentrifuged at 10,000 × g for 20 min to obtain a crude mitochondrial fraction.

The incubation (reaction) medium contains: Tris-HCl buffer (0.04 M), pH 7.3; magnesium sulfate (3.3 mM); sodium fluoride (10 mM); theophylline (10 mm); ATP (1-2 mm of ^{3}H-, ^{14}C-, or ^{32}P-labeled ATP; specific activity, 5-50 mCi/mmole); and the mitochondrial enzyme preparation obtained above (1-10 mg of tissue) in a final total volume of 0.6 ml. Incubation is carried out at 30°C for specified time intervals. After the addition of 0.1 ml (0.5 mg) of a carrier cyclic AMP solution, the reaction is terminated by immersion in a boiling water bath for 2 min.

The reaction vessel contents are centrifuged, and the supernatant is poured onto a previously prepared Dowex 50-H^{+} column. The column is eluted with water, and 2-ml fractions are collected. The UV absorption at 260 mμ is determined in each fraction. To the fraction(s) containing cyclic AMP, 0.2 ml of 0.25 M zinc sulfate and 0.2 ml of 0.25 M barium hydroxide are added, mixed, and the contents centrifuged. The supernatants are decanted into new tubes, and the barium-zinc precipitation step is repeated on these supernatants. After a final centrifugation, 0.5 ml aliquots are added to counting vials containing liquid scintillation fluor solution, and radioactivity is determined using liquid scintillation techniques.

Blanks are prepared by running incubations without the enzyme preparation or with heat-denatured enzyme. UV absorption at 260 mμ of aliquots of the final supernatants is determined in order to calculate the recovery of cyclic AMP. Adenyl cyclase activity is expressed in terms of the amount of cyclic AMP formed per unit of time, e.g., μmoles of cyclic AMP per minute per gram of tissue wet weight, or per unit weight of tissue protein.

Guanyl Cyclase

Guanyl cyclase is the enzyme that catalyzes the synthesis of cyclic 3',5'-guanosine monophosphate (cyclic GMP) from its nucleotide precursor, guanosine triphosphate (GTP). It is assayed by methods which are based on (a) determination of cyclic GMP by enzymatic cycling methods, (b) determination of radioactive cyclic GMP separated by thin layer chromatography, or (c) determination of radioactive cyclic GMP isolated with neutral aluminum oxide and Dowex-1 formate columns. All three methods involve measurements of the rate of formation of cyclic GMP. After brief descriptive summaries of the first two methods, the third will be described in some detail.

With first describe the enzymatic cycling method. The principle here is the conversion of cyclic GMP and GTP and then measuring the orthophosphate which accumulates during incubation of GTP in a cycling system containing myosin, pyruvate kinase, and phosphoenolpyruvate as follows:

1. Samples (i.e., brain homogenates) containing cyclic GMP are incubated in the presence of purified cyclic nucleotide phosphodiesterase, which catalyzes the hydrolysis of cyclic GMP to form GMP; and in the presence of ATP:GMP phosphotransferase, which phosphorylates GMP to GTP at the expense of ATP.
2. A mixture of adenylate kinase and myosin is added to the above mixture, and the resulting mixture is incubated. This step reduces to negligible levels any remaining amount of ADP or ATP left in stage 1 above.
3. A mixture of phosphoenolpyruvate, pyruvate kinase, and myosin is added to the above and incubation is continued.

The reaction is stopped addition of perchloric acid, and the orthophosphate resulting from the enzyme cycling system is measured in an aliquot of supernatant after centrifugation.

Second, we consider the use of thin layer chromatography in the separation of cyclic GMP from GTP, which has been described by White and Aurbach and depends upon detection of cyclic-^{32}P-AMP formed from α-^{32}P-GTP. The labeled product is separated from the labeled substrate by application of the reaction mixture to a Dowex-50 column and then by ascending chromatography on silicic acid medium, i.e., on ChromAR Sheet. The area corresponding to cyclic GMP is visualized with ultraviolet light, marked with a pencil, cut from the sheet, and prepared for liquid scintillation counting.

Third, we consider a more recent sensitive method using sequential chromatography columns. This method is outlined below.

The brain is quickly removed, chilled in an ice bath, and homogenized with 10 volumes of a 0.25 M sucrose solution containing 0.02 M Tris-HCl buffer (pH 7.4), 1 mM EDTA, and 10 mM 2-mercaptoethanol. The homogenate is centrifuged at 10,000 × g for 10 min at 2°C. The supernatant is decanted and centrifuged at 105,000 × g for 60 min at 2°C. The resulting supernatant is used as the crude enzyme preparation.

The reaction (assay) mixture contains the following: 60 nM of ^3H-GTP (0.02 μCi/nmole/1), 0.3 μM of cyclic GMP, 0.3 μM of $MnCl_2$, 30 μM of Tris-HCl buffer (pH 7.7), and 30 to 80 mg of the enzyme protein in a total volume of 0.15 ml. Following addition of the enzyme preparation, incubation proceeds for 15 min at 30°C and is terminated by immersing the reaction vessel for 2 min in a boiling water bath followed by chilling in ice.

To isolate the radioactive cyclic GMP, the reaction mixture is applied to a neutral aluminum oxide column. The column is then washed with 5 ml of 0.05 M Tris-HCl buffer (pH 7.4). The cyclic GMP passes through this column, while other guanine nucleotides remain adsorbed to the column. The eluant containing cyclic GMP is directly drained onto Dowex 1-X2 column. After all of the eluant is drained from the alumina column it is removed and the Dowex column is washed with 10 ml of 0.05 N formic acid. The cyclic GMP is eluted from this column with 6 ml of 0.2 M ammonium formate in 4.0 N formic acid.

Using this method and ^{14}C-cyclic GMP as the marker, recovery of cyclic GMP is reported to be greater than 85%. Units of enzyme activity are expressed in terms of the amount of cyclic GMP formed per unit time per weight of tissue, or of tissue protein.

Cyclic AMP and Cyclic GMP

The major problem encountered during assays of endogenous brain levels of cyclic AMP and cyclic GMP is that following decapitation, the levels of these cyclic nucleotides increase. The postdecapitation changes in cycline AMP are of a much greater magnitude than are the changes in cyclic GMP, and thus present a major complication in the determinations of brain cyclic AMP levels.

To obviate this difficulty by providing more rapid fixation of brain tissue, four methods have been tested in small animals for their usefulness in assay of endogenous cycle AMP levels. The methods used in order to decreasing effectiveness were: (a) microwave irradiation; (b) freeze-blowing (expulsion of brain tissue into liquid nitrogen); (c) immersion of the whole animal in liquid nitrogen; and (d) decapitation of the head into liquid nitrogen. Guidotti et al. have shown that microwave irradiation inactivates most enzymes in rat brain within 2 sec and has the same effect in mouse brain in 0.5 sec.

Cyclic Nucleotide Assays

The procedures for isolating cyclic nucleotides from brain are generally the same as described above for isolating the products of the cyclase reactions. Identification and quantitation of the endogenous cyclic nucleotides has only been feasible through the use of radioimmunoassay developed by Steiner et al.

The basic principle of radioimmunoassay is competition between radioactive antigen and nonradioactive antigen for a fixed number of binding sites on the antibody. In terms of the radioimmunoassay of cyclic nucleotides, the endogenous cyclic nucleotide to be measured is the nonradioactive antigen, which competes with a fixed amount of radioactive cyclic nucleotide for a fixed amount of specific antibody. This is represented schematically below (CN = cyclic nucleotide):

labeled antigen (CN) + specific antibody (Ab)

⇌ labeled antigen-antibody complex (Cn-Ab)

\+

unlabeled antigen (tissue CN)

⇅

unlabeled antigen-antibody complex (tissue CN-Ab)

The antigen-antibody complex is isolated and the radioactivity determined. The amount of radioactivity in the antigen-antibody complex is inversely proportional to the amount of cyclic nucleotide present in the tissue.

The radioimmunoassay of endogenous cycle AMP and cyclic GMP has become so popular that commercial kits based upon the method of Steiner et al. are now available containing all of the necessary components of the assays, and making it unprofitable (in terms of the time and money involved) for one to prepare one's own specific antibodies and immunoreactive tracer (labeled cyclic nucleotide).

Furthermore, the kits are highly specific, sensitive, and provide excellent recoveries in addition to their involving easy and rapid procedures.

Cyclic Nucleotide Phosphodiesterase (PDE)

The place of pride in assay of PDE undoubtedly belongs to the two-stage enzymatic procedure developed by Thompson and Appleman. This procedure is outlined below. Brain tissue is homogenized at 4°C in eight volumes of 10.9% sucrose for 1 min using a high speed tissue homogenizer at maximum speed. The homogenate is subjected to sonication in an ice bath for 15 min/30 ml of homogenate. The sonicated homogenate is maintained in the ice bath while its pH is adjusted to pH 6.0 with 1 M acetic acid. After centrifugation at 20,000 × g for 20 min, the supernatant is used as the enzyme preparation.

PDE Assay Procedure

Stage 1 consists of hydrolysis of the cyclic nucleotide to the corresponding 5' nucleotide by PDE. The reaction mixture contains, in a total volume of 0.4 ml, the following: ^{3}H-cyclic AMP or ^{3}H-cyclic GMP (approximately 200,000 cpm); unlabeled cyclic AMP (1.25×10^{-7} to 1×10^{-4} M) or unlabeled cyclic GMP (2.5×10^{-7} to 4.5×10^{-5} M); $MgCl_2$ (5 mM; Tris-Cl buffer, pH 8.0 (40 mM); 2-mercaptoethanol (3.75 mm), and the enzyme preparation. Incubation is carried out for 10 min at 30°C and terminated by immersion in boiling water bath for 2.5 min.

Stage 2 consists of the hydrolysis of the 5' nucleotide to adenosine or guanosine using the nucleotidase in snake venom. To the contents of the reaction mixture in stage 1, 0.1 ml of snake venom (*Ophiophagus hannah*) solution (1 mg/ml in Tris-buffer) is added. Incubation is resumed for 10 min at 30°C and stopped by the addition of 1.0 ml of a 1:3 slurry of Bio-Red resin, AG1-X2, 200-400 mesh, which binds all charged nucleotides, leaving only adenosine or guanosine. The contents of the reaction vessel are centrifuged in a low-speed (clinical) centrifuge, and a 0.5 ml aliquot of the supernatant is used for measuring the radioactivity due to ^{3}H-guanosine by liquid scintillation counting techniques.

The units of PDE activity are in terms of the pmoles of cyclic AMP or cyclic GMP hydrolyzed per minute per ml of assay volume. Alternatively, one may express PDE activity as milliunits per gram of tissue wet weight, one milliunit corresponding to the hydrolysis of 1 nmole of cyclic nucleotide per minute.

11

MINISEQUENCING AND MINISATELLITE

Since the discovery of DNA fingerprinting ten years ago, the direct analysis of DNA variation has been successfully used in a wide range of applications and has become an important tool in forensic science. Most DNA typing systems assay DNA fragment length at repeated loci showing tandem repeats, for example, minisatellites and microsatellites, which exhibit allelic variation in tandem-repeat copy number. However, despite the great discriminatory power and sensitivity of this approach, it has inherent limitations that have prevented its full potential from being realized. The most informative loci, hypervariable minisatellites, have quasicontinous allelelength distributions, with many more alleles than can be resolved by agarosegel electrophoresis, making unequivocal identification of individual alleles impossible. This has led to protracted arguments over the definition of match criteria and the extent to which allele-size estimates are prone to error. This problem can, in principle, be overcome by using microsatellites, which have fewer and smaller alleles that can be precisely sized on sequencing gels. Although microsatellites have now been widely adopted in the construction of investigative forensic databases, these loci also have attendant drawbacks, the most important being restricted allelic variability, as compared to hypervariable minisatellites.

MINISATELLITE

We have developed a technique that can, in principle, overcome many of these limitations by sampling sequence variation, rather than length differences, between hypervariable minisatellite alleles. In addition to variation in the number of tandem repeats in an allele, all minisatellites characterized to date also show variation in the sequence of the repeated unit. As a consequence, alleles at such loci can exhibit internal variation in the interspersion of the different repeat-unit types. The positions of *minisatellite variant repeats* (MVRs) along a tandemly repeated array define an MVR map that represents the internal structure of an allele with respect to the distribution of those repeat-unit types. We have developed a simple PCR-based technique (MVR-PCR) that can be used to obtain MVR map information from alleles at any suitable minisatellite locus.

MVR-PCR uses different MVR-specific primers to recognize and prime from different repeat-unit types along a minisatellite allele. Separate amplifications between the different MVR-specific primers and a primer at a fixed site in the DNA flanking the minisatellite generate complementary sets of PCR products extending from the flanking primer site into the minisatellite repeat array and terminating at each type of variant repeat unit. The sets of PCR products are then resolved side-by-side by electrophoresis through an agarose gel. The resulting MVR maps can be revealed by ethidium-bromide staining, by Southern blot hybridization, and detection with radioactive or chemiluminescent probes, followed by autoradiography, or by using nonisotopically labeled primers. The rungs on the MVR ladder can then be read off as a simple digital code. MVR-PCR of individual minisatellite alleles gives a binary code, with bands in one lane or the other. Polymorphic positions in the DNA flanking minisatellites can be exploited to design allele-specific flanking PCR primers that enable the mapping of single alleles directly from the genomic DNA of individuals heterozygous at such polymorphic positions. At rare loci where most or all repeat units are the same length, MVR-PCR can be applied to genomic DNA using a universal flanking primer, to give a diploid map of the interspersion patterns of repeats from two alleles superimposed. Diploid MVR maps can be described by a ternary code with bands in either or both lanes.

There are several criteria to which a highly informative locus for MVR-PCR must conform. It must be polymorphic, preferably with an allele-length heterozygosity >95%, to ensure that most or all alleles are rare. Repeat-unit heterogeneity must not be too extensive, and sites of variation must be suitably positioned to allow the design of repeat-unit-specific primers. Furthermore, there must be little or no repeat-unit-length variation if diploid MVR mapping is to be performed. Collectively, these criteria are rather stringent; only two out of 49 hypervariable minisatellites isolated in this laboratory, MS32 (D1S8) and MS31 (D7S21), have all of the aforementioned characteristics.

Single-allele MVR mapping of these two loci has shown levels of variability far in excess of those estimated from Southern-blot length analysis and has also revealed a gradient of variability along the alleles of these loci, with most MVR map variation confined to one ultravariable end of the array. The high heterozygosity of these loci combined with polar allelic variability make diploid MVR maps generated from the ultravariable ends of MS31 and MS32 highly informative, almost to the point of individual specificity.

Both MS31 and MS32 have two common sites of base substitutional polymorphism in their repeat units; MS32 has an A/G transition separated by 1 bp from a C/T transition while the variant positions at MS31 are adjacent, G/A followed by C/T. However, only the more informative of the two sites (MS32 A/G and MS31 C/T) is assayed in each case. For historical reasons, MS32 repeat units with the "G" variant are called a-type repeat units and those with the "A" variant are called t-type repeat units. To ensure compatibility with computer software developed for analysis and manipulation of MS32 MVR-PCR allele codes, MS31 repeat units are also designated a-type ("T" variant) and t-type ("C" variant).

Both pairs of MS31 and MS32 repeat-unit-specific primers have a sequence complementary to the minisatellite repeat unit plus a noncomplementary 20 nt 5' extension ("TAG") and are identical, except for the 3'-most base, which corresponds to either form of the variant position being assayed. At the correct annealing temperature, these primers only allow extension from repeat units that they match perfectly. The TAG sequence allows MVR detection and subsequent amplification to be uncoupled by using different primers for each process. This prevents the progressive shortening of amplified products down to the first few repeat units, because of MVR-specific primers priming internally within extant PCR products at each PCR cycle. PCR amplifications are carried out with a very low concentration of a repeat-unit-specific detector primer plus high concentrations of the two driver primers, one in the minisatellite flanking DNA plus the TAG sequence itself. 32-TAG-A terminates with a "C" and recognizes a-type repeat units; 32-TAG-T terminates with a "T" and primes from t-type repeats. 31-TAG-A ends with an "A" and detects a-type repeat units whereas MS31 t-type repeats are detected by 31-TAG-G, which ends with a "G". At each PCR cycle, an MVR-specific primer will prime from different cognate repeat units along the minisatellite input molecules and extend into the flanking DNA past the flanking priming site. At the next cycle, the flanking primer will prime synthesis of a strand complementary to these products back into the minisatellite, terminating by creating a sequence complementary to TAG, from which the TAG primer can now prime. The high concentration of the flanking primer and TAG now allows efficient amplification of this second PCR product during subsequent PCR cycles.

Since the same PCR parameters are used in diploid mapping of both MS31 and MS32, combinations of primers can be used to generate diploid codes from MS31 and MS32 alleles simultaneously. "Duplex MVR-PCR" uses both MS31 and MS32 flanking primers, one of the MVR-specific primers from each locus and TAG. 31 -TAG-A and 32-TAG-A are used in one PCR reaction with 31-TAG-G and 32-TAG-T in the other, to maintain the conventional order of a-type and t-type repeat-unit lanes on MVR-PCR gels. Examples of diploid codes generated from MS31 and MS32 by duplex MVR-PCR are shown. Southern-blot analysis by sequential hybridization with MS31, followed by MS32, reveals complete sets of PCR products from each locus with no evidence of interlocus interference or cross-hybridization, indicating that repeat units from both loci amplify, and are detected, independently.

Diploid profiles from both MS31 and MS32 are encoded in the same way. For individuals with alleles containing both a-type and t-type repeats, the diploid map is described by a ternary code in which each rung from the bottom of the ladder upward is coded as 1 (a band in the a-lane only), 2 (a band in the t-lane only), or 3 (a band in both lanes). Positions that cannot be scored reliably, for example, those corresponding to PCR products too small to hybridize efficiently with the probe, are designated as ambiguous by a "?". Coding commences from the second repeat unit, since the hybridization signal from the first repeat is often too faint to allow reliable scoring; this start position is confirmed by reference to a standard DNA sample of known code run on all gels. Diploid MVR profiles from both loci can generally be reliably scored at least 50 repeat units into the minisatellite array. Diploid MVR-PCR typing of MS31 and MS32 in several hundred unrelated Caucasians, followed by ternary-code comparison, showed that there were on average 30 code mismatches per pair of individuals over the first 50 repeat units. No two individuals shared the same MVR code at either locus and all individuals could be distinguished using only the first 17 repeat positions.

Both MS31 and MS32 alleles also contain a small proportion (around 1%) of repeat units that are not amplified by either MVR-specific primer. These "null" or 0-type repeats can be scored by dosage at MS32 creating three additional coding states, namely 4 (a faint band in the a-lane), 5 (a faint band in the t-lane), and 6 (no bands at that position). Bands corresponding to states 4 and 5 are half the intensity of those for states 1 and 2, while code 6 positions, which are rare, appear as a gap on the ladder. Coding states 4, 5, and 6 will also be generated beyond the end of the shorter of a pair of alleles, since the code above this position will be derived from only one allele. No PCR products will appear beyond the end of the longer allele, generating a66666 . . . code. Because of variation in band intensity at MS31, dosage cannot be used to identify reliably the positions of null repeats, except for code 6 positions. However, the potential problem of misscoring weak bands as nulls does not compromise the use of diploid coding for individual identification, since individual specificity at both loci remains when band-intensity information is removed by converting all code 4 (a0) and code 5 (t0) positions to codes 1 (aa) and 2 (tt), respectively, to generate quaternary codes (1, 2, 3, and 6) corresponding to bands present only in the a-track, only in the t-track, in both tracks, and in neither track, respectively.

Diploid MVR-PCR provides a novel and simple method for generating highly discriminatory digital information directly from human DNA and therefore potentially provides a powerful new DNA profiling system for use in forensic DNA typing. The technique overcomes many of the limitations associated with DNA typing systems that involve allele-length measurements and also offers additional advantages. Most importantly, MVR-PCR obviates the problem of DNA-profile matching and allele-size measurement based on error-prone DNA fragment length estimation. MVR maps are resolved on agarose gels but do not require band-size measurements, meaning that code generation does not require standardization of electrophoretic systems, is immune to gel distortions and band shifts, and does not require side-by-side comparisons of DNA samples on the same gel. Furthermore, MVR maps are simple to encode in a standardized digital format, making them highly amenable to computer databasing and analysis, simplifying sample comparison and facilitating rapid database searches and the dissemination of MVR information between laboratories. These codes are ideal for objectively determining a match between a forensic sample and a criminal suspect, since match critéria are unambiguous. Diploid MVR-map databases will provide a simple method for determining the statistical significance of a match between a forensic sample and a suspect, by counting the frequency (probably zero) of the particular MVR code in the appropriate database.

Besides providing enormous, although as yet unquatified, exclusionary power, preliminary investigations suggest that MVR-PCR is particularly well-suited to many types of forensic analysis. It is applicable to very small quantities of DNA as well as to degraded DNA and, importantly, to mixed DNA samples of the type often encountered in forensic casework. In the latter case, single-allele MVR-PCR can often be used to recover MVR information from each individual contributing to the mixture. The technique can also be used in parentage testing, with the caveat that these loci have relatively high rates (1%) of *de novo* mutation to new MVR structures. In addition, the design of the MVR system means that it is also suitable for automation. For example, the use of ethidium-bromide staining or nonisotopically labeled primers, together with in-gel or microcapillary tube detection by laser scanning, may allow the scoring of MVR codes directly into a computer database. As such, diploid MVR-PCR provides a DNA-typing system as widely applicable and sensitive as many currently used in forensic casework.

Materials

Hardware and consumables

All chemicals, reagents, glass, and plasticware used for MVR-PCR are standard and can be purchased from recognized suppliers of molecular-biology reagents.

Apparatus

PCR amplification from genomic DNA

1. Thermal Cycler. We use GeneAmp PCR system 9600 or DNA thermal cycler 480, Perkin-Elmer/Cetus
2. Spectrophotometer to determine the PCR primer and template DNA concentration.

Agarose gel electrophoresis

1. Horizontal gel electrophoresis tank.
2. Electrophoresis power pack.
3. Gel molds and combs.

Southern blot hybridization

1. An orbital shaker for gel pretreatments (depurination, denaturation, and neutralization).
2. Capillary-action Southern-blot-hybridization platform.
3. Hybridization membrane.
4. Chromatography paper. Whatman 3MM Chr.
5. Blotting paper.
6. 80° oven to dry hybridization membranes.
7. UV source for DNA crosslinking, e.g., UV Crosslinker, UV transilluminator.
8. Siliconized Pasteur pipets for probe recovery.
9. Containers for Southern-blot hybridization. For safety and convenience we use hybridization bottles mounted in a heated rotisserie oven; dedicated perspex boxes or sealed plastic bags may also be used. If boxes or bags are to be used, a 65°C shaking waterbath or hybridization oven will be needed.
10. A boiling waterbath or 100°C heated block are required for probe denaturation.

Autoradiography

1. A hand-held β-monitor to estimate required exposure times/ conditions.
2. X-ray film, cassettes, and intensifying screens for autoradiography. Standard films are suitable, and X-ray cassettes are available from numerous manufacturers.

Reagents and solutions

PCR amplification from genomic DNA

1. Human genomic DNA.
2. Oligonucleotides. Primers for MVR-PCR were synthesized using an Applied Biosystems Model 380B DNA synthesizer and were ethanol-precipitated and dissolved in PCR clean water prior to use. Kits containing MVR-PCR primers and probes are available from Cellmark Diagnostics.
3. PCR buffer. The buffer used for all PCR in our laboratory is prepared as an 11.1X stock containing: 499.5 mM Tris-HCl, pH 8.8, 121 mM $(NH_4)_2SO_4$, 49.95 mM $MgCl_2$, 74.37 mM β-mercaptoethanol, 48.84 μM EDTA, pH 8.0, 11.1 mM dATP, 11.1 mM dCTP, 11.1 mM dGTP, 11.1 mM dTTP (purchased as 100 mM solutions from Pharmacia and stored at -20°C), 1.254 mg/mL

bovine serum albumin (BSA) (enzyme-grade BSA, 10 mg/mL from Pharmacia, stored at -20°C). Buffer is stored as 200 μL aliquots at -20° and is stable for at least 3 mo with repeated freezing and thawing.

4. Thermostable DNA polymerase (Stored at -20°C).

Agarose-gel electrophoresis

1. Low-EEO, high-gelling-temperature agarose.
2. Electrophoresis buffer: in 45 mM Tris-borate, 45 mM boric acid, 1 mM EDTA, 0.5 μg/mL ethidium bromide (0.5X TBE, pH 8.3). This is prepared as a 10X stock and stored at room temperature. Ethidium bromide (stored as a 5 mg/mL stock at 4°C) is added to a concentration of 0.5 μg/mL before electrophoresis.
3. 5X gel loading buffer: 12.5% Ficoll 400, 0.1% bromophenol blue in 0.2 M Trisacetate, pH 8.3, 0.1 M sodium acetate, 1 mM EDTA (5X TAE).
4. DNA size markers: 100 ng/μL fX DNA digested with HaeIII stored at -20°C.

Southern blot hybridization

1. Depurinating solution: 0.25 M HCl.
2. Denaturing solution: 0.5 M NaOH, 1.5 M NaCl.
3. Neutralizing solution: 0.5 M Tris-HCl, pH 7.5, 1.5 M NaCl.
4. High-salt transfer buffer (20X SSC): 3 M NaCl, 0.3 Mtrisodium citrate, titrated to pH 7.0 with HCl.
5. Phosphate/SDS hybridization solution: 0.5 M sodium phosphate, pH 7.2, 7% sodium dodecyl sulfate (SDS), 1 mM EDTA. Sodium phosphate is made as a 1 M stock by dissolving 97.1 g anhydrous disodium hydrogen orthophosphate and 49.3 g sodium dihydrogen orthophosphate in 1 L water and titrating to pH 7.2 with orthophosphoric acid if necessary. This solution is stored at 4°C and prewarmed to prevent precipitation before adding an equal volume of 14% SDS and EDTA to make the working solution.

Radioactive probe labeling

1. Probe DNA: MS31A is detected by the 5.7 kb *Sau*3 AI minisatellite insert isolated from the plasmid pMS31; MS32 is detected by the 5 kb *DraI* fragment from plasmid pMS32. Kits containing MVR-PCR primers and probes are available from Cellmark Diagnostics. Probes are diluted to a concentration of 20 ng/μL with water or TE and stored at -20°C.

2. Probe-labeling buffer: Probes are labeled using the random hexamer oligonucleotide priming method to incorporate α-^{32}P-dCTP. There are many commercially available random hexamer probe-labeling kits.
3. Oligonucleotide-labeling buffer (OLB) is made by mixing the following solutions A, B, and C in the ratio 2A:5B:3C. A: 1.25 M Tris-HCl, pH 8.0, 125 mM $MgCl_2$, 0.18% (v/v) β-mercaptoethanol, 0.5 mM dNTPs, store at -20°C. B: 2 M HEPES titrated to pH 6.6 with NaOH, store at 4°C. C: Hexadeoxy-ribonucleotides (Pharmacia), evenly suspended in 3 mM Tris-HCl, 0.2 mM EDTA, pH 7.0, at 90 OD U/mL, store at -20°C. OLB is divided into 60 μL aliquots and stored at -20°C; it is stable for at least three months with repeated freezing and thawing.
4. Klenow fragment of DNA polymerase I.
5. α-^{23}P-dCTP (110 TBq/mmol).
6. BSA 10 mg/mL, enzyme grade.

Radiolabeled probe recovery

1. Oligolabeling stop solution (OSS): 20 mM NaCl, 20 mM Tris-HCl, pH 7.5,2 mM EDTA, 0.25% SDS, 1 μM dCTP.
2. 2 M sodium acetate, pH 7.0.
3. 3 mg/mL high-molecular-weight herring-sperm DNA (Sigma). Supplied as a powder, dissolved in water, and stored at -20°C.
4. 100% ethanol.
5. 80% ethanol.

Post-hybridization washing solution

1. Hybond-N (fp) membranes are washed to high stringency following hybridization in 0. IX SSC, 0.01% SDS at 65°C. This is made up as required from stocks of 20X SSC and 10% SDS.

Autoradiography

1. Proprietary X-ray developer, stop and fixing solutions; e.g., Kodak LX24 developer, FX40 fixer and HX40 hardener.

Methods

MVR-PCR amplification from genomic DNA

1. Aliquot 1 μL of 100 00 ng/μL genomic DNA into two tubes per individual. DNA from an individual of known MVR code is included on all gels to standardize code registration.
2. Two MVR-PCR reaction mixes are required per individual, containing either one or the other repeat unit-specific primer

together with the other reaction components. These are made up as master mixes that are aliquoted into the reaction tubes containing the template DNA and also into empty tubes for the appropriate zero-DNA controls. Add 6 μL of the following MVR-PCR reaction mixes per individual to the template DNA, using the appropriate flanking and MVR-specific primers for MS31 or MS32.

3. (a) Transfer the tubes to a thermal cycler; (b) Program 20 cycles of: 94° for 30 s, 68° for 30 s, and 70° for 3 min, 1 cycle of 68° for 1 min and 70° for 10 min.

Agarose gel electrophoresis

1. Prepare the gel plate and comb.
2. Make up a 1% agarose gel. Suspend 1 g agarose powder per 100 mL 0.5X TBE + ethidium bromide (200 mL for a 20 cm gel, 400 mL for a 40 cm gel), heat to boiling in a microwave until the agarose is dissolved, cool to 50°C, and pour into the gel former.
3. Once set, transfer the gel to the electrophoresis tank and add 0.5X TBE buffer + ethidium bromide to just cover the surface of the gel. Cover the top surface of the gel with a glass/perspex plate, so that the buffer covers the gel but not the upper plate, and the wells are not covered by the upper plate.
4. Add 2 μL 5X TAE loading dye to each PCR reaction and transfer to a well in the agarose gel. a-type and t-type reactions from each individual are run in adjacent lanes.
5. Run the gel until the lowest rung of the MVR-PCR ladder is estimated to be close to the bottom of the gel by comparison with 1 μg ϕX/ *Hae*III size markers. For diploid mapping, this is when the 118 bp marker is at the bottom of the gel. For a 40 cm gel this takes approx 16 h at 130 V.

Southern blot transfer and hybridization

Southern blot transfer

1. After electrophoresis, turn the gel, still between the glass plates, upside down and transfer to a plastic tray.
2. Add depurinating solution to just cover the gel, shake gently using an orbital shaker for 5 min twice, with a change of solution after 5 min.
3. Carefully remove the depurination solution and cover the gel with denaturing solution. Denature for 10 min twice, with a change of solution after 10 min.

4. Remove the denaturing solution and cover the gel with neutralizing solution. Neutralize for 10 min twice, with a change of solution after 10 min.
5. Prepare a Southern-blot hybridization platform. This is made by draping a wick of Whatmann 3MM paper, saturated with 20X SSC, over a glass sheet longer and wider than the gel to be blotted, into a reservoir of 20X SSC in a plastic tray. Put an additional piece of 3MM cut larger than the gel to be blotted onto the 3MM and carefully remove all bubbles by rolling with a glass rod or pipet.
6. Transfer the gel to the hybridization platform, remove any bubbles by rolling, and surround with clingfilm to prevent direct transfer of buffer between the wick and the dry blotting material above.
7. Wet a piece of hybridization membrane, cut to the same size as the gel, with 10X SSC. Float the membrane onto the surface of a tray of 10X SSC to ensure the membrane is wetted evenly and completely, then submerge.
8. Place the wet hybridization membrane on top of the gel and remove any bubbles by rolling.
9. Wet two pieces of 3MM cut to the same size as the gel with 20X SSC and place on top of the hybridization membrane, remove bubbles by rolling.
10. Place a stack of absorbent paper, e.g., paper towels or Quickdraw (Sigma) on top of the 3MM paper.
11. Cover with a glass plate and place an evenly distributed weight of approx 1 kg/20 cm^2 on top.
12. Leave the blot to transfer for 2.5 h, with a change of blotting towels after 0.5 h.

Fixation of DNA to hybridization membrane

1. Remove the hybridization membrane from the blotting apparatus, rinse in 3X SSC and dry in an 80° oven (approx 30 min).
2. Place the membrane in a DNA crosslinker or on a transilluminator, with the DNA side facing the UV source. The UV dose required for most efficient crosslinking depends on the type of membrane used and the strength of the UV source. Optimal exposure time can be determined empirically for a UV transilluminator or set with a UV crosslinker to deliver a measured UV dose.

Probe labeling

1. Aliquot probe-DNA solution containing 10 ng probe (10 ng probe DNA is sufficient to hybridize up to 5 hybridization membranes) into a 1.5 mL microcentrifuge tube, make up to 20 μL with H_2O.
2. Denature probe DNA by placing in a boiling waterbath or 100° heated block for 3 min.
3. Immediately add 6 μL OLB, 1.2 μL 10 mg/mL BSA.
4. Add 2.5 μL α-^{32}P-dCTP.
5. Add 2.5 units of the Klenow fragment of DNA polymerase.
6. Incubate for 1 h at 37°C or overnight at room temperature. We generally find better label incorporation with the latter method and routinely obtain specific activities of labeled probe $>10^9$ dpm/μg.

Probe recovery

1. Add 70 μL OSS to the labeling reaction.
2. Add 40 μL H_2O.
3. Add 30 μL 2 M sodium acetate, pH 7.0.
4. Add 30 μL 3 mg/mL carrier herring-sperm DNA.
5. Add 500 μL 100% ethanol, shake to coagulate precipitated DNA, carefully remove ethanol using a siliconized Pasteur pipet.
6. Rinse DNA in 80% ethanol to remove unincorporated α-^{32}P-dCTP, remove ethanol and dissolve in 500 μL H_2O.

Hybridization

1. Prewarm hybridization solution to 65°C.
2. Transfer crosslinked hybridization membranes to a hybridization bottle or box, add sufficient hybridization solution to cover the membranes, prehybridize by incubating at 65° with rotation/shaking for a minimum of 10 min.
3. Denature the radiolabeled probe by placing in a boiling waterbath or 100° block for 3 min.
4. Remove the prehybridization solution and add the minimum volume of hybridization solution that will just cover the membranes.
5. Add the probe DNA to the hybridization solution immediately after denaturation.
6. Incubate overnight at 65° in a rotisserie or shaking waterbath.

Post-hybridization washing

Excess and nonspecifically hybridized probe is removed by washing the hybridization membranes at high stringency.

1. Heat 1 L high-stringency washing solution to 65°C.
2. Add 100 mL wash solution directly to the membranes in their hybridization bottles, or transfer filters to a plastic box for washing, repeat every 10 min until washing solution is finished.
3. Remove membranes from the last wash into a tray of 3 X SSC to rinse off remaining SDS, transfer to an 80° oven to dry.

Autoradiography

1. Once the filters are dry, attach them to a sheet of 3MM cut to the same size as the X-ray cassette. A 35-43 cm cassette will take two 20-30 cm hybridization membranes.
2. Use a hand-held β-monitor to estimate the exposure time that will be required. The hybridized filters from MVR gels generally give 100 cps, in which case expose overnight at room temperature without an intensifying screen. If the membranes count <50 cps expose overnight at 0°C with an intensifying screen.
3. After developing the first exposure, adjust exposure times/conditions accordingly to give required band intensities for subsequent exposures.

MVR-code analysis

1. Diploid MVR-maps are converted into a digital code and entered into a database using software written in Microsoft QuickBasic by A.J. Jeffreys, available from the author or from Cellmark Diagnostics on request. For individuals with alleles containing both a-type and t-type repeats, the diploid map is described by a ternary code in which each rung on the ladder can be coded as, 1 (both alleles a-type at that position, a band only in the a-track), 2 (both t-type, a band only in the t-track) or (heterozygous, a band in both tracks).

Notes

1. The techniques of PCR amplification, agarose-gel electrophoresis, Southern-blot transfer and hybridization, with either radioactive or nonisotopic probes, are almost universally used in molecular-biology laboratories. The precise apparatus and techniques used to carry out these routine procedures may vary from lab to lab; therefore, the general items of equipment suggested for use here may be substituted for by a similar alternative without affecting the overall results of the MVR analysis.
2. MVR-PCR amplification from genomic DNA. Because MVR-PCR operates optimally over an annealing temperature window of around

2°, a thermalcycling machine capable of accurate temperature control is required.

3. We use custom-built gel tanks constructed in-house to take an agarose gel 40 cm long and 20 cm wide; however, MVR maps can also be resolved on standard 20 cm agarose gels in tanks from most molecular biology-equipment suppliers, e.g., BioRad.
4. We have extensively tested different hybridization membranes and found Hybond-N (fp) to be the best for MVR-PCR.
5. If a transilluminator is used for crosslinking, it should be regularly calibrated, using test blots to determine the length of UV exposure required for optimal crosslinking.
6. MVR-PCR amplification from genomic DNA. As with any PCR technique, precautions should be taken to ensure that all tools and reagents used for PCR are free of contaminating DNA, contaminants that may inhibit PCR, and from other DNA molecules (e.g., recombinant molecules, other human DNA or PCR products). This is facilitated by the temporal and spatial separation of DNA preparation and subsequent PCR amplification. To minimize sources of PCR contamination, all solutions used for PCR are made using reagents transferred directly from containers as supplied by the manufacturer using sterile 25 mL plastic sample bottles or plastic tips taken directly from the bags in which they are supplied. Dedicated pipets and plasticware contained in a laminar-flow hood are used in the preparation of all PCR reagents and in setting up PCR reactions. All reactions should be performed with the appropriate zero-DNA controls.
7. We have found that organically extracted DNA provides the best template for MVR-PCR. DNA is diluted to a concentration of approx 500 ng/μL with PCR clean water and stored at 20°C. MVR-PCR can be performed on 10 ng or less input DNA and is also possible using subnanogram quantities of DNA; however, in the latter case, some MVR code information may be lost. Control template DNA of known MVR code is available in an MVR-PCR kit from Cellmark Diagnostics. MVR-PCR can tolerate large variations in the quantity of input DNA; therefore, precise quantification is not needed. We generally estimate DNA concentration by comparison with size markers or genomic DNAs of known concentration on agarose gels.
8. We have tested several kinds of Taq polymerase and found Amplitaq and the thermostable DNA polymerase from Advanced

Biotechnologies Limited to be the best for amplification of minisatellite repeats in our particular buffer.

9. A high-stringency phosphate/SDS hybridization buffer is recommended for use with all highly repetitive minisatellite probes, since they have the potential to cross-hybridize to other loci at lower stringency.
10. Both radioactive and nonisotopic probes are suitable for MVR-PCR analysis. Since the precise methods used for probe-labeling are not critical, the labeling protocols and reagents already routinely used in your laboratory are probably best for using in MVR-PCR.
11. To reduce the overall consumption of reaction components to a minimum, 7 μL reactions are performed. Larger reactions can be performed and may be required when dealing with very low quantities of input DNA. In this case, the quantities given can be scaled up accordingly.
12. The quality of MVR mapping data was found to be improved by reducing Taq polymerase concentration. With less Taq polymerase, the signal from misprimed PCR products is reduced; however, the overall yield of genuine products also decreases; 0.25 U/70 μL reaction was determined by titration to be optimal for MVR-PCR.
13. Duplex MVR-PCR of both MS31 and MS31 can be performed simultaneously by using both flanking primers together with Tag and repeat unit-specific primers for one of the repeat types at each of these loci in the same tube.
14. All temperatures and times quoted are for the Geneamp 9600 Perkin-Elmer/Cetus, using thin-walled 0.2 mL tubes. PCR parameters are the same for MVR-PCR amplification of both MS31 and MS32. Denaturing and annealing times may have to be altered (probably increased) for optimal MVR-PCR efficiency in other thermal cycling machines, especially if thicker walled 0.5 mL microfuge tubes are used for PCR reactions.
15. By increasing the number of cycles (to 30), increasing the concentration of repeat unit-specific primers (0.7 μL 2.5 μM primer per reaction) and omitting the TAG primer, it is possible to visualize MVR maps on ethidium-bromide-stained gels. However, it is only possible to obtain information from the first 15 repeat units using this procedure.

16. The use of allele-specific flanking primers in MVR-PCR allows the amplification of single alleles directly from the genomic DNA of an individual previously identified as being heterozygous at one of several polymorphic positions in the DNA flanking MS31 and MS32.
17. Precautions should be taken to maximize MVR map resolution and minimize aberrant migration, e.g., "smiling," caused by local variations in voltage and/or gel thickness. Using a 40 cm-long gel rather than the conventional 20 cm format increases the resolution of minisatellite repeat units, particularly toward the top of the gel. However, adequate resolution for forensic analysis can be obtained using a 20 cm gel. We routinely use a comb to form 26 wells, approx 0.15-0.4-0.4 cm per gel. MVR-PCR gels are poured on 40-20 cm glass plates, using a piece of masking tape securely round the edge to contain the gel. Using glass plates reduces the possibility that variation in thickness across the gel will occur as a result of bowing of plastic gel plates when they come into contact with hot agarose.
18. A spirit level is used to ensure that both gels and gel tanks are horizontal before electrophoresis.
19. Gels are poured in a cold room and covered in a thin layer of 0.5X TBE buffer, once set, to prevent the upper surface from drying out.
20. A glass plate is put on the top surface of the gel to maximize the current passing through the gel. This not only improves resolution and reduces the loss of small fragments due to diffusion, but also reduces the extent to which the lanes spread out toward the bottom of the gel. The upper plate can be removed to observe the extent of migration of DNA size markers.
21. In practice, the use of size markers is not necessary once the distance moved by the bromophenol blue in the loading buffer is known relative to the position of the first repeat unit. However, ethidium bromide is still included in the running buffer to enhance resolution.
22. Gels are Southern-blotted from below, since the loaded DNA is closer to this surface of the gel and will therefore transfer from this side more efficiently. Inverting the gel while it is still between the glass plates is much easier than inverting it later.
23. The precise method used for Southern blotting is not critical for MVR-PCR. If duplex MVR-PCR has been performed, it is possible

to do a bidirectional sandwich blot to a hybridization membrane placed on each side of the gel, and subsequently hybridize each of these with a different probe.

24. Both radioactive and chemiluminescent probes have been used successfully in MVR mapping. The protocols described here are for radioactive probe labeling. Protocols and probes for nonisotopic detection of MVR maps are available from Cellmark Diagnostics.

Minisequencing

Single-base substitutions, which give rise to biallelic sequence polymorphism, have been estimated to occur on the average at one out of a thousand nucleotides in the human genome. Analysis of this allelic variation can be utilized in population genetic studies, in genetic-linkage analysis, for the discrimination between individuals and for tissue typing. Genotyping by analyzing single-nucleotide polymorphisms provides some clear advantages compared to genotyping by analyzing multiallelic microsatellite markers. The mutation rate of single nucleotides is lower, single-base substitutions can be detected by technically simple, automatable methods, and the computational interpretation of the results is simpler.

We have developed an efficient method, denoted solid-phase minisequencing, for the detection of known single-nucleotide variations or point mutations. The method is routinely used in our laboratory in genetic linkage and association studies for analyzing biallelic markers as a complement to microsatellite markers. We have also applied the solid-phase minisequencing method to the identification of individuals in forensic analyses and paternity testing by analyzing a panel of 12 polymorphic nucleotides located on different chromosomes. The power of discrimination between individuals using the selected marker panel is 0.99996 in the Finnish population, and the average probability of exclusion in paternity testing is 0.90. Because of the technically simple format of the method, more polymorphic nucleotides can easily be added to the marker panel to increase the discrimination power of the system.

The principle of the solid-phase minisequencing method is to identify a polymorphic nucleotide at a predetermined site in a DNA template by specific extension of a primer by a single nucleotide using a DNA polymerase. First, a DNA fragment spanning the polymorphic nucleotide position is amplified with one unbiotinylated and one biotinylated PCR primer. The amplified biotinylated fragment is then captured on an avidin streptavidin-coated solid support, the excess of

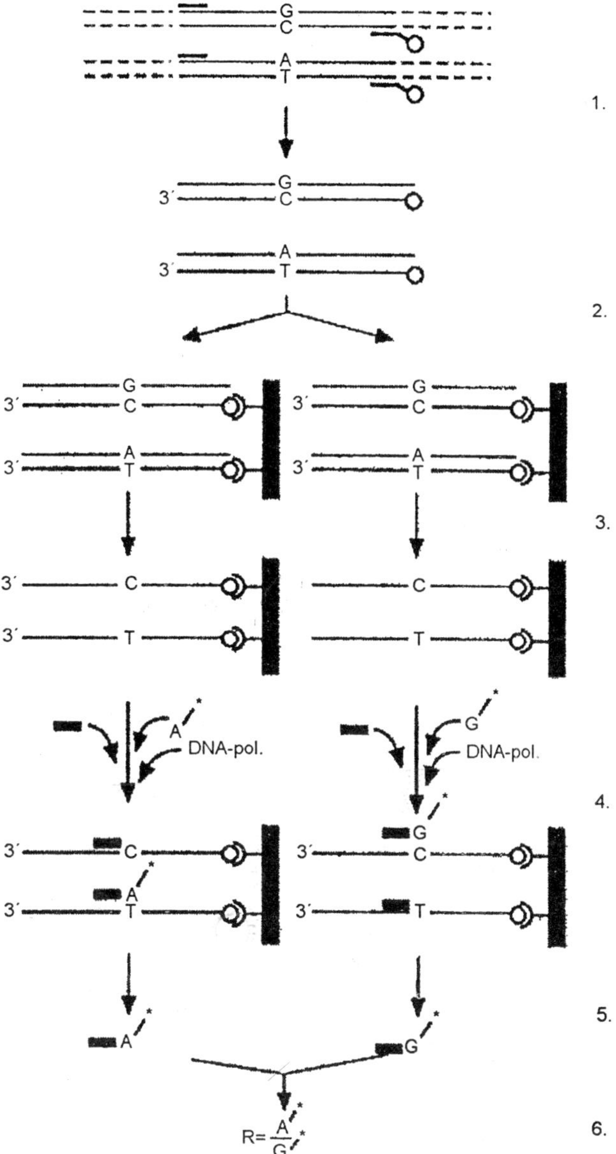

Fig. 11.1. Principle and steps of the solid-phase minisequencing method. (1) PCR with a biotinylated and an unbiotinylated primer. (2) Affinity-capture in streptavidin-coated microtiter plate wells. (3) Washing and denaturation. (4) Minisequencing primer extension reactions. (5) Measurement of the extended primers. (6) Interpretation of the result.

PCR reagents are removed by washing the support, and the captured DNA template is rendered single-stranded by alkaline treatment. The nucleotide(s) at the polymorphic site are identified in the remaining immobilized single-stranded DNA fragment by "minisequencing" reactions, in which a detection-step primer designed to anneal immediately adjacent to the polymorphism is extended with a single labeled nucleoside triphosphate complementary to the nucleotide at the polymorphic site.

The specificity of the solid-phase minisequencing method originates from the fidelity of the nucleotide incorporation catalyzed by the DNA polymerase, while the primer annealing reaction is carried out in nonstringent conditions. Therefore, all polymorphic nucleotides can be detected at the same reaction conditions, irrespectively of the flanking nucleotide sequence. The method can potentially be fully automated because it is carried out in a simple solid-phase format, and the results are obtained as objective numeric values that are easy to interpret and store. Furthermore, the solid-phase minisequencing method allows accurate quantitative PCR analysis of two sequences present as a mixture in a sample. This possibility has proven to be useful for rapid determination of the population frequencies of polymorphic nucleotides by quantitative analysis of large pooled DNA samples.

In the protocol for the solid-phase minisequencing method presented below, [^{3}H]dNTPs are used as labels, and streptavidin-coated microtiter plates serve as the solid support. All reagents and equipment required are readily available and generally applicable for detecting any polymorphic nucleotide.

Materials

Equipment

1. Access to oligonucleotide synthesis.
2. Programmable heat block and facilities for PCR.
3. Streptavidin-coated microtiter plates.
4. Incubator or water bath with shaker at 37°C.
5. Incubator or water bath at 50°C.
6. Liquid scintillation counter.
7. Multichannel pipets and/or microtiter plate washer (optional).

Reagents

1. Biotinyl phosphoramidite reagent for biotinylation of one of the PCR primers.

2. Thermostable DNA polymerase (e.g., *Taq* DNA polymerase, Promega Biotech or Dynazyme DNA polymerase, Finnzymes, Espoo, Finland) for PCR and the minisequencing reaction.
3. 10X concentrated DNA polymerase buffer: 500 mM Tris-HCl, pH 8.8, 150 mM $(NH_4)_2SO_4$, 15 mM $MgCl_2$, 1% (v/v) Triton X-100, 0.1% (w/v) gelatin. Store at -20°C, thaw completely before use.
4. dNTP mixture for PCR: 2 mM dATP, 2 mM dCTP, 2 mM dGTP, 2 mM dTTP. Store at -20°C.
5. Buffer for the capturing reaction (PBS-Tween): 20 mM sodium phosphate buffer, pH 7.5, 100 mM NaCl, 0.1% (v/v) Tween-20. Store at 4°C.
6. Washing buffer (TENT): 40 mM Tris-HCl, pH 8.8, 1 mM EDTA, 50 mM NaCl, 0.1% Tween-20. Store at 4°C.
7. Denaturing solution: 50 mM NaOH.
8. [^{3}H]-labeled deoxynucleoside triphosphates (([^{3}H]dATP, TRK 625; [^{3}H]dCTP, TRK 576; [^{3}H]dGTP, TRK 627; [^{3}H]dTTP, TRK 633).
9. Scintillation fluid.

Methods

Primer design

1. PCR primers that amplify a fragment, preferably between 50 and 200 base pairs in size, and contain the variable nucleotide position(s), are required. The PCR primers should be 20 nucleotides in size, have similar melting temperatures and noncomplementary 3'-ends. One of the PCR primers is biotinylated in its 5'-end during the synthesis.
2. The minisequencing-detection-step primer is designed to be complementary to the biotinylated strand of the PCR product immediately 3' of the variable nucleotide position. It should preferably be 20 nucleotides long and it should be at least five nucleotides nested in relation to the unbiotinylated PCR primer.

PCR amplification

1. Various types of DNA samples, treated as is suitable for PCR amplification, can be analyzed. PCR is performed according to a standard protocol, except that the concentration of the biotinylated primer should not exceed 0.2 μM (10 pmol/50 μL reaction).

Affinity-capture

1. Transfer two 10 μL aliquots (or four 10 μL aliquots for parallel assays of both nucleotides) of each PCR product to streptavidin-

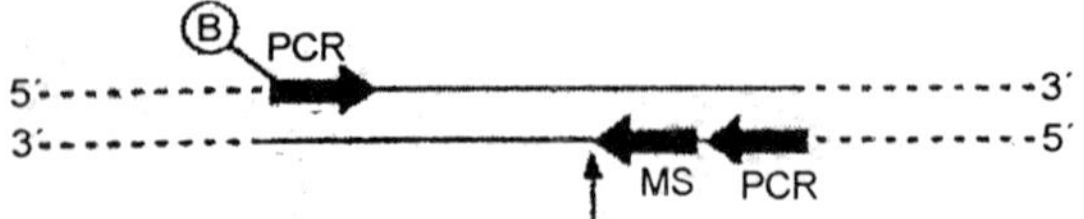

Fig. 11.2. Positions of the primers for solid-phase minisequencing.

coated microtiter plate wells. Include two negative controls containing DNA polymerase buffer only.

2. Add 40 μL of PBS-Tween buffer to each well and seal the wells with a sticker. Incubate the microtiter plate for 1.5 h at 37° with gentle shaking. Discard the contents of the wells.
3. Wash the wells manually three times at about 20° by adding 200 μL of TENT buffer. Empty the wells thoroughly between the washes by tapping the plates upside down against a tissue paper. The use of an automatic microtiter plate washer saves time and labor and improves the washing efficiency.
4. Denature the captured PCR product by adding 100 μL of 50 mM NaOH to each well, followed by incubation at 20°C for 2 min. Discard the NaOH and wash as in step 3 above.

Solid-phase minisequencing

1. Prepare the reaction mixtures for detecting each polymorphic nucleotide by combining 5 μL of 10X DNA polymerase buffer, 2 μL of 5 μM detection step primer (10 pmol), 0.1 μCi (usually 0.1 μL) of a [^{3}H]dNTP complementary to the nucleotide to be detected, 0.05 U of DNA polymerase and distilled water to 50 μL per reaction. It is convenient to prepare master mixtures for the desired number of reactions during the capturing reaction. The mixtures can be stored at room temperature until use.
2. For each amplified sample, add 50 μL of reaction mixture to the microtiter plate wells that correspond to the nucleotide to be identified. Seal the wells with a sticker and incubate the plate for 10 min at 50°C. Discard the contents of the wells and wash.
3. Release the primer by adding 60 μL of 50 mM NaOH to each well and incubate at 20°C for 2 min. Transfer the 50 mM NaOH solution containing the eluted primer to scintillation vials, add scintillation fluid, and measure the eluted ^{3}H in a liquid scintillation counter.

Interpretation of the result

1. The result from the scintillation counter is a numeric cpm value corresponding to the amount of [^{3}H]dNTP incorporated in a

minisequencing reaction. When the assay has been successful, the measured radioactivity will be 1000 cpm when incorporation of a [^{3}H]dNTP has occurred, and the background will be below 100 cpm.

2. Calculate the ratio (R-value) between the cpm value obtained in the reaction corresponding to one of the variable nucleotides and the cpm value obtained in the reaction corresponding to the other nucleotide. Calculation of the R-value eliminates variations in the amount of incorporated [^{3}H]dNTPs caused by variation between samples in the efficiency of PCR. The R-values fall into three distinct categories that unequivocally define the genotype of the sample. The R-value will be >10 or <0.1 in samples from subjects homozygous for one nucleotide and between 0.5 and 2 in samples from heterozygous subjects, depending on the specific activities of the [^{3}H]dNTPs used.

Notes

1. An obvious prerequisite for complete capture of the biotinylated PCR product in the streptavidin-coated wells is that the primer has been efficiently biotinylated (80%) during the synthesis. Normally the biotinylated primer can be used without further purification, but if necessary, biotinylated oligonucleotides can be purified from unbiotinylated oligonucleotides by HPLC, PAGE, or with the aid of disposable ion-exchange chromatography columns.
2. Because [^{3}H]dNTPs that are of low specific activity are used as labels in the minisequencing reaction, it is important that the PCR amplification be efficient. Ten microliters of the PCR product should be clearly visible on an agarose gel stained with ethidium bromide.
3. The biotin binding capacity of the microtiter plate wells sets an upper limit to the amount of biotinylated PCR product (and excess of biotinylated primer) that can be present during the capturing reaction. The biotin binding capacity of the wells is 2 pmol of biotinylated oligonucleotide. Therefore, in our standard protocol, the biotinylated primer is used at 0.2 μM (0.2 pmol/μL) concentration, and 10 μL of the PCR product is analyzed per well. If products of multiplex PCR reactions are to be analyzed, the amount of biotinylated primer during PCR and the volume of the analyzed aliquot should be reduced. If a higher biotin binding capacity is required, another affinity matrix with higher biotin binding capacity, such as avidin-coated polystyrene microparticles

(Fluoricon assay particles, 0.7 .9 μM) with extremely high biotin binding capacity (>2 nmol/mg of particles) or streptavidin-coated magnetic polystyrene beads can be used.

4. It is important for the specificity of the minisequencing reaction that all dNTPs from the PCR be completely removed by the washing steps. The presence of other dNTPs than the intended [^{3}H]dNTP during the minisequencing reaction will cause unspecific extension of the detection-step primer.
5. Other than thermostable DNA polymerases (e.g., T7 DNA polymerase), and dNTPs or ddNTPs labeled with other isotopes, haptens, or fluorphores, can also be used in the minisequencing reaction.
6. If a scintillation counter for microtiter plates is available, streptavidin-coated microtiter plates manufactured from scintillating plastic can be used as the solid phase. This will simplify the procedure in that the final washing and denaturing steps and the transfer of the eluted primer to scintillation vials can be omitted.
7. If, despite thorough washing, the R-value obtained in a sample does not fit into one of the three distinct categories defining the genotype of the sample, this indicates the presence of a mixed sample, e.g., contaminating DNA or a PCR contamination.
8. The R-value obtained in the solid-phase minisequencing method reflects the ratio between two sequences when they are present in a sample as a mixture in any other ratio than that in samples from homozygous subjects (allele ratio 2:0) or heterozygous subjects (allele ratio 1:1). Since the two sequences are identical, with the exception of a single nucleotide, they are amplified with equal efficiency during PCR. Thus the ratio between the sequences in the amplified sample measured by the minisequencing assay directly reflects the initial ratio between the sequences in the original sample. The ratio between two sequences in a sample can be calculated from the R-value, taking into account the specific activities of the [^{3}H]dNTPs used in the minisequencing reactions. If the sequence contains one (or more) identical nucleotides immediately next to the nucleotide at the variable site, one (or more) additional [^{3}H]dNTP will become incorporated, which obviously affects the R-value. Both of these factors are known in advance and can easily be accounted for. Alternatively, the ratio between two sequences can be determined by comparing the obtained R-value with a standard curve prepared by analyzing

mixtures of known amounts of the corresponding two sequences. The high specificity of the single nucleotide incorporation catalyzed by the DNA polymerase allows detection of one sequence present as a small minority (<1 %) in a sample. The use of a standard curve corrects for differences in specific activity and the number of $[^3H]$dNTPs incorporated, but also for a possible small misincorporation of a $[^3H]$dNTP by the DNA polymerase, which may affect the result, particularly when a sequence present as a small minority of a sample is to be quantified.

12

FORENSIC ANALYSIS OF DNA

Since their introduction into forensics some two decades ago, DNA-based genotyping technologies have revolutionized the science of human identification. Initially, panels of '*variable number tandem repeats*' (VNTR) probes were used in Southern blot applications and represented, at the time, a quantum leap over serological testing in their ability to discriminate between individuals. The invention of the *polymerase chain reaction* (PCR) fostered the introduction of the much shorter hypervariable '*short tandem repeats*' (STR), the major forensic DNA typing tool currently used, as well as mitochondrial DNA sequencing and, more recently, Y-STRs and *single nucleotide polymorphisms* (SNPs). Compared to VNTR analysis, PCR-based assays are better suited for the often-compromised nature of crime scene samples, they consume 1000-fold less sample and they reduce the sample processing time from weeks to less than 24 hours. Despite these significant advances in analytical methods, improvements in throughput have largely been offset by increased specimen collection at crime scenes and through expansion of legislated mandates for criminal offences. Although the existence of backlogs in many jurisdictions may be associated with high local crime rates, the resource-consuming, manual nature of forensic casework as it is performed in most laboratories remains a significant factor contributing to the backlogs. Additional opportunities for improving processing capacity and turn-around time reside in the development of faster evidence screening tools and in the introduction of automation for liquid handling and data analysis.

The elimination of offender and casework backlogs and the timely processing of incoming submissions are necessary steps towards achieving the true potential of DNA typing tecnnologies. No less necessary is the development of informatic tools not only to provide support for automation technologies necessary for improvements in process quality, reliability and throughput, but also to take full advantage of the information content of processed data sets. Although the resolution of many casework situations resides in direct matching of genotypes obtained from crime scene evidence and suspect(s), applications requiring more intricate data analysis have emerged in response to challenges of increasing complexity encountered in the field. Current laboratory information system (UIS) developments on the offender data banking front have largely dealt with supporting parallel processing pathways and automated data review to increase the reliability of uploaded offender genotype data. Other activities on that front aim at extending direct match capabilities to 'familial' search capabilities, as many offenders have been found to have next-of-kin already included in offender data banks. Data analysis applications are emerging on the crime scene front to assist with data interpretation of mixed profiles that often necessitate software-assisted, mathematical deconvolution for resolution. In situations where recovered human remains must be identified, significantly different approaches are required because a reference biological sample from the victim is often not available. In *mass fatality incidents* (MFIs), entire families often perish, making it necessary to use large-scale kinship analysis to reconstruct family pedigrees from within the victim's genotypic data set. The UIS applications have been built to address these numerous complexities on the path to identification in large-scale MFIs and ongoing developments aim at providing computing capabilities for even larger scale and more complex events. Much of the UIS infrastructure used for MFIs can be leveraged into the development of Missing Persons Databasing applications as very similar complexities are encountered.

This chapter presents the developments and applications of laboratory information systems that have promoted the growth of genetic forensic identification over the last decade. First, the major DNA analytical platform used in forensics is discussed to identify areas where automation technologies can provide improvements in the platform's qualitative and quantitative performance. Next, specific implementations of computing support to different forensic applications are reviewed. Finally, conclusions are presented regarding likely future directions for the adoption of technology and development activities by forensic laboratories.

Specifications of Forensic Genotyping Assays

The choice of genetic markers and assay technologies needs to be carefully considered if these technologies are to be employed in forensic genotype data banking. A decade ago, the forensic science community recognized in autosomal STRs a general genotyping technology with the potential for responding to data banking and casework needs. Since then, forensic laboratory facilities have developed considerable experience and invested heavily in an installed base of this technology. The platform has proven robust and cost-effective, performs well in a variety of operational contexts and, importantly, allows for casework mixed-source samples to be analysed. Although many other genetic markers, e.g. mtDNA, SNPs and Y-STRs, have been developed and are put to use in specific operational contexts, the current autosomal STR system is likely to remain the reference platform for forensic DNA analysis platforms for the foreseeable future. This will not impede development work on wet chemistry components of this assay as throughput improvements are expected to emerge from the implementation of thermal cycling and electrophoresis capabilities embarked on micro-fabricated devices.

Single tandem repeat genotyping is accomplished through multiplex PCR reactions designed to amplify up to 16 genetic markers or 32 different allelic targets in a single reaction. Its range of alleles and the presence of 1 bp variants confer high discrimination potential to the system and can be resolved with electrophoresis instrumentation designed for DNA sequencing applications. Several multiplexes configured for forensic application are commercially available and produce electropherograms balanced for intra- and inter-locus signal strength over a variety of forensic sample types. Precision and accuracy in allele calling are achieved on electrophoresis platforms with floating bins through the use of commercially available allelic ladders. A variable and generally small percentage of samples will either experience some random processing anomaly or present a rare but normal feature, both of which will be detected on electropherograms. These anomalies (e.g. '*spike*', pull-up, saturated and split peaks, elevated baseline, heterozygote ratio imbalance, elevated stutter, profile slope), at times, may interfere with accurate allele calling, or cause the affected sample to fall outside of quality control specifications.

Rare features may prove to be variant alleles, tri-allelic loci or unfavourable heterozygous ratio at a given locus as a consequence of a sequence polymorphism under a primer annealing site. The interpretation uncertainty associated with both random processing anomalies and rare genetic features is normally resolved by re-working the sample through the analytical platform: the latter condition will be replicated, the former will be resolved.

From an automation design perspective, the STR technology is stable – a desirable attribute as it limits the scope and costs of software maintenance/upgrades. The labour-intensive procedure involved in STR typing offers substantial opportunities for quality, reliability and productivity improvements through the introduction of automated solutions.

Automated Pipetting

As with any analytical platform, manual pipetting is best suited for the handling of very few samples at a time, and quickly becomes error-prone as throughput escalates. Automated liquid handling is the ideal solution in large-sample volume applications, such as convicted offender data banking. Proven robotic technologies tested in genome sequencing and clinical environments can be readily implemented in forensic environments, and their application can provide benefits in process precision and reproducibility, increased sample tracking confidence through reduction of error-prone tasks, the reliability of movements generated from computer programs and sample throughput.

Sample tracking confidence is an important aspect of data quality that automated pipetting can improve compared with manual processes. High-density assay plates are required for high-throughput applications involving the low reaction volumes of PCR-based assays, an environment where the high positional accuracy and reliability of automated pipetters are considered a prerequisite to secure sample tracking. The majority of robotic instruments can integrate barcode scanning devices to record the location and identity of all barcoded containers on the instrument work surfaces, assuring correct container addressing by pipetting or transport heads. A powerful feature available through this enhancement is operator-independent sample and reagent tracking. Many of these robotic systems offer logging capabilities that support quality assurance and chain-of-custody objectives by recording pipetting steps associated with specimen processing.

More sophisticated implementations support communication with external systems such as LIS applications. Logic can be introduced to permit the LIS to control many aspects of sample flow management. Client-based applications can be designed to initiate a transaction containing information about specimens, reagents, operators, instruments, etc. prior to initiating a processing step. After the LIS has confirmed that sequential processing steps are completed in order, reagents are appropriate and have passed quality control tests, operators and equipment are validated, as well as making other important confirmations, a transaction is returned to the client application to signal that processing can proceed. A final transaction is sent back by the client application to the database to record that the process is complete. Since queries to the database can be incorporated at the outset of various processing steps, the LIS can track the progress of every sample, prevent inappropriate processing and alert operators about detected incongruities.

A further level of integration brings under the management of LIS applications the control of robotic instrumentation through worklists – large yet simple text files that contain the required pipetting commands for the execution of a routine – written in language supported by the robot's control software. Pipetting and sample flow management logic can be integrated to transform isolated instruments into components of fully integrated processing platforms. If the intuitive approaches of trained forensic analysts can be understood in sufficient detail to permit their description in a rules-based system, then the system can dynamically alter default processing schemes when certain pre- or mid-process conditions are met. This type of customization can include every aspect of automated pipetting, such as changing source and/or destination containers (i.e. cherry-picking), altering transfer volumes and changing liquid pipetting specifications.

Sample flow management logic can manage sample re-processing queues to regroup samples that share the same point of reintroduction in the processing scheme or similar modified pipetting schemes, and build batches optimized for pipetting efficiency. An integrated capability promotes higher first-pass processing success by reducing wasteful analytical attempts under non-ideal conditions, which may prove mission-critical for many scarce casework samples. Such a system provides flexibility with the processing platform that exceeds what may normally be achieved manually.

Convicted offender databanking was the first forensic process to employ extensive automation. These specimens are collected under controlled conditions similar to those employed for clinical genetic testing, making for ideal specimens for genetic analysis. As most of the wet chemistry is similar from one forensic application to the next, the experience from automated processing of large numbers of convicted offender specimens has been leveraged into other areas of forensic processing. However, variation in sample input attributes greatly increases the processing contingencies that must be handled and thereby increases the design complexity for an automated processing system. In that respect, casework and MFI samples, being collected at crime/ disaster scenes, often present compounded problems linked to substantial variation in substrate, cell/tissue type and quality/quantity of recoverable biological material, which calls for chemistries and robotic pipetting schemes supporting a larger range of quality/quantity of input material. The increase in precision and reproducibility afforded by automated pipetting devices provides a consistency that may improve the quality of STR data generated from compromised samples.

Casework samples also present additional intricacies at the evidence screening step as many samples need to be localized and cut away from larger pieces of evidence, all samples need to be assessed to confirm human origin of the recovered material, the body fluid involved, their suitability for ensuing DNA extraction and genetic analysis, and the amount of material to be processed in order to meet processing platform sample input range specifications. A substantial, largely manual front-end processing step is necessary to qualify the samples for further processing and direct them to an appropriate wet chemistry processing protocol. Throughput improvements for this front-end step may come from improved stain visualization technologies, streamlined presumptive tests and clerical technologies (i.e. LIS-supported voice recording, speech-to-text software, digital photography and tactile computer screens) to facilitate and ex pedite accurate information capture.

In summary, substantial improvements in throughput can be readily realized through the implementation of LIS-supported automation of pre-data analysis steps. Development activities should focus on enhancing efficiencies through aids to evidence screening, and on the extended integration of automated liquid handlers with LIS systems. Continued progress in these fields is essential if reductions in casework backlogs are to parallel those for convicted offenders.

Analysis of STR Data

The review of STR data can be relatively straightforward for pristine, single-source specimens such as those collected from convicted offenders. Still, regardless of sample type, a number of samples will present some anomalous features that may interfere with the final allele call and genotype assignment. Most anomalies (e.g. pull-up, saturated and split peaks, elevated baseline, heterozygote ratio imbalance, elevated stutter, profile slope) will present electrophoretic data signatures that can be recognized by suitably designed algorithms and quality metrics. In fact, automated quantitative assessment of quality metrics is likely to be more efficient at enforcing quality control thresholds than through human review. However, not all qualitative problem scenarios can be anticipated and coded into quality control algorithms intended for automated data review systems. In order to ensure that all anomalous results are scrutinized, the experience of trained analysts must bear on the final interpretation of the data. Historically, it has been customary for all data to be subjected to dual review by separate analysts, although the practice can become a limiting throughput factor in certain environments.

Many large data banks have developed automated data review packages, or '*expert systems*', integrated in their LIS systems, and several software packages are commercially available as well. Quantitative measurements used to affirm quality control thresholds form the basis of these review applications. Detection of the presence of mixtures, genuine or due to cross-contamination within a processing batch, are additional features available in current applications. Electrophoretic data signatures of frequently encountered anomalies, commonly referred to as '*rules*', are used to filter data sets and flag electropherograms that require a second, human review.

The available published data on the performance of these systems on convicted offender type samples indicate that, on average, 30% of allele calls are flagged by at least one rule. This significant number of flagged allele calls may reflect the removal of subjectivity of human review from the process, resulting in more consistent examination of every locus, as well as the enforcement of more stringent thresholds to ensure the capture of all problematic data. However, very high allele call concordance (>99.9% in most studies) between manual and automated review results was reported, which provides support to the feasibility of replacing a two-person review process with a single reviewer assisted by a computer algorithm.

Casework data review presents additional complexities linked to the often-compromised nature of the casework specimens. Increased slopes across profiles, dropped-out alleles and mixtures are regularly encountered with these specimens. An automated data review system configured for data-banking needs may indicate which casework samples need further review.

Analysis of Mixtures

Some of the most complex crime scene evidence samples from a data analysis standpoint contain biological material from multiple contributors, typically encountered with sexual assault evidence. The simplest and most common mixture scenario stems from a contamination of the differential lysis sperm fraction with the epithelial fraction originating from the victim. These are the easiest analytical circumstances since the known genotype of the victim may be subtracted from the mixed profile to establish a list of obligate alleles for the perpetrator. If the male contributor to the mixture represents the major profile in the mixture, it may prove possible to deduce a complete male genotype, which is ideally suited for a search of both the convicted offender and crime scene indices of data banks.

The next most common mixture situation involves a sperm fraction holding two male profiles – the perpetrator's and the victim's consensual partner – reflecting consensual intercourse in the hours/days preceding the assault. In the much rarer instance of collective sexual assaults, multiple male contributors may be recovered from the sperm fraction, generating a much more complex STR profile that may prove impossible to deconvolute with technologies available at this time. Under these last two scenarios, no procedure akin to differential lysis can alter the major : minor contributor ratio to facilitate discrimination between contributors.

When the investigation has produced individual(s) suspected to have contributed to a mixture, a first investigative step is to attempt to exclude the suspect(s) as contributor(s) to the mixture. In the absence of suspects, the perpetrators' genotypes must be dissected out from the mixed profile to allow for a search against a convicted offender data bank. The deconvolution of a mixture involves three steps: the ascertainment of the number of contributors, the estimation of the proportion of the individual contributions to the mixture and the establishment of a list of possible contributing genotypes that could explain the mixed profile along with probability estimates. When the ratio of components of a two-contributor mixture is more than 1:3, peak height or peak area information may allow an analyst to visually resolve the major and minor components of the mixture.

With other ratios of contributors, the ascertainment of the number of contributors can prove a challenge in itself, and an incorrect assessment may have dramatic effects on the interpretation of testing results. Many approaches to mixture deconvolution have been proposed over the years, but a consensus on mixture interpretation guidelines has yet to emerge.

Several LIS systems designed to assist with mixture deconvolution are being evaluated in the community. Bill *et al.* (2005) proposed a computerized algorithm to estimate the proportion of the individual contributions in two-person mixtures and to rank the genotype combinations based on minimizing a residual sum of squares, eliminating unreasonable genotypic combinations.

Perlin and Szabady (2001) and Wang *et al.* (2002) have proposed *linear mixture analysis* and *least square deconvolution* models, respectively, to estimate mixture proportion and enumerate a complete set of possible genotypes that may explain the mixed profiles. Cowell *et al.* (2006) have proposed a model unifying, under a single Bayesian network model, many of the elements of the above-mentioned models. No model currently takes into account all potential technical complications such as dropped-out alleles, stutter and excessive profile slopes.

Bioinformatics

The comparison of genotypes is an intrinsic component of all forensic genetic analysis. Comparative analysis can link crime scene to suspect, victim to relative and reveal cases that share perpetrators. Most computations performed in data banks involve searches for perfect or partial genetic matches between a query and an entry in one of the data bank indices. System innovations currently focus on 'familial searching' algorithms. As nearly half of jailed inmates in the USA are reported to have at least one close relative who has been incarcerated, the use of likelihood ratio computations to detect potential parent–child or sibling relationships between an unknown perpetrator's genotype recovered in crime scene evidence and that of a catalogued offender offers new investigative possibilities, and could lead to a substantial increase in cold hit rates, if implemented.

Over the last decade, the forensic community was confronted with several challenges, unique in scope of work and technical complexity, in the wake of large- scale MFIs. From airliner mishaps to the World Trade Center attacks to tsunamis, large increases in the number of victims and extreme fragmentation and/or decay of recovered remains have led to a considerable paradigm shift in the way that identification initiatives are conducted and in the laboratory infrastructure needed to handle such events. DNA typing has taken a major role in large-scale events involving high body fragmentation. The complexity of these initiatives is such that bioinformatics have become a crucial component for identification mandates to be met.

All MFIs are unique in the circumstances of the incident, and the required identification solutions will vary between incidents. There are common limitations to these events that create unique demands on LIS applications to support DNA-based identifications. The first limitation pertains to unavailability of a reference genotype, usually generated from trace biological material recovered from a personal effect (i.e. personal hygiene items), for a proportion of the victims of MFIs as probative personal effects are often destroyed in many events (e.g. air crashes). This limitation makes it necessary to supplement direct matching algorithms with computationally-intensive large-scale kinship analysis and parentage trio searching routines.

The second limitation is linked to the obligation of performing parentage trio searching routines, and results from the inaccuracy of some reported biological relationships as a consequence of incorrect information capture. Traditional triangulation methods, by which the third member of a parentage trio can be quickly located within a genotype data set with the help of a list of obligate alleles derived from the two surviving members of the trio, rely on the accuracy of next-of-kin self-reported biological relationships. An alternate procedure is required to detect parentage trios solely on a genetic basis, immune to sample accessory information errors. This is especially important for *missing persons databasing* (MPD) initiatives as, contrary to MFIs, MPDs are open-ended, long-term initiatives and, as such, problematic data may go undetected indefinitely.

The alternative procedure is also crucial for events where families are among the victims (e.g. most airliner mishaps) as pedigrees must be re-assembled, solely on a genetic basis, from within the victims' genotype data set. This alternative procedure calls for the evaluation of every possible parentage trio involving each victim and every pair of related and unrelated next-of-kin, an evaluation that may amount to a very substantial and escalating computing workload.

Many additional event-related limitations add more complexity still. More often than not in MFIs, remains recovery is partial, a proportion of recovered remains has incurred significant thermal/chemical/bacterial decay leading to the production of partial genotypes during analysis, many potential contributors to parentage trios involving older victims may be pre-deceased and many victims may have few next-of-kin who can be used as genotypic references. Computing solutions are expected to provide ways to mitigate the lack of complete STR profiles from the recovered remains and the absence of important reference genotypes.

Finally, the scale of the incident has significant impact on computing parameters. As pair-wise comparisons are the mainstay of computing efforts in MFI victim identification, the computing load increases nearly exponentially with the number of victims. These complicating factors add considerable complexity to the design of bioinformatics tools required to produce the necessary identification inferences.

As much as the World Trade Center appears to have been the most demanding identification initiative to date, the circumstances of the incident could have substantially increased the complexity of DNA-based identifications. The data processing contingencies would have been very different if the collapse of the World Trade Center towers had trapped the normal weekday occupancy of 50000 instead of 2749, or had included families. High body fragmentation/high remains dispersal incidents involving 100000 or 1000000 casualties as a result of natural, accidental or terrorist activity are within the realm of possibilities.

Bioinformatic tools that can handle this sample load have been developed, however it is unclear whether the STR loci currently in use in forensics would provide sufficient discrimination power to support large-scale kinship analysis and parentage trio searching algorithms. These scenarios can be simulated and conclusions drawn as to the genetic marker set and computing capabilities that would be required in varying circumstances.

The scale and complexity of current forensic projects, such as large backlogs of data bank/casework samples, large-scale MFIs or MPDs, have reached a level where these projects can greatly benefit from the utilization of LIS-assisted automation technologies. The throughput and sample tracking capabilities afforded by LIS-driven automated liquid handlers will contribute to substantial reductions in backlogs and improvements in process quality, sample tracking confidence and turn-around time. Although these instruments have tremendous capacity, they address aspects of laboratory processing that tend not to limit throughput.

The labor-intensive procedures of data review, data collation, enforcement of quality control standards and formatting results for submission to databases stand to benefit from the introduction of automated data review applications. Expert systems to assist with casework mixture deconvolution are emerging and will benefit from a consensus on mixture interpretation from the forensic community. Familial searching algorithms would provide investigative assistance in cases where perpetrators are not yet registered in offender data banks. The victim identification of large-scale MFIs and MPDs has greatly benefited from LIS-based large-scale comparative genotyping applications to achieve their mandates, and larger throughput capabilities are being developed. These LIS-based technologies will continue to evolve and take full advantage of the information content of available forensic genotypic data.

13

Application and Measurement

Pharmacogenomics encompasses several major areas: the study of polymorphic variations in drug response and disease susceptibility, identification of the effects of drugs/xenobiotics at the genomic level, and genotype/phenotype associations. The most common type of human genetic variations is *single-nucleotide polymorphisms* (SNPs). Several novel approaches to detection of SNPs are currently available. The range of new methods includes modifications of several conventional techniques, such as PCR, mass spectrometry (ms), and sequencing, as well as more innovative technologies such as *fluorescence resonance energy transfer* (FRET) and microarrays. The application of each of these techniques is largely dependent on the number of SNPs to be screened and sample size. The current chapter presents an overview of the general concepts of a variety of genotyping technologies, with an emphasis on the recently developed methodologies, including a comparison of the advantages, applicability, cost efficiency, and limitations of these methods.

The human genome is made up of approx three billion nucleotides that code for all the macromolecules necessary for human life. The most common types of human genetic variations are single-nucleotide polymorphisms (SNPs), which are defined as DNA sequence variations that occur when a single nucleotide (A, T, C, or G) in the genome sequence is changed. It is estimated that only one in every thousand bases is different, or that the DNA code is approx 99.9% identical between human subjects. SNPs occur in both coding and noncoding regions and may or may not result in altered gene expression or gene products. Even SNPs that do not themselves change protein expression and cause disease may be in close physical proximity on the chromosome, or "linked" to deleterious mutations. Because of this linkage, SNPs may be shared among groups of people with harmful but unknown mutations and serve as markers for them. Such markers can help uncover the actual functional mutations and accelerate efforts to find therapeutic drugs.

One of the initial applications of the recent advances in the human genome sequencing project is the emerging field of pharmacogenomics. Pharmacogenomics encompasses several major areas: the study of polymorphic variations to drug response and disease susceptibility, identification of the effects of drugs/xenobiotics at the genomic level, and genotype/phenotype associations. The promise of pharmacogenomics is that studies using genome-based technology will lead to the identification of novel SNPs and the characterization of their impact on human health. The development and application of screening technologies is therefore of high priority.

The last decade or so has witnessed a veritable explosion in the design and development of molecular genetic technologies that can be used in pharmacogenomic and molecular toxicological studies to understand the biological basis of complex traits and diseases and their relationship to environmental exposures. It is well-recognized that characterization of DNA sequence variation will enable the identification of novel genetic risk factors for disease, novel targets for drug therapies, and avoidance of adverse drug reactions. The SNP consortium (a group of pharmaceutical and bioinformational companies, five academic centers, and a charitable trust) is currently producing an ordered high-density SNP map of the human genome.

For the last 25 yr, the most commonly used approach to identify genes that influence traits has been meiotic or linkage mapping. All linkage analysis methods involve the assessment of the transmission and cosegregation of alleles at regions on the genome known as marker loci, with disease alleles assumed to be carried by family members exhibiting the disease of interest. Unfortunately, linkage analysis has not proved powerful enough to detect genes influencing many common multifactorial diseases, primarily because the study of genes with a small to moderate effect on a trait or a disease requires the collection of hundreds if not thousands of families for reliable results.

There are a variety of reasons why SNPs have emerged as an alternative form of sequence variation for gene identification and mapping studies. Primary among them is the high frequency with which

SNPs are found in the genome, lending utility for the discovery of disease-related genes. SNPs are found throughout the genome, in exons, introns, intergenic regions, promoters, enhancers, and so on. Therefore, they are likely to be associated with a functional or physiologically relevant allele. Because SNPs occur in such great abundance over the genome, groups of neighboring SNPs may have alleles that show distinctive patterns of linkage disequilibrium and may create a haplotypic diversity that can be exploited in both genetic linkage and direct association epidemiologic studies. Another advantage to studying SNPs is that since they typically have only two variant alleles, SNPs will have allele frequencies that will drift as a function of the dynamics of different populations, creating allele frequency differences that can be exploited in population-based studies. Lastly and most importantly, owing to their simple structure, the development of technologies that enable rapid, efficient, and cost-effective genotyping of thousands of individuals for hundreds of SNPs has become possible.

A number of novel, high-throughput genotyping technologies have recently been developed, including various microarray formats, matrix assisted laser desorption/ionization time of flight (MALDI-TOF) mass spectrometry (MS), and TaqMan allele discrimination approaches. However, these current state-of-the-art approaches do not yet meet all of the requirements for maximum utilization of genotyping information. A major issue with each of these approaches is the cost per SNP detection. Currently, most procedures involve polymerase chain reaction (PCR) amplification of a target sequence, a somewhat costly and time-consuming method that limits possibilities for automation. As the scale of genotyping analyses increases, the cost per genotype will need to decrease from the current level of approx $1–3 to pennies or tenths of pennies. A second key requirement for any genotyping technology is flexibility. As new SNPs are identified, there will be a need for rapid inclusion of the novel SNP within the screening procedure. For several currently commercially available, preconfigured microarrays, this is a major problem. Although it is now possible to reconfigure an existing microarray or develop a new custom array more rapidly, these technologies are still associated with high costs for synthesis and further assay validation requirements. Additional requirements for an optimal genotyping approach include sensitivity (requiring less than 1 ng genomic DNA/genotype), scalability and automation compatibility, and efficient turnaround times. For most of these newer technologies, DNA template amount is not a problem, although the amount of input DNA for microarray analysis is relatively higher.

PCR-Based Techniques

SSCP-PCR

Single-strand conformational polymorphism (SSCP) analysis is one of the most widely used methods for mutation detection. DNA regions with potential polymorphisms are amplified by PCR, the products are denatured, and the single strands thus formed are electrophoresed on a polyacrylamide gel. A fragment with a single base modification migrates differently than wild-type DNA. Alternative conformation-based mutation screening methods include conformation-sensitive gel electrophoresis, chemical or enzymatic mismatch cleavage detection, *denaturing gradient gel electrophoresis* (DGGE), and denaturing *high-performance liquid chromatography* (HPLC). The underlying principle of these methods is that the melting characteristics of double-stranded DNA are defined by its sequence, and hence a single-base mismatch can produce conformational changes in the double helix that cause the differential migration of homoduplexes and heteroduplexes containing base mismatches during gel electrophoresis. This method is highly sensitive for identifying mutations in areas of highly GC-rich sequences.

PCR Mismatch Cleavage Detection

Mismatch cleavage detection takes advantage of the fact that mismatched bases are sensitive to cleavage by enzymes and chemicals. After PCR amplification, wildtype and variant alleles are subjected to denaturation/renaturation to create heteroduplex molecules. The products are electrophoresed side by side to detect the presence of mismatch cleaved molecules following incubation with resolvases.

Denaturing Gradient Gel Electrophoresis (DGGE)

In denaturing gradient gel electrophoresis, the PCR products are resolved on a denaturing gradient gel containing formamide and urea under temperature control. SNPs are revealed by their migrational differences from wild-type homoduplexes. The major advantage of this method is its accuracy; however, its disadvantages are low throughput and difficulty of optimization.

Denaturing HPLC

In this method, polymorphisms are detected by analyzing the mobility of DNA heteroduplexes using chromatography under denaturing conditions. The variant sample is first hybridized with wild-type DNA to form a mixture of homo- and heteroduplexes. The heteroduplexes can be separated from the homoduplexes by column chromatography at a temperature that partially denatures the mismatched DNA.

Restriction Fragment Length Polymorphism (RFLP)-PCR Analysis

For *restriction fragment length polymorphism* (RFLP)-PCR analysis, a specific target region of genomic DNA is amplified by PCR. The product is then digested with appropriate restriction enzyme(s) and visualized after being gel-electrophoresed. If the SNP produces a gain or loss of restriction site, the restriction pattern is altered, and homozygous wild-type, mutant, or heterozygote carriers are easily identified. A major limitation of this method is the requirement that the polymorphisms result in an altered restriction enzyme site.

Oligonucleotide Ligation Assay (OLA) Genotyping

The *oligonucleotide ligation assay* (OLA) approach is based on the premise that hybridization with specific oligonucleotide probes effectively discriminates between wild-type and variant sequences. Three probes are used in this assay, two allelespecific probes and a common fluorescent probe. The 5'-end of the common probe is immediately adjacent to the 3'-end of the allele-specific probe. The PCR product is incubated with the three probes in the presence of thermally stable DNA ligase. Ligation of the fluorescently labeled probe to the allele-specific probe occurs only when there is a perfect match between the probe and the template. The wild-type and the variant genotypes are differentiated following electrophoresis of the ligated products. The major disadvantage of this method is that highly GC-rich regions make the allelespecific ligation step difficult to optimize.

Branch Migration Inhibition (BMI)

The *branch migration inhibition* (BMI) technique is based on the fact that spontaneous strand exchange is inhibited by sequence differences between two DNA molecules. Genomic DNA is amplified using four primers. The two forward primers are 5'-labeled with either biotin or digoxigenin. The two reverse primers have similar priming sequences but different tail sequences, which consist of 20 nucleotides that are not complementary to the genomic target but are incorporated into the PCR products. The PCR products are then subjected to heat denaturation and reannealing of single strands to form, eventually, a doubly labeled, four-stranded cruciform DNA structure. When there is no mutation, the two arms of this structure are identical, and strand exchange via branch migration leads to its complete dissociation into two duplex molecules, producing no signal. In the presence of a sequence difference, as in mutation or polymorphism, branch migration in the presence of Mg^{2+} is inhibited, and the cruciform structure does not get resolved. Thus, the stable association of biotin and digoxigenin is detected by standard *enzyme-linked immunosorbent assay* (ELISA) techniques. One of the primary limitations of BMI is that it cannot distinguish between homozygotes for two alternative alleles. It only detects heterozygotes and therefore requires an additional step, in which a reference amplicon is added to each amplified sample corresponding to one of the two possible homozygotes. The denaturation and branch migration steps are then repeated.

PYROSEQUENCING

Pyrosequencing is a DNA sequencing technique based on the detection of released pyrophosphate (PPi) during DNA synthesis. In a cascade of enzymatic reactions, visible light is generated that is proportional to the number of incorporated nucleotides. The cascade starts with a nucleic acid polymerization reaction in which inorganic PPi is released as a result of polymerase-mediated incorporation of nucleotides. The released PPi is subsequently converted to ATP by ATP sulfurylase, which provides the energy to luciferase to oxidize luciferin and produce light. Since the added nucleotide is known, the sequence of the template can be determined. Pyrosequencing uses the Klenow fragment of *E. coli* DNA *Pol*I. The ATP sulfurylase used in pyrosequencing is a recombinant version from the yeast *Streptomyces cerevisiae*, and the luciferase is from the American firefly *Photinus pyralis*. One picomole of DNA yields 6×10^{11} ATP molecules, which generates more than 6×10^{9} photons at a wavelength of 560 nm. A charge-coupled device (CCD) camera easily detects this light. Two different pyrosequencing strategies are currently available: solid and liquid phase. Solid-phase pyrosequencing utilizes immobilized DNA, and the excess substrate is washed off after each nucleotide addition. In liquid-phase pyrosequencing, a pyrase, a nucleotide-degrading enzyme is introduced, thereby enabling the removal of the solid phase support and intermediate washing. For SNP analysis using pyrosequencing, the 3'-end of the primer is designed to hybridize one or a few bases before the polymorphic position. Each allele combination provides a distinct pattern on the program readout. These programs can be analyzed manually or by pattern recognition software.

Array Pyrosequencing

Pyrosequencing can be applied to both ordered and random arrays; for example, the PSQ 96 System employs a DNA array, a nucleotide delivery module, and a CCD camera. A sprayer is used to deliver all four different nucleotides. Current imaging technologies require a minimum of more than 5000 template molecules. Several optimizations are still under way to allow the use of this technology for reliable high-throughput DNA sequencing, but the range of applications is growing as more institutions acquire the technology.

Specialized software has been designed to automate the classification of genotypes for samples screened by pyrosequencing in a microtiter plate using a SNP genotyping algorithm. Based on pattern recognition, this algorithm both scores the genotype and provides a value for the quality of each SNP that is scored. The assignment of this value is based on a number of different parameters, including differences in expected and obtained sequences around the SNP, signal-to-noise ratio, and variance in peak height and peak width.

Dynamic Allele-specific Hybridization (DASH)

Dynamic allele-specific hybridization (DASH) is essentially an enhanced form of allele-specific hybridization that uses a convenient microtiter plate format, a simple duplex-DNA intercalation for signal production, and a dynamic low–high temperature sweep to capture all phases of probe–target–DNA melting. For the purpose of DASH assay design, one needs to anticipate target-DNA secondary structure problems, and a maximum negative threshold of –4.0 kcal/mol should be expected. Furthermore, probe target ratios of C+G percentages should be more than 1.0. Two probes are designed for each SNP, representing both allelic sequences complementary to the biotinylated strand of the PCR product. The plates containing the bound product, the probes, and a DNA intercalating dye are subjected to a range of different temperatures, to follow the decrease in fluorescence as the temperature increases. The assay is repeated by using alternative allele-specific probes, and genotypes are scored from the fluorescence curves obtained. Devices that support the DASH procedure have been used to analyze 89 intragenic SNPs.

Allele Discrimination Using Fluorescence Resonance Energy Transfer Detection (FRET)

Fluorescence resonance energy transfer (FRET) occurs when two fluorescent dyes are in close proximity to one another and the emission spectrum of one dye molecule overlaps the excitation spectrum of the other fluorophore. Commonly used FRETbased technologies include the TaqMan assay and Molecular Beacons.

TaqMan Genotyping

The basis for FRET allele discrimination and quantitation is to measure PCR product accumulation continuously using a dual-labeled fluorogenic oligonucleotide probe, called a TaqMan probe. This probe is composed of a short (~20–30-base) oligodeoxynucleotide labeled with two different fluorescent dyes. On the 5'-terminus is a reporter dye, and on the 3'-terminus is a quenching dye. This oligonucleotide probe sequence is homologous to an internal target sequence present in the PCR amplicon. When the probe is intact, energy transfer occurs between the two fluorophors, and emission from the reporter is quenched by the quencher. During the extension phase of PCR, the probe is cleaved by the 5'-nuclease activity of DNA polymerase, thereby releasing the reporter from the oligonucleotide quencher and producing an increase in reporter emission intensity. The Applied Biosystems Sequence Detection systems use fiberoptic systems that connect to each well in a 96-well PCR tray format. The laser light or tungsten–halogen lamp excitation source excites each well, and a CCD camera measures the fluorescence spectrum and intensity from each well to generate real-time data during PCR amplification. The system software examines the fluorescence intensity of reporter and quencher dyes and calculates the increase in normalized reporter emission intensity over the course of the amplification. The results are then plotted vs time, represented by cycle number, to produce a continuous measure of PCR amplification. Several other companies also market real-time PCR detection systems including Stratagene and Bio-Rad.

Lee et al. first demonstrated that the 5'-nuclease assay could be used for allelic discrimination. In the assay, two TaqMan probes as described above are included in the reaction, one specific for each allele. The probes are distinguished through the use of different fluorescent reporter dyes (usually 6-carboxy-fluorescein [FAM] and 6-carboxy-4,7,2',7'-tetrachlorofluorescein [TET]). A mismatch between probe and target greatly reduces the probe hybridization efficiency and specific cleavage. Following PCR, an increase in the level of a FAM fluorescent signal without an increase in the TET-specific signal indicates that only the FAM-specific sequence (allele) was present and that the sample is homozygous (and vice versa). An increase in both reporter signals indicates heterozygosity. The software makes three separate calculations to arrive at the result for allele discrimination. First, using multicomponent analysis, the software determines the contribution of each component dye to the observed fluorescence spectrum. Following this, these dye component results are normalized based on control reactions (which have no template), known allele 1 template, or known allele 2 template, which are run on the same plate. An allele 1 score (on a scale of 0–1) and an allele 2 score are calculated for each sample. Finally, the allele 1 and 2 scores are normalized for the extent of the reaction, based on the results of the no-template control. A number of factors contribute to allelic discrimination based on a single mismatch. First is the thermodynamic contribution owing to the disruptive effect of a mismatch on hybridization. A mismatched probe will have a lower melting temperature than a perfectly matched probe. Second, the assay is performed under competitive conditions; therefore the mismatch is prevented from binding because stable binding of an exact match probe blocks hybridization of the mismatch. Third, the 5'-end of the probe must start to be displaced before cleavage occurs. Once a probe starts to be displaced, complete dissociation occurs faster with a mismatch than with an exact match.

Molecular Beacons

Molecular beacons are oligonucleotide probes that have two complementary DNA sequences flanking the target DNA sequence and a donor/acceptor dye pair at opposite ends of each probe. The probe adopts a hairpin loop conformation with the reporter and the quencher dyes close together when it is not hybridized to the target, and therefore, no donor fluorescence is generated. When hybridized to the right target sequence, the two dyes are separated and the fluorescence increases. Thermal instability of the mismatched hybrids increases the specificity of molecular beacons. For SNP genotyping, two molecular beacons with exact sequence matches to the wild-type and variant alleles are used in the same PCR. The use of two differentially labeled molecular beacons in the same PCR reaction allows the simultaneous detection of three possible allelic combinations.

Multiplex Automated Primer Extension Analysis (MAPA)

Multiplex automated primer extension analysis (MAPA) is a semiautomated fluorescent method that can accurately and easily genotype multiple SNPs simultaneously. This technique is a modification of a commercially available protocol that uses the extension of a primer designed to end one nucleotide 5' of a given SNP with fluorescent ddNTPs, followed by automatic sequencing on an ABI PRISM 377 Sequencer. The MAPA modification includes the incorporation of several primers corresponding to several SNPs in the same reaction and loading the primer extension products on a single gel lane. There is a limit to the number of SNPs one can multiplex with this method, dictated by the range of primer lengths (16–50 nucleotides) and the minimum spacing in the primer length that allows for separation.

Therefore, the maximum number of SNPs this method can multiplex is approx 10–12 SNPs per sample. Another drawback is that primer orientation appears to affect the accuracy of genotyping heterozygotes, perhaps because of the formation of strandspecific secondary structures.

Capillary Electrophoresis

In 1981, Jorgenson and Lukacs were the first to demonstrate electrophoretic separation of samples inside narrow-bore capillaries filled with electrophoretic media. Capillary electrophoresis (CE) was found to separate small molecules with a very high resolution. In recent years this technique has been modified for the detection of point mutations and SNPs. The most widely employed of several modifications is a technique known as *constant denaturant capillary electrophoresis* (CDCE), coupled with high-fidelity PCR. This application has lent itself extremely well to high-throughput analysis of samples. CDCE combines the principles of CE and *denaturing gradient gel electrophoresis* (DGGE) in linear polyacrylamide matrices. The denaturing conditions in CDCE are achieved by heating a section of capillary in a temperature-controlled water jacket. CDCE offers high resolution and amenability to automation, and, coupled with high-fidelity PCR, it is possible to measure point mutations at frequencies as low as 10^{-6} in human genomic DNA. The CDCE instrument has been further improved by the addition of a two-wavelength detector. This allows the use of two sets of samples labeled with two different fluorescent dyes, thus permitting comparison of two separate channels. Separation of PCR products is generally conducted in capillaries with an internal diameter of 75 μm at a constant current of 9 μA. Future integration of multiple capillary arrays and automation systems should increase the speed and the scale of this technique.

MALDI-TOF Mass Spectrometry

Karas and Hillenkamp first introduced MALDI-TOF MS in 1988 as a revolutionary method for ionizing and mass-analyzing large biomolecules. They discovered that irradiation of crystals formed by suitable small organic molecules (called the *matrix*) with a short laser pulse at a wavelength close to a resonant absorption band of the matrix molecules caused an energy transfer and desorption process, producing gas phase matrix ions. They also found that when a low-concentration of a nonabsorbing analyte, such as a protein or a nucleic acid molecule, was added to the matrix in solution and embedded in the solid matrix crystals, the nonabsorbing, intact analyte molecules were also desorbed into the gas phase and ionized upon irradiation, allowing their mass analysis.

Originally, MALDI-TOF MS was proposed as an alternative high-throughput technology for DNA sequencing to replace the conventional method. Enzymatic DNA sequencing coupled with MALDI-TOF MS analysis has been shown to be effective at discovering previously unknown SNPs. However, there is a loss of signal intensity and mass resolution with increasing DNA size, owing to the size-dependent tendency of the phosphodiester backbone of DNA to fragment during the MALDI process. Consequently a robust MALDI-based approach to SNP discovery, which requires sequencing of PCR products up to 300 bp in length, has not been demonstrated. This limitation has also hampered attempts to analyze PCR amplicons containing SNPs directly. Additionally, during the MALDI process, double-stranded PCR products can dissociate into single strands of slightly different masses, which as a result are poorly resolved. Minisequencing has become the most widely used MALDI-TOF MS-based method for SNP analysis. It involves annealing of a primer to a template PCR amplicon downstream of a SNP. A mix of deoxynucleotide triphosphates and dideoxynucleotide triphosphates are added to a PCR template and primer, along with a DNA polymerase.

The polymerase extends the 3'-end of the primer by specifically incorporating nucleotides that are complementary to the sequence of the PCR product. Extension terminates at the first position in the template where a nucleotide complementary to one of the ddNTPs in the mix occurs. MALDI-TOF MS-based methods have been developed in which extended primers are solid phase-purified and detected by MS; the identity of the polymorphic nucleotide is determined by measuring the mass of the extended primer.

The greatest promise of MALDI-TOF MS for SNP analysis lies in its ability to genotype many SNPs rapidly, accurately, and simultaneously. Recently, another approach to MALDI-TOF MS has been developed that does not require a PCR amplification step. This direct approach involves the sequence-specific hybridization of two oligonucleotides to form an overlapping structure at the polymorphic position. Enzymatic cleavage and amplification of an allele-specific, short oligonucleotide signal molecule, which is derived from this overlap structure, follow this. The signal molecules produced in this reaction contain a biotin group, enabling solid-phase sample preparation by capturing these molecules on streptavidin-coated magnetic beads. They are then washed to remove contaminants, and the clean signal molecules are eluted for MALDI-TOF MS analysis.

MICROARRAYS

The DNA microarray chip has revolutionized the application of high-throughput genotyping in the last few years. A DNA microarray is a small chip, generally about a square centimeter, most commonly made of glass, plastic, or silicon. SNP analysis with the DNA microarray chip is a hybridization-based genotyping technique that allows the simultaneous analysis of many polymorphisms. High-density microarrays are created by attaching hundreds of thousands of oligonucleotides to a solid surface in an ordered array. The DNA of interest is PCR-amplified to incorporate fluorescently labeled nucleotides and then hybridized to the chip. Each oligonucleotide in the array acts as an allele-specific probe. Well-matched sequences hybridize more efficiently than mismatched sequences and therefore give stronger fluorescent signals. The signals are quantitated by high-resolution fluorescent scanning and analyzed by sophisticated software programs. Many biotechnology companies have developed and are marketing DNA microarrays. The unique features for several different microarray approaches currently available are described in the following sections.

Affymetrix GeneChip Technology

Affymetrix uses light-directed synthesis for the construction of high-density DNA probe arrays using two methods: photolithography and solid-phase DNA synthesis. Synthetic linkers modified by photochemically removable groups are attached to a glass substrate, and light is directed through a photolithographic mask to specific surface areas to produce photodeprotection. This is followed by the chemical coupling of hydroxyl-protected deoxynucleosides at the illuminated sites. Next, light is directed to different regions of the substrate by a new mask, and the chemical cycle is repeated. Thus, for a given reference sequence, a DNA probe array can be designed that consists of a highly dense collection of complementary probes. The amount of nucleic acid information encoded on the array in the form of different probes is limited only by the physical size of the array and the achievable lithographic resolution. Because the arrays are constructed on a rigid material (glass), they can be inverted and mounted in a temperature-controlled hybridization chamber. A fluorescent-tagged nucleic acid sample injected into the chamber hybridizes to complementary oligonucleotides on the array. Laser excitation enters through the back of the glass support, focused at the interface of the array and the target solution, and the fluorescence emission is collected by a lens and passes to a sensitive detector through a series of optical filters. A quantitative 2D fluorescence image of hybridization intensity is obtained by simply scanning the laser beam or translating the array.

Different flow-through systems have been developed to allow a continuous measurement of real-time hybridization to an array, by adding cell lysis and amplification to a miniaturized fluidics system. This approach extends the two dimensions of the lateral microarray resolution by the time-resolved analysis of the binding process as a third dimension. Real-time hybridization also allows the calculation of binding kinetics for every spot under different temperatures and changed hybridization conditions.

Nanogen Biochip Cartridges

Nanogen has developed a microchip cartridge, called the *Nanochip*, to facilitate rapid identification and precise analyses of biological molecules using a process based on the electrical properties of biological molecules. This technology, termed *electronic addressing*, places DNA fragments at selective sites on a silicon microchip and involves active hybridization as opposed to the passive hybridization process described above. After the DNA is addressed, a test site or multiple test sites are electronically activated with a positive charge. The negatively charged probes move to the positively charged test sites, where they are concentrated and bound by a chemical process to that site. The microchip is then washed, another set of DNA probes is added on, and different sites are activated. Therefore, an array of specifically bound DNA probes can be assembled or addressed in a user-defined order. The highly advantageous feature of the Nanochip compared with other array approaches is its flexibility in experimental design. Because you can hybridize only the sites you want by specifying particular sites for electronic concentration and hybridization, you can run multiple experiments on the same chip. The current configuration of the Nanochip contains 100 sites on a single cartridge.

Single-Base Extension-Tag Array on Glass Slides

Also called minisequencing or template-directed incorporation, single-base extension-tag array on glass slides (SBE-TAGS) involves extension of a primer located adjacent to the position of the SNP, using DNA polymerase in the presence of fluorescently labeled ddNTP. The SBE-TAGS method marks each primer with distinct 5'-end sequence tags that allows separation of a multiplexed SBE reaction by hybridization to a microarray. Depositing unmodified nucleotides on a glass slide with routine spotting equipment can easily generate these arrays. Arrays are scanned using external argon lasers, and a matrix is applied to correct for the crosstalk between multiple overlapping fluorophores. This method has been used to genotype over 100 SNPs accurately.

Microsphere-Based Technology

Microsphere-based techniques have been described in the literature for a number of applications but have been further developed by Luminex. The Luminex technology couples existing flow cytometric technology with color-coded microspheres, each of which carries an individual assay. The approach is rapid and extremely flexible. The first use of flow cytometry for analysis of microsphere-based immunoassays was published in 1977 and was reviewed by McHugh in 1994. The flow cytometer is able to discriminate different particles based on size or color, providing the potential for multiplex analysis. The Luminex system is based on the principle that panels are created by combining up to 100 different microsphere-based assays into a single sample test. Multiplexed assays can be run on sample volumes as small as 5 μL. Each assay is individually constructed around a single microsphere set with its own identifying fluorescent color. Each set of microspheres is manufactured with unique relative proportions of red and orange fluorescent dyes. The system consists of 100 distinct sets of fluorescent microspheres and a standard benchtop flow cytometer interfaced with a personal computer containing a digital signal-processing board. Individual sets of microspheres can be modified with reactive components such as oligonucleotides, antigens, or antibodies and then mixed to form a multiplexed assay set. A further advantage is that the system is extremely flexible and permits easy incorporation of new endpoint measures. This contrasts with DNA microarray chip technology, which is not only more expensive but has less flexibility in making new probes available as new polymorphic alleles are identified. So instead of requiring the reconfiguration and synthesis of a new chip when a new allele is to be added to the screening panel, the Luminex system simply requires the addition of an additional oligonucleotide-hybridized microsphere.

The Luminex technology is very amenable to studies of SNP genotyping owing to its flexible format. One can visualize an assay in which a bank of prelabeled probes is held in reserve and an investigator or clinician can pick and choose the SNPs for which to screen. One drawback of the technology, however, is that it requires a considerable amount of time for assay optimization and validation, particularly in the multiplex format. For this reason, many investigators have decided to wait for the availability of commercial kits for use on the instrument.

Another method using the microsphere-based Luminex assays has also been developed for successful multiplexing of SNPs. The conventional Luminex assay using *single base chain extension* (SBCE) has been modified into an allele-specific primer extension reaction (ASPE). This method utilizes a pair of allele-specific primers that differ from each other at the 3'-end and encode different "ZipCode" sequences at the 5'-end, in the same reaction. The DNA polymerase extends only one primer if the template DNA sequence is homozygous, whereas both primers are extended in heterozygotes. The ASPE reaction eliminates the necessity of post-PCR cleanup and the addition of unlabeled nucleotides.

Genotyping Analysis of the CYP2D6 Gene

As mentioned above, the application of SNP genotyping analyses to pharmacogenetic endpoints is of growing clinical importance. The genetic polymorphisms associated with specific human CYP and phase II enzymes typically occur with variable frequency in different populations or ethnic groups and may result in *poor metabolizers* (PMs) or *extensive metabolizers* (EMs) for specific substrates. CYP2D6 metabolizes up to 20% of commonly prescribed medications, including antidepressant/psychotics, antiarrhythmics, and β-blockers, as well as many environmental agents. There is a wide intersubject variability in the pharmacokinetics of all CYP2D6-metabolized substrates, which exhibit variations in clearance over a 20–200-fold range depending on the agent under study. To date, over 74 allelic variants in the human CYP2D6 gene have been identified, many of which are associated with either decreased or enhanced metabolic activity. The CYP2D6 gene represents a challenge for genotyping: the numerous known polymorphisms are not caused only by single-nucleotide substitutions or deletions but also by gene deletions, duplications, and the presence of pseudogenes.

For CYP2D6, the 74 known variants are associated with 60 different polymorphic regions. The number of SNPs within a particular variant allele range from a single SNP (for example, CYP2D6*1B) to eight SNPs (for example, CYP2D6*4G). Four unique SNPs in exons 3, 4, 8, and 9 are observed among the *6 variant allele subfamily. Although the T1707Del SNP would identify a *6 variant, genotyping analysis would require the screening of all four of these SNPs to distinguish among the *6 A, B, C, and D variant alleles. Screening for only 4 of the 60 currently known possible SNPs results in redundant variant allele classifying information, i.e., screening for 56 SNPs is required for the accurate and complete elucidation of the CY2D6 genotype.

A number of novel, high-throughput genotyping approaches have recently been developed, yet these do not yet meet all the requirements for maximum utilization of genotyping information. For example, PCR-based techniques such as PCR-RFLP, PCR SSCP, OLA, and others are time-consuming and labor-intensive and do not provide large amounts of information quickly, i.e., it is not possible to multiplex using any of these techniques. Furthermore, gene duplications and gene deletions such as those present in CYP2D6 cannot be identified.

Sequencing-based techniques such as minisequencing and pyrosequencing are extremely accurate but, again, are laborious and not cost-effective. Furthermore, when multiple SNPs are necessary to define a variant allele and they lie in different regions of the gene, as they do in CYP2D6, numerous fragments would have to be sequenced in order to genotype an individual. FRET-based techniques do not provide a solution for multiplexing either, as the time and cost of optimizing assays far outweighs the ability to genotype for all the various SNPs. However, TaqMan-based assays are extremely useful in genotyping for the common variants of CYP2D6 using commercially available kits. Microsphere-based methods using both SBCE and ASPE techniques coupled with flow cytometry and microtiter-based assays are promising in their applications for multiplexing. Multiple PCR products can be screened simultaneously using specific probes, thus allowing detection of SNPs that are far apart. CYP2D6 genotyping, for example, therefore poses a great challenge, especially since none of the latest techniques allows for the detection of gene duplications and deletions in a speedy and cost-effective manner.

Measurement

The analysis of gene expression is an integral part of any research characterizing gene function. A wide variety of techniques have been developed for this purpose, each with their own advantages and limitations. This section seeks to provide an overview of some of the most recent as well as conventional methods to quantitate gene expression. These approaches include Northern blot analysis, *ribonuclease protection assay* (RPA), reverse transcription polymerase chain reaction, *expressed sequence tag* (EST) sequencing, differential display, cDNA arrays, and the *serial analysis of gene expression*

(SAGE). Current applications of the information derived from gene expression studies require assays to be adaptable for the quantitative analysis of a large number of samples and end points within a short period coupled with cost effectiveness. A comparison of some of these features of each analytical approach as well as their advantages and disadvantages has also been provided.

Gene expression analyses have long been used to provide insights into gene function. Many environmental pollutants, toxicants, and heavy metals affect cellular function by causing drastic changes in gene expression patterns. For both toxicological screening and chemical-specific mechanism of action studies, a wide range of approaches is available to evaluate changes in gene expression at the molecular level that may occur because of a toxic response. These approaches are not unique to the analysis of endpoints of interest in molecular toxicology, as for example, the expression of biotransformation enzymes, but are extremely valuable tools for all genomic studies. The recent rapid technological advances in this field were prompted by the ability to identify genes at the nucleic acid level, rather than proceeding from a known protein to its chromosomal counterpart. Expression studies have previously relied on techniques such as Northern blot analyses or the ribonuclease protection assay, each of which measures the expression of only a small set of genes at a given time. More recent technologies, including *serial analysis of gene expression* (SAGE), quantitative *reverse transcription polymerase chain reaction* (RT-PCR), cDNA microarrays, and high-resolution 2D gel electrophoresis, allow for the expression levels of tens to thousands of genes to be screened at once. The number of samples and number of genetic endpoints to be analyzed and taking into account both cost and throughput capability, one analytical approach for RNA expression analysis may be more appropriate for a particular application or research study.

Prior to any expression analyses, it is essential to verify the integrity of the RNA and to obtain accurate measurement of RNA concentration levels. The feasibility of obtaining meaningful quantitative gene expression data is dependent on the utilization of a validated approach with multiple quality control measures in place. These include the inclusion of either endogenous or exogenous standards or positive controls to assess reproducibility of all steps of the assay; verification of the absence of genomic DNA contamination by DNase treatment and/or in the case of PCR-based methods, the use of primers that span intron/exon junctions for amplification of cDNA only; quantitation analysis of samples collected during the exponential phase of PCR amplification; and negative controls to verify absence of contamination and specificity of the probe used for detection of target mRNAs.

Northern Blot Analysis

Northern blotting was developed as the RNA counterpart of Southern blotting. This technique mainly involves separation of RNA species on the basis of size by denaturing gel electrophoresis followed by transfer of the RNA onto a membrane by capillary, vacuum, or pressure blotting. The RNA is then permanently bound to the membrane either by heating at 80°C or by UV crosslinking. These membranes are then probed with partial or complete cDNA oligonucleotides that are labeled by radionucleotides or chemiluminescent moieties. Nonspecific hybridization is removed by washing, and then the blots are audioradiographed. The resulting visible band(s) indicates the size of the RNA, and the intensity corresponds to the relative amounts of the RNA. The band intensities are quantitated by densitometry using the appropriate image analysis software. Northern blotting is perhaps one of the few techniques that permits mRNA size determination and therefore is useful for the detection of alternatively spliced transcripts or mutations that result in modified mRNA sizes. One of the primary drawbacks of Northern blotting, however, is that the technique yields semiquantitative results. The other limitations involve the requirement of very high quality intact RNA concentrations, variability in transfer efficiencies, and high background levels on the audioradiograms. Typically, the expression of various housekeeping genes with similar copy numbers are used as external controls for sample loading variability and blot-to-blot comparisons. However, the expression of these housekeeping genes may vary with different stages in the cell cycle or among different cell, tissue, or disease types. Variations of the Northern blot such as dot, slot, and fast blots have been developed in an attempt to increase quantitation and simplify the assay. However, before any of these alternate procedures can be used, it is imperative to demonstrate, via the Northern blot, that the probe used in the application is specific to the target RNA, as there is no scope for size fractionation with these methods.

Ribonuclease Protection Assay (RPA)

The *ribonuclease protection assay* (RPA) is a variation of the Northern blot approach, except that it is performed in a solution containing a labeled antisense target RNA probe and the target mRNA without prior gel fractionation or blotting. The unhybridized probe and the sample RNA are degraded enzymatically following incubation for several hours. The remaining hybrids are electrophoresed on a denaturing polyacrylamide gel and visualized by autoradiography. Alternatively the RNase-resistant hybrids are precipitated and bound to filters for direct quantitation by scintillation counting. RPA is considered to be 10-fold more sensitive than Northern blot analysis.

Several issues need to be taken into account when one is designing RPA probes. If the RPA products are to be analyzed using gel electrophoresis, the RPA probe should contain some terminal sequences that will not hybridize with the target mRNA, so that undigested probe can be distinguished from probe-RNA hybrids on the basis of size. As is the case with Northern analysis, quantitation requires the concurrent hybridization of an invariant control mRNA. Probes may be multiplexed together in a single hybridization reaction if the sizes of the products do not overlap. This holds true if the products are analyzed by electrophoresis. However, if RPA products are going to be analyzed by the scintillation counter method, then the use of two different radionucleotides solves this problem. The two main advantages to RPA are sensitivity and the ability to determine absolute RNA levels. The disadvantages are difficulties encountered in designing adequately sensitive internal controls, and the high quantity/ quality of RNA required for the assay.

Expressed Sequence Tag (EST) Sequencing

The concept of *expressed sequence tag* (EST) sequencing was first described in 1991. The underlying goal was to create cDNA libraries, pick random clones, and then carry out a single sequencing reaction with a large number of clones. Each reaction generates approx 300 bp of sequences that represent a unique sequence tag for a particular transcript. EST sequencing can be carried out using both normalized (in which each transcript is represented in more or less equal numbers) and nonnormalized cDNA libraries. The advantage of using normalized libraries is that redundant sequencing of highly expressed genes is minimized. The advantage of nonnormalized libraries is that the abundance of the transcript in the original cell is accurately reflected in the frequency of clones in the library. Hence these libraries can be used to identify highly expressed but unknown genes as well as to compare the expression of highly expressed genes in different cells or tissues.

There are currently over 1.5 million human ESTs in the publicly available database of ESTs (dbEST) provided by the National Center for Biotechnology Information. These ESTs are derived from approx 1200 human cDNA libraries. In addition to public databases, several companies have generated larger collections of ESTs. These include Human Genome Sciences, Incyte Pharmaceuticals, and Celera Genomics Group.

Subtractive Cloning by Representational Difference Analysis (RDA)

Subtractive cloning methods have been in use for many years and offer an inexpensive and flexible alternative to EST sequencing and cDNA array hybridization. The PCR-based method commonly used is known as *representational difference analysis* (RDA). In this analysis, double stranded-cDNA is created from the two cell or tissue populations of interest (for example, tumor and normal tissue), linkers are ligated to the end of the cDNA fragments, and then the cDNA pools are amplified by PCR. The cDNA pool from which unique clones are desired is designated as the "tester," and the cDNA pool that is used to subtract shared sequences is designated as the "driver." Following PCR amplification, the linkers are removed from both cDNA pools, and unique linkers are ligated to the tester sample. The tester is then hybridized to an excess of driver DNA, and sequences that are unique to the tester cDNA pool are amplified by PCR. The primary limitation of this method is that subtle quantitative differences are missed because the cDNAs identified are usually those that differ significantly in expression level between the cell populations. In addition, because each experiment is a pairwise comparison, and the subtractions are based on a series of sensitive biochemical reactions, it then becomes difficult to compare a series of RNA samples directly.

Reverse Transcription-Polymerase Chain Reaction (RT-PCR)

RT-PCR is an in vitro method for amplifying defined target sequences of RNA. It is an extremely sensitive method and can be used to compare levels of mRNA in different sample populations and to characterize patterns of mRNA expression. RT-PCR analyses have been modified to increase its sensitivity and accuracy; some of the modifications include semi-nested, nested, and even three-step nested RT-PCR techniques. There are also a number of detection methods that can be used, yielding either semiquantitative or quantitative results. All of the components of an RT-PCR reaction and subsequent product detection are interdependent and require careful optimization to ensure specificity, sensitivity and reproducibility of the assay. Typically, all measurements are standardized to a calibrator sample so that data collected at different time points can be compared directly.

The first step in RT-PCR is the *reverse transcription* (RT) of the RNA template into cDNA, followed by its exponential amplification in a PCR reaction. Separation of the RT and the PCR steps is advantageous for long-term storage of the cDNA or analysis of multiple targets. The RT step can be primed using specific primers, random hexamers, or oligo-dT primers. Specific primers can sometimes cause marked variation in estimates of mRNA copy numbers; while random hexamers can overestimate mRNA copy numbers by about 19-fold. Numerous RT enzyme preparations are commercially available and vary in terms of efficiency and in range of primers that can be used for first-strand synthesis. In all RT-PCR applications, it is critical to include a no-RT template control to avoid the quantitation of false positives.

Like other methods for RNA quantitation, RT-PCR can be used for relative or absolute quantitation. Absolute quantitation, using competitive RT-PCR, measures the absolute amount or number of copies of a specific target mRNA sequence in a sample. In competitive RT-PCR, increasing amounts of DNA highly homologous to the target, but distinguishable by either size or restriction sites, are added to the PCR, and both target and competitive template are quantified. It is assumed that the amplification efficiency of both templates is identical; however, this may not be the case. Most gene expression analysis studies utilize a relative expression calculation similar to those used in standard assays such as the Northern blot. Expression of the gene of interest is reported relative to expression of an endogenous control gene, which is assumed to have equal expression in all tissues in the study. In this way, expression levels can be compared from tissue to tissue. The endogenous internal control in relative RT-PCR may be analyzed in a multiplexed reaction or in two separate reactions. Common internal controls include 18S rRNA, β-actin, β-glucuronidase, and GAPDH mRNAs.

Critical to either absolute or relative RT-PCR is quantitation of the product during the exponential phase of PCR. This represents a challenge because internal control RNAs are typically constitutively expressed housekeeping genes of high abundance, and their amplification reaches the plateau phase with very few PCR cycles. It is therefore difficult to identify comparable exponential phase conditions in which the PCR product from a rare target mRNA is detectable. Detection methods with low sensitivity, like ethidium bromide staining of agarose gels, are therefore not recommended. Detecting a rare message while staying in exponential phase with an abundant message can be achieved in several ways: (i) by improving the sensitivity of product detection; (ii) by decreasing the amount of input template in the RT or PCR reactions; and/or (iii) by decreasing the number of PCR cycles.

Modifications involving the application of fluorescence probes and instrumentation have led to the development of kinetic RT-PCR methodologies that facilitate the quantitation of nucleic acids with improved sensitivity and throughput and overcome many of the problems described above. There are currently at least three manufacturers of fluorescence resonance energy transfer detection (FRET)-based instrumentation systems.

The ABI PRISM 7700 contains a built-in thermal cycler with 96 wells and a fluorescence reader that can read wavelengths between 500 and 660 nm. The fluorescent light source in this case is a laser, and the emission is directed to a spectrograph with a *charge-coupled device* (CCD). The most recent commercially available model, ABI PRISM 7000, uses a tungsten–halogen lamp, and the fluorescence emission is directed through four optical filters to a CCD camera. The rest of the features are similar to the 7700. On the other hand, the ABI PRISM 7900HT has a 384-well capacity and allows the use of multiple fluorophores in a single reaction owing to the feature of continuous wavelength detection.

The LightCycler uses small-volume glass capillary tubes that are heated and cooled by an airstream. A blue light-emitting diode is the light source, and the fluorescence is read by three photodetection diodes with different filters. It can analyze up to 32 samples per run.

Bio-Rad has recently launched an optical module that fits into their conventional thermal cycler. This device can scan up to 96 samples simultaneously and at present can monitor four different fluorescent reporters.

To date, there are four different competing techniques available to detect the amplified product with the same sensitivity. The simplest method employs fluorescent dyes that bind specifically to double-stranded DNA. The other three utilize the hybridization of fluorescently labeled probes to specific amplicons. These four methods are molecular beacons, DNA binding dyes, hybridization probes, and hydrolysis probes.

Molecular beacons

Molecular beacons are probes that have a loop structure complementary to the target nucleic acid molecule and a stem structure that is formed by the annealing of complementary sequences on the ends of the probe sequence. A fluorescent marker is attached to one arm, and a quencher is attached to another. In solution, the free molecular beacons have a hairpin structure, with the stem keeping the arms in close proximity, thereby resulting in the efficient quenching of the probe. On encountering a complementary target, they undergo a conformational change that results in the formation of a probe-target hybrid. This hybrid forces the stem apart, leading to the separation of the fluorophore and the quencher and consequently the restoration of fluorescence, while the free molecular beacons remain nonfluorescent. The main drawback of molecular beacons is their ability to form alternate conformations that fail to place the fluorophore next to the quencher, resulting in large background signals.

DNA-binding dyes

DNA-binding dyes such as SYBR green, which exhibit no fluorescence alone in solution, can be incorporated into double-stranded DNA during the PCR elongation step. Detection of the fluorescence of the DNA-binding dyes therefore increases during the elongation step and decreases during denaturation. The specificity of target detection largely depends on the specificity of the PCR primers, and a separate probe is not added. An important failing of this method is that the number of dye molecules that are incorporated into the PCR product may vary with each PCR cycle and from sample to sample, and therefore the analysis is semiquantitative at best.

Hybridization probes

The LightCycler uses hybridization probes. One probe has at its 3' end a fluorescein donor, whose emission spectrum overlaps the excitation spectrum of an acceptor fluorophore, which is attached to the 5' end of the second probe. This acceptor labeled probe is blocked at its 3' end to prevent its extension during PCR. Fluorescent light is produced from FRET following excitation of the donor. The two dyes are apart when in solution; however, following hybridization of the probes to the target sequence, they are brought into close proximity, and FRET occurs. Therefore, the increasing intensity of wavelength of the second dye is directly proportional to the amount of DNA synthesized. Furthermore, a melting curve analysis can also be performed for multiplex analysis, as the probes are not hydrolyzed.

Hydrolysis probes

Hydrolysis probes are usually used in TaqMan assays; they use the 5' nuclease activity of the DNA polymerase to hydrolyze a hybridization probe after it has bound to its target. The PCR step, which follows the RT step, increases the specificity of the reaction by the use of three oligonucleotides complementary to the DNA. Two primers amplify a specific amplicon, followed by the use of a probe that hybridizes to the product during annealing/extension. The probe has a fluorescent dye at the 5' end and a quencher at the 3' end. If no complementary amplicon is generated, the probe remains intact. Conversely, if the probe binds to the complementary sequence as it is being amplified, it is eventually cleaved, thus separating the reporter and quencher dyes, causing emission of fluorescence. Because of the high Tms of the probe, the TaqMan system PCR annealing and extension steps can be combined and most reactions are carried out at 60–62°C. This also ensures maximum 5'-3' exonuclease activity of the Taq polymerase. The increase in the length of the annealing/extension step, coupled with increased Mg^{2+} or Mn^{2+} for longer amplicons, makes this system less efficient and flexible than others. Real-time RT-PCR assays are conclusively more reliable than conventional ones and can easily be adapted to a high-throughput setup.

Differential Display

Another widely used PCR-based method that is extremely popular is differential display or RNA fingerprinting. Differential display involves RT primed with either an oligo-dT or an arbitrary primer, in conjunction with the RT primer to amplify cDNA fragments that are then separated on a polyacrylamide gel. The presence or absence of bands on the gel visualizes differences in gene expression. Differential display has also been adapted for use in fluorescent DNA sequencing machines. It is efficient for analyzing as little as 5–10 ng of total RNA. A limitation of this method is the generation of false positives either during PCR or in the cloning of differentially expressed PCR products. Large amounts of RNA are required to discriminate true positives from false positives. A modification of the technique based on the analysis of 3'-end restriction fragments claims to result in fewer false-positive signals. In this method, double-stranded cDNA is prepared and digested with a restriction enzyme with a four-base recognition site. Linkers are then ligated to the restriction fragments, and the entire pool of transcripts is amplified by PCR. Gel electrophoresis of the 3'-end fragments reveals the differences in gene expression. The distinct advantage this modification offers is that every gene in the cell can be identified by the use of a series of restriction enzymes; furthermore, because the migration of the bands in the gel is determined by the restriction site at the 3'-end, known genes can simply be identified by measuring the size of the restriction fragment.

cDNA Microarrays

In a cDNA array, many gene-specific polynucleotides derived from the 3'-end of RNA transcripts are individually arrayed on a single matrix. This matrix is then simultaneously probed with fluorescently tagged cDNA representations of total RNA pools from test and reference samples, allowing one to determine the relative amount of transcript present in the pool by the type of fluorescent signal generated. An internal control is provided for each measurement. The adaptable nature of the fabrication of the array and hybridization methods allow the technique to be widely applied—the limitations being cost, the availability of clones for the solid phase, and the quality of the RNA extracted from cell lines or tissues. The targets for the arrays are labeled representations of cellular mRNA pools. A labeled product from the 3'-end of the gene is produced by RT with an oligo-dT primer. The purity of the RNA is critical, particularly when using fluorescence, as cellular proteins, lipids, and carbohydrates can mediate significant nonspecific binding of fluorescently labeled cDNAs to slide surfaces. For adequate fluorescence, the total RNA required per target, per array, is 50–200 ng. For mRNA present as a single transcript per cell, application of target derived from 100 ng of total RNA over an 800-mm^2 hybridization area containing 200-μm-diameter probes will result in approx 300 transcripts being sufficiently close to the target to have a chance to hybridize. Therefore, if the fluorescently tagged transcripts are 600 bp, have an average of 2 fluor tags per 100 bp, and hybridize to their probe, approx 12 fluors will be present in a 100-μm^2 scanned pixel. Such low levels of signal are at the lower limit of fluorescence detection and can easily be rendered undetectable by assay noise. A variety of means by which to improve signal from limited RNA have been proposed. For example, efficient mixing of the hybridization fluid should bring more molecules into contact with their cognate probe, increasing the number of productive events. Posthybridization amplification methods have also been reported in which detectable molecules are precipitated at the target by the action of enzymes "sandwiched" to the cDNA target.

A critical challenge of the high-throughput technologies available to measure gene expression is the accurate and adequate analysis of the vast amounts of data generated. At present the most widely used computational approach for analyzing microarray data is cluster analysis.

This analysis groups genes based on similar expression profiles and compares them with other clustered genes, providing clues to the function or regulation of the genes. The three broad categories of cluster analysis include a tree-based approach that uses a measure of the distance between genes such as a correlation coefficient to group genes into hierarchical trees. The second category minimizes variation within clusters so that between-cluster variation is maximized. The third category groups genes into two basic blocks, one in which the correlation is maximized and one in which the correlation is minimized. All these categories basically utilize the intensity differences between the mean intensity for each of the groups. However, relative mean comparisons ignore the premise that differences in expression level of less than 100% may exert meaningful biological effects. Various statistical models have been designed to approach the problem of gene expression data analysis, and several problems still remain associated with each of the strategies. Although technological advances have simplified the ability to study thousands of genes at once, the interpretation of this data and its subsequent analysis continue to pose a challenge.

Serial Analysis of Gene Expression (SAGE)

Serial analysis of gene expression (SAGE) utilizes isolated sequence tags from individual mRNAs that are concatenated serially into long DNA molecules that are then sequenced. Initially double-stranded cDNA is synthesized from mRNA using a biotinylated oligo-dT primer. The cDNA pool is then cleaved by a restriction enzyme, also known as an anchoring enzyme, and is then separated on a polyacrylamide gel. The total number of tags identified by this method to date number close to 5 million. SAGE requires relatively higher concentrations of RNA compared with RT-PCR or microarray analyses, and it is relatively technically difficult to create tag libraries. There are two major concerns when using SAGE. One concern is identifying sequencing errors, and the second is making valid tag to gene assignments. Several modifications have been developed to increase the utility of SAGE in terms of both methodology and data interpretation.